BORN
TO BE
WIRED

Lessons from a Lifetime Transforming Television,
Wiring America for the Internet, and Growing Formula One,
Discovery, SiriusXM, and the Atlanta Braves

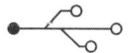

JOHN MALONE

Simon & Schuster

New York   Amsterdam/Antwerp   London
Toronto   Sydney/Melbourne   New Delhi

Simon & Schuster
1230 Avenue of the Americas
New York, NY 10020

First Simon & Schuster hardcover edition September 2025

SIMON & SCHUSTER and colophon are registered trademarks of Simon & Schuster, LLC

For information about special discounts for bulk purchases, please contact Simon & Schuster Special Sales at 1-866-506-1949 or business@simonandschuster.com.

The Simon & Schuster Speakers Bureau can bring authors to your live event. For more information or to book an event, contact the Simon & Schuster Speakers Bureau at 1-866-248-3049 or visit our website at www.simonspeakers.com.

Interior design by Hope Herr-Cardillo

Printed and bound in India by Replika Press Pvt. Ltd.

10 9 8 7 6 5 4 3 2 1

Library of Congress Cataloging-in-Publication Data is available.

ISBN 978-1-6680-5153-5
ISBN 978-1-6680-5155-9 (ebook)

To Leslie, the love of my life

CONTENTS

CHAPTER 1

KEYS ON THE TABLE

I had done this a hundred times before in a dozen different bank boardrooms, and each time the scene was the same: a cavernous, wood-paneled room with a long mahogany table polished to a sheen. Around it sit a dozen or so aging men in starched white shirts and neckties, frowning and looking up periodically from the financial numbers on the documents in front of them.

But on this afternoon in 1975, the banks had requested the meeting, not us, and far from a polished boardroom, it was in our brown, flat, single-story office building in the long shadow of the Rockies. I knew this meeting would be different.

The past couple of years had been pure hell for both of us. Bob Magness was the chairman of a struggling cable company on the outskirts of Denver named Tele-Communications Inc., and he had brought me in as the new CEO two years earlier.

TCI had been a bright young star in the rapidly growing cable television business. We were hanging coaxial cable across the country to provide rural areas with better reception of broadcast signals from CBS, NBC, and ABC, and eventually hundreds of new TV channels and the internet.

One day, this would lay the foundation for the largest cable operator in the U.S., serving one out of every four homes, and give rise to a robust, two-way digital communications network in the U.S., providing the platform for the likes of Amazon, Facebook, and Google, and unlocking immense value in a new digital economy.

Bob and I had no idea of any of that potential back then. That morning, we merely were hoping to survive the day. Bob, a World War II vet and part-time rancher and cottonseed broker, had launched his cable company in Memphis, Texas, in 1956, after a chance conversation with two strangers in a cotton gin, where Bob did business.

Sold on the idea, Bob and his loving and loyal wife, Betsy, sold their cattle, mortgaged their house, and jumped in. He and a small team of friends started climbing telephone poles and hanging wire, with Betsy stationed at the kitchen table as head of accounting. Several years later, Bob moved operations to Denver and took TCI public in 1970.

When I first accepted the offer to come work for Bob, the pitch was solid: Come out West and run one of the largest cable operators in this new industry! Long-term contracts to wire big cities were worth millions of dollars. This set off a land grab across the country, and TCI had taken on crushing debt to finance furious growth. Around this time, TCI reached more than 621,000 subscribers through 151 systems in 33 states, with annual revenue around $34 million a year—and $84.8 million in debt.

Almost immediately after I arrived in 1973, several things started breaking the wrong way for us: oil prices quadrupled, the inflation rate shot up to double digits, and interest rates skyrocketed to 12 percent in July 1974, more than doubling borrowing costs year over year. That hit the cable business especially hard, because for us more debt was like rocket fuel. The variable cost of stringing wire from pole to pole above ground had doubled, thanks to new regulations and price increases from suppliers. In big cities, where cable had to be buried underground, the costs could run as high as tens of thousands of dollars per mile.

Now the banks were balking at any more lending, yet we already had pledged TCI to pour half a billion dollars into new construction to win cable franchises from local governments in Tennessee, Washington, and elsewhere. On top of that, in return for franchise agreements to operate there, we had inherited promises made by systems TCI bought to build community centers and parks.

Despite healthy revenue gains and operating margins of 40 percent, our debt was closing in fast, and for the first time in my career, I was scared. To consolidate the loans he had already accumulated, Bob had drawn a

$77.5 million bank line of credit in 1972, just before I joined. And we had borrowed $76.5 million of it.

A week earlier, I had called a loan officer to arrange the meeting where we would ask to borrow the final $1 million. Before I could even get the words out, he cut me off.

His tone on the other end of the line struck me as a little rude: "By the way, don't ask for that other million. If you don't want the house of cards to come down, don't ask."

What was I thinking? I was educated at Yale, I had worked in the most famous laboratory in the world at Bell Labs, I had trained at the fabled McKinsey & Company, and I had been CEO at Jerrold Electronics, the dominant (and highly profitable) supplier and financier to the cable industry. I had turned down a plush job with an absurdly big salary in New York, with a car and driver, to take this job instead.

I had joined a bunch of cowboys and a near-bankrupt former cottonseed salesman who had bet his farm, literally, on a newfangled business called cable TV. I had uprooted my family, moved across the country, and taken a pay cut—on a promise. I had risked everything.

I even had taken out a $60,000 loan from the Bank of Denver to buy TCI stock at $7 a share when I joined—a year later, the stock had fallen to $3, weighed down by high interest rates, wild inflation, and an unrelated industry scandal, briefly bottoming out at 78 cents. My start date at the company should have been my first clue: April Fool's Day.

We were minding every nickel at the office, and my wife, Leslie, and I were counting pennies at home, using coupons at the grocery store, never eating out, and going for a month without a home phone at one point.

The vise grip of home and work was squeezing my brain. We had already started slashing salaries at the office, and we were doubling up in hotel rooms and flying economy to every new city. I had not expected this.

The worst, though, was that I wasn't the CEO people had expected me to be, the father I had wanted to be to my kids, or the husband I had promised to be for my wife.

In honest moments, Leslie would let her frustration show: "You promised me after McKinsey and Jerrold you'd be home more, and that we'd have dinner together like a family, and you're not, and we don't."

As we waited for the bankers to arrive, I realized that this one meeting would determine the fate of the company, our employees, and my career. The imminent risk of losing the company and going bankrupt was an existential threat that had resurrected old demons of self-doubt, particularly the fear of letting everyone down.

As the bankers arrived, they fanned out around the table in our cramped conference room. The only friendly face among the gaggle of them was that of Donne Fisher, our treasurer at TCI, and he looked like a man in the back of a long line at the DMV—irked and impatient, yet keeping it all in check.

I opened the meeting with an introduction heavy on promises and light on numbers, because I knew the numbers couldn't save us. Then Donne and I left them to deliberate privately.

Bob walked into my office and asked how things were going. He still looked every inch the laconic cottonseed salesman he had been a decade earlier, with a molasses-slow Texas drawl and dressed, almost always, in a white Western dress shirt, a bolo tie, and a cowboy hat that was perched atop neatly combed white hair.

As Donne and I gave him a read on the room, he just stared off into the distance. In Bob's eyes I couldn't tell if I saw fear or despair that afternoon, maybe a bit of both. He was genuinely stoic, as if he were witnessing an accident in slow motion. In many ways, I guess, he was.

The first thing the bankers decided was that one of their members had to leave: the representative for the Teachers Insurance and Annuity Association of America, which had different agreements than the banks; he was now regarded as being too close to the company. The man walked out of the meeting, stunned and a little stung, and joined Bob, Donne, and me.

As we were all sitting on a couch waiting in my office, with the clock literally ticking, Bob finally stood up and said to no one in particular, "I can't take it anymore. I'm leaving." And he drove home.

After an eternity, representatives of two of the largest debt holders, the Bank of New York and Philadelphia National, came to my office. Donne and I looked at each other, then looked at them. Tom Renyi, who would later become the CEO of the Bank of New York, revealed the verdict.

"Well, the banks have conferred, and we're prepared to give you the extensions that you've requested," he declared. And then came the sucker punch: "However, we think because of the deteriorated nature of the credit, the banks are entitled to an increase in the interest rate."

The damned fool. When I heard those words, I knew it was over. I lost my breath and felt my skin go numb.

"Tom," I said quietly, "I was afraid you were going to say that. I've got every knob in this company turned down as tight as they'll go." Then my voice started to get louder. "We've got people working sixty-hour weeks and getting paid for thirty. We're working overtime to just get over this hump. And that's all it is—a hump. We can get over it." I sounded like a gambler with a hot tip.

"But if you do this now, it will kill us," I continued. "It'll so demoralize everyone. I just can't continue to run the company if you're going to do that!"

"And so if *you* think *you* can extract this little bit more juice out of the company . . . here's the keys to everything." I pulled my ring of office keys out of my front pants pocket and threw it down on the table in my office. "You run it and let me know how you make out."

I had pulled the keys out for effect, but the truth was I was dead serious. I also knew that all banks dread having to seize a customer's business, because they know nothing about running any business; they'll just screw it up. They know only money.

Plus, in our loan accord with the banks, they were allowed to boost the interest rate on our debt only with our approval. So I told them straight-out: "You can put us in the tank, you can put us into bankruptcy, and you can call a default, but you can't raise the interest rate unless we agree to it . . . and we're not going to agree to it because I think it's the wrong thing to do at this time."

Silence.

"Thank you for your time, John."

And just like that, the meeting was over.

And they all left without saying goodbye. *Are we done? Is this the way it ends?*

That night I was so wired I couldn't sleep, my brain busy with unsettling scenarios. We arrived in the office the next day waiting for the phone to ring with the verdict. The call lasted less than a few minutes. The banks had decided to forgo raising our interest rate. It was good news, but there was nothing to celebrate. We could only exhale.

The meeting, and that moment, would stay with me forever, and that sharp pang of fear at the imminent prospect of crushing failure has never really left me. It remains with me to this day, like a nettlesome and negative old friend I must abide, albeit I am better at keeping it in check now.

It made me realize that the adage is true: in every crisis lurks opportunity. So if I could learn something from a near-death experience, maybe the whole thing was worth it. That day, now fifty years ago, I made a promise to myself that I never have broken: *If we get out of this alive, I will never bet the whole farm . . . on anything. No deal is ever worth doing that.*

Without saying it aloud, Bob and I knew the bankers saw us as just numbers on a balance sheet—and they would never understand what drove us. Bootstrapping the business over the past two years had forged a strong bond between us all at TCI. This was our life's work, something built on grit, optimism, and a trust that ran deeper than any balance sheet could reflect.

Wall Street bankers debate which metric is best for divining the intrinsic value of a company. Is it revenue growth or the bottom line? Forward-looking earnings estimates or shareholder equity? What about any one of the alphabet soup of acronyms they so love to spout—EBITDA, ROE, ROI, ARPU, CAGR, EPS, P/E, P&L?

But none of these is right.

I have spent my career negotiating deals in telecommunications, music, sports, horses, land, media, and more. I have been a buyer and a seller, depending on the deal and the moment. Altogether, over a lifetime, I figure I have had a hand in hundreds of transactions, maybe thousands.

Now, in a lot of those deals, we focused hard on one measure: cash flow, or specifically, EBITDA (earnings before interest, taxes, depreciation, and amortization). It gives a clearer picture of operating performance and a firm's ability to borrow or invest. Some people say I all but invented the term. I can't swear to it, though it is true that I helped make it a whole new form of currency on Wall Street.

But it turns out that cash flow is the wrong answer, too, in placing a value on a company, or any deal for that matter.

The most valuable assets in any business are people and relationships.

I may have neglected to appreciate this at the time, when we were down in the fray. Now that I am a bit older and slowing down, just a little, I have realized that, all along, the most important element was *who* was involved, not what. The people whom I befriended, learned from, and fought against— rather than the deals or the payoff—gave me the most satisfaction. And the right people produced the highest upside—giving my journey meaning and enriching my knowledge of the world.

Along the way, I have been the beneficiary of extraordinary mentors, partners, and employees. If not for their support and dedication, none of the experiences I share here would have been possible. This book is a thank-you note to those people. Without these characters, I might be on an entirely different path. But through a few chance encounters, seemingly small at the time, I found myself at the heart of a technology revolution. What started with coils of coax and threads of fiber became the largest private construction project in the U.S. since World War II. And through it all, their influence echoed—proof that the right people, at the right moment, can change everything.

It has been enormously exciting and at the same time gratifying to play a role in the digital revolution. Our original intent was to deliver broadcast TV signals to far-flung rural valleys and mountainous terrain that antennas couldn't reach. That very same cable evolved into the backbone of the broadband network better known today as the internet, three decades after we at Tele-Communications began laying down lines.

As chairman of Liberty Media and Liberty Global, one of the largest broadband companies in the world, I now have diversified holdings in content, sports, digital media, broadband, ranching, forestry, farming, horses, and hospitality.

Contrary to the clichéd image of a rapacious business titan, I never sought to build a conglomerate, or family empire, and I can just as easily be a seller or a buyer. I believe in creating value while you own the assets you build or buy, and doing it in the most efficient way. All the stakes that I have owned in a wide array of cable channels, overseas cable systems, and other assets are less an empire than a mutual fund with a desirable portfolio of properties.

I built this portfolio with one clear goal—the same one that I believe anyone who is an active member of the management of a public company should share: to maximize the value of the shares of the company over a medium term. Because that is why you were hired—to maximize shareholder returns. The recent fad of "stakeholder capitalism" relegates shareholders to merely one of myriad groups a company is obligated to serve, and it is simply impractical to serve multiple masters and remain productive. You have to honor your obligations to your employees, yes, and you must honor your obligations to your lenders. But you must *maximize* the value for your shareholders.

I navigate by rational analysis of the hard data, but also by my sense of the people who are sitting at the table in front of me. I have come to appreciate those relationships more. As far back as I can remember, I have always perceived myself as different because I was such an introvert. And for much of my life, I thought of that as an impediment.

I regarded myself as mismatched to the world to some degree, handicapped by an absence of social skills or the drive to socialize, and envious of the people who felt at ease in crowds and parties.

Even the people I think I am close to sometimes see me as cold and aloof. I have come to realize later in life that, like other members of my family, I am a high-functioning autistic.

As a result, I have come to appreciate more and more the lasting connections I have still managed to make with others. I know now what I should have known all along: the people in my life are the most critical asset of all.

People like my most trusted partner of sixty-two years, an auburn-haired beauty with a quicksilver mind who can outwit most executives I know.

Everyone in business benefits from a partner who listens, whom they trust, and who will offer unconditional love. I have Leslie. Beyond her beauty and her devotion as a mother and wife, she is blessed with keen intuition. She once saw a visitor for me park his car across three spaces in our driveway and wondered aloud how he treated his partners. Turned out she read him right; the deal didn't work because there was no reciprocal respect from the start.

People like Monty Shapiro, my first business mentor, when I was in my twenties, who told me, "Son, always ask, 'What if not?' What if things do *not* go as planned?" He taught me to assess the worst that could happen and ensure that we could live to fight another day, advice that I hear in my head thinking over every big deal.

Bob Magness, my first partner, a cowboy from Texas, taught me how to take big risks and fight through the fear of tough decisions by sharing the load, and the confidence that comes with control in a company.

Or Marty Flessner, my assistant of thirty-eight years, who knows more about my business affairs than I do, and has taught me empathy and humility. She is not shy about telling me precisely how I screwed things up when I really need to hear it. I'd be lost without her.

And my first teacher, my father, who taught me an engineer's love of problems—not to fear them, but to see them as puzzles waiting to be solved. And through it all, he passed on a stoic view of the world, reminding me that strength comes not from avoiding life's storms but from standing firm in the wind.

Often in business, and in life, I was able to apply the lessons I learned from these people, even as I have made my share of mistakes, including a couple of real whoppers.

To my chagrin, I was unable to convince Netflix founder Reed Hastings to merge his then-upstart company into DirecTV when I was chairman. Waiting for dinner to be served at a party hosted by Herb Allen at his annual Sun Valley retreat in 2011, Reed explained to me that he was betting the entire company on a rapid switch to distributing movies over the internet. I could see that he was close to cracking the code on streaming content ahead of cable TV, satellite companies—everyone. He passed. Sometimes it's hard to catch lightning in a bottle.

I also have had the rare opportunity to help some gifted entrepreneurs with great ideas, like Bob Johnson, who came to me with a concept for a cable channel appealing to African Americans called Black Entertainment Television (BET). After a thirty-minute meeting, I loaned Bob $320,000 and gave him $180,000 for a 20 percent stake in BET. He later became one of the first Black billionaires in America. And John Hendricks, who called me in 1985 in a last-ditch play to help save his struggling but promising network called Discovery. TCI wired John $500,000 within forty-eight hours after I hung up the phone with him. Prior to its merger with Warner Bros., Discovery reached a market cap of $16 billion and could be seen in more than 220 countries and territories, in fifty languages.

I found a lifelong friend in Ted Turner, a funny and fearless maverick who created a new "Superstation" to compete with the Big Three broadcast networks, which had held a lock on over 90 percent of viewers since television was invented. It was Ted who taught me one of the most enduring lessons in my life: about the power of wealth to do good in society and the absolute necessity to save this planet, specifically the most beautiful open spaces in this country.

News Corp. Chairman Emeritus Rupert Murdoch, who at various times has been my competitor—or my consigliere, gave me a master class in business strategy. I am still learning the black magic of programming from Barry Diller, who is a bona fide genius and a maestro of television and internet content. And I am reminded of my own ambition when I counsel Mike Fries, who is one of the hardest-working, team-building, risk-taking entrepreneurs I ever have seen, helping to build one of the biggest broadband companies in the world with Liberty Global.

All of these people, and the companies they drove, pushed the boundaries of modern communications and helped reshape our world. Woven together, their incredible stories help explain how we have arrived at this moment of disruption and the incredible velocity of change in how we communicate, educate, and entertain ourselves.

It is a rather astonishing business tale. One of the most sophisticated networks in the history of humankind was first laid out by a ragtag group of risk-takers, idealists, and "cable cowboys." They strung wire across the country, driven by their own aspirations for a better life and fueled by vivid dreams of success in a free market.

Few of those cable cowboys stringing wire from the mountains could have imagined they were laying the infrastructure for the profound trans-formation in society that continues even today.

I know, because I was there in the beginning.

CHAPTER 2

DIFFERENT WIRING

Mowing the yard around my house was always a bit of a death-defying feat when I was a boy.

During summers in the early 1950s, in our middle-class neighborhood in Milford, a small town along the rocky coastline of Connecticut, it was my job to mow our half-acre lot, on a beast of a contraption we called the lawnmower.

The lawnmower was assembled from spare parts, with precious few safety features, by my father, a born inventor who loved to build and repair things in the cavernous, white wooden building behind the house that he called simply "the barn." But it never held a farm animal that I know of, and there was no hay. A more appropriate name would have been the laboratory, a place where he could repair—or invent—virtually anything. It was one of innumerable mechanical projects started by my father, many of which lay half-completed on the work benches in the barn, including some of the first models of working TV sets. Embedded in the things he built, or the motors that he repaired, were lessons for solving complex issues that lay ahead. My father was a soft-spoken man, but his expectations were clear, and I yearned for his approval. No matter his mood, he remained stone-faced and unflappable.

Looking back, I can now understand that he was a high-functioning autistic, which limited his social prowess but allowed him to immerse his mind in the complexity of whatever mechanical conundrum sat before him. It is a way of seeing the world I have inherited.

At six feet, two inches and 250 pounds, Daniel Malone was a hulking presence with a head of white hair and a matching mustache that gave him the handsome air of a distinguished professor at some Ivy League school. He was an introvert, so stoical that to this day I can't remember hearing him raise his voice or get truly angry at anyone, not even the time he fell wearing a suit and tie into a three-foot-deep mud pit "trap" dug in our backyard by me and my best friend from the neighborhood, George Hanlon.

My friends called him the gentle giant, and I can remember sitting in his lap as a toddler as he told me stories. He was a farm boy from York County, Pennsylvania, one of five who all left home with advanced degrees. My father went to the University of Michigan for his master's in electrical engineering, and he and my mom met in Philadelphia while in school.

My mother was a counterbalance to my father's quiet ways. Jule Custer Malone was energetic and radiated unconditional love, and she tended to scraped knees, bruised egos, and the troubled heart of a teenager whenever I needed to talk. Adventurous in her youth, she had been an incredibly talented swimmer, and was asked to try out for the Olympics. Her brush with greatness came when she trained with Johnny Weissmuller, a five-time Olympic gold medal winner who played Tarzan in the movies in the 1930s and '40s.

My mom had a thirst for learning like my father's. She had been a teacher in the Atlantic City high school system after graduating from Temple University in Philadelphia before she married my dad. She gave up teaching when my sister and I were young, and by the time I was twelve, she had gone back to school, earned a master's degree, and started teaching physical education in the Stratford, Connecticut, public school system for years before she retired. She was proud of me no matter what, and I would spend a lifetime trying to find inside myself just a fraction of the empathy she showed me.

Some of the happier moments of my preteen years came on Saturdays, when I would stand outside late in the day and gaze down our tree-lined street, waiting to spot my father's yacht-sized black 1947 Fleetwood Cadillac, with its proud chrome goddess hood ornament. He commuted weekly from our home in Milford to General Electric, a mammoth conglomerate that made lightbulbs, refrigerators, dishwashers, and washing machines and dryers, along with airplane engine parts and some of the earliest versions of the mainframe computer and the TV set. GE had offices in Syracuse, Schenectady, and Utica, New York, and moved him around.

My father didn't express emotions the way other dads did. He spoke in silences, leaving me to decode pride or disappointment through the smallest gestures—a nod, a slow exhale, or a smile that lingered. His peaceful presence in our home comforted me, and over time his stoicism became mine.

We were Presbyterian in name mostly; my father had no patience for the small talk and handshakes that came with Sunday mornings. Instead, our religion was practiced quietly at home, anchored in his strict, simple code: You are responsible for your life. Do your best. No shortcuts. No loafing. No cheating. Catholics had it easier, he'd tell me—they could sin, confess, and be forgiven with a fresh start. But for my sister and me, there were no excuses. The pressure to get it right the first time lingers still. I learned to forgive others easily, but forgiving myself was always a silent negotiation with the ghost of my father's expectations.

I missed him then as I miss him now. The unfulfilled need for his approval, maybe more than anything, is a major element of what drives me, and over a lifetime, with male mentors, bosses, and friends, I've tried to prove my worth.

My first real job was a long paper route slinging *The New Haven Register*, my bicycle loaded with papers in big saddlebags. I would hoard my earnings with the same frugality as my parents; I hung on to the first dollar I made until the day I got married.

My first entrepreneurial opportunity came when I was around twelve years old. GE's small appliance division in Bridgeport was unloading hundreds of small, broken radios that had been returned for various reasons. The price couldn't be beat: $1 apiece. Using money from the paper route, I bought the surplus radios. Using Dad's equipment in the barn, I repaired the radios on nights and weekends and sold almost all of them for $4 apiece— a 300 percent profit!

During those years, most of my free time was spent back behind the house in the barn, helping my father service our cars, boat motors, or the appliances from our house. It was like a quiet apprenticeship in mechanical engineering. All these things came to the repair shop in the barn like patients to a hospital, with my father playing the cool and calm head surgeon. I was the assistant, passing him tools or grabbing parts that lay on the table.

The air was always cooler under the big barn's tall ceiling, even during steamy summer days, when I would shimmy on the cold cement floor underneath our old Fleetwood to get a look at the oil pan. Often I held the trouble light above the car engine for Dad, listening as he described how the pistons moved up and down because of tiny explosions, which in turn moved the rods connected to a crankshaft.

My father reveled in the joy of figuring things out, especially anything mechanical. He could hold his own with the smartest person at the party but preferred to be in the quiet of his shop; he was an intellectual in white sports socks.

There were few items we couldn't take apart and put back together. When he got his '47 Fleetwood, we dropped the oil pan and changed the main bearings. Just going and buying bearings for his Cadillac was too easy. He was convinced a new quasi-exotic metal was better for bearings than the usual metal coating, and that's how the bearings got to be too tight: he electroplated them with just a touch too much metal. One family vacation we spent hours sitting by the side of the road waiting for the Cadillac to cool. My parents would never fight in front of us, but you could almost see the smoke coming out of my mother's ears. My dad was only mildly embarrassed. That was Dad.

He passed down his knack for inventing and assembling things to me, and by the time I was a teenager, we often had to compete for space on the workbench in the barn.

My father had a background in radar, and when the Korean War started in 1950 he did some classified work for GE with the U.S. Navy. When the war ended, he continued to work in the development program as an engineer in the research division. General Electric made some of the earliest TV sets, in the 1940s, and my dad quickly gained a reputation as the resident expert on the new technology, occasionally being asked to visit the living room of a GE bigwig to fix the family TV.

Often, my dad took me along for those visits. I started out as the gofer, running out to the car to a get a tool. Eventually, I could change the tubes myself and was assisting in the diagnosis, which often transpired in the barn, where we had an impressive collection of TV parts, tools, and special devices that measured the sets' vital signs. Dad and I would stare into the nest of wires and parts in the back of a TV's hulking wooden cabinet and carefully dissect the problem. My father had pulled the curtain open behind the magic of television.

But as magical as it was, the old vacuum tubes were unreliable, the picture was grainy, and the screen was small. Our family was often the field test team for the latest TV set my father had just fixed; my mom would complain that we had five different sets piled on top of one another, and only one might work.

I walked with my buddies to the local public school, where I genuinely enjoyed learning. I loved to read, and in my fourth-grade year, I developed a schoolboy crush on my teacher. My nine-year-old brain decided the way to her heart was through sheer literary stamina, so I plowed through a hundred books over the year.

In September 1954, I was accepted into a prestigious private prep school in New Haven called Hopkins School on a work scholarship that paid 60 percent of the tuition if I kept my high marks and worked for an hour a day during the week and half days on Saturdays. My parents had worried about my previous public school as the academic rigor declined, but I think my dad was pleased that the deal for the new private school included an element of hard work. I spent many afternoons sweeping classrooms, washing dishes in the cafeteria, fertilizing the fields, or mowing fields (under much safer conditions than home). I felt proud I could contribute. Some of my oldest friends to this day are the people I met in that work scholarship program.

The move to the new school in eighth grade, something I hadn't requested or expected, turned out to be a pivotal moment in my life, and a lifelong reminder for me of the power of education.

Founded in 1660 in a one-room building on the New Haven Green, the school was named after Edward Hopkins, a governor of the original Connecticut Colony, who left money for schools in American colonies dedicated to teaching "hopeful youths for the public service of the country." The school's mission rings as relevant for me even still: "learning how to learn, how to think clearly, how to express ideas effectively, and how to work independently."

In some ways the mental tasks in class were like the ones that occupied my weekends in the barn, fixing a radio. To this day, I can get lost in thought while figuring out a problem and be completely content. My wife says I overthink and extrapolate for everything, from menu choices to movie night. I was a loner in my teen years, and I could bury myself in books while isolating myself from the high school social scene.

It was a long day, leaving home by 6 a.m., commuting the half hour to New Haven from Milford, and getting back home around the same time in the evening. On weekends, I would make the transition from a preppie wearing buttoned-down collars and ties to a tough-guy greaser, complete with a heavy mop of pomaded hair. I would come home to the neighborhood in a tie and jacket to glares and taunts from neighborhood kids, who would threaten to kick my ass.

I enjoyed fencing: the power of the épée, the self-reliance the sport required, and the competitive thrill of a one-on-one duel—in one bout the tip of a sword broke off in my shoulder. I soon became undefeated against other prep schools in Connecticut, in part because I was stronger and faster, but more because I learned early that calm beats rage, and control beats pride.

Anticipating your opponent's next response is critical. In fencing, "second intention actions" entail blade movement and footwork to draw out a counterattack from your opponent. Your first attack is the diversion, and it has to be convincing enough to draw out your opponent's reaction. Once you know their reflexive move to a particular attack, then you can go in for the kill. Business can work that way, too.

All the while, I was changing physically, growing fast, and pumping iron to get even stronger. My real sweet spot was in high school track and field, throwing the discus, and I eventually broke the state record. My friends nicknamed me "The Bat" after seeing my lats flexed and my long arms out-stretched, spinning before the release. Beneath my muscular build and my black leather jacket, I was more shy than tough.

Everybody hung out at Paul's Drive-In in Milford, a place not unlike Mel's Drive-In in the old movie *American Graffiti*. The small parking lot was a beehive of activity, with hot rods cruising through, girls clustered around car windows, and the sounds of Buddy Holly and Bill Haley blasting from car speakers into the night air. And the hamburgers—juicy, salty, dripping cheese, and made to order—are, to this day, without doubt, still the best I ever have tasted in my life.

A lot of kids sneaked beer, but I didn't get into alcohol, in part because I thought of myself as an athlete and in part because I didn't like being out of control. I would still hang out at beer parties on the beach, and there was always a guy who wanted to prove how tough he was by challenging me, but I avoided conflict.

When it comes to emotions, I am more of a stoic like my father. Happiness seems to me a relative measure, because it must be juxtaposed to expectation. If you walk through life expecting everything to be wonderful and trouble-free, you will never be what most people consider happy.

I was a quiet kid in and out of class, and respectful to my teachers. I excelled in calculus, cheered on by an inspiring math teacher named John Heath, but I struggled in French.

It was one of the oldest, finest schools in the Northeast, but I didn't care about the reputation back then. All that mattered was that I was saving my parents money and, perhaps more than anything else, that I was making my father proud—I hoped.

As pleased as my parents were, I felt in many ways that I didn't fit in at school. Though I was challenged intellectually and stimulated by the learning environment, the awkwardness I felt made it hard to feel sure about myself.

I can appear to be distant and unapproachable at times. But my autism, wherever it is on the spectrum, has gifted me with the ability to hyper-focus on intricate challenges and pursue a goal with dogged determination. From a young age, I saw patterns, connections, and solutions others overlooked, and this attention to detail helped me identify opportunities early and gave me a competitive edge. With a virtually photographic memory at the time, I could recall verbatim entire sections of books.

Little by little, the contradictions in my life stopped feeling like mistakes and started to feel like information. I didn't "overcome" my thoughts— I learned to understand them, to use them. In time, what once felt like disorder became direction.

What I knew about big business then was through the prism of my dad's experience at GE. He got kicked around inside GE, and too many years there had soured him on giant corporations. In the 1950s and '60s, he was moved from pillar to post, never getting recognized for his contributions, which were often meaningful to the company, and then ultimately losing stature when the group he worked for got blown out by some reshuffling or political move.

I think he finally got disgusted with the commute and the hassles of working at the company, and so late in his career there, he started a business on the side—an appliance store in nearby Fairfield. He wanted to sell and repair TV sets and radios along with refrigerators and washing machines, the staples of modern life. He had hired a manager and had assigned the job of bookkeeper to my mother. But it didn't work out, and the store closed.

After another unsuccessful effort, with a military electronics company, my father took a third shot with a business deal that showed promise, this time with an electronics manufacturer. He was the junior partner, and the venture lasted a couple years and went public. Once again, somewhat wealthier this time, my dad ended up leaving the business, largely because he disagreed with the senior partner's determination to go ahead with a big transaction (which would ultimately tank the company).

Maybe he was too naive or simply too focused on mechanics, and not enough on finances. Throughout his career, my father was considered an extremely good problem-solving engineer, but the people who were controlling the business, whether his employer or his partners, focused on the money side. This left him with a lingering belief that he had been taken advantage of, and that, in turn, left him feeling less than competent.

I vowed to avoid ending up like that, with no control, no sense of the business-finance side, and no partner I could trust.

If our makeshift garage was a university, my thesis was the 1954 Jaguar XK-120 coupe I had bought with savings from my paper route. The car looked like something James Bond would drive—sleek, curvy, and built for speed—but mine was more of a jalopy when I got it. The previous owner had modified it for track racing, but it didn't run, and the gears jammed. My father and I towed it home one Sunday morning—him in his big black Caddy, me at fourteen behind the wheel of the old Jag, as proud as ever.

We got the engine running, and I even figured out the problem with the four-speed synchro transmission, which I repaired by welding a chipped tooth on the synchro sleeve. I tore that motor apart so many times that by sixteen, I could fix damn near anything.

I continued to find respite around the barn on weekends. My father would observe and advise as we tinkered, quizzing us with open-ended questions like he was Socrates. He enjoyed showing us how to disassemble the complex parts of a motor and then put it back together. He could "see" an engine in his mind even though most parts were scattered on the concrete barn floor.

George and I spent a lot of time repairing boats. We started racing hydroplanes—small, flat speedboats with open cockpits that skimmed the water's surface at forty to fifty miles per hour. I loved the thrill of speed, as the outboard engines created a rooster tail of cut diamonds twenty feet high in their wake.

It was an idyllic life in a classic suburban American neighborhood in the 1950s, a stone's throw from Long Island Sound and the Atlantic Ocean, which has always been a source of solace for me. The waves, the salt air, the gulls, and sand of Long Island Sound hooked me from an early age. And the feeling I got driving a boat on the water was one of absolute freedom.

I loved the sheer scale of the ocean, the endless miles of undulating blue water, all of it moving in a connected, harmonious rhythm that comforts me to this day.

I miss those days still. George would eat supper with us, and we'd stay up late watching TV, with Mom knitting, and Dad dozing nearby, still in his work clothes, which were dusty and oily from the barn.

On one sunny afternoon, my father agreed to chaperone a practice drive before my driver's license test. So we drove the Austin down the Merritt Parkway, a double ribbon of parallel one-way roads separated by trees.

On the straightaway, brimming with confidence, I let my foot get too heavy on the gas pedal. George was in the back seat, peering over my shoulder at the speedometer, and his voice signaled his alarm: "John," he called out as we were about to race past the exit we were supposed to take. "John? . . . JOOOOOOHN!!!!"

It was too late to make the turn off the highway, but I decided to take the exit anyway, jumping the median at roughly double the speed limit and coming within inches of clipping the exit sign—and at least one other car. The Austin bucked like a wild horse over the curb of the median, and George screamed: "I don't want to diiiiiiiiiiiiiiie!!!!!"

When I got the wheel under control and slowed the car down, I glanced over at my father out of the corner of my eye. He had braced his big frame against every immovable square inch of the front cabin and looked nonchalantly ahead. Slowly relaxing his body, he said, calmly as could be: "A little too fast . . ." As if he had just looked up from his newspaper. That was my father.

Moments later, I looked in the rearview mirror to see George, having recovered his composure, smirking at me. That is how I remember my friend decades later: smiling mischievously, always ready for our next adventure. George and others taught me that the friends you make are the measure of your life. And even the people you leave behind, you never really lose, because those moments are preserved in memory, and they fortify the bonds of friendship over time and space.

As my father and I both got older, we got into a habit of sitting in these aluminum chairs out in back of the house. I relished these moments and basked in his attention, and found myself asking his direction long after I left home.

Then the news came one day in a phone call, in the middle of an afternoon, out of nowhere, after I had taken a new job. My father had suffered a heart attack. They had found him in one of those aluminum chairs.

CHAPTER 3

MEETING MA BELL

About the only thing I didn't have at the time was a girl. And there was a very good reason for that. I could explain far more easily how to rebuild a carburetor than tell you how I was feeling at any given moment. And I was stumped at making polite conversation. It's just not how I am wired. To this day, I am not a fan of cocktail parties or big crowds. I'm better with people one-on-one, and even then I can run into trouble with awkward silences and stammering.

All that would change in the summer of 1958. One afternoon, I was killing time down on the beach with a group of friends, including my sister. I saw her talking to a girl I knew but did not immediately recognize.

"Hey, sis."

"Hey, John, you remember Leslie, right?"

Time froze. She was the most beautiful creature I had ever seen, and I could not stop staring. Auburn hair. Just days away from her Sweet 16 birthday. In a two-piece green swimsuit.

At first I was tongue-tied, but Leslie started talking to me in a way few other girls did. I felt so at ease. We walked the beach and chatted for over an hour, and for the first time in a long time, I felt connection. I didn't want it to end. I worked up enough courage to ask her to see the premiere of the movie *South Pacific* at the New Haven Theatre with me.

Walking back to the car that day with George, I was still tingling with all the physical and emotional energy a seventeen-year-old could handle. Dancing electrons. I was in love.

"I think I just met my wife."

"Suuuuuure you did," he laughed.

"I'm serious," I said.

I stopped on the spot and stared him down for effect. Then I pulled a coin from my pocket, cocked my arm back, and hurled it into the surf. "There's my bet."

A little over four years later, my prophecy came true. She is the same woman I met as a teenager, but today, more than sixty years later, so much more than the partner I bargained for. If you were to chart my personal highs and lows, like the daily price of a stock, I could point to a steadily ascending peak that begins with meeting Leslie.

Leslie is still today the love of my life, as beautiful to me as the day I met her, artistic, intuitive, empathetic, mentally sharp, and physically strong, and in many ways, on many topics, my complete opposite.

My drive to constantly prove myself would create difficulties for us later on and distract me from the true value Leslie has brought to my life. That day on the beach was the first time I ever had such an overwhelming feeling for another person, and I couldn't focus on much else. The distractions would find me soon enough.

I did well enough at the Hopkins School to get a National Merit Scholarship upon graduation in 1959, and my application to Yale was accepted, which made my parents proud.

Brilliant ideas never came to me like a bolt of lightning. Creative genius for me was the constant assemblage of prior exposures and putting those things together for a solution.

I was never a fast learner, but I was diligent and focused, and I had the intellectual grit to stick with a problem. So, by the second year at Yale, I was pretty competitive with the smarter kids in class, and by the third year I was outrunning them. It was my persistence more than anything. I stayed with it, and by the end of the term, I had the answers before most others in class.

Though the university was only fifteen miles or so from our house, living on campus that freshman year, a requirement for the academic program, was the first time I had ever lived away from home. My closest friends at

Yale were a motley crew of guys who had come with me from prep school: a genius nuclear physicist, a gambler, and some serious engineering geeks. I missed my dear friend George, who had joined the navy and was in Europe most of the time I was in college.

The workload felt light since most of my classes were in engineering—all clean lines and logic, the kind of structure my mathematical mind felt at home in. I was driving a Jaguar, flush with freedom, and head over heels in love. Time felt elastic then—and there was a sense that everything good was still ahead. It was one of those rare stretches in life when everything clicked.

By the time I got to Yale, I had very strong beliefs about what made the world work. And in many ways, I was out of sync with the prevailing political attitude, so I often found myself at odds with professors. Many of the economics courses leaned toward socialism, in my opinion.

One of the main textbooks was Paul Samuelson's *Economics*, a respected introduction to Keynesian theory—the idea that government can manage the economy by intervening in markets, such as by spending to boost economic growth. But I didn't buy it. I believed in free markets. To me, people act in their own self-interest—it's just human nature—and that's what really drives the economy. I remember thinking: this all sounds nice on paper, but it's not how the real world works.

Some of the professors promoted Russian mathematicians who had built models supporting "orderly" centralized economic planning, considered more efficient than America's "chaotic" free-market system. And because I questioned these concepts, I often got poor grades in those classes.

At the time, it felt like the whole country was drifting toward socialism. When John F. Kennedy was elected, he went after U.S. Steel for raising prices—basically telling them to back down or face consequences. Even Republicans favored more government control. Belief in free markets, it seemed, was fading.

Looking back, my concerns about Yale's liberal and Keynesian slant seem almost rather quaint given where we are today in universities. Since then, universities have shifted even more, with some professors teaching economic theories that, in my view, miss the mark—often to students who haven't yet had much real-world exposure to business or capitalism.

Today I'd call myself a libertarian by nature, a fiscal conservative, and a somewhat social liberal.

I graduated Phi Beta Kappa from Yale in 1963 with a bachelor's degree in economics and electrical engineering. I wanted more practical knowledge than anything, but I wondered if I needed to get my doctorate degree to do more. I wanted to avoid burdening my parents with debt, and at the time, three big companies offered to pay for graduate education for a Yale engineering student like me as part of the employment contract: Bell Labs, Hughes Aircraft, and United Aircraft.

Of those, Bell Labs seemed the best option, the famed blue-sky research division of the old American Telephone and Telegraph Company, which operated the Bell telephone system as a monopoly for most of the twentieth century, before federal government trust-busters broke it up into pieces in 1984. I had begun to see myself as a scientist or engineer, in part because I loved the empirical data, cold logic, and indisputable science that governed how technology works. The undeniable certainty of mathematics fueled my curiosity as I tried to engineer new ways to solve problems.

Bell Labs was building a discipline in a new field they called operations research, a new way of applying scientific modeling to complex problems in business, engineering, and other fields. First, break the problem into manageable parts, then apply relevant disciplines—mathematical modeling, data analysis, and computer simulations, all while considering real-world constraints like time and money. The result: firms make smarter, faster, and more cost-effective decisions.

I wanted to learn more. Bell Labs offered to cover all the expenses of school and pay a decent wage. I would finish my education in Baltimore at Johns Hopkins University, one of the finest and oldest research university in the country, founded in 1876 with a record philanthropic gift from entrepreneur Johns Hopkins.

I loved operations research. It seemed to fit my view of the world and business: applying math and science to maximize profit, minimize cost, build wealth. It was a way to think about business, and I loved the efficiency of it. Though some of its tools are obsolete now decades later, its way of thinking still resonates.

I would get a master's degree in industrial management from the Johns Hopkins University in 1964 and an additional master's degree in electrical engineering, in part through a classroom program provided by New York University, then graduate with a doctorate in operations research at Johns Hopkins. There was another big reason Bell Labs fit so well: Leslie and I were still dating, we were madly in love, and we wanted to get married. It fit our life plan.

Long before the emergence of Silicon Valley, Bell Telephone Laboratories was the hotbed of activity for every young, tech-obsessed geek. As part of the program at Bell Labs, you started as soon as you graduated.

What a fabulous place Bell Labs was in 1963, with some fifteen thousand engineers, scientists, and mathematicians. Long before it was fashionable, the labs employed many women in the ranks. Operated in a monolithic building on Mountain Avenue in Murray Hill, New Jersey, inside Bell Labs was some of the most advanced futuristic research and development (R&D) anywhere in the world. These were the golden years of R&D: the first laser was invented at Bell Labs, and the transistor, and the Unix computer operating system, among many other advances. I was in heaven. In my early years there, I was working in economic planning and R&D under the tutelage of Doug Barnes, who became a mentor to me.

After a few years at Bell Labs, I began to feel the gnaw of a familiar force that I wanted something different, yet I didn't know what. Many of my colleagues, all in our mid-twenties, highly educated, thought life's path had now been fully determined. You could have a great career in the protective fortress that was the Bell System, and that is what most people wanted—security.

I had promised Leslie stability in the form of a family, and a career at Bell Labs would help make that possible. The Bell System, a gigantic monopoly, offered great security, but I wanted more. My dad's experience at GE had soured me on big bureaucracies because suddenly when you are closing in on age forty, when the company switches directions and your skill set no longer matters, you have nowhere else to go.

I looked around and saw a lot of people who were doing, in the end, useless jobs, which created huge overhead. I remember debating them, telling them they might *think* their jobs were secure, yet they were working in maybe the most insecure spot in the world—they were in such narrow disciplines that they would lack the broader skills to survive if the company shelved their projects. And then I would give 'em my favorite line: "You will be dinosaurs."

As I was finishing my coursework for my PhD, I was assigned to work on some large-scale models of the Bell System for AT&T. Many of the projects allowed me to study ways to make significant improvements not just in operations, but finance as well: debt leverage, depreciation schedules, taxation—the big-picture stuff I loved to contemplate and calculate. This gave me the opportunity to build a mathematical model of the Bell System itself.

One of the highlights of my new career was when I was asked to make a presentation of my work to the entire AT&T board of directors (a board I would join thirty years later). I had coauthored published papers on "The Impact of Regulation on a Monopoly Firm" and "Profit Maximization at a Regulated Firm," which analyzed profit objectives, return on capital, and asset allocation. During my presentation, I used some of these mathematical models to justify making sweeping changes to the financial strategy of AT&T, suggesting an unorthodox approach to its prodigious, pristine balance sheet—one reason for its top-notch, triple-A debt rating. AT&T was underleveraged, and undervalued, so I urged the board to shift its debt-equity ratio, borrowing billions of dollars to invest in buying back its own stock on the open market.

This buyback program proposed to reduce the total number of shares of AT&T stock on the market and available to the public since more shares would be owned by the company. That, in turn, would increase the company's earnings per share, a key metric on Wall Street. The downside was that a higher debt load might result in a modestly lower credit rating for AT&T and increase its interest costs. We dismissed that worry, arguing any impact would be minimal because interest payments are tax-deductible. So AT&T essentially would boost earnings and fund the carrying costs of its stock buybacks with money that it otherwise would pay to the tax collector. This was a more efficient use of AT&T's cash.

It was a bold idea, and I was sure it could help the company. In fact, this big idea would play a role in driving the strategies, mergers, and financial alchemy that would come to define the rest of my career. It's the strategy I used to help grow the cable industry by focusing Wall Street and bank lenders on cash flow instead of taxable earnings.

I was only twenty-seven years old and addressing a board for the first time, yet I felt pretty confident of my case after vetting my remarks with multiple levels of management. Still, my gut growled with nervousness as I entered the boardroom at AT&T's headquarters at 195 Broadway in downtown Manhattan. By the time I had finished delivering the report, maybe twenty minutes later, I had convinced myself it had gone well.

Afterward, the chairman of AT&T at the time, Fred Kappel, came over to me with a big smile on his face. He wrapped an arm around my shoulders and walked me out of the room, telling me, "Son, that was great! Stimulating! A lot to think about!" My smile widened, until he continued: "But if in your whole career, you can do a single thing that changes the Ma Bell system in even the smallest way, you would be very successful." With a genuine smile and a pat on my back, he had swatted away the idea as if it were a housefly.

I realized that at AT&T I would spend my career belowdecks, and that any raise I got would depend on other people. I would lack control over my own life. So I immediately began writing my résumé.

When I told friends at work I was looking to leave Bell Labs, they told me I was crazy, while I thought they were making a mistake by staying. I wanted something more out of life. And so I bailed, much to their shock. I was a young, rising star in the Bell System and my advancement there was all but guaranteed, and yet all I could think about was: *I can't get out of this place fast enough.*

Around this time, I had applied for a job at McKinsey, the global white-shoe consulting firm. I figured the life of a consultant might provide a more realistic education about how businesses work.

When I got the offer from McKinsey, though, I was panicked at first, and suddenly I felt buyer's remorse. I wondered whether I had just jumped from the biggest, safest vessel I would ever board. I fell ill, ran a fever for weeks, and had a series of diagnostic medical tests run. *What the hell was wrong with me?*

CHAPTER 4

MY MENTOR MOSES

On the first day of my new job at McKinsey & Company, I arrived at my desk to find a note waiting for me: "John, if you can't be in Montreal by 1:30 p.m. to have lunch with the chairman of Bell Canada, please call this number . . ." Attached to the note was a plane ticket.

I lacked the social skills then to travel to another country and talk casually with CEOs of big firms and advise them what to do. Hell, before joining McKinsey, I had never been in an airplane—my family never flew. But that first day I took a car to LaGuardia and flew to Montreal. Four hours later, I was in the dining room of Bell Canada interviewing the chairman. I would spend the next six weeks in Montreal, assessing Bell Canada's entry into the hot new field of microelectronics. I interviewed the executives involved, to analyze their strategy.

And that was a large part of the job: listening, a severely underrated talent in business. It should be a class unto itself in business schools. Most people in a conversation are waiting for their turn to speak. Everyone wants to be heard, but few people in business engage in listening to understand.

I have learned an awful lot about business over the last sixty-plus years by asking dumb questions and then keeping my mouth shut, more than I ever learned by saying something. Sitting down with major executives across a desk or at lunch, asking them questions, and listening hard to comprehend their most critical issues provided me with the answers I sought—and more insight that I expected.

Often the answer was hiding in plain sight, and you were opening the leaders' eyes to something staring at them. Sometimes CEOs are plagued by doubt and indecision and want outside counsel. Other times the CEO already knows what action he or she wants to take, and the consultant provides the data to support their call.

McKinsey was filled with Harvard Business School grads, polished presenters with big Rolodexes and even bigger vocabularies. The culture there offered a startling change from the educational environment that had shaped me. Now I was asking the questions, not the professors. It was exhilarating and terrifying. CEOs were now seeking *my* advice on big, complex problems.

Typically, I was a shy guy, unwilling to talk in social circles. Now, because of my new role, fueled by my genuine and growing curiosity and my love of solving problems, I could interview some pretty senior people without feeling intimidated or awkward. And it went very well; most of my clients walked away happy, and it was very instructional for me.

We looked at all sorts of corporate problems, but the thorniest case I worked on was a reorganization of General Electric. One of the biggest companies in America, it was also the same company that had employed my father for most of his career. Connecting with people, understanding their biggest concerns, and mapping their universe proved far more valuable than reading GE annual reports. You have to go in and talk to people to understand why something's not working. And again, you listen.

It became clear quickly that the teams at GE were frustrated by having to go through five or six layers of approval to get anything done. Plus, the people in charge of signing off didn't really understand the business or the problem. Suddenly a culture of second-guessing had emerged throughout the organization.

The solution, as I saw it, was to create strategic business units that could operate independently in terms of decisions and budgets within the conglomerate. GE previously had defined departments and divisions based on size, and they were bloated.

GE was top-heavy, and that was impeding innovation and efficiency, so we urged management to trim corporate staff. Laying off people is painful for all involved, but sometimes a necessary strategy for survival. GE would later adopt McKinsey's recommendation and ultimately ended up with a small corporate headquarters in Stamford, Connecticut.

Despite the great experience I was getting at McKinsey, the travel and hours amounted to a marriage-killing schedule. And the culture was not particularly warm, built more on performance than relationships. The guy I reported to was an icicle; one year he had me deliver his Christmas presents to his kids because he had emergency meetings during the holidays. It was becoming clear that if you were going to work at McKinsey, you were going to give up having a family life.

I felt like I spent more time in airports than in the office. Back home, Leslie struggled in my absence. We had moved from North Jersey to Weston, Connecticut, a country hamlet just an hour on the train from the office in New York City, for the sole purpose of settling down. But it may as well have been a million miles away for the little time I spent at home.

This felt even worse after Leslie gave birth to our daughter, and later when we had a son on the way. I wanted things to slow down just as the pace was speeding up, and I wanted to keep my promise to Leslie.

By 1970, two years after joining the firm, I knew I had to move. One of my last clients at McKinsey connected me to was someone who would change my thinking forever. A company called General Instrument had started as a sleepy electronics firm in New York in 1923 and had evolved into being the owner of assorted electronics businesses. GI had just bought a Philadelphia-based company called Jerrold Electronics; it was a massive acquisition for a company that size, roughly 40 percent of its value at the time.

GI was one of the first companies to market with UHF tuners, introduced in the 1950s and '60s to allow TVs to receive ultra high frequency (UHF) channels (13 through 48) beyond the original very high frequency (VHF) band (channels 1 through 13). GI had stock that was overvalued at the time, and the company wanted to use it to buy something. Jerrold, it was discovered later, had some financial irregularities, always to the upside, of course, since accounting "errors" rarely make a firm's finances look worse rather than better. So GI had used inflated paper to buy an inflated business. Less than a year after the Jerrold acquisition, GI was in trouble. It had bought a series of businesses, which wasn't working, and, worse, now General Instrument was struggling to stay current on its loan payments.

It was a common scenario: senior executives call in consultants to fix a fast merger. Everything looked right when they bought the company. Once the contract was signed and the backslapping was over, suddenly the plan all went to hell. It was up to McKinsey, or one of a number of other consulting firms, to untangle the mess. McKinsey sent me to General Instrument's base in Philadelphia to figure out what was going on.

I studied the situation for six months, traveling back and forth between Connecticut and Philadelphia. Finally I reported back to the chairman of GI, one of the smartest businesspeople I have had the pleasure of working with, Moses "Monty" Shapiro.

He was a former labor lawyer who spouted Talmudic wisdom, and he would become my first true mentor after my father. He could spot opportunity that was light-years away, and he played a pivotal role in the commercialization of cable TV in the U.S.—and ushered me into it. I am forever grateful.

Jerrold quickly became one of the first providers of parts for broadcast and then cable companies, and its founder, Milton Shapp, would reap millions of dollars from the sale and would later become governor of Pennsylvania. In the late 1940s, a few inventive entrepreneurs had discovered they could deliver better TV reception to whole communities by essentially sticking the equivalent of a big roof antenna atop a hill, wiring the signal down to individual homes, and charging them a monthly fee for the service. They managed to sell broadcast TV shows that local stations were beaming to their audience for free. But in small towns where hilly topography prevented broadcast television signals from reaching customers' homes, this was big news and caught the attention of national media, including *The New York Times* and *The Wall Street Journal*.

Robert Tarlton, who started using Jerrold's amplifier for apartment complexes to wire entire communities for television antenna service, was one of a handful of innovators creating such a system. Intrigued, Shapp visited Tarlton, his longtime customer, and suddenly realized Tarlton's grand vision.

In 1950, with a group of retailers in Lansford, Pennsylvania, who were eager to sell more TV sets, Tarlton began to offer antenna service from Philadelphia broadcast TV stations to homes in Lansford for a fee.

From that day forward, Shapp was convinced of the promise of this new market, and he overhauled his company to deliver parts and services to the growing community antenna TV business. Two years later, Tarlton went to work for Jerrold, and he would go on to become a cofounder of the industry's first national cable-TV trade group, known today as NCTA—the Internet and Television Association.

Tarlton's account is just one thread in the origin story of cable television— a quiet revolution that began not in boardrooms or broadcast towers but in the foggy hills and wooded hollows of Pennsylvania, Oregon, and Arkansas, which broadcast signals struggled to reach and where multiple pioneers laid claim to being first.

With the post–World War II economy roaring, Americans craved entertainment and connection. Facing a flood of applications for broadcast stations and technical challenges to map them, the FCC imposed a "freeze" on new TV licenses from 1948 to 1952—leaving millions of Americans in a television void.

Into that vacuum stepped plucky pioneers who devised a bold solution: hoist towering antennas atop the highest peaks to capture faint transmissions from distant stations. From there, they strung wire, pole by pole, down into the shadowed towns below.

Jerrold Electronics began building components of these community antenna systems and selling them as turnkey businesses to eager entrepreneurs. After the war, a lot of the coaxial cable manufactured for communications was sold in surplus, and much of the cable in the early days came in odd sizes. By the 1950s, Jerrold had standardized cable wire and had begun making or buying connectors that could hook up these wires to large antennas. One huge strength Jerrold had over rivals was a team of crack-shot engineers, who had a head start on competitors, and were first to market standardized fittings with almost no leakage in the signal. As an enticement, the company would guarantee that as new equipment was developed, Jerrold would replace the original equipment you had installed at no extra cost.

The company accepted promissory notes from customers, a legal promise to pay the bill—and sold the notes to financial institutions at a discount. Most banks wouldn't touch loans for such a risky business. When a lot of those early entrepreneurs overextended themselves and faced financial trouble, Jerrold took over their systems. Consequently, Jerrold became one of the largest "community antennae TV" operators in the country.

Television, the spectacle unveiled at the 1939 World's Fair, remained a luxury in 1950, present in just a few million homes. Yet by decade's end, it was a national fixture, glowing in over 50 million living rooms. Cable TV was a quiet accomplice in this revolution, an improvised, ingenious solution born of necessity. And it spread like windblown seed, propelled by tinkerers, dreamers, and hometown entrepreneurs.

At first I thought costs had skyrocketed at Jerrold Electronics, but with a little sleuthing, I found the truth: the company had been posting fraudulent, inflated numbers. So I flew again to Philly to give Moses, who also went by the more secular name Monty, the news. After going through the misdeeds, I finally sighed, "Monty, GI overpaid for a real turkey here." His displeasure with the business was obvious. Monty was as coarse as he was colorful, often using expressions from WWII: "You don't know shit from Shinola" and "Quit beating your gums." I was terribly fond of the old guy, and we had developed a strong bond.

One day I happened to be in the room as he was dressing down a lieutenant in sales; minutes earlier, he had literally turned the heat up on the thermostat in the room for effect. "Burt! God damn it. Your business is just not getting it done!" Monty was all over the poor guy.

As we were talking through the troubles at Jerrold one day, Monty asked me straight-out if I'd like to run GI's Jerrold myself. I was getting tired of being a consultant and never seeing my family. If Leslie and I moved to a nice neighborhood in Philadelphia, maybe we could build a more stable home life without all the traveling. I could be president of Jerrold, the third-largest U.S. cable operator and one of the largest divisions in GI. I'd be the one making the decisions, rather than simply whispering in the CEO's ear.

With a daughter now and a son on the way, I liked the idea of no more trains, planes, and automobiles. I would be home, like a regular parent, and I'd be there to give my kids presents at Christmas.

So, with absolutely zero hands-on experience running a business, I quit my job at McKinsey and set about trying to fix a money-losing company called Jerrold.

Running a business, it turns out, is harder than *telling somebody how* to run a business. I learned by following Moses's Talmudic wisdom, a bit of trial and error, and asking endless questions of the engineers and executives around me. I was basically a technology-trained engineer, with a bit of high-level strategic exposure, now dealing with the nitty-gritty of running a very large and complicated company. Jerrold posted $80 million a year in revenue, employed thousands of people, and was deep in parts manufacturing, cable-TV system construction, and financing.

One major pain point for General Instrument initially was a big debt suddenly due because of a bad currency bet. GI had borrowed a bunch of money in deutsche marks, Germany's currency before the euro, which had then appreciated. And the only thing that they had that was liquid was Jerrold's cable systems, so they were forced to sell.

Not long after I arrived at Jerrold, I had mentioned to Monty, then the chairman of General Instrument, that Bob Magness, who was then a customer of mine, desperately wanted to buy the Jerrold/GI systems at a time when Bob's TCI's stock was frothy from acquisitions. I still recall Monty's response, more than fifty years later: "Yeah, but I don't want any Portuguese escudos from Magness. I want coin of the realm: cash."

At that time, an entrepreneur named Charlie Sammons was one of a few guys around with real cash, and he was willing to part with it. Jerrold sold the systems to Sammons for $28 million, and that was a lifesaver for GI. It would also prove to be a smart investment by Sammons—twenty years later, after buying more systems, he would sell the company to various buyers for $1.8 billion.

I was focused intently on the business, but it was Monty who, from time to time, made me look up. One lesson I learned from Monty that would save me time and again in the future, even to this day, was to ask on every big deal, a simple three-word question: What if not? What if this doesn't work? What if this venture or idea falls apart completely?

I started seeing risk through a different lens: When you focus on the opportunity and genuinely deconstruct the hazards ahead, the fear of taking a leap begins to fade. Knowing with certainty that the risk won't kill you is what liberates you to take it.

Jerrold faced serious issues—chief among them was inflated numbers tied to a corrupt purchasing department taking kickbacks. Productivity at the main factory was also poor. We overhauled purchasing, shut down the Philadelphia plant, and moved operations to more efficient locations in Nogales, Mexico; Springfield, Massachusetts for high-end parts; and Asia for low-cost components. By committing to large-volume buys, we cut costs dramatically.

While some may criticize the shift overseas, it made sense—U.S. plants are better suited for advanced, high-margin manufacturing.

We focused hard on offering the lowest prices on volume products the industry needed, down to the little connectors to join or plug in cable wires. So that every time a Jerrold salesperson greeted a client, there was a reason for the order book to come out. And just by doing a better job of running the business, we saw the results start to improve and our market share go way up. Monty was thrilled.

In pursuit of market research, I joined the board of the newly formed trade association for cable TV, and right away I became aware of a new product opportunity.

Cable TV was about to catch a big break from the government. The trade association was pushing the government to loosen restrictions on cable, promising to create two-way interactive services with downstream and upstream signals. So I directed the folks in our R&D labs to start working on two-way amplifiers.

When the government finally agreed to loosen restrictions and deemed that all systems built after 1972 had to be two-way, everyone in cable TV wanted a two-way amplifier. And guess who was the only company with a practical, deployable two-way system? General Instrument's Jerrold division.

Orders took off, and our market share in cable-TV equipment exploded, shooting from around 40 percent to 80 percent. Our margins went from 20 percent to 70 percent, and profitability followed. I started to pile up cash at Jerrold.

In two years, we took Jerrold from a laggard to the leader of all of General Instrument—generating more than all the earnings of the parent company. We could barely keep up with demand.

We were so successful that during my second year there, the Federal Trade Commission opened an investigation into charges (made by a competitor, Magnavox) that we were selling below cost to monopolize the market. The FTC investigated, and we showed them our cost information and product strategy, arguing we had simply outmaneuvered our rivals. The agency seemed to agree: the investigation ended.

To really get inside the business, I launched a key account system—each top client had a Jerrold exec on point. I took the top five myself.

The new cable-TV world was filled with original characters—mostly men, dreamers from all walks who'd caught the scent of opportunity. Each had their own way of doing business. When one colleague struggled with Gene Schneider, a sharp-tongued, charismatic cowboy from Oklahoma, I took over. I listened to his plans to build in Wyoming and quickly discovered that endless specs on amplifiers were useless.

I flew to Tulsa, drove to Gene's house, drank brandy, and shot pool. That was the sales pitch. And then Gene would say, "Let's go get some steaks for dinner. You can stay over, we've got a spare bedroom." Soon, I was selling Gene cable boxes and whole systems, turnkey, with an ironclad promise to stand behind our word. One-on-one worked well for me. Jerrold was booming.

I'd fly out to Colorado and visit Bob Magness, my future cohort, a Stetson-wearing, cigar-chomping cowboy, who by then had built Tele-Communications Inc. into a multisystem operator out West.

And on the East Coast, my biggest client was Alfred R. Stern, who had left a good job at NBC to found Television Communications Corp. (TVC), which he would grow into a big publicly held cable company that sold to Warner, which formed the core of its cable television division.

Before he became the largest broker of cable deals, Bill Daniels was a Golden Gloves boxer and a WWII navy fighter pilot, earning a Bronze Star for heroics aboard the USS *Intrepid*. In 1952, he made history by beaming the first commercial TV signal via microwave from Denver to Casper, Wyoming—and later became the cable industry's ultimate matchmaker, connecting buyers and sellers across the country.

Their stories were legend. Glenn Jones, a former U.S. Navy underwater bomb expert who was also a piano-playing poet, borrowed $400 against his beat-up Volkswagen to buy his first cable system in Colorado, and became the tenth-largest cable operator in the U.S. Alan Gerry, born to Russian immigrants, started a TV repair and sales business in a converted grain elevator in 1951 after focusing on electronics in the Marines; he then built a cable system to increase sales in the mountainous region surrounding his hometown of Liberty, New York, which grew into the eighth-largest U.S. cable operator. Ralph Roberts, the former owner of Pioneer Suspender Company, founded Comcast in 1963 with the purchase of a tiny cable-TV system in Tupelo, Mississippi—it would become for a time the largest cable operator in the United States.

Something about this collection of entrepreneurs drew me in. They all were part of the communities they were serving. They all faced similar obstacles. They were also dealing with unfair regulation coming out of Washington, D.C., and it seemed to strengthen their camaraderie. There was a pioneering, entrepreneurial spirit, and I began to identify more and more with it.

I had come to know the newcomers and the veteran pole-climbers alike, and had become good friends with some. The mechanics of the budding new cable-TV business spoke to me. I understood the underlying and interlocking pieces of the entire business. And I loved it.

It was mostly a man's world back then, with hardly any women or minorities running cable-TV operators, which were more akin to construction companies at the time. Back then, it was simply the way things were, and most of us didn't question the lack of diversity. I can't erase the past. But I can acknowledge it, learn from it, and try to ensure my actions today align with the fairness and opportunity everyone deserves.

Notoriously hard to please, Monty was happy with my progress, and I quickly got a taste for the confidence that comes after a making a good business decision. While most of the divisions at General Instrument were struggling, our group was exceeding expectations handily.

That summer in 1971, I had never felt more liberated—and congratulated—in my life. Having started out as an unknown at Jerrold, an ailing company, I was now running what had rapidly become the biggest and most profitable division of GI. It was the feeling I'd had as a boy in Long Island Sound, struggling to right the big wooden water skis attached to my feet underwater, then suddenly pulling up and gliding on the surface behind the boat.

Just as my future looked brighter than ever, Monty called me into his office and told me the board wanted him to retire soon because of his age. The only smart move for him to do, in my humble view, was to make me the CEO of the company. Monty had other plans. "John, you are too young to run the entire company no matter how successful you've been here."

I took great pride in his approval and was devastated by his conclusion. I was even more distressed by what he said next: "I'm looking to hand things over to Frank." Frank Hickey, already on the board, was next in line to become CEO of GI. I loved Monty and my team at GI; the problem for me was Frank—for reasons of personality, management style, and business prowess.

"This won't work," I said to Monty. "I have nothing in common with him."

I accepted the inevitable. Hickey became CEO, and once again I began looking for another job. I wished Monty well and opened my book of contacts in the fast-growing industry known as community antenna television. In very short order, I had three offers, one of which would entail meeting Howard Hughes.

The first call I got was from the King of Cable himself, Irving Kahn, the founder of TelePrompTer, an electronic, scrolling cue-card device. It was founded in 1950 by a trio of unlikely partners: a Broadway theater actor, an electrical engineer, and Irving Berlin Kahn, named after his famous music-composing uncle. Hub Schlafly, the engineer, had invented the now iconic TelePrompTer device to help a soap opera actor recall his lines. TelePrompTer had sold its eponymous business in the 1960s and invested the gains in cable and broadcast services.

Kahn, a gregarious CEO, started buying cable systems in the late 1950s, then merged with H&B American Corporation in 1970, creating the largest cable-TV company in the country. He offered me the top job at the top company: CEO of TelePrompTer.

My enthusiasm for the possibilities was short-lived. Irving Kahn was in the middle of the biggest trial of his life, a scandal that would cast a long, dark shadow over the new industry. He was accused of bribery, paying $15,000 to city officials in Johnstown, Pennsylvania, to win the cable television franchise for TelePrompTer. Kahn pretty much conceded making the payment—and he argued, to the end, that city officials had extorted *him*, knowing the value of the exclusive franchise to serve the city. It was extortion at work, he argued, not bribery.

TelePrompTer had recently grown even bigger by buying some cable systems controlled by Jack Kent Cooke, a renowned Canadian-born businessman who owned the now Washington Commanders and the Los Angeles Lakers. And while Cook was the largest shareholder of TelePrompTer, Kahn had control of the board of directors, which included, among others, Howard Hughes.

So when Irving called to say, "John, I hear you're not too happy with the succession over at Jerrold. What do you think of the idea of coming over and running TelePrompTer?" I cut him off: "I've kind of had it with New York, Irving, and TelePrompTer's in New York."

"We'll provide a limo from Connecticut to New York, or we could move the headquarters to Connecticut. We want to make you happy," Irving assured me. I told him I would consider it, but I wanted to talk to some of his directors first. Soon after, I had a brief, polite conversation with Howard Hughes, who at the time was less reclusive than later in his life.

Then I learned in a conversation with Irving that he believed he was going to be indicted. "And if I have to let go of this company, I want to have someone in the company I can trust." Irving was so eager for me to join he had already held a board meeting where I was approved to be named president. Before even contacting me.

"Irving, before I accept this honor, I need to talk to Jack Kent Cooke," I said.

"John, if you insist on talking to Jack, the deal's off."

"Why is that, Irving?"

"Because it would be like Jesus and the Devil in the Garden of Gethsemane. Jack will spin your head and fill you full of bullshit."

While the lure of running the largest cable operator in America was tempting, I had seen too many fights for control at companies, public and private, and I did not want to get caught in the cross fire. Kahn would be convicted of bribery in 1971, and forever maintain the firm was extorted by city officials. In 1973, he began serving a twenty-month prison term, and three years later, he jumped back into the cable industry.

As word got out I was looking, I got a call from Steve Ross at Warner. He was an impeccably dressed and roguishly charming media visionary charging against the Big Three television networks (ABC, CBS, and NBC) that dominated broadcasting with unprecedented news and entertainment choices. Ross had parleyed his early start in the funeral parlor business into what would one day become one of the largest entertainment companies in the world, Time Warner.

In 1972, Ross was appointed CEO, president, and chairman of Warner Communications. He had a reputation as a CEO who delegated responsibility, supported his lieutenants, and gave them lucrative financial incentives, all of which inspired loyalty. He graciously offered me the job of head of Warner's growing cable division. "We'll buy you a limo, a house anywhere you want. And we'll pay you a lot of money." Steve Ross would have been a great guy to work for, no doubt, but the downside was I would be a division head, not president, and worse, I'd be commuting to New York City.

Around this time, I also got a call from Bob Magness, my old Jerrold customer who ran an outfit called Tele-Communications Inc. He wanted

to know if I'd like to move out to Denver and "run the show." I had gotten
to like Bob a lot and the people who worked for him, but I knew he was
dealing with debt issues.

Bob had the best backstory of all. He was a part-time cattle rancher and
cottonseed broker who had stumbled on an idea for cable TV by helping
strangers one day on the job. As he told an interviewer for his oral history
at the Cable Center:

> I was at a cotton gin one evening, and two gentlemen came walking
> in. They had lost a rod in a pickup down on the Four Sixes Ranch.
> We were down kind of in the middle of nowhere, where the Pitch-
> fork and the Four Sixes and Wagner and the Matador all kind of
> comes together.
>
> ... It was 30–35 miles to a village from there. They were afoot
> and I thought, I've got a flat tire in my trunk and I could be afoot too,
> so I took these guys back to Paducah, Texas, and stayed on the high-
> way. During the time we were going back, they were talking about
> this new community antenna system they just put into their town.
>
> So I listened and thought a little bit about it. About a week
> later ... I went down and looked them up and talked to them some
> more. The gentlemen were very kind to help me and show me every-
> thing they were doing, tell me where you buy these things, where
> you learn how to do this and so forth. So about thirty days later, we
> were stringing wire.*

At his first cable system in Memphis, Texas, TCI caught three TV stations from nearby Amarillo, about 80 miles away, and Lubbock, about 140
miles away. Bob paid $100,000 to a Forth Worth company to erect a thirty-
story tower on a sixty-foot rise near town. Subscribers paid $33 to get hooked
up, plus a $6.60 monthly fee. From their kitchen table, they started off with
Betsy handling billing and Bob managing construction.

When they couldn't build, they bought, merging the cable company

---

* Bob Magness, Oral History, Barco Library, Cable Center.

with a large common carrier microwave company, whose big dishes could transmit TV signals to cable-TV headends far away by line of sight. By the time the company went public in 1970, TCI was already the tenth-largest cable operator in the country. But the sudden growth had left TCI bloated with debt.

The challenge drew me in like seeing a stalled car on the side of the road. I would come in as president and CEO. No more number two. And I liked the team of Western cowboys Bob had assembled. Straight shooters and plain talkers. No fancy suits, no MBAs, and no elaborate business jargon. And no New Yorkers.

There is such a thing as a Cowboy Code, and they had it: you finish what you start, stand up for what's right, and take pride in your work. It appealed to me. The one thing they didn't have at all was any of my kind of training or background. They were people I liked, but it was a challenge.

The thought of moving out West to Denver, without a long commute or office politics, where I might have time for my family, was compelling. The one drawback was compensation. Bob Magness told me in that first call, "I can't pay you very much, but you've got a great future here if you can create it." It would be up to me.

So, I turned down Steve Ross's offer of $150,000 a year and lots of perks, and Irving's offer to run the largest cable operator in the U.S., to join Bob Magness, a down-on-his-luck cable operator whose company was running fast but deep in debt. Starting pay: $60,000 a year. I look back on that decision, and I smile at how naive I was at the time. You are unafraid of what you don't know.

I had no way of knowing then that, only weeks after I took the new job, a dark new reality would crush the optimism I had for the company. TCI was at the top of a long, slow climb on a rickety roller coaster, and it had paused long enough for me to hop into the head car.

CHAPTER 5

CABLE COWBOYS

That dramatic day in the bank boardroom where I had thrown down my office keys on the table had rattled me.

Although the unrelenting fear of bankruptcy in the early 1970s scared me, it also forced me to quantify risk with precision, weigh every deal with a clear head, and make bold moves without ever putting everything on the line again.

I see how my restraint runs counter to the bet-it-all mindset of some of the current business stars. Elon Musk, a brilliant mind and inveterate risk-taker, has famously doubled down again and again. He poured roughly half of his entire fortune into SpaceX when it was near bankruptcy, as he did with Tesla.

But in my constitution, if the financial numbers fail to support the big bet, it is time to make a smaller one instead. This cautious, but calculated mindset would define my dealmaking for the next thirty years or more. We started building out TCI when I went there in 1973 and vastly accelerated our expansion efforts in 1979. We grew mainly through acquisitions, and by 1982, nearly ten years after I arrived, TCI was the largest cable provider in the U.S., with 2.5 million subscriber homes. And that was just the start, though I am unsure we knew this at the time. By one count, we acquired 482 companies from 1973 to 1989: a rate of one new deal every two weeks.

At the beginning, the one skill I lacked was the one I needed most: mergers and acquisitions. I was an introvert, an engineer, a problem-solver who preferred the quiet company of another builder, rather than a rainmaker, backslapping and jawboning my way through deals. So, I listened.

The cable-TV industry got its start as a patchwork of tiny local operators rather than a handful of conglomerates. The industry emerged to fill
a need for TV reception in rural areas after the mass market for broadcast
TV took off. So these family-run businesses had limited access to funds to
grow—typically a bank loan for the cable and equipment—yet each system
enjoyed a "natural" monopoly. Towns typically granted a new franchise to
only one provider because having a second company rip up streets or run
duplicate wire was impractical.

The real value, we recognized, would lie in assembling a whole bunch
of local-monopoly cable systems and growing them enough to create scale
efficiencies, even as they were being managed by a crew of independent,
iron-willed cable cowboys. Happily, in the ensuing years, we would make
scores of family owners wealthy beyond their giddiest expectations.

Quickly I sensed the takeover game required so much more than just
my focus on the numbers. Negotiating is all about understanding what the
seller wants and how you can satisfy the seller and still make the transaction
work for you. Empathy is a big part of being a good negotiator, friend, or
teacher, and something I struggle to recognize and refine in myself at times.
Listening saved me. As the saying goes, someone doesn't care what you know
until they know that you care.

I had left a job at Jerrold when it was booming and joined a company that
I thought was growing in an industry with access to capital. Now, poring
over the numbers, I realized the enormity of the task at TCI. Anybody in
their right mind who assessed the resources at TCI or the outlook for the
industry would have run out at breakneck speed.

Our brinkmanship with the bankers was just the beginning of a series
of calamitous events that followed my arrival at TCI in 1973.

President Richard Nixon, who had been re-elected in a landslide, would
draw the country into a political crisis with the Watergate scandal, which
played out in Congressional hearings on television almost daily in the summer of 1973. The stock market crashed in 1974, losing nearly 45 percent of
its value by some estimates, as inflation roared, interest rates shot up past 12
percent, and an oil embargo by Arab countries left many Americans idling
in long lines at the gas pump.

Meanwhile, around this time, Wall Street's confidence in the cable industry was further dampened when accounting irregularities surfaced at the largest, most successful operator, TelePrompTer.

With no bank willing to lend us more money, no government loans, and no rich uncle, we had no other choice but to learn the art of perseverance, tugging at invisible strings of hope until they carried us to the next quarter. For the next five years, obstacle after obstacle would pop up like dandelions in spring, and nothing had really prepared me for it.

I relied on creative problem-solving skills I had honed at Jerrold and in my days at Bell Labs and McKinsey. Some days I felt energized by the challenge, like a young mechanic back home piecing together parts on the garage floor and trying to get a dead engine to come sputtering back to life.

At the office, I was under a lot of pressure to perform. I was the outsider, the East Coast, Ivy League, suit-and-tie whiz kid mixing in with cowboys who preferred horses and cattle to cocktail parties. And while I was president, I still felt like the new ranch hand in the bunkhouse. People at the office had started calling me a nickname from a popular soap opera back then, "Young Doctor Malone," which I found awkward.

Well into the 1980s, cable-TV operators still had few females or people of color as executives, due in part to ingrained biases, but also the industry's roots in technical and operational fields, which were traditionally male-dominated. Our spartan crew was mostly all white guys from the West. Bob was our leader, a contemplative cowboy with the wits of a business tycoon and the quiet stability of a ranch boss. He had the final word on big decisions, and I looked to him for advice and approval.

Larry Romrell, a lean and quiet mustachioed engineer from Idaho, maintained the company's microwave transmitters and headends. Having teamed up with Bob Magness almost from the start, Larry was a strategic thinker, and he was tough as nails. He carried a gun to shoot rattlesnakes or cougars as he hiked five miles or more up the side of a mountain to make repairs on headends, where, in the winter months, Larry's crew stored venison in the headend sheds on some mountains in case they were hemmed in by snowstorms. Larry is also a great listener—and more than fifty years later, he remains my best friend.

Donne Fisher, a friendly number cruncher who first met Magness when he was a carpet-layer in Bozeman, was our treasurer, and Gary Bracken, an accountant from a Big 8 accounting firm, was our comptroller. They would stay as busy as anyone helping us sort through partnerships, buyouts, and bank debt.

Our skill sets were strategically complementary. Over time, for me, the acquisition strategy became one of mine. For JC Sparkman, TCI's chief of operations, the integration of the acquired cable systems became the specialty. And for Gary and Donne, managing the financials became their expertise. So we were all learning together, in a company that was struggling, in an industry that was changing.

JC Sparkman was more responsible for getting TCI out of the hole than just about anyone around. He was a straight talker with a head of wavy black and silver hair and the raspy voice of a late-night DJ. JC had joined a cable-TV company on October 15, 1956, just one day after he had left the U.S. Air Force. He had worked at Jerrold before I did, and he was a customer of mine when I worked there selling components to TCI after Bob hired him. We were on the same frequency.

What we needed more than anything was to convince banks of our creditworthiness by delivering consistent financials. So JC and I began creating key targets based on the performance of our leanest and most profitable systems. After comparing results and noting basic measures such as cash flow, down to how many installers needed per mile, or marketing people per city, we set benchmarks for each new franchise we bought.

JC was notoriously demanding. "If you're off by even one percentage point, don't even wonder—know you'll be in my office to explain," he told teams. He enforced the financial benchmarks with military precision, always setting a realistic but aggressive budget, then beating it. Poor performers were not tolerated.

It is a simple lesson for any person graduating college, starting a new job, or beginning a relationship: you will go incredibly far in life if you simply do what you say you will do.

Tough as he was, JC also knew how to talk to people. He could speak the language of the barracks or the boardroom or the bar. He courted the regional managers who performed, played golf with them, and fought for them on resources. And he was brilliant at stepping aside to let them take credit for success. I watched him build a stable, loyal group of disciplined managers, without a single Harvard MBA in the mix.

JC and his lieutenants—Larry Carleton, Art Lee, and Marion Nowack— were nice but could have easily passed as modern Vikings when taking over a cable system in those years, cutting cost and enforcing the TCI way. Once, JC drove from the Newport Beach, California, system to Denver in a fairly new Oldsmobile Ninety-Eight, previously driven by the head of the cable company we had just acquired. To the victor go the spoils.

Even before I could find my way around the squat one-story office in Denver and settle into the financial problems at TCI, I stumbled into a political showdown in November 1973. The city council of Vail, Colorado, a tourist town built on ski resorts and condos a couple hours west of Denver, had refused to renew TCI's contract unless we met certain demands. TCI had then failed to meet deadlines to rewire the system. So the council called a meeting, and with no public hearing or due process, canceled our franchise agreement with the city.

I felt like the town was playing hardball, which many cities were willing to do when it came to the cable franchise, so we played hardball, too. Since we couldn't legally operate a franchise, we opted to pull the plug on the system after 6 p.m. on November 2, 1973, about ten minutes into *Bullitt*, an action flick with Steve McQueen. In its place, we ran a scrolling text of the names of the mayor and the city manager, with their phone numbers. The blackout continued Friday through Monday, eclipsing a Denver Broncos game.

It didn't take long for the phone lines to spur the politicians. By Tuesday, we had hammered out an agreement with the council. We were also putting cities on notice if they were mulling franchise renewals for TCI: don't threaten our livelihood and expect TCI to simply roll over.

In this and all other issues, my aging cowboy boss, Bob Magness, was glad to hand the reins over to me. He had borrowed big-time to buy or build more than two hundred cable systems in twenty-one states, with all the headaches of running them. Those headaches were all mine now—meeting with seven banks to get credit for TCI, five banks for a subsidiary called NTA, and two banks for a cable company called Athena, which Magness had bought from Gulf+Western a few years earlier.

By the end of 1974, our debt was around $150 million, and our interest payments had doubled to $12 million a year. TCI's annual revenue was less than $35 million. The debt ate at me, sure, but it literally raised Bob's blood pressure and his tolerance for whiskey. He took it personally when bankers pressed us, feeling umbrage at the inference that we weren't good for the money.

Bob liked to joke that "We're lower than whale shit, John." But the truth was we were closer to the Mariana Trench, six miles down, where it is dark and cold, and extreme pressure makes it difficult for anything to survive.

Some companies went bankrupt during this period. TCI was damn close—our stock had gone from around $16 at the IPO to a high of $37, but bottomed out at around 75 cents in 1974. The market capitalization—the value of all the shares at the time—was $3.9 million. We had halted hiring, cut back hours to meet payroll, and I was personally approving any expense in the company over $500. It wasn't much different at home.

We squeezed and squeezed, and finally got enough juice to pay the interest on outstanding loans. From late 1973 we were scraping for every last penny to pay the banks, and by 1976, we actually started making principal payments.

Still, the threat Bob and I feared most was a corporate raider pouncing with a hostile takeover. If we didn't get the stock in friendly hands, we would be toast.

One of TCI's largest shareholders, homebuilder Kaufman & Broad, which owned close to 20 percent, had whispered to Bob that they were ready to get out of their investment in TCI, which was understandable. Bob had given big investors in TCI his inflated stock, assumed the debt of the construction on the business, and committed to building out these underdeveloped franchises. Now, with the stock in the tank, those investors were rethinking their position.

The ownership of TCI was spread out: in addition to Kaufman & Broad's stake, Bob and Betsy owned 12 percent; Gulf + Western owned about 7 percent; Kearns-Tribune had about 6 percent; and his friend George Hatch had around 9 percent.

Neither Bob nor I could buy any more shares because we lacked the cash, and TCI's bank agreements blocked the company from borrowing money to buy back shares. At the end of one particularly long day at the office, we were both nursing drinks and commiserating about our plight. We could think of no one to trust with K&B's 11 percent of the company.

Magness looked up at an old ranch dog, a lethargic mixed beagle named Tiger, sleeping by the fire. "About the only one we can trust in the whole world is Tiger . . . ," Magness said.

I laughed. Then . . . lightning struck.

TCI, too, had a sleeping asset that could save the day. By happenstance, we had an unrestricted subsidiary that was not on the balance sheet of TCI, a small cable system down in Brazoria, Texas, that for some reason was not covered by the bank agreements. If we could leverage the balance sheet of that company to purchase stock, we could buy the shares back at a bargain and redeem them into the treasury.

And that is exactly what we did, buying back almost 20 percent of the company at a big discount, redeeming shares, and shrinking the equity through an entity called Tiger Inc., which included the stock held by Gulf+Western and Kaufman & Broad. The move allowed us to keep more than 40 percent of TCI shares in friendly hands. We later moved the Tiger shares over to Jerry O'Brien, publisher of *The Salt Lake Tribune,* an early TCI investor and Magness friend.

Several years later, another person was eager to unload TCI shares, but for different reasons.

George Hatch—a Utah broadcaster who had helped Bob cofound Western Microwave, the precursor to TCI—was anxious to make a bid for TV stations owned by the Kansas State Network in the 1960s. But because Hatch owned cable systems in some of the same markets through TCI, FCC cross-ownership rules meant he would be forced to sell his TCI shares, which could put a big block of shares in unfriendly hands.

Hatch was concerned because a rival cable company, Heritage Communications, had accumulated a 25 percent stake in the Kansas State Network. But Heritage was blocked from buying the company after a friendly acquisition turned hostile, and was now stuck with a big position.

Bob and I had known Heritage chairman Jim Hoak for years, so we flew out to Des Moines, Iowa, to check his temperature. Bob and I had doubled up in a single room at the local Holiday Inn, and the night before we met Jim, we made a beeline for the hotel bar after dinner, still chewing over the issues of control.

"What if we did this with two classes of stock?" I asked Bob. "TCI can split its stock, then issue a class B share for every share that exists." Bob looked at me, his empty face begging for an explanation for this unprecedented maneuver.

"And the only difference after this two-for-one stock split," I told him, "is that the class B shares would have ten votes per share, giving holders of that stock ten-to-one voting power over regular class A shares." If we could redeem Hatch's B shares and buy enough class B shares on the open market, we could safeguard control.

So TCI split the stock, and Bob swapped all his class A shares for Hatch's super-voting B shares, and then exchanged as many class A shares as we could on the open market.

Hatch then used his shares in TCI to acquire the 25 percent stake in KSN from the Heritage company in Des Moines. To facilitate the trade, TCI bought an interest in Heritage, whose stock shot up when it sold its KSN position. Eventually we would acquire all of Heritage.

The idea for two classes of stock was a seminal solution for TCI and one of my prouder moments. Magness was able to double his 20 percent voting control of TCI at the time to around 40 percent, Hatch got out of TCI. And TCI ended up with a profitable stake in Heritage—all tax-free because the deals were stock swaps.

While I could handle the high finance, Bob was the better negotiator. I remember one day I had a lot going on and asked Bob to handle a visit from potential sellers of the Cheyenne, Wyoming, cable system. When he peeked through the door of our adjoining offices to update me on the terms, it seemed like we were buying the company with their own money.

I said, "Geez, Bob, you ought to go in there and give them something back!" The guy could really cut a hell of a deal.

We needed Other People's Money, or capital, to build out the cable systems we had promised. But Wall Street investors and analysts were having a hard time coming up with a way of assessing the intrinsic value of cable companies. The industry was embryonic, with no real history or following, and the chief way Wall Street put a value on most things, earnings, was scarce.

I had always looked at the cable-TV business as being fundamentally different from other industries, and more akin to the real estate business, where you buy property and collect rent or lease payments in the form of monthly fees. It was obvious to me that if we were going to be measured on earnings, it would be real tough to stay in the cable industry and grow. We needed to promote a different metric to get investors interested.

Government tax laws gave cable companies a big advantage over phone companies: they could "depreciate" their systems quickly over a shorter life, treating the gradual loss of value in their equipment as an expense, even though it wasn't an actual cash cost, with greater tax advantages. This accounting method reduced their reported earnings and, in turn, their taxes. On top of that, they could also deduct real cash expenses like interest payments before calculating taxable income, cutting their tax bills even more.

So, when investors pointed out that TCI had high interest payments, big cable equipment budgets, and no earnings, I would point out that these accounting-based losses resulted in TCI hardly paying any taxes to the government. And as long as cable operators collected predictable "rent" in the form of monthly fees from customers, and they met interest payments and grew from acquisitions, the value of the company's stock would increase.

I started to rely on a single powerful metric, almost like blood pressure in a human, that I thought could instantly, accurately reflect the health of a cable operator: cash flow. The shorthand for this metric would become known as EBITDA—"earnings before interest, taxes, depreciation, and amortization" (and pronounced "ee-bit-dah"). That is, earnings before we deducted all those expenses to lower our tax bill. Robust, tax-sheltered cash flow became the lifeblood for early cable operators, enabling them to manage big upfront capital and operating costs, service their debt, and invest in growth despite the long timelines often required to achieve profitability.

I would proselytize cash flow to investors at shareholder meetings and elsewhere, making it a stump speech of mine for years, until Wall Street embraced it as a rational barometer for cable TV. There is a big difference between creating wealth and reporting income, and the investors with patience for TCI's long view were rewarded.

For investors, I would argue this is a "tax-sheltered growing annuity." If a company can borrow money and buy cable systems with an interest rate that is less than the growth rate of the cash flow, the present value of that stream is technically infinite—as long you reinvest the capital into acquiring still more cable systems.

Net income—a company's earnings, aka the bottom line—was an invention of the priesthood of accountants. I was challenging conventional wisdom, and it was tough for investors and analysts to embrace a totally different strategy and mindset.

Many big public companies were using an earnings-per-share metric to evaluate these new cable systems, including some of the larger media firms that were buying into cable TV, such as Westinghouse, GE, and Warner-Amex. They were issuing equity in the form of their own stock to buy more cable systems, diluting the value of their stock in the long term. Eventually, many of these earnings-based companies would bail out of the capital-intensive cable-TV business. And when they sold, we bought—and their stock price typically rose.

I could always count on a good laugh at shareholder meetings when an investor would ask a question about the prospects for earnings. I would listen, then deliver the politest of punchlines: "I think you're in the wrong meeting."

One of the more valuable lessons I learned back then was the value of doing someone a favor. A newly hired lawyer at TCI told us about some insurance companies that had financed cable systems that were so badly managed the insurers had taken ownership control over them, and now they owned assets they had no experience running.

When I quizzed the lawyer further, he said a group of life insurance companies including Connecticut General, John Hancock Life Insurance Co., and Phoenix Mutual had originally financed some cable systems in a complicated limited partnership. But they had foreclosed on the businesses, and they were really stuck because few investors wanted to untangle it. And they didn't have a plan B in terms of management. The properties were scattered in the Midwest, and they had no scale—but many were located near systems we owned.

So I called the principals. "I could offer to buy these properties from you, but I don't have any money," I told them. "But what I can offer to do is run them for you for free. We can make them worth enough that you'll get your money back."

At the very least, we could get the systems turned around so they would show positive cash flow. My thinking was we might one day buy an adjoining system, plus it wouldn't hurt for us to know some potential new lenders.

JC went in there with one of his best regional managers, Jim Oswald, and within months, not years, the businesses were generating meaningful free cash flow and servicing the debt, paying back principal on the loans. And the insurance companies were both impressed and grateful.

Two years later, the favor was returned. We got a call from a representative at Teachers Insurance, a longtime lender to TCI that still held warrants on our stock. The representative said that Teachers, Travelers, Equitable Life, John Hancock, and the others would be willing to lend $78 million to TCI, one of the largest loans to the cable industry at the time, at a rate nearly two points cheaper than the banks were offering, with much more flexibility.

The insurance companies had seen how consistent our returns were over several years and felt confident to commit to a new line of capital for us. We first flew to New York to finalize the paperwork and celebrated, then quickly called a meeting in Denver to give the news to our banks.

I'm sure Bob wanted to tell them all where they could go, but I stepped to the front of the room and said politely, "I'm happy to announce TCI has arranged for alternate financing, so it's going to be possible for any bank that wants to reduce their exposure to do so on a timely basis."

Then we let the banks know that their interest rates weren't good enough. "From this day forward, the company is a prime-rate borrower," I said, meaning TCI deserved lower rates than other companies were getting. Five of the seven banks wanted to stay in, and they rewrote their covenants with more flexible terms and lower borrowing rates.

After five or so years of growing without a single new bank loan, we began to get access to capital. The stock price started to edge up, and we could afford to buy more systems and give people raises. Most importantly, we were beginning to discover cost advantages from economies of scale.

In the winter of 1979, I was once again on a plane, away from family, when JC and I flew to Anaheim, California, for the Western Show, a popular annual cable convention. Several networks were preparing to launch cable systems, and we were eager to see what channels were out there to draw more subscribers.

JC and I had an early meeting at the convention center, and we walked the show floor before. What we saw opened our sleepy eyes—workers setting up booth after booth for new channels, including HBO, Showtime, ESPN, Nickelodeon, and MTV—more than we had ever seen before and nothing like we had expected. No longer would cable TV be a community antenna service merely bringing in the Big Three broadcast networks (ABC, CBS, and NBC). These companies were coalescing into a completely different business, an unprecedented platform for networks of all kinds: movies, music, news, history, education, food, and so much more. Millions of TV homes in America would want more choice in the channels they watched.

We weren't ready for it. On the spot, we canceled the meeting we had scheduled and rushed home to Denver instead.

"We've got to get a lot bigger," I told Bob and others the next morning in his office. We needed to get bigger because the bigger we were, the more cheaply we could buy everything: parts, debt, and programming. Economies of scale bring costs down. And if we didn't get big fast, someone else would—scale economics was going to determine who was going to survive.

"If you can buy 'em and finance 'em, I can drive synergies," said JC, instantly reminding me why I was grateful he was with us. From that day forward, we made a goal of rapidly growing through acquisition and organic growth.

Soon, I got the hang of M&A negotiation by realizing that often the people involved were concerned with issues beyond just the sale price. From the shoes of the seller, maybe it was the taxes on the deal, or a parent with a good-for-nothing kid, or a dream of retiring in Palm Beach.

Whatever was important to the seller, I tried to resolve it. Instead of going about the negotiation through force, I began to see that a touch of empathy and a bigger worldview gave me more context and a better chance of a win-win transaction.

Typically, a small mom-and-pop cable operator would take out a bank loan to buy the cabling and equipment required to bring service to a rural area out of range of the nearest broadcast signal. No government subsidies or free spectrum existed to help them, things the big broadcasters were given to create their businesses. These were entrepreneurs driven by determination, sweat equity, and lots of debt.

We started rolling up small and regional cable companies, cashing out first-generation owners, and at least initially, avoiding big cities where other big companies were fighting for franchises. JC and his team would go in, slash overhead, integrate management, and most times, increase revenue by 15 percent each year.

When we started to grow and finance that growth, predictability was what gave banks the confidence to lend more money for bigger purchases. We saw patterns, which led to some simple rules at times: for example, never pay more than five times the annual cash flow generated by a cable system, figuring in the savings from synergies. This helped us decide instantly if a property was worth the asking price.

It was all quite simple—a virtuous circle that would help us gain the advantages of scale economics. Buying more cable systems would bring in more paying subscribers. More paying customers meant higher cash flow and lower costs in the form of bulk discounts for networks. Increased cash flow allowed TCI to borrow more money and pay the higher total interest costs on it, which we used to buy still more cable systems.

With the cable industry growing, the government had begun to finally clarify some rules surrounding it in the mid-seventies, issuing standards for broadcast signals to be imported into cities, capping the franchise fees cities could demand, and fixing the length of franchise agreements to fifteen years, which lifted the uncertainty for franchise renewals. Many big media companies jumped in, buying cable companies, including Cox Enterprises; a division of the Westinghouse Electric Corp.; and Storer Broadcasting. Some stayed. Many more would sell.

Launching in big cities was messy initially. The franchise renewal process was still often corrupt, with costly demands by local politicians. Costs were higher to bury coaxial cable lines under city streets and avoid existing power, sewer, and phone lines. And customers were harder to attract since most could easily receive broadcast channels.

Warner Communications chairman and CEO Steve Ross brought in American Express to become a fifty-fifty partner to bankroll Warner's expansion into cities with a war chest of more than $800 million. Warner and others promised to wire the cities of tomorrow with advanced new services, and investors and lenders began to warm to their vision.

A popular book at the time, *Wired Nation* by Ralph Lee Smith, painted a picture of cable's potential as an interactive, two-way platform—unlike its one-way predecessors, radio and broadcast TV. By connecting society through an "electronic highway," cable could allow viewers to one day get newspapers, books, mail, banking, college courses, shopping, and more from home. The notion was growing in the public consciousness, with studies by the RAND Corporation and the Sloan Foundation making similar predictions.

Inspired by a closed-caption TV system in a Tokyo hotel room he saw, Warner-Amex's Ross launched a new TV service called QUBE, in Columbus, Ohio, in 1977, boldly promising this future without waiting: an advanced cable system that allowed subscribers to watch pay-per-view movies, see rock concerts, play interactive games, and watch local high school sports or educational programs. By pressing buttons on a cereal box–sized console, QUBE viewers could select from classical symphonies on demand to a feature allowing citizens to "vote" their opinions on local issues. QUBE turned out to be a great sales tool for winning franchises. In the early 1980s, Warner deployed the QUBE system in Cincinnati, Dallas, Houston, Pittsburgh, and St. Louis, accumulating 325,000 subscribers.

Ross was a visionary, seeing trends in entertainment long before most people. But these were just fleeting glimpses of the future. QUBE turned out to be too early and too expensive to maintain or scale up, and by 1983, the QUBE experiment would cause Warner to rack up $875 million in debt before getting shuttered.

That year, Warner-Amex CEO Drew Lewis brought in McKinsey, which confirmed what he suspected—recent acquisitions like Pittsburgh weren't delivering returns. Under pressure, he renegotiated franchise terms and sold MTV and Nickelodeon to Viacom for $690 million in 1985.

Seeing an opening, I pitched him a clean exit: "we'll return every nickel you've put into the system."

I knew we could make Pittsburgh work. The systems were weighed down by overhead, over-engineered tech like QUBE, and flashy marketing. Our strategy was simple: strip it to the essentials, run it efficiently, and focus on fundamentals.

We borrowed every penny, and within two years—thanks to JC's crew and regional manager Marion Nowak—we had it running on its own cash. Leverage dropped fast—we had essentially bought the cable system with its own cash flow. We ran the same play in Dallas with Warner-Amex.

We would do the same thing buying the Dallas franchise from Warner-Amex.

As I looked around the media world for allies, few companies were willing to do business with us. Theater owners had been historically against cable operators from the earliest days, running ads before the start of movies about the evils of "pay TV." Telephone companies saw us as future competition and famously charged cable operators usurious rates to hang wires on their poles. And, of course, powerful broadcasters were aligned in spending millions of dollars to lobby the government to restrain the power of cable pretty much anywhere they could.

One group that seemed approachable was the newspaper and magazine industry, which was competing with local TV stations for ad revenue. They had cash to invest and enough political power to blunt the blade of the broadcasters in battle, especially because government's cross-ownership rules kept them out of the broadcast business. They could, however, get into cable TV.

At TCI, we would host newspaper executives for a daylong catered seminar, painting a future with newspaper subscribers reading on screens. Out of these meetings, we engineered joint ventures with the newspaper publishing giant Knight Ridder, where we would match every dollar of equity they put in with a dollar of equity of our own, and they would receive shares of preferred stock, which paid them a quarterly dividend. And then we would leverage that equity structure and acquire another cable system. We applied our Knight Ridder template to similar partners—E.W. Scripps Company and Taft Broadcasting—to buy jointly owned cable systems, which we would put into separate operating entities, and use them to buy still more franchises. Eventually, we would buy them all out.

By 1982, cable-TV was big business, and TCI had become the biggest cable operator in the U.S. With cities handing out exclusive, long-term franchises, given the high building costs, cable had become a natural monopoly: win the rights, and you owned the market. Once the dust settled on a franchise fight, operators rarely competed for customers. What started as a scrappy local business was now a strategic chessboard. We kept growing, often teaming up with former rivals on acquisitions. If you could find a way to buy together, you avoided bidding wars—and everyone came out ahead.

This made for a much more fun industry to be in, unlike some industries where it is kill or be killed. Each cable system was a natural monopoly awarded by the local government, which allowed us to spend more time lobbying jointly on regulatory issues and solving thorny technological issues.

Most of all it led to a collegial, almost familial industry, where friendships grew.

What a dream it has been to build a company with those relationships.

At TCI, these cable cowboys carried more than their share of the work, and those sacrifices built character. And they are respected and loved not just by me but by their families. It broke my heart when JC passed, but I got a call from JC's great-grandson the other day wanting to know stories about his great-grandfather. What more can you ask for in life?

They say you live life twice. You live it first in your life, and second in your memories, and when I visit these places in my mind from time to time, I am filled with gratitude for the sacrifices of my friends and family in those early days.

CHAPTER 6

ECONOMIES OF SCALE

B y the late 1970s, we knew instinctively that the key to victory at TCI was in our ability to gain scale and grow ever larger through acquisition. We had three key goals in the 1980s: accumulate cable systems as fast as possible, aggregate them into contiguous clusters, and refinance the debt terms based on our bigger size and bigger cash flow.

Now, at first, you might think it was all about the numbers: penetration rates, total homes that could be serviced in the market, average subscriber price per home, gross profit margins, free cash flow after improving the lines—all that stuff, given my mathematical inclinations and engineering background, as well as my awkwardness in dealing with people I don't know well.

What I learned, though, as we did more deals, was that an equally important factor was people. The people who had built the business we were buying. And the people who would be working with us after we made them part owners.

And even with my somewhat lesser people skills, I got pretty good at the people end of dealmaking, too, and that made me feel pretty good about the whole effort. I learned not only that you have to put yourself in the other person's shoes to figure out what they want, you also have to always leave something on the table for the other person in the deal.

We put together hundreds of deals that made millionaires of dozens of cable-system owners, often family businesses whose owners had worked most of their lives to build what they built. The motivation to sell is different for every person. For some it's the money. For some, it's a family thing. Most are just retiring, sapped from juggling all the headaches of a small business.

We believed our stock was undervalued, and I avoided using cheap currency to buy assets—a mistake many start-ups make by giving up too much equity early, instead of waiting to raise capital when their value is higher. And we didn't mind cash deals because the step-up in basis gave us larger depreciation deductions, which helped offset future taxes. At TCI, we thought we were just scaling up for efficiency and cash flow—but in chasing margins, we unknowingly laid the fiber backbone for the internet itself, paving the future for broadband before we knew what it would become.

Throughout the 1980s, while the rest of America was watching *Cheers* and *Family Ties* on broadcast television, I had no time for TV shows, the bar, or even my family for that matter. We were building TCI, brick by brick. The stress of my time away from home began to eat at my relationship with Leslie. I wanted her to know I was doing all this work for her and the kids for the future.

"I want you here now," she'd say, "not some distant date in the future."

Then Leslie would look at me—steady, unblinking, those pale blue eyes searching mine for something I couldn't give—and I'd turn away. I would leave feeling justified because I knew I was providing, but anguished by the guilt of knowing I was hurting someone I so dearly loved. Worse, I'd be a thousand miles away in a lonely hotel room while Leslie took care of business. The weight of family obligations left me with a constant ache of missing out on the life I was working so hard to support.

On the road, a consistent traveling companion was Paul Gould from the boutique banking firm of Allen & Company, who was soft-spoken and polite for a New Yorker. I trusted his judgment more than my own at times.

On a typical deal, we'd pay off the owner/CEO of the systems, who was typically thrilled to get out of a game that was increasingly corporate. Then we would turn to the next person in charge at the company: Do you want to be the new boss? Often they did.

Then we would go down the list of questions:

"Okay, how many on the team are good workers worth keeping? Can you match the targets we've set here? How much more can you cut the overhead?"

Then JC Sparkman would come in to help us deliver scale efficiencies, ordering equipment in greater bulk, teaching managers how to adapt to the changes in operations so that TCI was absorbing these businesses with very little disruption.

After so many negotiations, a funny thing started to happen for me personally: a lot of the awkwardness that I had initially felt began to dissolve. We were doing so many deals, I began to relax more, and I actually started to embrace the uncertainty of each one as another problem to solve.

Like the baseball player in batting practice, you finally get so many pitches you relax enough to start "seeing" a fastball. And when you start hitting the ball enough, you know it is within you to knock it out of the park.

I began to polish my skills as a negotiator, as a money raiser, as a manager of an executive team made up of mostly cowboys, and each of these roles began to feel more comfortable as time went by, and I learned something new in every deal. I found that I was learning, growing, and happier. I saw more possibilities, and that fed into itself and *created* more possibilities.

Demand for cable service was compounding, spreading from its rural roots as an antenna service and into some of the largest urban centers, from New York City on down as a source of new and unique programming. It had taken the young industry thirty years to sign up 13 million subscribing homes by 1978. Just four years later, that number had doubled to 27 million subscribers. And the total had doubled again to 54 million six years later, up fourfold in a decade.

In 1978, only eight cable programming networks were in business; by 1984, there were forty-seven. From 1976 to 1987, revenue industry-wide expanded more than twelvefold, from $900 million to almost $12 billion. America liked the taste of cable TV.

Like most cable operators, we invested a great deal of profit in upgrading our wired networks. By doing so, we could make more off the wires: more robust, reliable networks cut down on truck rolls, saved money on amplifiers, and allowed more channels on a system. Not to mention, it was immediately depreciated for tax purposes.

This means the investment in the infrastructure was deducted from earnings right away, reducing our taxes on any profit, even though the benefits of the investment would last for years. It thereby provided a great incentive to keep investing in our own systems to make them better.

Compared to a telephone company's "twisted pair" of thin copper strands, cable TV relied on a coaxial cable with a thick center wire, ringed by solid foam insulation inside of a metal tube—all of this covered by a black plastic jacket. A wire within a hollow wire. If you cut off a section, each end would be a circle with a dot in the center. It's all a little thicker than a broomstick.

What gives this pipe near-infinite capacity is that the signal ricochets between the two axes, not through the wire like it does with thin telephone wire. And while this quantum leap in capacity is marvelous, these electromagnetic waves pulsing between the wires degrade as they travel. So they need the help of expensive amplifiers every two thousand feet or so to maintain the signal strength.

The introduction of fiber optics in the 1980s would advance the industry to a new level of transmission capacity, allowing us to carry more channels more cheaply. Fiber optics are glass wires the thickness of a strand of human hair, with hundreds of times the capacity of coaxial cable, less susceptible to interference, and the signals—light vs. electricity—can travel faster, longer, up to fifty miles or more before they begin to degrade. Fiber optics could eliminate signal interference and the need for amplifiers and filters.

Taking a cue from AT&T, Verizon, and others, cable operators upgraded their systems, replacing the "trunks" of the systems' "tree and branch" architecture with fiber optics, which carried voice, video, and data over beams of blinking light, connecting with coaxial cable "branches" that stretched into subscribers' homes. Higher reliability lowered costs on service calls—and gave us more channels.

This was just the beginning of what this wire could carry. This hybrid fiber-coaxial (HFC) system would become the backbone of the internet in the U.S. over time.

We raised money from everywhere—banks, insurance companies, publishers, Wall Street, anyone with capital—to fuel TCI's growth, because

I knew the advantage would go to the biggest company. Scale economics drove every decision.

While we were figuring what to buy, we also were figuring out how to pay for it, so I was learning a lot about managing—and even harder, leading. I had become the main spokesperson for our "road shows," to raise capital with banks and finance companies. I was learning to come out of my shell, motivated by the desire to get in front of a field of fast-moving companies.

But I still felt awkward stepping out and glad-handing strangers. I have never, to this day, felt the desire to impress, to make someone feel a certain way about me. I'm comfortable in my own skin. And I found it difficult trying to sell someone on an idea I thought was obvious if only they had taken the time to study it. At times, I may have let my impatience show, or let potential investors walk out the door rather than chase them.

With potential investors, you often summoned the courage to get up in front of an audience to talk about a business that they don't really understand or care much about. Often you would look up to a sea of blank faces. We even traveled overseas to raise money, but the rest of the world was never that impressed, either.

When we were at our limit with our usual suspects of lending, we turned to still more alternative means of financing. One of those was a controversial financier named Michael Milken, who was known for creating a new market for high-yield "junk" bonds.

The rise of Milken and the firm Drexel Burnham Lambert created a revolution in deal financing for us. Their agility to buy and price offerings dramatically changed the acquisition game—and saved me incalculable hours in front of clients on road shows. We knew what level of debt and the terms that were available if we had Drexel on our team.

Milken was made the poster boy for Wall Street excesses after the Crash of 1987. In a plea bargain deal in 1990, he pleaded guilty to six felony counts, including securities fraud, mail fraud, and tax evasion, and served twenty-two months of a ten-year sentence after cooperating with authorities and getting time off for good behavior. He was fined $200 million and ordered to pay $400 million in restitution to investors.

His issues with Uncle Sam notwithstanding, what I know is that Mike

Milken proved his thesis that non-investment-grade bonds were under-valued relative to investment-grade bonds. And he helped TCI raise a lot of money perfectly legally, just as he had done with Ted Turner and many other U.S. companies. After we started dealing with Milken, we didn't have to do as many road shows anymore.

The term "junk bonds" is a misnomer because they can be a company's treasure, too—as they were for TCI. Typically issued by a company with a lower credit rating, a junk bond has a bigger risk of defaulting compared with bonds issued by a blue-chip company. To reward the investor for taking on this higher risk of default, a junk bond pays a higher interest rate.

Junk bonds were used in a variety of ways in the 1980s, good and bad—to defend against a hostile takeover, or to launch one, to expand a business organically or merge it with another one. For us, they were a lifeline.

I am thankful for Milken's theories on finance born out of his obsession, and also grateful for his funding for new treatments of prostate cancer, which he had been diagnosed with himself. His Prostrate Cancer Foundation has benefitted many men, including Rupert Murdoch.

In this flurry of dealmaking, we were doubling in size every eighteen months, JC Sparkman pointed out to me at one juncture. It was like Moore's Law, which states that the number of transistors on a microchip doubles every two years, and so does its computing power. And so did ours.

By 1982, TCI had built itself into the nation's largest cable company, but the biggest deals were yet to come. More scale equals more savings, which gave us more buying power to buy more systems and build more scale, which equaled more savings—a virtuous growth cycle.

When I wasn't raising money in the 1980s, I was flying from city to city, making promises to politicians where we owned cable-TV franchises, or where we were trying to buy them. Big established media companies were now elbowing in to buy or build cable systems—not in the rural towns where the industry was born but in the big cities where urbanites were eager to explore the new national networks like HBO and TBS.

TCI initially steered clear of most of the contentious battles in the rush to wire big metro areas, mainly because we lacked big money. Because a franchise was so valuable, typically awarded for ten to fifteen years as a government-decreed cable monopoly, companies spent hundreds of thousands of dollars on advertising, presentations, and expensive dinners to woo a city, promising state-of-the-art cable systems. The battle to win these long-term franchises became known in the industry as the "Franchising Wars."

Local politicians who could vote to oppose a new franchise might insist on "extras" from companies: Can you plant trees in the city green? Can you build a small municipal building? Sometimes, in return for the franchise, local pols simply demanded cash under the table. The very charges that put Irving Kahn behind bars—bribery—were common in negotiations, as was Kahn's defense: extortion by crooked politicians.

Charging a new cable company 5 percent or more of gross receipts was an easy way to bring in nontax revenue for the cities, and the pols could boast of the cheap cable-TV channels they'd won for citizens.

All too often, big companies eager to lock in a ten-year franchise would gladly abide. One popular tactic to get an edge was a ruse called "rent-a-citizen," in which cable operators offered local politicians a chance to become investors in the new cable franchise. No money? No problem—we'll loan the money to you! When the franchise was approved, the "investors" were bought out at a profit.

For example, a half dozen companies spent $500,000 each preparing bids in 1980 for the Dallas franchise, one of the largest in play at the time, with four hundred thousand homes in a city busting at the seams. The franchise ultimately went to Warner-Amex, which had touted its new interactive QUBE system, and promised eighty channels, including channels for city government and schools. (True to the times, Warner-Amex officials had worked with police to arrest someone who had offered to sell them information to win the franchise.) Even after it was awarded, Sammons Communications, covetous of such a big win, contested the decision and tried unsuccessfully to reverse it by gathering signatures for a referendum.

We tried to avoid playing these games even though our competitors were. Giveaways became common, even ridiculous, before reality set in. We had channels for reporting bribery or extortion attempts, and we had to call in the FBI on franchise competitions in Miami and New Orleans because of bribery proposals we received.

Of all the dustups, one of the costliest for TCI was fought just twenty miles northwest of our Denver headquarters, in the city of Boulder, Colorado. In May 1979, TCI informed the mayor of Boulder that we were planning to expand our coverage area in the city as planned. We were installing an earth station for receiving and sending TV signals from satellites in February 1980 to deliver more channels to the entire city.

But when some local residents launched a new company called Boulder Communications Co., the city decided to kick us out and declared a moratorium on TCI's expansion plan. The council opened up the bidding for the franchise for the rest of the city, despite the fact that TCI was in a twenty-year franchise for Boulder and still had another four years left in our contract.

No. Hell no.

I told JC to tell the crews to proceed with their plans for the day to wire the streets. "Roll the trucks."

Shortly after, a city utility truck followed a TCI truck on a Boulder street and, almost as soon as TCI employees hung the coaxial cable, Boulder public works employees pulled it down.

We'd hang up the wire, and they'd rip it down.

Police arrested *our* construction crews. At that point, I had to give up. We finally called the trucks back to the office. After all, their side had guns.

Eventually, we found justice when the case reached the U.S. Supreme Court. TCI sued the city on antitrust and First Amendment grounds. Lower courts had ruled the city did not have the authority, and by 1982, Boulder, fearing that a protracted legal battle would postpone cabling the city for years, settled out of court, letting TCI stay in place. TCI wired the rest of the city within months.

A similar fight erupted in Jefferson City, Missouri, when the city requested new bidders for the franchise in 1981. A new bidder, Central Telecommunications, was awarded the franchise, meaning TCI would be forced to sell the cable wires already lining Jefferson City streets.

To me it amounted to illegal government seizure of private property.

More practically, it would cause TCI to break loan agreements that would stymie the company further. In March that year, TCI sued in federal court again.

Finally, in April 1982 after talks with the city, TCI was awarded the franchise. Central Telecommunications, then sued TCI, alleging restraint of trade and tortious interference. TCI counterclaimed, and we kept the franchise.

These problems kept me up at night as I was trying to finance further growth at TCI. We would have a similar fight, and a rare loss after seven years in federal court, with the city of Morganton, North Carolina.

These days, the names of the cities we fought still ring clearly in my head, like the names of old battlefields so far gone I struggle to remember all the details. But I have the scars to prove I was there.

The entire setup between cities and cable operators was unsavory, and soon it attracted the attention of Congress, which had become more keenly interested in the budding antenna industry and the labyrinth of local and state laws that dictated everything from what a cable operator could charge to what types of channels it could show. This localized control handed great power to small-time politicians and gave rise to bribes and insider deals common in the nascent days of this industry.

The National League of Cities lobbied to retain local oversight (and the cities' tax-free revenue stream—tacking on a fee of 5 percent of our total revenue locally). Our trade group, the National Cable Television Association, pushed hard for new federal laws to liberate cable companies from onerous, often unfair rules market by market.

Two of the cable TV industry's strongest supporters were U.S. senators Barry Goldwater (R-AZ) and Tim Wirth (D-CO). Recognizing the FCC's favoritism toward broadcasters, they advocated for cable TV, highlighting its diverse programming and potential for two-way communication.

The handcuffs finally came off the industry when President Ronald Reagan signed the Cable Communications Policy Act of 1984 into law, the first national legislation establishing the federal government's authority over cable TV. Its biggest impact was the deregulation of monthly cable rates where there was "effective competition" from at least three over-the-air broadcast signals in the market, which included most markets. Cable operators could now charge what the market would bear. Cities could still grant franchises, but fees paid to government were capped at 5 percent. Incumbent cable operators, usually the ones who had laid down the wire, were favored in franchise renewals. And phone company giants like AT&T were forbidden from owning cable operators, removing a competitive threat.

Suddenly Wall Street had the one thing it craves: certainty. With demand for cable TV strong, and capital more available at banks and lenders, the industry suddenly had momentum.

As the deals got bigger, we started doing them in partnerships with other cable operators. In 1986, we helped assemble one of the largest cable sales in the industry with Westinghouse Broadcasting, which owned more than 2 million subscribers in thirty-four states, after gobbling up TelePrompTer, then the largest cable operator in the U.S.

Westinghouse had paid $650 million for TelePrompTer's cable operations in 1981 but found it hard to eke out a profit. Nick Nicholas at Warner-Amex floated the idea to make an offer first to me and then to a couple of people he knew on the board at Westinghouse.

We knew the price could be close to $2 billion, but how to afford it? "Clusters" had become a buzzword in the industry, adding adjoining systems in a certain geographic area like pieces in a puzzle. It was the first time we began to think about the potential to buy or swap systems with other cable operators who owned systems near the markets we were newly acquiring, a tactic Tryg Myhren, the CEO at Time Inc.'s American Television and Communications Corporation (ATC), had popularized. Instead of fighting over it, why not buy it together and divvy it up?

So we reached out to cable operators I knew with nearby systems, including Comcast Corporation chairman Ralph Roberts and his son, Brian, among others. And that's how a consortium of cable operators—TCI, Comcast, ATC, Daniels & Associates, and Century Southwest Communications Corp.—pooled $1.6 billion in cash and $500 million in debt for Group W, the cable division of Westinghouse.

The Westinghouse deal was complex and moving fast, like all group deals. For that, you need a great lawyer, and we had one in Jerry Kern, a lawyer at Baker & Botts at the time. Jerry was the most gifted lawyer I've ever known, and could draft a perfect memorandum, contract, or court challenge in a chaotic room, people coming and going, and still finish with a smile—usually because he'd found a way to make everyone happy. He was our secret sauce.

Once Nick Nicholas and I convinced Westinghouse CEO Dan Ritchie that they would be better-off monetizing the business—selling it—rather than running it, then identified parts that didn't fit TCI or Time/ATC, we invited other friends into the deal. We could assemble the purchasers based on fit.

There was a sort of Pax Romana after the franchise wars. Franchises were largely claimed, so a period of relative peace and stability followed, with nearly 60 percent of the country subscribing to cable-TV service. When Nick and I agreed on a deal, the rest of the players understood that they were lucky to get in on it. Certainly we had to be fair—not unlike a family sitting at a meal—and everyone bought in.

By selling the stock in the company in one fell swoop versus having to sell the actual assets piecemeal, Westinghouse was able to minimize taxes according to the U.S. tax laws at the time. TCI and other buyers could use the existing depreciation rates to mitigate short-term tax liabilities.

Soon after the Group W deal, we turned to another longtime cable-system operator I hoped would take our call: Robert and Marshall Naify.

Two publicity-shy brothers born of Lebanese immigrants, the Naifys had started out as ushers in their father's movie theater in Atlantic City and eventually grew a small group of screens into the nation's largest movie theater chain, United Artists Theaters. Along the way they had aggressively assembled one of the largest cable-TV operations in the country, with more than 750,000 subscribers in fifteen states. Like us, the Naifys believed in scale economics.

One day their investment banker, Paul Gould at Allen & Company, called me out of nowhere to say, "I think they're ready to sell." The brothers were tiring of the day-to-day oversight headaches in the fast-moving cable business. They were also getting older, so they wanted more liquidity, or more cash on hand.

TCI was growing fast, and each visit I made to San Francisco, I tried to convince the Naifys that the strategy TCI was pursuing, which was scale driven, with small investments in content, was a sound economic strategy.

We made the brothers an offer in 1986: $140 million in cash and $250 million in notes convertible into TCI stock for 51 percent control, and an exchange offer to existing shareholders at the same rate, which valued the deal at close to $760 million. Bob Naify would become a friend, and his sage advice was always welcome. He joined TCI's board, and he held on to TCI stock through every split, spin-off, or new offering.

Later, we merged United Artists Communications into a similar-sounding company we controlled called United Cable Television, run by my old friend Gene Schneider, in a $2 billion stock swap. And we sold the theater chain to Merrill Lynch Capital Partners Inc.

The public loved the novelty of cable TV, but many customers were justifiably upset about customer service: long wait times on the phone and for service calls.

There was a good reason for the disconnect: Cable-TV operators were in the distribution industry, but up until that point, TCI and most other cable operators could only think of themselves as being in the *construction* business. Climbing poles, hanging wire, and giving little attention, and hardly any budget, to customer service.

As we were bulking up, big, traditional, earnings-oriented media companies, including Westinghouse, Dow Jones, and American Express, were selling out. They learned that metropolitan areas were far more costly to wire, and residents could easily tune in broadcast channels in big cities. In 1988, we took aim at a target I had missed two years earlier, when Kohlberg Kravis Roberts (KKR), a big private equity firm, bought Storer Communications, the fourth-largest cable operator in the country, in a hostile leveraged buyout. Henry Kravis at KKR wasn't a cable operator—they were financial investors betting on cable's growth—and they had hit the timing just right.

Once again we teamed up with Ralph and Brian Roberts at Comcast in Philadelphia. TCI and Comcast paid $1.5 billion and assumed $2.2 billion in debt, splitting the cable systems between the two companies. For twice what we had been willing to pay two years earlier. It would prove to be worth every penny.

The deal grew our subscriber base by 20 percent. And we made overhead expenses disappear. Gone were the luxury offices, corporate dining rooms, and company cars. And while we inherited regional employees and managers in each acquisition, we didn't add a single person to corporate HQ. Aside from the cable systems that were wholly owned, TCI was a minority partner in more than thirty-five cable companies, all of which got the same price breaks in programming that TCI got.

Many of the deals I made were built on the camaraderie of friendships within the industry. When Heritage Communications was the nation's tenth-largest cable company, it was still run by James M. Hoak Jr., the man who had played a key role in the deal over a decade earlier that created two classes of stock for TCI. Hoak was a Midwesterner who had graduated Yale, interned at the FCC in 1968, graduated from Stanford University's law school, and started a cable company—at twenty-six years old.

Under Jim, Heritage operated cable systems in Dallas, Philadelphia, San Jose, and elsewhere. In the mid-1980s, an investor out of Texas named Robert Bass had begun buying up stakes in Heritage, accumulating a 9 percent stake. The word on Wall Street was that he was plotting a hostile takeover.

Soon after getting a phone call from Jim, I was on a plane to Des Moines, again, and within hours of landing, we shook hands on a deal for TCI to buy Heritage in 1987. Jim and I structured a deal that satisfied everyone, especially the public shareholders: TCI paid $1.5 billion in cash, stock, and assumed debt, and a premium to the price of the stock at the time. By that time, TCI was decentralized to the point that decisions were delegated to six different regions, each with their own accounting, engineering, and maintenance teams. Layered on the owned systems, we were operating systems through more than fifty partnerships, most of which were with the original operators we trusted to keep running more systems. If you buy a property and find a manager motivated by ownership in the company, keep them in power and trust them.

By one tally, we had spent $3 billion by 1987 for more than 150 cable companies, giving TCI reach into nearly 20 percent of U.S. homes. We had a sufficient lead—nearly twice as large as the number two player, Time Inc.'s ATC. A year later, we had no earnings but posted cash flow of $850 million— more than the cash flow of ABC, CBS, and NBC combined.

With TCI getting some room to breathe, I began to feel more confident about the industry's future and TCI's prospects. I would need that confidence for what was coming.

CHAPTER 7

MEDIA MAVERICK

I'd like to think I played an important role in helping Ted Turner build a fledgling local TV station into a media juggernaut worth nearly $8 billion, but the fact is Ted played just as large a role in my own career and life. Of the hundreds of people I have done business with, Ted Turner stands out as one of the most driven, iconoclastic, irrepressible, hilarious, unrelenting, and visionary leaders I ever have encountered.

I have known the man well for the better part of fifty years. He turned to TCI in the 1970s, and we became the linchpin to his securing national cable coverage for his TV station in Atlanta, WTBS, which became the foundation of Turner Broadcasting System (TBS) and spawned CNN, TNT, TCM, the Cartoon Network, and other channels. Then in the 1980s, my cable allies and I bailed out Ted when his own bankers balked at lending him even more money.

My financial gamble on him paid off handsomely. He was also the first person to introduce me to the idea of ownership in something versus just drawing a paycheck. This advice helped inspire me to form Liberty Media, the holding company for many of the channel ownership stakes TCI was accumulating. Since I now had skin in the game, my wealth grew alongside the rising value of the company, benefitting thousands of our shareholders, as well; this is the way it is supposed to work, and for us, it has worked wonderfully.

While I don't socialize much with most business colleagues, Ted and I became fast friends, and over the years we've hiked, hunted, fished, and flown together. And here's the funny part: Ted Turner and I are as different as two people could possibly be. I am an introvert, and I am quiet—for the most part—at meetings. Public speaking for me can be a mild form of punishment. But Ted has the intensity of a revival preacher when he believes in something, pacing the room and occasionally quoting Shakespeare or Alexander the Great to annunciate his points.

Politically, Ted evolved into more of a progressive Democrat, while I am more of a libertarian. I have an engineer's mentality that compels me to plan crucial details, fully calculating every possible outcome so that all risks are known ahead of time. Ted's life seemed to be a string of risky bets, based on the instinct and impulse of a mad, creative genius.

In my voyage with Ted, there are key waypoints that led us where we are today: in the 1970s when he arrived at TCI seeking national distribution on our cable systems; in the late 1980s when he almost went bankrupt and was in danger of losing everything; in 2000 at the peak of the internet bubble, when Ted's bosses at Time Warner decided to merge with America Online; and, more recently, in 2020, when Ted asked me privately to consider joining up with him to buy back his most beloved property of all, CNN.

Old habits die hard, right?

Each moment was classic Ted Turner: total transparency, not a single emotion or thought held back. This man shared everything in real time, and then some. And he did it regardless of whether you were looking to hear his thoughts. This made me admire Ted's daring escapades even more. There was no stopping him.

One day in the fall of 1975, all seventy-five people in the spartan Denver offices of Tele-Communications Inc. were expecting a special visitor. Folks in our front office, a carpeted area furnished like a cheap hotel lobby, were on the lookout. Those of us in the linoleum-tiled back office weren't quite sure what to expect—that feeling when you're looking on the horizon for an approaching storm.

None of us had ever met Ted Turner, and all we really knew about him was what we had heard and read. Ted Turner was from Atlanta, and his nicknames hinted that this was no wallflower: "Captain Outrageous" and "Mouth of the South."

Ted had asked to meet with TCI's executive team to hear him out on an audacious plan, something unprecedented in the broadcast television industry at the time. He wanted to transmit his struggling local Atlanta TV station to a satellite twenty-two thousand miles above the earth—and then beam it back down to cable systems everywhere in the U.S. to create the first "superstation." His weak-signal UHF station, WTCG (for "Watch This Channel Grow"), later renamed WTBS, would usher in many original cable channels and vastly expand the cable-TV business.

Ted could see, early on, the benefit of befriending the cable industry. Already he was extending the signal from his broadcast tower beyond its forty-mile range by using microwave transmitter towers, a technology adopted from World War II communications. So, when cable operators emerged, he had a natural ally in his mission to reach more customers than just those in Georgia's rural hill country.

We knew Ted wanted our subscribers. At that point, TCI was the second-largest cable operator in the country behind TelePrompTer, and it now served 650,000 customers in 149 cable systems in 32 states.

The entire executive team assembled. When Ted finally arrived, he entered the room like a tornado, bringing our dusty office on the edge of Denver to life. After hearty handshakes, everyone started to take their seat except Ted, who stood at the head of the room.

When it got quiet, he unloaded: WTCG was reaching 460,000 homes in central and southern Georgia and in surrounding states by bouncing a signal from microwave tower to tower in the hills and valleys. He could go nationwide, overnight, he said.

Just getting warmed up, Ted started pacing back and forth as he spoke, like a tiger in a cage, a recurring behavior that I came to recognize as a sign that his synapses were firing in overdrive.

Ted explained that he had agreements in place with a new channel called HBO to share space on Satcom I, a new communications satellite going up later that year. With assurances from HBO president Gerald "Jerry" Levin, Ted told us, "There's room on the bird for us."

At one point Ted stopped mid-stride and declared, "I promise you I'm gonna take this superstation and I'm gonna put it up on that satellite and beam it back down!" His voice rose as he added: "All the cable companies are gonna carry it. We're all gonna get rich together. It's gonna be wonderful!" Like any good salesperson, he emphasized the hope more than the hurdles.

After about ten minutes, an assistant poked her head into the conference room and asked us, "Does anybody need coffee?"

From the back of the room came JC's gravelly voice: "Ted sure as hell doesn't!"

Then I interrupted Ted's pitch. "There appear to be a couple roadblocks," I said. First, current government rules banned cable operators from "signal leapfrogging" over nearby towns to get distant signals, a rule to protect local broadcasters and maintain order in the TV market.

"TCI would only be able to carry you in the markets where you're the closest—just a fraction of our base," I told Ted and the group.

"And number two, permits are required for a satellite-receiving antenna, which has to be a minimum of ten meters, which costs upwards of $100,000— a lot of money for most cable operators."

Half listening to me, Ted waved his hand, swatting away the pesky regulations like a fly in the room. Ted didn't really want to hear any objections or any questions. He wanted more than anything to leave with a handshake to carry his network to reach all of TCI's subscribers.

With my questions hanging in the air, all eyes were on Ted. Instead of calmly responding to the issues, Ted, in suit and tie, dropped down onto the floor on his hands and knees and started crawling around as if he had dropped something.

Groveling on the floor, he crawled over to JC Sparkman, head of operations, and kissed JC's shoes, telling him, "JC, I'll kiss your feet if you carry this station! Please carry my channel!" It was quite a show, acted out in dramatic fashion, and he had the entire office hooting, howling, and laughing at the theatrics. He had won the crowd.

When Ted figured out he wasn't walking away with an agreement, though, he made his intention clear: "Well, I'm ready to do it myself if I can't get anybody to help."

Impressive. Here's a guy who is unafraid of walking into the cage and poking the tiger. Here was a broadcast station essentially planning to take on the broadcast industry, which had had its boot on the back of the neck of cable operators for years.

Is this guy fearless or crazy? I thought at the time. *Probably a little bit of both.*

Ted was hoping to get onto the satellite with HBO, a premium cable channel launched in 1972 by the Manhattan cable-TV franchise owner Charles "Chuck" Dolan, whom I knew. As the owner of the first franchise in the city—and the first (more expensive) underground cable system—Chuck was not bringing in enough customers. Inspiration struck him on vacation for a programming service of first-run commercial-free movies packaged with the Knicks and the Rangers games. With backing from the publisher Time Life, he launched HBO, which juiced the subscriptions to cable TV.

Both HBO and Ted's WTCG had faced the same dilemma: they bounced their signals along a daisy chain of microwave towers to extend the market to other cable operators, but the signals were vulnerable to interference and limited to line-of-sight communications.

Satellite technology would solve this problem with efficiency and simplicity. A geostationary communications satellite moved in orbit at the exact same speed as the rotation of the earth, while appearing to "hover" in one spot, thereby reaching every antenna in a given area. Cable-TV networks could for the first time transmit high-quality signals to cable operators nationwide, bypassing the limitations of microwave or even terrestrial broadcasting. We had gotten our first peak at a live demonstration of satellite TV at the 1973 cable show in Anaheim, California. What really convinced everyone was the commercial demonstration in September 1975, when HBO aired the "Thrilla in Manilla" fight between champion Muhammad Ali and Joe Frazier, live from around the world, to a handful of cable systems who had agreed to buy and install big dish earth stations. Driven by a young executive named Gerald Levin, Time Life's HBO struck a deal with RCA Americom to lease a transponder on Satcom I—which was to launch at the end of 1975.

What Ted was doing—distributing his signal far beyond what any of his programming suppliers had imagined—wasn't illegal on its face. But his programmers saw it differently, including Bowie Kuhn, the commissioner of Major League Baseball. Kuhn testified to Congress that Ted Turner had illegally flooded the regional market with Braves games and infringed on clubs' rights. Never mind that it also had brought a national audience of new fans to the team, raising its value significantly. Likewise, the Motion Picture Association of America accused Ted of reselling movies to cable operators, sales that should go to the Hollywood studios that owned the film copyrights.

When Congress held hearings on the future of cable TV in 1976, Ted was invited to speak alongside Gene Jankowski, the president of the CBS Broadcast Group, who testified it was unfair that CBS paid big rights fees for content, while "cable interests use the same program material by paying a token statutory fee" to the U.S. Copyright Royalty Tribunal.

But Ted served it right back. Rattling off figures for the robust pretax profits of CBS, NBC, and CBS and the movie industry's record box-office revenue, he went on the offensive: "They want to stop all competition and keep the little club the same way it is, just the three of them monopolizing what the American people see and hear."

"What alarms me most," Ted added with dramatic flourish, "is that when a small businessman comes in, works hard, plays by Mr. [FCC Chairman Charles] Ferris's rules and has a few successes, the first thing these huge organizations do is try to use their power and influence to change the name of the game."

Politicians were keenly aware that local broadcast networks were gate-keepers to local voters, so they made sure to placate station owners with political favors. Powerful and politically connected lobbyists at the ABC, CBS, and NBC networks had crusaded for draconian rules that held down the programming side of the upstart cable industry.

One of the more arcane and punitive laws I ever have seen was the Anti-Siphoning Rule, a government fiat that benefitted broadcasters. New cable channels were blocked legally from airing any sports event that had been on broadcast TV in the past five years. Networks also were prohibited from showing movies that were less than ten years old. On this one, HBO took the FCC all the way to the Supreme Court and won, citing violation of its First Amendment rights.

The FCC, beholden to concerns of the broadcasters, expanded its jurisdiction as the industry expanded. As a result of new restrictions, there was a chilling effect on the development of cable TV, hindering access to badly needed capital. Money got scarce.

None of which was daunting to Ted Turner. Before he even showed up at TCI to ask for our help, he had defied the odds at every major moment in his life. The stories were told so often they sounded like legend, but they all were true.

One of the most famous was when Ted told his father, a successful businessman, of his decision to study the classics at Brown University. His dad balked and responded with a long, blistering letter to his son on the irrelevance of the degree, at one point calling Ted a jackass: "My dear son, I am appalled, even horrified, that you have adopted Classics as a major," Ted's father wrote. "As a matter of fact, I almost puked on the way home today." Ted retaliated by giving the letter to the Brown University newspaper, which reprinted it, word for word.

A few years after Ted left Brown before graduating, his father, the owner of a thriving billboard advertising business, committed suicide in 1963, when Ted was twenty-four. This is when Ted, despite his grief, took on a heap of debt to take control of the company, which his father, Ed Turner, had arranged to be sold.

Ted renamed the company Turner Communications Group and bought two small independent UHF television stations in the Atlanta and Charlotte markets, and began to build a company that would affect the world of television in new and irrevocable ways. His Channel 17 in Atlanta was the underdog to local affiliate stations of the Big Three broadcast networks. UHF stations had weaker signals and weaker finances, generally speaking, than VHF stations in the cities, whose more powerful signals got better reception throughout markets.

Ted's WTCG showed reruns of old gems like *I Love Lucy*, *The Andy Griffith Show*, *The Three Stooges*, World Championship Wrestling, and cartoons: *The Flintstones*, *The Jetsons*, and *Scooby-Doo*. He broke TV norms from the start, holding telethons to keep the network afloat and counter-programming old movies on Sunday morning while the networks were airing religious shows. Ted even hosted one of the more popular shows, *Academy Award Theater*, on Saturday nights. He would be introduced as "R. E. Turner" and mosey over to an easy chair to sit down and present the movie.

The station began broadcasting Atlanta Braves baseball games in 1973. Three years later, realizing the hometown team's importance to his programming strategy, Ted bought the money-losing franchise for $10 million, financing it in part with the TV rights money that WTBS already had paid to the team.

In 1977, frustrated by the team's sixteen-game losing streaking, Ted Turner named himself team manager and emerged from the dugout with a wad of tobacco in his cheek. He was directly reprimanded by the baseball commissioner for violating league rules prohibiting owners from managing their properties.

Ted reveled in outrageous promotions. He bloodied his nose once in a race with Phillies pitcher Tug McGraw to push a baseball around the field, on hands and knees, using only their noses. In front of thousands of fans, Ted furrowed the field to get the ball to home plate.

Another time, dressed in jockey silks, he raced a sportswriter in buggies pulled by ostriches around the field. And in a marketing coup that showed his familiarity with the Middle America audience he sought, seventeen couples were married on the field before the game, and a wrestling event was held afterward. The promo: "Wedlock and Headlock!"

A year after he bought the Braves in 1976, Major League Baseball commissioner Bowe Kuhn suspended Ted for a year for trying to sign a free agent before his contract was up. Ted protested, pleading ignorance. The very next day, Ted acquired the Atlanta Hawks franchise of the NBA for the same reason he'd bought the Braves—programming.

Ted was equally outrageous and competitive in yachting. In the trials for the 1974 America's Cup yacht race, the sailing world's most prestigious contest, Ted was dismissed by the mucky-mucks of Newport after he captained the losing Mariner. Ted came back three years later and won, then promptly celebrated by getting drunk on national television.

By 1979, he captained the winning boat in the Fastnet race, considered the most dangerous race in the history of sailing. In seas as high as fifty feet, fifteen people died in the 650-mile race, and of the 303 boats that started the race, only 86 finished. In driving sheets of rain and violent waves, Ted was so obsessed with competing and winning that he was unaware of the death and trauma behind him as he crossed the finish line.

During this time, as I got to know Ted, I was intrigued by what a character he was. A good ol' boy from the South, yet he was Ivy League–educated, and he liked to quote great literature. A favorite was Thomas Babington Macaulay's poem "Horatius at the Bridge," and Ted loved delivering particular lines with dramatic gusto:

"Hew down the bridge, Sir Consul, with all the speed ye may! / I, with two more to help me, will hold the foe in play. / In yon strait path, a thousand may well be stopped by three: / Now, who will stand on either hand and keep the bridge with me?" Ted loved voicing the role of the outnumbered Roman soldier, an apt analogy for his own career.

Ted also cultivated the attitude of the screen hero he so admired, Rhett Butler in *Gone with the Wind*, right down to the character's pencil-thin mustache. And frankly, my dear, Ted didn't give a damn about what other people said about him. Like me, Ted could get lost mid-thought—he'd take these epic pauses, let out a long "aaaaaaaaaaaahhhhhhh," like he was buffering, then suddenly drop a one-liner so sharp you couldn't help but laugh.

Amused at first, I became inordinately impressed by how Ted had bucked the odds in business and government. The more business I did with him, the more convinced I became that he possessed some preternatural sense of timing, a phenomenon I still marvel at so many years later. Like a cartoon character on one of his networks, Ted would start walking directly off a cliff—and a path suddenly would appear beneath his feet, as if he'd known it would materialize.

After his performance at TCI's home office, by the time we saw Ted again, in just a matter of months, many of the rules I had cited to him had, almost magically, changed in his favor. With concerted lobbying by the industry, the government dropped the license and size requirement for the expensive satellite receivers, for example.

In fact, the mid-to-late 1970s could not have been better timing for Ted, or the budding cable industry. On December 17, 1976, WTCG became America's first satellite "superstation" capable of reaching every cable operator in the continental U.S.

In Ted's own words, it was "an independent voice offering more choice and more variety. While the broadcasters were filling the public airwaves with a lot of garbage—sensationalized news, violent dramas, and such—the superstation, with its wholesome movies, sitcoms, and sports, would provide a welcome alternative."

By 1979, Turner changed the call letters to WTBS, rebranded it as Superstation TBS, and started to attract much larger advertisers. It was a breakthrough moment for the cable industry—the debut of the first free, ad-supported national programming network on cable systems that previously merely retransmitted local broadcast signals. Now, instead of dealing with a long list of local agreements, HBO, TBS, and other cable networks could negotiate national deals with the largest operators like TCI.

By literally flipping a switch, a cable channel could reach every viewer in America with a TV signal on this platform, and it set off a chain reaction that would reverberate for decades, changing forever the way people around the world entertained and informed themselves.

For viewers, it marked the beginning of unlimited choice for news, sports, and entertainment, delivered instantly, and they signed up in droves. For incumbent broadcast networks, fat with profits from advertisers, the newcomers were a pest at first, but soon the Big Three would feel the sharp sting of competition for the first time—and start objecting more loudly to politicians.

Ted's launch of TBS on the satellite sparked a land rush for viable cable network ideas by eager entrepreneurs. TCI would come to invest in many and carry most all of them. Christian Broadcasting Network (CBN) was our first investment in 1977. Founded by a born-again Christian named Pat Robertson who bought a small Christian TV station in Portsmouth, Virginia, it was the first basic cable channel. Airing mostly televangelists, old westerns, and family fare, CBN, aided by loyal viewers who warmed to a new religious variety program called *The 700 Club*, grew its subscriber base to 10 million households by 1981.

Two years later, we invested in C-SPAN, the cable-TV industry's gift to the American people. Funded originally by a consortium of cable companies and carried voluntarily by all cable operators, a TV camera captures the proceedings of Congress, unfiltered, with no ads, no on-air personalities, and no commentary. Politicians can say what they want on the campaign trail, but if you want to see how they use the power we give them in real time, watch C-SPAN. The network was the brainchild of Brian Lamb, a Washington, D.C., bureau chief for the upstart *Cablevision* magazine at the time.

The quickest decision I ever made in those days was with Bob Johnson, a young lobbyist on the staff at the cable industry's lobby group, NCTA. He buttonholed me after a board meeting and asked, "Do you think there would be any hope for a channel aimed at the Black demographic?" We both knew that there was enormous opportunity to create content for African American audiences, who up until then had largely been overlooked in programming.

After a thirty-minute meeting, I promised to give him half a million dollars for his idea. TCI agreed to give Bob $180,000 for a 20 percent stake in Black Entertainment Television (BET) and loan the remaining $320,000.

I wasn't just an investor in Bob Johnson—I believed in his mission to entertain and empower Black audiences. BET launched in 1980 and, within a decade, became the first Black-controlled company on the New York Stock Exchange. When Bob sold it to Viacom in 2001 for $3 billion, he became a billionaire—and in turn made many Black shareholders millionaires along the way. In 2003, he broke another barrier, becoming the first Black owner of a major U.S. sports team with the NBA's Charlotte Bobcats. I didn't just back Bob with capital—I opened doors. He built a brand, lifted others with him, and earned every bit of the value he created.

In 1980, Ted showed up again on our doorstep at TCI in Denver, having doubled down with his latest cause, Cable News Network, known today as CNN. Before anyone else, he was pitching a channel airing twenty-four hours a day of news, when America seemed just fine with an evening newscast for half an hour per night on the Big Three.

Ratings for local broadcast news were fair at best, and besides, what kind of news can you cover for twenty-four hours? Critics piled on, even before the launch. Broadcasters dubbed the fledgling channel the "Chicken Noodle Network." But once again, Ted would jump first and take on the establishment. He trusted his gut and pushed ahead with the idea, pouring more than $100 million into it.

Not long after CNN launched on June 1, 1980, American Broadcasting Companies and TV station owner Westinghouse Broadcasting announced plans to launch their own news network, the Satellite News Channel, with updated stories like news radio—free to cable operators. With $100 million already invested in CNN, which was still bleeding money, and two large, well-funded media companies coming at him, Ted said he felt CNN "had a dagger pointed at our heart."

He reminded me that we could not allow a broadcaster to come in and kidnap our ideas, warning, "If you and the cable industry don't carry CNN, I'm dead."

For the first time, Ted needed to charge cable operators to carry one of his channels, if CNN was to survive. TBS had been a distant signal offered free of charge to cable operators. On a discussion panel at a trade show in the early 1980s, I had been openly opposed to paying a subscription fee to certain channels, such as MTV, in part because I knew they were making a healthy profit margin on the videos. I added pointedly that TCI was willing to entertain subscription fees for basic cable channels—if the channels fit a unique niche that would help us grow the number of subscribers.

In any case, I concluded that ABC and Westinghouse would have to charge us for their news channel, sooner or later. Nothing of value is ever free. And Ted was right—if the broadcasters got a toehold in the market, they would exploit it against us and other operators.

Ted poured on the charm offensive to the cable industry, trying to get CNN carried and reminding the cable operators of his loyalty. He hired a country band, made a video where he sang parts in a "I Was Cable When Cable Wasn't Cool" song, and rented a billboard at the annual trade show in Las Vegas, featuring a photo of himself wearing a cowboy hat and holding an acoustic guitar. It was a funny gimmick, lined with a plaintive appeal, a reminder that Ted had been a partner to cable from the early days.

Ted ultimately would invest a quarter of a billion dollars in CNN before it turned a profit, and while entertainment networks would require much less, they would require payment from cable systems, too. If we wanted to create demand for this product, we had to show quality programming, and that meant we had to belly up and be willing to pay the tab.

By 1983, after beating the broadcast giants to market with a news channel, Ted agreed to buy the bones of Satellite News Channel, eliminating CNN's main competitor.

The press portrayed him as a lucky daredevil in business, but Ted wasn't so much reckless as he was fearless—there's a difference. He was the same in sailing. At the helm, Ted would steer the speeding boat directly into the rocks before he would tack at precisely the right moment, shaving seconds off his run time. Behind the playboy image, Ted was a hard worker and a smart businessperson who saw things on the horizon that others could not: how technology, public policy, and consumer interest were shifting and aligning to create new opportunities in this new industry.

CNN did more than bring cable into American homes—it redefined news. With unprecedented live, global coverage and groundbreaking use of satellite technology, CNN outpaced the networks and changed how we watched world events. Its defining moment came in 1991 with the Persian Gulf War, capturing the nation's attention and cementing its place in the media landscape.

To me, the early days of CNN fully manifested the concept of freedom of the press. The immediacy of CNN would have a profound impact on journalism, and an even bigger role in proving the power of the press, helping fuel the fall of Communism abroad and changing American opinions about the idea of war back home.

I almost hung a poster that said, "We listen to all ideas for networks." Our rationale at TCI was that if your network comes to us to be carried, we'll pay you like everyone else, but we will expect a meaningful volume discount as in any other business. So then if someone had a good idea, and they were looking for an equity holder, why not strike a deal for TCI to own 20 percent of that company instead? We reached roughly 20 percent of the industry's subscribers. Over time, that became a model for several such deals.

Critics in the government and the press howled, accusing TCI of "squeezing" new networks, demanding unfair terms. But anyone interested in the creation of value, and what each party brings to the table, would follow the flow of money: a network charging 25 cents per customer, per month, wanting to launch across TCI's 8-million-customer universe, would be charging $2 million per month, $24 million a year—for an unproven service! The risk was lopsided.

Was I a tough negotiator? Damn right I was. The cable company down in Slippery Rock who's got only one thousand customers will pay you 25 cents, and it will take you years to build up critical mass. How much does that help you? But you're asking me for real money and a real commitment and this really launches you into orbit, and has real value. What is it worth to you in start-up losses, if it takes three years or so, whereas TCI can launch tomorrow? What is that worth to you?

The doors opened even wider for the industry thanks to the passage of the Cable Communications Policy Act of 1984, which effectively unshackled the industry from punitive rules.

Up until then, cable TV was regulated by FCC rules in the Communications Act of 1934, written five decades earlier and intended for radio. And because cable operators needed public right-of-way access to string wire or bury it beneath streets, the industry was caught in the cross fire of ancient federal rules and the demands of local governments. Along the way, telephone companies imposed steep fees to attach our wires to their poles—an unfair "pole tax" that hampered cable's growth in the 1970s until leaders like Continental Cablevision founder Amos Hostetter helped win concessions.

Senator Barry Goldwater (R-AZ), one of the new law's sponsors, called the previous rules a "patchwork of Federal, State, and local regulations and court decisions" that had resulted in a "an unstable regulatory environment that has been bad for the cable industry, bad for the local and state franchising authorities, and bad for consumers."

So after more than two years of lobbying, compromises, and with a big push from Representative Tim Wirth (D-CO), the new act was passed, outlining clear rules for municipalities to award franchises to cable companies—or revoke them. The 1984 act also required cable operators to set aside channels for public, educational, and governmental use.

Perhaps most importantly for cable operators, rates could be regulated only if no "effective competition" existed, which was defined as having fewer than three over-the-air broadcast stations. It was a huge victory for cable operators—few markets in the U.S. had three clear signals from all three networks at the time.

The 1984 Communications Act broke many of the chains holding back cable, unleashing eager entrepreneurs and innovation. Engineering advances improved signal quality and boosted the capacity of set-top boxes, driving demand in urban and suburban markets. With looser regulations, cable companies raised capital, expanded services, and attracted more customers. Major operators began consolidating smaller ones, leveraging scale economics to reshape the industry. By decade's end, growth surged, and TCI emerged as a rising star.

CHAPTER 8

SHOPPING FOR ANSWERS

High tea at the old Helmsley Palace Hotel was a well-known tradition in New York City in the 1980s, with harp music playing in the background, and butlers serving guests from tiered carts loaded with finger sandwiches, scones, and crumpets—whatever those are.

I felt a little sheepish having flown in from Denver, where real work was going on, to hail cabs and dodge tourists to sit waiting on a velvet-covered chair at a dainty round table in the hotel. I looked around at the tables nearby, waiting to talk to the founders of a new cable network.

It was the summer of 1986, and I had flown to New York with Peter Barton, a new young recruit at TCI who had shown promise, to explore investments in a new, fast-growing genre that was making money. A lot of money. We were there to meet Irwin Jacobs, a corporate raider from Minnesota who had founded a mail-order company that dealt in closed-out merchandise. Irwin was a shrewd, motivated businessman who had found opportunity in the detritus of companies that had failed, or needed cash, or had bought too much of one product. He had been called a corporate raider in the press, accused of greenmail by public firms, and was known as "Irwin the Liquidator" in local business circles and on Wall Street.

We were there to hear more from Irwin, who had supplied a solution to the very quandary that we were eager to solve in programming: how to break into the shopping-over-TV business. The Home Shopping Network had just gone public, and Wall Street loved it.

Just months earlier, I had experienced a genuine epiphany that brought me to the Helmsley. When I had shaken hands with Drew Lewis, CEO of

Warner-Amex, I had heard that Warner was planning to launch a new stock offering for MTV, their hot new teen-targeted music channel. Investment bankers had convinced Lewis that the new network could capitalize on its viral popularity by charging cable operators more money per subscriber than anyone had ever dared to charge before—50 cents per subscriber. Alarm bells went off in my head.

Holy shit.

HBO was a premium service, around $10 a month, but most others were free to consumers, and ad-supported, like TBS and USA. I had always expected nominal fees from networks, but, until hearing about MTV's plans, I never had imagined that cable networks would have the market power to create a dual revenue stream: fees from the distributors carrying their network, on top of the money that advertisers paid to air commercials on it. All this time, I had valued the *distribution* part of the company, and now more of the future value might well lie in *content*.

TCI had a new worry: we'd be held hostage to ever-increasing fees from networks that attracted the biggest audiences. This changed the economic model in my mind, and in an instant I saw our big distribution company differently. We would have to become owners of content.

Quality programming was critical for the industry, and I understood most content providers were price constrained, which is why we stepped up for Ted Turner and why we invested in BET, Discovery, and the Family Channel.

The conversation was always the same: What is your programming service worth? If the answer was, say, $20 million, we'd say, "Okay, we'll pay you $5 million for a 20 percent stake, and we'll pay you 5 cents per subscriber home per month—but we want to freeze that rate flat for the next fifteen years." An implicit part of this discussion was TCI's reach as the biggest cable operator in the country. By signing on with our cable systems, new channels instantly could reach 20 percent of the nation from the get-go.

I personally wanted to encourage the programming companies and entrepreneurs to create content exclusively for cable TV. The industry had been feeding on leftovers from the broadcasters for nearly twenty years; in the early 1980s, the top-rated cable programs included ancient reruns of

The Andy Griffith Show from the sixties. I knew if the new cable networks had access to the same scale and financing as we did, they could exceed the quality of what the broadcasters were producing.

We wanted to be the first ones at the buffet table. So we adopted a strategy that we wanted to own 20 percent of the best networks, because that's all the government would let us own at the time.

We did not have the skill to run channels on our own, but we could be an investor and justify our investment with vast distribution. We needed to protect TCI's interests—and, by extension, those of our customers—by limiting the ability of networks to raise prices. We would do this by demanding a volume discount and/or long-term price guarantees on a carriage contract. We wanted a "Most Favored Nation" clause, a guarantee that we would get the lowest prices a programmer was charging to any cable operator. This simple tactic could give us a real edge.

I could see what was coming: once Warner got everyone hooked on free content with MTV, it was going to increase the price down the road. So I needed to throw a monkey wrench into their IPO plans for MTV.

So I wrote a letter to Warner that stipulated that, absent a mutually acceptable agreement, we were dropping MTV from all of our systems. I knew this would interrupt the MTV prospectus (the offering document for the IPO), because it would be considered a material change if the largest distributor planned to discontinue carriage.

Drew, whom I liked, was on the plane and sitting in my office the next day, and Warner and TCI struck a long-term deal that protected us against the increase in rates. Quality content would become much more valuable. Already cable was outgrowing its amateur-hour status compared with the broadcast networks. CNN was now in 26 million homes, with a George Peabody Award in journalism. HBO would win its first Emmy in 1988 with a documentary.

Audiences were grouping around networks with specific demographics, like ESPN, Lifetime, and MTV, as well as updated information channels such as the Weather Channel, the Financial News Network, and C-SPAN. Advertisers rushed in.

And in retail, cable TV offered something called "home shopping."

While it's hard to imagine what life was like before websites like Amazon, the only way back then that you could get a product you could not buy in person at a physical store was to order it from a paper catalog, either by mail order or by telephone (one connected to the wall with a cord). The notion that you could now see on TV a necklace on a live model, or watch a power saw buzz through a board, and order it up sparked the imagination of retailers, and literally dozens of shopping networks jumped into the race within months. As we sat in the Helmsley, Irwin said all the right things, claiming he had plenty of inventory, big warehouses, and "everything we need to make it happen fast."

He was as eager as we were to get into the home-shopping business and wanted to harness the powerful new reach of cable TV. He was in business with an equally colorful character named Ted Deikel, the president of Fingerhut, a popular mail-order catalog cofounded by Ted's father-in-law, Manny Fingerhut.

Peter was cracking jokes as we waited for Irwin and Ted, and we knew they had chosen this extravagant hotel for the theatrics. Peter and I had already flown to Minneapolis once when Deikel picked us up in his own Rolls-Royce, which he proudly drove to a warehouse filled with closed-out merchandise.

As we sat there in the Helmsley, I was sizing up Peter Barton, too. I had invited Pete to Colorado after opening an unusual letter in the mail—a Harvard Business School graduate offering to work for free for ninety days. And at the end of ninety days, we could hire or fire him. We hired him.

Peter had spent his formative years assisting New York governor Hugh Carey, so he knew how to navigate the corridors of power. A bantam-weight athlete with coal-black hair, he also had a wilder side: he was a radio disc jockey, painter, and avalanche rescue team skier who jumped from helicopters. And he was funny as hell.

When Irwin and Ted finally showed up, we had a good laugh at the setting. We did not nibble long on the cucumber sandwiches as I remember: within minutes, after warming up on the broad strokes of a deal, we discussed how the ownership would look to launch a new network called CVN: Cable Value Network.

Later, when Peter and I were alone, I offered him an assignment I thought would be the perfect test for his skills. "Okay, Pete, this is your first shot at running a business. You're going to Minneapolis, to be the first president of CVN. You're gonna have Irwin and Ted up there to help you out. We'll take care of the cable industry side of things. You take care of getting CVN on the air."

Peter jumped in with both feet. He had coincidentally fallen in love with one of our top marketing executives, Laura Perry, who, seduced by Peter's charm, moved to Minneapolis with him and married him.

Peter was perfect for the job. Competition fired him up, and he was racing against other companies with the *exact same idea*. He was so confident he would succeed that he placed a bet with Ted Deikel: Peter would take ownership of Ted's beloved Rolls-Royce if CVN signed up 10 million subscribers before the launch date.

So Peter flew around the country selling cable operators on the idea of both carrying our new shopping channel and owning a small stake in it—and with it a percentage of the annual revenue.

We were late to the home-shopping industry by 1986, but within a year, Peter had managed to sign up cable operators representing more than 14 million subscribers, more than enough for profitability, based on our crude projections, and commitments from even more.

He had won the bet with Ted Deikel by landing at least 10 million subscribers, and Ted had happily paid up, knowing the far greater prize was his stake in a big television shopping retailer.

Peter liked to tell the story of driving home with the new Rolls-Royce, thinking he would soon just drive it back to Denver and be done. I broke it to him on the phone. "Now you have to make it work."

Retailing on TV, it turned out, wasn't as easy as it looked. Within minutes of CVN's going on the air in September 1986, customer orders overwhelmed the old batch-processing computers that the staff had been using to record sales. Everything had to be stopped for the night simply to process the day's orders. At one point, inventory was so screwy that Peter sent employees down the street to Kmart to buy goods to put on the air so we'd have something new to sell.

Eventually, the ordering system was replaced, and sales grew. But we were still not up to par with the Home Shopping Network. And over in Philadelphia, a fellow by the name of Joseph Segel was doing a much more elegant job of selling merchandise on a network call QVC. Joe was a polished businessperson who had founded the Franklin Mint, which ran sophisticated ads in magazines to sell commemorative coins, medallions, figurines, and other collectibles.

He, too, had seen HSN and launched QVC as the Saks Fifth Avenue to HSN's Walmart. QVC's hosts were smoother, and its merchandise comprised of more high-margin products. So TCI took an equity stake in QVC, along with Comcast and others.

Literally dozens of companies announced new shopping networks, far too many for the market to support. And the market quickly thinned out. The Fashion Channel, in which TCI owned a stake, would go bankrupt and be folded into CVN. Many retailers saw the vision, but few could make it work in time. Still, there was opportunity for the right player.

Since what we knew about retailing you could put into a thimble and shake around, we decided to invest in someone who did it better.

QVC under Joe Segel, a seasoned merchant, with backing from Comcast, had outperformed CVN on margins, operational efficiency, and product quality. So, in July 1989, after conversations with Comcast chairman Ralph Roberts, his son Brian, and vice chairman Julian Brodsky, we struck a deal to sell our Cable Value Network to QVC, even though CVN was the much bigger network.

Roberts really wanted to retain effective control, and it was clear Joe Segel was his person. I knew we'd make more money as an investor, not an operator. Sometimes it helps to know what you're good at and what you're not.

By the fall of 1988, more than half of the estimated fifty shopping channels had gone out of business. Months later, the field would dwindle down to just two players: QVC and HSN. We were on the leaderboard.

Both Ted and Irwin were handsomely rewarded for their stakes when we did the deal. Ted Deikel would go on to negotiate the sale of Fingerhut and today operates his own luxury real estate design and development firm with his wife in California.

I continued to talk with Irwin for years afterward. He became a philan-thropist, part owner of the Minnesota Vikings, and owner of Genmar Corp., the largest privately held boat company in the U.S. Our shared fondness for boating kept the lines open between us before he passed away.

We would ultimately merge QVC with HSN more than twenty years later. And even with the rise of Amazon and online shopping, TV shopping remains a valuable business, with QVC, HSN, and online retailer Zulily delivering nearly $11 billion through the QVC Group.

Yielding to a better, smaller competitor taught me that when you lack a special expertise, it is better to own a small piece of a thriving enterprise rather than to own 100 percent of a struggling one you don't know how to run.

That day at the Helmsley Hotel, I found myself quietly taking stock of four very different individuals. Funny how, over time, the people who cross your path—often by chance—end up altering the course of your life. Irwin Jacobs and Ted Deikel were larger-than-life figures and introduced us to the retail business. Joe Segel at QVC stood out for his quiet integrity and a forward-looking vision of what television retail could be. And then there was Peter—facing long odds but driven by sheer instinct, creativity, and a sense of humor that shined even in the toughest moments. I took a chance on each of them, and looking back, they all turned out to be the right kind of risk.

CHAPTER 9

CRAZY LIKE A FOX

"Rupert's in a tough spot."

I had just picked up the phone to hear the voice of Paul Gould, a managing director at Allen & Company, one afternoon in 1988. Paul was an old friend, occasional sailing partner, and a fellow introvert with whom I enjoyed endlessly deconstructing deals.

In his easy way, Paul explained the situation in bare terms: the Australian media magnate Rupert Murdoch, after pulling off a string of business conquests in the U.S. for his News Corporation, was caught in a bad cash crunch that could topple his company.

Rupert had borrowed close to $5 billion from banks to acquire some pricey new properties, including the iconic 20th Century-Fox movie studio, the Metromedia broadcast TV stations, and a bunch of consumer and trade magazines owned by Ziff Davis. He had defied conventional Wall Street wisdom and launched a fourth broadcast network in 1987. Then in 1988, he pledged $3 billion to buy Triangle Publications, which published *TV Guide*, the largest and most profitable weekly at the time.

TV Guide was a cash cow that could help pay off the mountain of takeover debt that Murdoch had built up in a flurry of deals. It also could serve as a bullhorn to promote his TV properties, with a finely tuned distribution system reaching 17 million readers each week that he could leverage to expand the circulation and reduce costs for other News Corp. publications. It was a great asset—if he could afford it.

The late 1980s were a heyday for business mergers, with the help of big bank loans, junk bonds, and leveraged buyouts. Nabisco Brands and R.J.

Reynolds Tobacco Company merged in 1985, for example, and three years later, RJR Nabisco was bought by KKR in what was at the time the largest leveraged buyout in history.

The media industry was at the forefront of this consolidation. Warner Communications bought Time Inc.; Viacom bought Showtime and MTV; Sumner Redstone bought Viacom; Capital Cities bought the ABC network; GE bought NBC; Turner bought MGM.

Then the federal government, after a decade of watching these Wall Street–inspired acquisitions, began clamping down on highly leveraged transactions (HLTs). Rupert's short-term money borrowed from U.S. banks to buy Triangle fell under this new definition.

The regulators had changed the rules for Rupert in the middle of the game. It is, unfortunately, government's way.

To pay for the deal, Rupert had borrowed around $1.5 billion, on top of more than $4 billion in News Corp. debt, and still he had been forced to sell around $1 billion in assets. And now Paul was on the phone with me, brainstorming his way through a problem once again, this time to help out a client: "John, what about investing in News Corp.?"

I was just getting to know Rupert. Was this someone I was willing to bet big money on?

My gut said yes—Rupert's confidence and strategy spoke volumes to me. I told Paul we were in for as much as he needed. TCI made its first investment in News Corp. that year, putting up $75 million in return for redeemable preferred stock, a type of stock that allows the company to buy back the stock under certain conditions, thereby raising money without giving up permanent ownership.

Looking back on it now, I did it for two reasons: (1) I wanted to help a new friend, and (2) I wanted to invest in something I was sure would grow.

When banks under HLT restrictions became concerned about News Corp.'s creditworthiness in 1998, as a board member of the Bank of New York, one of News Corp.'s creditors, I reassured them, and lobbied on Rupert's behalf.

In the end, Rupert got his balance sheet in shape, the banks were paid off, and we watched the value of our stock grow. At various times over the years, when their stock was cheap, I'd throw a few bucks at increasing our stake.

I had heard about Rupert long before I met him. He was an unwelcome arrival to the media business in the U.S. Many people conflated his name with that of Robert Maxwell, a more infamous press baron with the same initials, who was competing with Rupert at the time over media properties in the UK. After Maxwell's body was found in the Atlantic Ocean in 1991, apparently after falling off his yacht, news emerged that he had stolen from his company's pension funds, which began the unraveling of his publishing empire.

Rupert was catching some backlash for being another overleveraged, swashbuckling CEO with media properties and an accent.

Still, Murdoch's influence in the media business was rippling across markets on a global scale with News Corp.'s vast holdings in film, television, newspapers, and publishing in the UK and US—the spoils of death-defying bets he had made since taking over a handful of newspapers after the death of his father in Australia in 1952.

Federal law forbids any noncitizen from owning TV stations, so Rupert Murdoch became a naturalized U.S. citizen in 1985 and quickly set about assembling a formidable media empire. He brazenly bought up some of the crown jewels of American media, such as the 20th Century-Fox movie studio. And amid the sneers of skeptics, Rupert launched a fourth U.S. broadcast network, the Fox Broadcasting Company, challenging the dominance of ABC, CBS, and NBC. After buying Metromedia's TV stations, securing a foothold in key markets, he enlisted as CEO Hollywood heavyweight Barry Diller, who crafted a strategy around younger audiences and unconventional shows like *The Simpsons* and *Married . . . with Children.* Fox defied the odds and reshaped the American television market in the process. I learned from Rupert's approach—aggressive and direct, the kind of competitor who was deadly because he was so quick to draw and fire. He tackled challenges head-on—whether from regulators, competitors, or his own team—and always found ways to navigate around obstacles. And he's never, ever been afraid to buck the system. I respected that.

In six decades of dealmaking, I have accrued a list of impressively formidable opponents on the global stage of telecommunications. By comparison, the list of friends in business, people I was close to outside the office, people with whom I've genuinely connected, is short. Rupert is the one person who tops both of those lists.

We first met in 1983 at a media conference in Sun Valley, Idaho, run by Allen & Company's namesake founder, Herbert Allen. One of the few get-togethers I looked forward to attending, it was private, with no press, so it gave a me a chance to learn from CEOs outside the cable-TV industry. Mostly, the setting was undeniably peaceful: hiking trails, horseback riding, and fly-fishing against an endless horizon of grassy peaks and picture-perfect valleys.

As president of the nation's largest cable operator, I gave an informal presentation about our simple strategy: (1) continue to grow by acquisition, while at the same time (2) invest in new programming ventures, and all the while (3) test new theories about what we could do over our many miles of networks.

The invite list for the first conference was small—only five companies— compared with the large media-covered Allen conferences of today. I was one of the presenters, as I recall, to a limited attendee list, all of whom were business legends in their prime, including Bill McGowan, founder of MCI, the man responsible for breaking AT&T's stranglehold on the long-distance market; Gerald "Jerry" Levin, the CEO of Time, the publishing empire with *Time*, *People*, *Life*, and over one hundred other magazines; Roberto C. Goizueta, a Cuban immigrant who had climbed the ranks to become chairman of Coca-Cola; and a charming Aussie named Rupert Murdoch.

What I first noticed about Rupert was just how very focused he was, even in our first conversation. He listened intently, a sign of someone gifted with perception, which is rare in business. He offered some reasonable assumptions about the growth of U.S. markets, and a few thoughtful open-ended questions.

That night, enjoying the solitude of the star-filled walk back to my room, I was fascinated by this fellow, who was ten years my senior and one of the smoothest operators and smartest strategists I had ever seen up close.

Rupert had a ton of ambition, and not an ounce of fear. Perhaps he had earned the nickname "The Great White Shark" from Australia.

For many years after that first deal, if I got to Sun Valley again, I'd get together with the Murdochs and Rupert and I would spend the afternoon just talking about the industry and what we could do together. Our view of the world is similar. Generally speaking, we both are libertarians, we both believe in self-reliance, maximizing individual rights, and minimizing the role of the state. And we both believe in the strongest defense possible because the government's principal purpose is national security. We are both concerned with America's future and its ability to thrive amid global, state-backed competition.

And while Rupert is more comfortable in the role of pushing a conservative ideology on the platforms he owns, I prefer not to proselytize, personally or through the various media companies we own.

As our conversations grew deeper in business, our friendship got closer. In the years that followed, that friendship would be tested in ways neither of us could imagine.

Sometimes in business, a strategy doesn't appear to work at first, but the knowledge you gain is more valuable because it informs decisions down the road. In late 1988, Rupert called with a very particular request. "John, you know about computers and networks and so on, and there's a company called Prodigy . . ."

We had been closely watching the "computer information services," as they were called back then. Rupert wanted to explore joint acquisitions using TCI's networking and News Corp.'s programming. "There must be something here for us," he said.

Personal computers were just taking off in the late 1980s, a precursor to the internet explosion soon to follow. Before the arrival of broadband, networking for those early computers was limited. Computers "talked" to one another using telephone modems, which made contact only after connecting though a series of screeches and chirps via a plain old copper phone line.

Prodigy was an early player looking to connect personal computers on a private subscriber network. Prodigy's owners were IBM and Sears. IBM, the largest computer maker in the world at the time, and Sears, one of the biggest retailers, were offering news, sports, weather, entertainment, and home shopping through Sears and other retailers. Members could "message" one another only on the proprietary, closed Prodigy network.

The biggest of these new networking services was AOL, followed closely by CompuServe, owned by H&R Block Inc. and General Electric Company. They were all clunky, closed-off networks or "walled gardens." Simple connections took a few minutes and required special software and modems, and some services charged per minute for usage!

From the outside, it looked a lot like cable TV—a network of interconnected customers—but when we tried to reverse engineer how it was being done, we did not see a role for the cable industry. TCI passed. Our conclusion: Prodigy could not scale up quickly with high costs, slow modem speeds, and limited network infrastructure. I'm glad we passed—none of these services from back then exist in the same form today, although strands of their DNA were injected into other companies. Almost a decade later, after investing $1 billion in Prodigy, IBM and Sears sold the service in 2001 to SBC Communications, formerly Southwestern Bell.

Rupert was smart enough to pass on buying Prodigy in the early 1980s, but he resumed a shopping spree for media companies as if checking off a giant grocery list, buying the *Chicago Sun-Times*, Metromedia's TV stations, and the HarperCollins book publishing company.

He launched Sky Television network, the first satellite service in the UK, in 1989, beaming Sky News, the first twenty-four-hour news network in

the United Kingdom, which he would merge with British Satellite Broadcasting to form BSkyB in 1990, which would become the largest digital TV
subscription company in the UK. And in 1993, he took News Corp. to a
fourth continent, buying Star TV in Asia for $525 million.

I was fascinated by Rupert's business acumen and his willingness to push
everything to the center of the table on a bet. He went all in, over and over,
and each time, he walked away with his pockets stuffed with million-dollar
chips.

I knew that Rupert and I would have to navigate a complicated relationship, one that would ebb and flow based on where our investments or
companies were at the moment. The world was too small.

We were already competing with Rupert's TV business in different parts
of the globe. For example, in the UK, TCI's TeleWest, which operated
much like a U.S. cable operator, in the early 1990s was getting its lunch
eaten by News Corp.'s Sky, which had moved to digital much faster, with
more channels and better picture and audio.

Soon I fell into a simple philosophy that helped me deal with Rupert.
The way I saw it, sometimes he was playing on my team. A lot of times he
was playing for a different team but not opposing us. And in certain games
he and his team were playing against us—and hard.

The press later would dub us "frenemies," but that hardly describes the
respect I had for Rupert. I was fairly skilled in the sport of fencing back in
high school, and going back and forth with him was a lot like facing the foil
of a skilled opponent whose style meshed well with mine. Every time with
Rupert, I relished the match.

CHAPTER 10

SWEET LIBERTY

Nearly every big deal we announced in the 1990s, either the Justice Department or the Federal Trade Commission jumped in to scrutinize it, partly because of required reviews, but also because they were curious about TCI's size and market power.

In 1991, we were trying to buy a 50 percent stake in Showtime, the number two premium service and a good hedge against the dominant premium service, HBO. But TCI's offer for Showtime sat stalled under review at the FTC for more than a year. After the commission ultimately OKed the deal, both sides had already moved on. A few years later, Liberty and TCI would instead launch Starz, a "multiplex" of several premium movie channels, sourced by Turner Broadcasting's New Line and other studios, with founding CEO John Sie—the same sharp strategist who had penned the digital HDTV white paper, and was now a core force within the company's leadership.

Still, the government's treatment of the industry was near schizophrenic: Cable TV started under a patchwork of onerous local rules in the 1970s. The Cable Communications Policy Act of 1984 essentially deregulated the industry, freeing operators of oppressive local rate regulation. By 1991, Congress, in all its long-range wisdom, was seriously considering *re-regulation*. CEOs in the relatively young cable-TV industry were getting whiplash.

Besides technology, the only force that has consistently shaped the destiny of the cable-TV industry over time is government. Over the next several years, federal regulators, led by misguided politicians, would end up brutally punishing the cable-TV industry and rewarding incumbent broadcasters with billions of dollars in undeserved payments, all the while claiming to do it in the name of helping consumers.

The problem, as the government saw it, was that since the cable-TV industry had been deregulated, rates for the most popular basic service had risen 61 percent on average, according to one big federal study. Complaints of rising monthly cable-TV bills and sloppy service were sprouting nationwide like cheatgrass on the plains. Some increases were due to speculative owners who jumped in to buy fast, raise rates, and sell for a quick buck.

Few in Congress could see, as we did, that most increases were long overdue, to cover the cost of bringing in ever more satellite-delivered TV networks and upgrading our plant to improve service. By 1990, more than half the homes in the country subscribed to cable, and the number of cable networks had jumped to seventy-nine, from just twenty-eight in 1980. All of this was done without a penny from the government, unlike broadcasters, who were given their licenses. Are you not entertained?

I was, however, so focused on growing the company that I ignored how poor our customer service had become. TCI's primitive outage alert system was reflective of the industry: we offered a discount to the first home on the wire coming out of the head end, a transmission hub for cable-TV signals, if they notified the main office when their signal went out. Amid consolidation in the industry, TCI was the biggest, and managed to stand out like an ugly duckling. Complaints piled up. Congress noticed.

On Capitol Hill, the campaign got louder to crack down on cable-TV rates by groups claiming to represent consumers, and an assortment of proposals had been whittled down to a bill in each house of Congress.

Seeing an opening, our competitors piled on. The Big Three broadcasters (to reiterate: ABC, CBS, and NBC), who were bleeding advertising dollars and audience share to what they saw as these new piranha-like cable networks, wanted more than anything to kill the upstart industry. Broadcasters funded a multimedia lobbying effort to get a cable regulation bill passed under the pretense of helping consumers, with letters, meetings with key senators, and ads in newspapers warning, "If cable wins, consumers lose."

Broadcast networks lobbied Congress to require all cable operators to begin paying new fees to retransmit broadcast network programming, rather than the cheap copyright fees Congress had signed off on years earlier. Never mind that broadcasters sent the same signal free everywhere in the U.S. over the air to literally tens of millions of rooftop antennas.

Regional telephone companies looking to offer video service lobbied the FCC to order rates cut up to three times the 10 percent rollback others had proposed. Satellite-dish TV companies pressed for access to programming on the same terms as we offered our best customers.

The bills also raised concerns about our size, specifically about getting too big in two ways: *horizontally*, by controlling too many cable systems across different areas, and *vertically*, by owning both the cable networks and the systems that distribute them.

By that time, TCI, Warner Communications, Cox Cable, and other large operators all owned stakes in networks, and TCI owned stakes in some of the biggest—CNN, Discovery, the Family Channel, and the second-largest shopping channel, QVC, among others. We supported Discovery's acquisition of The Learning Channel and were on the lookout to buy several networks, losing out on the Financial News Network to a joint bid of Cablevision and NBC.

TCI was a convenient villain for politicians. We had grown into the largest cable operator in the country, reaching nearly one in four cable-TV subscribers in the U.S. We were too big to ignore, and in the fall of 1989, I got caught in the government's net. I was called to testify on TCI's behalf before a Senate subcommittee considering a bill to address rising cable rates, service complaints, and market power of the cable industry.

I would rather tap dance in a minefield than speak in a crowded room to a dais of senators eager to pepper me with trapdoor questions—all while cameras are rolling for people to parse my words.

But there I was on November 16, 1989, cramped and sweating at a table before senators questioning the industry's pricing power, in a gallery filled with people, including the press. Quite literally, my worst nightmare.

On my right was Jim Robbins, the highly regarded and affable president of Cox Communications, a family enterprise in Atlanta that also owned newspapers and TV stations. On my left was Jim Mooney, the silver-haired, golden-tongued head of the NCTA who led the effort to secure the 1984 Cable Act, which allowed the industry to prosper.

Even though I had studied my prepared words, I was woefully unprepared for the public humiliation that would slowly unfold over the next couple hours. I did not like being called to the carpet to answer for every bad actor out there, especially by politicians preening on an issue like lower rates for cable television.

Making matters worse, while the stately Senator Daniel Inouye (D-HI) headed up the committee, members seemed to give free rein to a brash young Tennessee senator named Al Gore, whose rural constituents were upset over higher cable-TV rates. Before I had even walked into the room, Gore had already softened the crowd, dubbing me the "King of the Cable Cosa Nostra," an unkind reference to the Sicilian mafia, and likening me to Darth Vader.

I never responded to it. We were discussing the price of MTV, not the end of the planet. Bob Magness said it best: you cannot win a pissing contest with a skunk, so there's no point in defending yourself or saying anything.

I had a history with Gore, and I'm sure he remembered. Several years earlier, HBO and other cable-TV networks, and even broadcast networks such as CBS, with full support from Hollywood, had announced plans to scramble signals, which caused static in Washington, D.C., in the 1980s. I, too, feared owners of big "TV Receive Only" parabolic dishes in rural areas would pirate content. In a private meeting, I urged Al Gore to support a plan for Primestar, owned by TCI and other cable operators, to offer scrambled signals to these C-band homes more efficiently. But Gore, backed by dish-makers and rural voters, pushed the 1988 Satellite Home Viewer Act, allowing big-dish owners in remote "blind" areas to access broadcast networks for free.

So now, as I sat shifting in my seat, Al Gore commanded the microphone. What had Gore particularly peeved was that cable rates had shot up in his home state of Tennessee after a company called Multivision had jacked up rates, which he detailed in a large chart before the dais. I breathed easier when I saw TCI was not on the list.

"Well, what's going on, Mr. Chairman, is that some people say, 'Well, that's just the marketplace at work; if they want to raise their rates 117 percent, that's just market economics. Well . . . it's a monopoly! And the federal government has come in and told the local governments which grant the monopoly franchise, 'Hands off! Let them fleece the consumers as much as they possibly can.'"

Sounding more like a prosecutor instead of a questioner, Gore continued, "TCI for one—we'll hear from its CEO today—is obviously hell-bent toward total domination of the market as it buys up not only more and more cable systems, but more and more major programming services, and even movie studios."

When it came my time to speak, I conceded that after the Cable Act of 1984, cable companies had raised their rates, but instead of generating large profits, the increased cash flow was reinvested into the business, funding upgrades to cable systems and new programming. Based on our cash-flow metrics, the cable-TV industry had the lowest return on invested capital of any media or communications industry. "Years ago, we had some of the largest industrial companies in America in the business—General Electric, Westinghouse, American Express, Capital Cities—they all exited the industry over the last five or six years, and all of them cited low return on investment below their corporate objectives as their reason to exit."

The same government report that showed big rate increases, I pointed out, also showed that "the cost per channel of cable has gone down since deregulation in real terms and stayed flat in inflationary terms."

Sure, the industry had raised rates, but look at what that investment had yielded: the number of new national cable networks had exploded, and with far more selection than broadcasters ever dreamed of offering: old Hollywood films, new movies, financial news, religious programming, regional sports, live coverage of Congress, programming for Hispanic and Black audiences, the arts—and we were just getting warmed up.

"Further proof in our market economy that our product is successful, the penetration of cable TV has actually been accelerating rather than decelerating," I pointed out. If so many people were unhappy about the cost of cable TV, I wanted to ask more bluntly, why was it that every day more people were signing up for it?

The proportion of subscribing households *tripled* between 1976 and 1988; by 1990, 52 million households subscribed to cable—57 percent of TV homes. In the early 1980s, cable networks' share of the audience was less than 10 percent of TV sets in use during the prime-time hours of 8 p.m. to 11 p.m. against the Big Three networks; by 1991, it was 24 percent and climbing fast. The cable industry was collecting over $20 billion in annual revenues, the value of cable systems had doubled, and cable networks were accounting for nearly a third of U.S. viewing.

As powerful as the Big Three broadcast networks were, Wall Street had decided they were prey, not predators, and in 1985, Capital Cities bought ABC, and General Electric bought NBC. CBS became a target in hostile takeover attempts from a rogues' gallery of 1980s dealmakers, including Ivan Boesky, Marvin Davis, even Ted Turner briefly, and eventually, Loews Corp. chairman Larry Tisch, who became president and CEO in 1986 and slashed costs. Little wonder the broadcasters were so eager to crush our revenue stream.

I tried to tell the assembled D.C. crowd who we *really* were: long-term investors and builders, not a force led by a galactic overlord hell-bent on world domination.

The goal was smart capital allocation, looking for the best way to increase our efficiency, maximize our cash flow, and ultimately increase shareholder value. "We have been in business twenty years as a public company. We have never paid a cash dividend to our shareholders. We have invested every dollar that we've been able to scrape together through equity sales or borrowing back in the cable business. Our cumulative retained earnings in that time has been zero. We have plowed everything back into growth and renewing our technology. Cable companies are cash-capital alligators. Our technology is evolving so rapidly we can't wait the fifteen-year franchise renewal cycle. We have to constantly reinvest, expand channel capacity . . ."

Addressing our ownership of cable networks, I tried to paint a picture: It was necessary to own networks as a hedge on price gouging from other networks. "We are a purchasing agent primarily for our subscribers. And if we don't have some market power to perform that function right now, we are very vulnerable to just being nothing more than a collection agency as we have very little ability to resist price increases."

Most networks started out promising to be ad-supported and free, but with each renewal came ever larger charges "often on a take-it-or-leave-it basis," I told the committee, one reason TCI now required long-term contracts.

If lawmakers stepped back, I explained, they'd see a window to create a new two-way platform with incredible opportunity for the country, and it would last only so long. "I think, Senator Gore, our market system works in a wonderful way. [Companies] can be excessive for a little while. Technology moves on and competition moves on and ultimately competition does represent the real limit."

And competition for viewers' attention was all around, not just from satellite firms and telephone companies. American viewers had just discovered the joys of recording network shows for watching later as VCRs in U.S. households rocketed from 11 percent in 1983 to 67 percent in 1989.

"Nothing is forever, not even cable . . . and there will be competitive services evolving. I would not put this industry in such a box that it cannot follow evolving technology."

The senators sat unfazed, as if I had just been reading out the ingredients from a cake recipe. "We can't close our ears to the shouts from our constituents," Senator Inouye said. "They're pretty loud."

These politicians were about to step on a sprouted seed. Without a dime from government subsidies, from 1984 to 1992, the industry would spend more than $15 billion wiring up America's homes, considered to be the largest private construction project in the U.S. since World War II.

At one point, I called out Gore in the politest of ways. "I know Senator Gore has referred to me in public as Darth Vader, a cause for great humor . . . I guess . . . for my friends and employees," I joked that my wife found me to be more like the Wizard of Oz, "credited with a lot more influence and power than I actually wield."

What genuinely spooked me was when my family and I were threatened by mail and calls by wackos who heard this verbal mudslinging, and the attention robbed us of our privacy, forced us to put up gates at the driveway, and made our kids start to fear encounters with strangers.

I did not play the political game as well as I should have in Washington, D.C., and my uneasiness was surely detected in meetings. I got to know a few legislators I liked, including Senator Fritz Hollings (D-SC), a smart, charming Southern gentleman with hair the color of snow. He enjoyed tennis, and when I told him I had played before, he asked if we could reserve a court.

I stiffened. "I'm sorry, Senator, I've got to get back to Denver."

The truth was the thought of donning tennis whites and making small talk on a country club tennis court terrified me. My spot on the spectrum will not allow me to pretend to be interested in something I'm not, particularly in group settings. It transports me immediately to prep school, with my mother in her soothing voice encouraging me to be social with the kids in class.

Throughout my career, I've had wonderful opportunities to be part of the gang, to join elite social clubs, to leave the meeting with a group of CEOs for dinner, or simply schmooze with politicians in a social environment. I've never done it. I knew I should play the game, but I was unequipped. It's not me.

As I was leaving Senator Hollings's office, he could tell I was troubled by what I saw as the unfairness, but more the inevitability, of the new law.

"John," he said, grinning, "you know, even Thomas Edison had to accept the fact that he was gonna be in a regulated industry." The line drew a smile from both of us.

TCI had come a long way since its earliest days. We had bootstrapped our way out of bankruptcy, grown revenue twenty-four-fold, increased subscribers to 8.5 million from 1.1 million, and given shareholders a 386 percent return for the ten-year period. After more than fifteen years of grinding it out, we had finally built the largest, most efficient cable operator in the country, far bigger than any of us had imagined. Most importantly for me, Bob was pleased.

But as Congress mulled these new bills to regulate the industry, uncertainty hung over all cable stocks. The market for junk bonds had all but washed out, there was a savings and loan crisis in the U.S., and federal regulators began zeroing in on "highly leveraged" transactions, known as HLTs. Lenders pulled back, and with just a trickle of financing available, cable deals slowed to a halt.

TCI was now the biggest cable-TV battleship, and the government was aiming a torpedo at it. We didn't just need more bulkheads, we needed a lifeboat. I believed, and our lawyers agreed, that government regulators might try to force TCI to sell assets or split TCI into two separate businesses: distribution (cable operators) and programming (networks).

And so if cable distribution was going to get regulated, and programming (cable networks) were not, then maybe we should be more into programming, with a vehicle to buy and build more of it. And if the government was thinking of forcing a divestiture of the programming assets . . . why not do it for them?

By 1990, in addition to our cable systems, TCI owned a grab bag of miscellaneous assets that the market really was not valuing properly—mostly noncontrolling programming stakes, including a note from News Corp. for the Family Channel and a stake in Lenfest Communications and other cable-system assets.

It was my own kitchen drawer of nonconsolidated or partially owned equity assets with virtually no debt. I was investing in opportunities, but a big downside was that investors would look at it and say, "What's Malone doing? Why is he putting down money to own 25 percent of this company or that one, with no interest in controlling all of it? Why is he investing in that instead of buying back his own stock?"

And as much as I preached EBITDA and how this was like real estate, investors and analysts were not giving us the kind of valuations I thought TCI deserved. So we were in an earnings-based market that did not fully appreciate our underlying value. And in my efforts at smart capital allocation, I had complicated things a bit by this whole big collection of various cats and dogs we had invested in.

So in 1991, we solved two nagging problems with one solution.

First, we beat the government to the punch. In hopes of preempting further scrutiny, or worse, a move by the DOJ to split up TCI, we carved out more than $600 million worth of assets from TCI—roughly half in cable networks and the other half in cable systems where we owned a minority interest. Looking to get out from under the government's thumb, we called the new company Liberty Media.

I told Bob he should participate because it could be a life raft for TCI. "The whole idea of a life raft is you set it afloat, and at least you're safe if the ship hits an iceberg." Bob would eventually buy into Liberty, but most of his wealth stayed in TCI.

We could not simply spin Liberty off into its own company—it did not meet the spin-off rules at the time, which required majority ownership of the entity for five years. So with the help of a smart accounting advisor, we came up with the idea of a "simultaneous incorporation," in which a newly spun-out entity is legally incorporated at the time it receives the assets and stock of a qualifying business from the parent—and is tax-free under IRS rules.

Liberty Media would hold the stakes in programming networks, including 50 percent of American Movie Classics, 16 percent of the Family Channel, and 30 percent of QVC, and interests in fourteen regional sports networks, as well as fourteen cable systems.

TCI shareholders would get the "right" to buy one Liberty share for every two hundred shares of TCI they owned. And each right allowed an investor the option to swap in sixteen shares of TCI stock for a single share of Liberty Media. Liberty was expected to own 10 percent of TCI's outstanding shares on a fully diluted basis.

Every TCI shareholder was given the opportunity to own shares in the new company as if it were a spin-off, but we had a slightly more complicated way of getting there. The new Liberty was essentially buying these assets from TCI at cost, so there was no gain or loss. And in the end, Liberty was able to create enough juice to pay TCI back.

In the Liberty prospectus, we estimated that, net of debt, the market value of Liberty's assets was $625 million. On 2.1 million shares, that works out to nearly $300 per share. The Liberty Media subsidiary had reported pro forma, nine-month revenue ending September 30, 1990, of $52.4 million.

I was planning to put everything I owned into it. Up until then, I was one of the lower-paid CEOs in the business. I was making $300,000 a year by 1991, and after the conversation I had with Ted about wealth, I thought this lifeboat could also be my ship that comes in . . . one day.

As chairman of the new company, I needed someone fast on their feet as president because I was still running TCI. Peter Barton had proven himself by launching CVN, negotiating with cities over tough franchise renewals, and adding levity in the awkward moments of deal discussions. He was a helluva salesperson, too, but he was terrible with numbers. How he got through Harvard Business School I have no idea.

Nonetheless, I named Peter the CEO of Liberty Media under one condition: Robert "Dob" Bennett would be vice president and principal financial officer, and he would handle all financial details. Dob and Peter are about as different as people can be. Peter had the risk tolerance to think big, then move aggressively on a target acquisition. Dob, who had been director of finance at TCI since 1987 after leaving the Bank of New York, assiduously weighed the probability of success against the downside risks.

But Dob and Peter worked together like they were brothers, occasionally bickering but silently complementing each other's strengths. Sometimes one person can do two jobs. Other times, you need two people to do one.

We tried to explain to investors that the Liberty spin-off would simplify the balance sheet, giving investors more choice on which part of the TCI empire they thought held more promise—pure distribution with TCI or more content with Liberty.

When we put out the prospectus, we were criticized for the complexity, despite exhaustive explanations about our prognosis for the stock.

As Peter later described a meeting with analysts immediately after the release, "We had this [337-page] prospectus that was this thick and so we stood up and we tried in very simple terms to explain Liberty, which was a relatively simple concept. It just didn't write that way once you complied with all the SEC requirements for reporting. We went out of our way, John and I, to say, 'Forget what you read. There's only this many pages that matter.' I think we even said which pages. Read those, the rest of this stuff is not important.

"So I went to the back door and as everybody walked out, all the major analysts, I asked twenty-three of the top analysts, 'Are you participating or not? Are you recommending or not?' Twenty-one said no. I was astounded."

Peter got nervous. I was indifferent to, not disappointed by, the response. I reassured him, saying, "People have to make up their own minds. You can get yourself into trouble convincing people to get into things."

On March 25, 1991, we officially created Liberty Media as a separate company.

Only about a third of the TCI investors swapped their shares for Liberty stock. After my talk with Ted, I bought as much of Liberty Media as I could, swapping in a third of my TCI shares for what amounted to nearly 9 percent of Liberty shares in return. After borrowing $25.6 million to exercise the options I was given, I would come to control 20 percent of Liberty's class B stock, which was allowed ten votes per share. And using rights Bob transferred to me, I would control close to 40 percent of the shareholder votes at Liberty.

Among the few longtime TCI shareholders who bought into the Liberty deal was Gordon Crawford, portfolio manager at the Capital Group; the Naify brothers, who had taken TCI stock for their cable systems; Myles Berkman, an early TCI board member; as well as investors from Oaktree Capital Management.

Investing in networks would turn out to be a smart investment, which the price of all programming stocks reflected, including Liberty. Liberty initially traded at $256 a share and more than tripled to $770 in less than a year of trading. By the summer of 1993, the shares would be worth $3,700 unadjusted for splits. My own investment of $42.1 million, most of it borrowed, grew to more than $600 million in the tax-free stock trade.

Over the next two years, Liberty Media would release more shares to increase liquidity and make it more affordable, splitting Liberty stock 20-for-1, then 4-for-1, and then 2-for-1. Our theory of making money was similar to

Berkshire Hathaway—a portfolio of companies run by a lively mix of driven and dedicated entrepreneurs.

All cable networks were benefitting from the dual revenue stream of advertising and cable-carriage fees. Dual revenue strength and pricing power associated with branding meant that quality networks could pay for better content and draw more viewers. Programmers began staking claims in adjacent categories. E.W. Scripps would launch HGTV and, later, the Food Network and DIY Network. Discovery would include in its family Animal Planet, Discovery Science, Travel Channel, and Discovery International.

For me the creation of Liberty was capital allocation, but more simply, creative problem-solving. Sometimes a complex problem deserves a complex answer. In many ways, Liberty represented a clean canvas to draw on and freedom from regulators poring over TCI. Liberty would become a vehicle to build personal wealth and the progenitor of everything we run today.

With none of the history or the drag of groupthink, decisions at Liberty were streamlined, without the typical friction, often just a quick phone call between a few people—typically Peter, Dob, and me.

Most of the boats I have owned over the years—*Liberty*, *Ragtime*, *Leslie Ann*, and others—passed for a traveling boardroom of sorts. Peter, Paul Gould, Gordon Crawford, Gerry Lenfest, or some different cadre of investors would set sail on a long trip, from the Bahamas up to Maine, or back down to Florida. You get to know people pretty well on a long boat ride. There was freedom to explore new ideas about the future of programming, potential combinations, or threats on the horizon.

Although more than once I was awakened from a perfectly sound shipboard sleep by the shenanigans of Peter Barton and an occasional willing accomplice. Once on a long trip to Maine from Florida, aboard the *Leslie Ann*, a fifty-nine-foot Hinckley Sou'wester, Peter gave an Academy Award–worthy performance swearing he saw a sea monster in the distance. As I squinted into the distance, he and Paul started giggling as I realized I'd been pranked.

Funny/not funny.

After sputtering in 1991, a bill came surging through the Senate like a freight train to restore rate regulations on cable operators in 1992, and by the fall, many in Congress, some looking for an easy issue in the elections, jumped to support the Cable Consumer Protection and Competition Act of 1992. The bill required the FCC to establish "reasonable" costs for basic service through rate cuts, with the proposed legislation predicted to result in $3 billion in savings to customers.

In September 1992, both houses of Congress voted for the bill. President George Bush, predicting that a new law would not lower rates, promptly vetoed it, but like a zombie from a Hollywood film, the bill would not die. Congress overrode President Bush's veto—the first such occurrence in his presidency.

We felt the effects of the new law fast. The new rate restrictions would crimp the industry's cash flow and send stocks tumbling initially. The first day the new law took effect, TCI shares dropped almost 10 percent in value, to the $20 range, and other cable stocks fell along with us.

The FCC was assigned by Congress the untenable task of creating a framework for cities to regulate eleven thousand cable systems, based on complicated mathematical formulas for new rates. Cable operators were forced to freeze rates, and in the spring of 1993, when more rules were released, we were forced by the FCC to roll back rates for "basic cable" by 10 percent.

The 521-page Report and Order explaining the rules was "longer than the Old Testament and more confusing than the tax code," said Steve Effros, who led a trade group of small and mid-sized cable operators called the Cable Telecommunications Association.

A year later, under pressure from Congress, the FCC called for another rate rollback—this time an additional 7 percent, for a total of 17 percent in rollbacks. Ouch.

Commodities that are measurable, like water and electricity, are much easier to regulate than entertainment TV networks, and the FCC struggled to apply complex mathematical algorithms to simulate basic cable prices where cable operators faced competitors such as satellite-TV services. In response, some cable operators reacted by simply offering another nonregulated "expanded" tier of service, which was more popular, leading to rate *increases* in some areas.

Did the 1992 Cable Act lower rates? Yes, most consumers found some relief—but not to the extent and scope that Congress had wanted.

The cable-TV industry suffered lasting effects, though, with a section of the law called retransmission consent, which allowed broadcasters to choose if they would prefer to be carried for nothing, called "must carry," or negotiate a rate for "retransmission consent." If these payments were not allowed, broadcasters argued, it would "threaten the future of free, over-the-air television broadcasting."

The intent was to preserve local broadcasters and codify their rights when they negotiated the terms of cable carriage—not to serve as a subsidy for major networks. Cable operators were already paying a copyright fee, but big broadcast networks took advantage of the law and used it like a cudgel against cable operators.

Instead of taking cash, initially some broadcast networks offered their own cable networks for cable operators to carry instead, resulting in America's Talking (now MSNBC), FX (Fox), and ESPN2 (ABC). But by the mid 2000s, broadcast stations began to demand cash carriage fees from cable/satellite "pay-TV" operators, and by law these costs could not be passed to customers.

Today, retransmission consent has turned into exactly what it was not intended to be: a subsidy for the national broadcast networks and their affiliated cable channels rather than a source of support for local broadcasting. Retransmission consent fees from cable, direct broadcast satellite, and telco video operators surged from $1 billion in 2010 to $10 billion in 2018, and now hover at $16 billion annually, reflecting broadcasters' reliance on the fees to buttress stations' ad revenue.

In a perverse distortion, though, the big broadcast networks now demand "reverse compensation" from their local affiliates—stations they do not own—completely flipping the arrangement that existed in 1992.

And if cable operators dare refuse a big increase, the broadcasters threaten to legally withhold their signal even today, leaving viewers in a "blackout." These retransmission consent disputes reflect how the law has become obsolete. In 2010, broadcast stations forced eight blackouts because of retransmission consent disputes; in 2023 there were 253. It made little sense to me: Broadcasters, which are granted a license by the government, are withholding the same signal to be retransmitted to more people.

This wasn't the last of the government's intrusion into the industry—a new national law would be passed only four years later.

With the 1992 Cable Act ankling the industry, and phone and satellite competitors on the horizon, the cable industry was beginning to look like a leaky boat headed for rough seas. The cable-TV industry's Western Show was scheduled for December 1992, and at TCI we were working on a new development at CableLabs (the industry research consortium) compressing digital signals.

I wanted to do three things at the Western Show. I wanted to let Washington regulators who were tweaking new rate rules know that we were building an Information Superhighway. I also wanted to divert investors' attention away from the nightmare of the new regulations. And I wanted to lift the morale of the industry by showing that our platform was far superior to the much larger phone companies.

At the Western Show, where tens of thousands of the cable industry faithful gathered annually in Anaheim, California, TCI called a press conference. I took the small stage off the main conference floor to share some surprising findings from our labs. Engineers at CableLabs had figured out a way to squeeze ten channels into the space typically required for one, or "digital compression." So on an average TCI cable system with fifty channels, viewers could theoretically expect some five hundred channels with the new technology: more movies on demand, interactive shopping, news and sports channels, and online communications. TCI had signed a letter of intent to buy up to a million digital set-top terminals from GI and AT&T, with delivery to the first customers in July 1994.

"This is just the beginning," I told reporters. "This first round of products is the first of an evolution. We want to deliver a broad range of services adapted to the individual needs of the consumer." Technology would save cable as it had done so many times before. I had wanted to raise the curtain only a little. The next morning, the news made the front page of nearly every American newspaper. "Need more TV? TCI may offer 500 channels," read *The Wall Street Journal*. *The New York Times* trumpeted it on the front page: "A Cable Vision (Or Nightmare): 500 Channels." Even in the doldrums of reregulation, cable stocks, including TCI, took off.

Somehow, I had just pulled a rabbit out of a hat.

CHAPTER 11

COMPRESSION OBSESSION

Though "500 channels!" appeared to be a sudden "Eureka!" moment, this breakthrough was, in fact, the outcome of an unlikely sequence of events and people that had played out over several previous years.

This included a TV-set war with Japan, an act of Congress to let rival cable operators cooperate on tech innovation, a trip to Tokyo, a World War II hero, as well as a group of engineers with ever-present pocket protectors, who would summon astonishing new capabilities from the same old cable wire.

Our ability to compress digital signals to get to five hundred channels grew directly out of the feverish race to deliver the first commercial high-definition TV signal—and avoid losing out to Japan, yet again. That old saying comes to mind: necessity is the mother of invention.

Before HDTV—or what most people now simply call TV—the best picture was an analog color TV set with roughly a quarter of the resolution (produced by dots or pixels of light on the screen) most people see today. By the late 1980s, creating the first commercially viable high-definition TV system had become a point of national pride for Japan.

With brands like Sony, Toshiba, and Hitachi, Japan had long reigned as the global leader in electronics of every kind, especially TVs. Japanese broadcaster NHK introduced the first analog high-definition TV sets in the 1980s with its MUSE system, which displayed pictures that were double the standard resolution.

If Japan persuaded the rest of the world to adopt its high-definition standards, NHK—and Japanese electronic companies—stood to reap the lion's share of sales and royalties for decades, leaving U.S. makers with scraps. And in June 1989, before the U.S. and Europe, NHK began transmitting the world's first commercial daily HDTV programming to viewers. "Television was initiated by the United States," NHK chairman Keiji Shima said before flipping the switch. "But Hi-Vision [HDTV] will be led by Japan."

Early reviewers were impressed with the eye-catching clarity of the NHK system, which could display tiny dew drops on the petals of a flower. But the NHK scheme relied on souping up existing technology, and this was a key drawback.

Meanwhile, the American effort to build a high-definition TV set was led by competing teams using *digital* technology, which was largely untested commercially. Those competing companies, including AT&T, General Instrument, Philips, Sarnoff Corp, Thomson SA, and Zenith, would ultimately join forces in a group called the Grand Alliance. Leading the charge at GI was a brilliant engineer from Korea named Woo Paik, who with his team developed the DigiCipher HDTV system in 1990, considered to be the first working encrypted, all-digital HDTV system.

Digital technology, rather than analog, would be far superior in terms of requiring less storage, producing less noise than a real analog signal, and improving distribution capabilities. And making the jump to digital transmission was how the U.S. would miraculously leapfrog over Japan to create the standard for HDTV.

Many industry players, including me, lobbied the FCC and Congress to convince them of this superior digital HDTV standard. TCI's John Sie wrote an influential white paper for the FCC explaining that an analog standard was more expensive and would be obsolete—just as a digital solution was on our doorstep. His thesis would set off several lightbulbs for me as I read it over later: digital was simply more efficient, adaptable, and resilient.

I was genuinely concerned we would be handcuffed with an inferior, outdated analog standard. In the end, the U.S. HDTV standard won out based on its exceptional transmission capability, and over time, it would gain global recognition as the superior standard. It was a landmark decision by the FCC, and it makes me proud that the heart of the digital HDTV standard used today is the result of Yankee ingenuity.

This turn to digital would end up unleashing billions of dollars in new capital spending, subscription revenue, and stock market value. This wellspring began even before the mainstream arrival of HDTV sets themselves.

Only later did I realize the odd truth of this: The race was to produce a prettier picture, sharper in resolution, and able to show lifelike images. But in reaching for this goal, my industry ended up producing something of far greater value: the capability to deliver hundreds of extra channels of programming, new on-demand shows, internet access, and even phone calls to U.S. homes. Right away.

Using digital technology, engineers could convert the continuous waves of video, audio, or data signals into strings of ones and zeroes, which could be compressed, transmitted, modulated, decoded, and stored for later retrieval. It also solved an urgent problem for TCI and the cable-TV industry: the ablity to offer the public dozens of new channels and movies on demand, increase revenue, and get us out of the hole the government had dug with the 1992 Cable Act.

For me, the moment onstage in Anaheim announcing five hundred channels was the direct result of asking a simple question: Why can't we do this right now? In the U.S., if digital compression was proven for HDTV, why couldn't this same technology be applied to existing analog cable systems to expand channel capacity ASAP?

I had been pressing like hell for a real shift in the business, trying to drive solutions that would favor us as an industry, and digital compression of TV signals—a by-product of HDTV research—clearly was one of them. I knew it worked. I could sit down with a piece of paper and analyze the bit rates, and I knew it was feasible.

An important preliminary step in this effort came in 1984, when as a way of encouraging innovation Congress passed a law permitting rival firms to collaborate on research and development efforts without risk of antitrust violations. Up until then, strict antitrust rules had forbidden businesses in the same industry to meet to discuss anything.

The timing of the new law was ideal for the cable industry, which was particularly fragmented, with hundreds of systems served by different hardware providers and equipment brands. We lacked a broad set of industry standards.

And operating on an industrial scale was the only way we could create something truly valuable. Vendors often sold different hardware components that were incompatible with one another. This hampered purchasing of advanced electronics for big companies with cable systems using different brands and models in various states of repair.

The 1984 act allowed us to converge on protocols and standard designs. It also cleared the way for the creation in 1988 of CableLabs, the industry research consortium whose engineers would give us five hundred channels and architect the industry's future.

On the cable side, the effort to form a new industry laboratory started as many of my projects always have begun: with a phone call from an old friend.

His name was Richard Sully Leghorn, and I knew him from the board of the National Cable Television Association. He had been an early proponent of the 1984 law and now he wanted to make use of it. Leghorn was a genuine World War II hero who owned cable systems in five states, including some systems up in Cape Cod that we later bought from him.

He had been talking with the association president, Jim Mooney, about starting an industry research group that could help develop new technologies, a concept backed by a RAND Corporation project he personally funded outlining the merits.

A big man with a head of thick gray hair, Richard still resembled the handsome pilot he was back in World War II, when he played a crucial role in one of the most significant battles in Europe. After graduating with a physics degree from the Massachusetts Institute of Technology, he worked in photographic research at Eastman Kodak and learned to fly. After joining the air force, he eventually led low-flying missions with the 30th Photographic Reconnaissance Squadron to help plan the D-Day invasion of Normandy, earning a Silver Star.

After the war, he pushed public policy issues such as national security and advocated for the "Open Skies" doctrine, pressing to open satellite communications for television and other commercial services, then joined the industry he had helped to enable.

Richard called me one day in 1988 to discuss the new industry consortium, and days later he was in my office in Denver, making me an offer I shouldn't refuse: given my tech background and TCI's number one pole position in cable, I should head this new industry effort to establish a standard design and protocol all of us could adopt and follow.

I accepted his overture without hesitation. Now that TCI had grown into the largest cable operator in the U.S., I had an obligation to the industry I had helped build. Even though the new job description sounded like dance choreographer for a chorus line of elephants.

Richard Leghorn made several trips to Denver, and we quickly started sketching a structure for something we called CableLabs, a research and development consortium that would create specifications (flexible technical guidelines), rather than formal, accredited standards, for the products the cable operators were looking to buy at scale. I shook hands with Richard and became the founding chairman, a position I would hold for ten years.

In May 1988, I wrote a letter to the largest cable operators, inviting them to join Cable Television Laboratories, Inc. Consumer demand was expanding for our product, I said, and technology could unlock the value.

For a CEO, we recruited Richard "Dick" Green, who had run broadcast engineering at PBS, a consortium of public stations, as well as the CBS Laboratories, helping broadcasters develop digital TV standards. Experienced and confident in his science, Dick also had a hair trigger for genuine belly laughs. He was calm, curious, and creative, and he loved math—my kinda guy. Dick had experimented with all sorts of transmission methods, using lasers, fiber, and digital compression; he also wrote musical scores for movies in his spare time. He was fabulous at keeping everybody in the tent, and he was keenly aware of our intention to drive technology at scale.

CableLabs evolved into a place where the leading engineers in- and outside the cable industry could solve challenges, innovate our platform, and, most of all, ensure interoperability, which would have a transformational impact on the television industry in the U.S.

So now, instead of vendors coming to operators with proprietary designs, CableLabs could go to *them* with the specs and ask, "Would you like to build this for us?" Dick Green set up headquarters in Boulder, Colorado, where hundreds of companies could test their equipment on a model cable system in a lab and have it analyzed for efficiency.

I wanted the CEOs of the largest cable-TV operators to commit personally, and Dick, with his genuinely humble demeanor, made this easier by sowing trust among their CTOs and engineers. In its high-tech workshop, CableLabs was driving collaboration while at the same time ensuring standards; it was a place where engineers could crowdsource a nitty-gritty software bug or hardware issue. The resulting cooperation led to many other beneficial relationships—deals, trades, and joint ventures that brought colleagues in the industry even closer together. We were now driving solutions with the collective brainpower of the industry and the firepower of scale economics.

This new, legally authorized level of camaraderie was on display in 1991 when the executive committee of CableLabs took a trip to Tokyo to check out NHK's much-hailed analog format for HDTV while attending the largest annual IT and consumer electronics trade show in Japan, held every fall in Tokyo.

This was our chance to get a close-up view of the most advanced TV technology in the world, and our entourage included CEOs and tech chiefs from the top companies: Jim Chiddix and Joe Collins from Time Warner; Brian Roberts and Mark Coblitz from Comcast; Bill Schleyer from Continental Cablevision; and Larry Romrell and me from TCI. We all took the same plane—I briefly shuddered at the prospect that a crash would set the industry back ten years.

A few hours after lifting off from JFK in New York, as restless executives wandered the cabin, Comcast president Brian Roberts, the ambitious son of founder Ralph Roberts, took the seat next to mine. He was a bespectacled thirty-one-year-old who had sold cable TV door-to-door in his hometown of Philadelphia during boyhood summers before graduating from Wharton. Brian had jumped at my invitation to be vice chairman of CableLabs. He had been named president of Comcast a year earlier (in 1990) when Comcast's annual revenue was $657 million. Flash-forward to today, and Brian has done one hell of a job: Comcast has 182,000 employees worldwide and more than $122 billion in annual revenue.

In the quiet of the cabin, while the rest of the entourage slept, we talked pretty much for the next dozen hours or so, without taking a nap or watching a movie, and stopping only to eat. Brian and I discussed the architecture of the industry and what was possible in the next ten years, from HDTV and cable modems, to Wi-Fi and outflanking the telephone companies, to the tax logic of Liberty.

We probably should have slept since we had big meetings in the coming days with Sony, Toshiba, and other electronics firms to analyze their latest product offerings in digital.

After dinner one night, CableLabs CEO Dick Green suggested we stroll through an area in downtown Tokyo known as Akihabara Electric Town, a bustling, neon-lit district of electronics retailers, filled with storefronts and stalls selling TVs, camcorders, VCRs, electronic gadgets, and hardware of every kind.

We spotted a high-definition television set sitting out on a table on the sidewalk. Up until that point, I had been underwhelmed with the smaller high-definition pictures I had seen in the lab, unable to easily discern notable differences in the clarity. This TV set was different. It was bigger than most screens I had seen, around forty inches, and it was receiving a high-definition signal directly from the NHK satellite above our heads. And on the screen was a news anchor so three-dimensional, so *real*, I felt like I could reach through the screen and touch the anchor's desk.

Well, I said to myself, finally convinced, *it* is *a better picture.*

The very next day, we were scheduled to meet with the founder and chairman of Sony, Akio Morita, along with his team at the Sony building in Tokyo. Before we arrived, Dick Green had carefully briefed us on protocol for how to greet our hosts. I was in the middle, flanked by Richard and the other executives.

When the Japanese executives walked into the room, they were all wearing lab coats, and the man in the middle was Mr. Morita. Richard Green and I opened with some flowery comments, and introductions were made.

I was aware that Sony was struggling with a programming investment. So I asked a pointed question: "How do you like your Columbia investment these days?"

Less than two years earlier, in 1989, Sony Corp. had plunked down $3.4 billion to buy Columbia Pictures Entertainment, and the studio had subsequently spent billions to bring on new leadership and settle lawsuits, then taken painful write-downs on big box office flops.

Dick gasped at the question, unaware of my intent. Morita, a World War II vet from the Japanese Navy, was very western, but he had the calm reserve of the East, and he smiled a confident smile. Sony had weathered many storms, and it had learned lessons the hard way: Sony had led the world with the superior Betamax standard, only to lose the videocassette war to the VHS format, which was cheaper and ran longer and won wider distribution with Hollywood studios. In admirably polite style, Morita explained the strategy behind the Columbia investment. Sony wanted to supply content, particularly movies, to its hardware customers, and though Columbia faced some headwinds, patient management there would see increasing returns. Thirty years later, Columbia Pictures remains part of Sony's entertainment group, one of the Big Five in Hollywood.

I liked him instantly. My comment, while brusque, got us past the small talk and endless formalities. Within minutes we were deep in conversation about market demand, productivity, and production of HDTV sets and digital video recorders.

"You've built an impressive HDTV set," I said to Morita. "What if we were to buy ten thousand of 'em? What would it cost us?"

Morita talked to his deputies and they retreated to a corner for a moment.

When we reconnected minutes later, Morita smiled politely and said, "We can build them for seven thousand U.S. dollars apiece." Which was a great price at the time, because in Japan they were not yet the commodity that they are now. We had seen ads for HDTV sets for $30,000.

Then the visiting cable team was off by themselves, too. "Hey, John, we didn't bring our checkbook, and I'm not authorized to spend anything!" said one CTO, concerned we were in the middle of a purchase order.

The intention wasn't to buy HDTV sets, I explained. A simple question like that will get you answers from Sony about how they're thinking about high-volume production. What are they pricing sets at, how many can they make, and how quickly can they penetrate the market? All these things, just by asking a question.

In the end, there were too many unknowns, and we couldn't get consensus on such a large investment on such short notice, but the visit had convinced all of us of one sure thing: the migration to high-definition television was inevitable.

To me the real trick in the invention of HDTV wasn't the TV set itself, but how the picture was sent to it. The practical problem of transmitting in high definition was that it was a bandwidth hog, requiring somewhere around six times as much bandwidth as a normal standard-definition signal requires.

Cable engineers were already scrambling to squeeze more channel capacity into their old analog systems because that meant more networks, which meant more subscribers, which meant more revenue.

In the early 1990s, most cable operators increased channel capacity by upgrading with fiber for a hybrid, fiber-optic/coaxial cable (HFC) network, and building channel capacity incrementally, with most big analog systems up to fifty channels.

Cable engineers knew that adding fiber to coaxial lines cut noise and reduced the need for costly amplifiers. Though expensive upfront, replacing main trunks with fiber saved money long-term with better signal quality, fewer outages, and less equipment.

Fiber increased reliability and, happily, channel capacity. And it was fast becoming the backbone of the architecture of the cable-TV industry. In 1992, Jim Chiddix, the gifted SVP of engineering and technology at (Time Warner's) ATC, the second-largest cable operator, built a fiber-rich system in Queens delivering 150 channels for $23.95 a month called Quantum. Customers loved it—and so did the press.

But fiber alone would not allow enough bandwidth for HDTV. Compressing the signal was the only way it could happen, and for years it was a theoretical process that engineers were trying to perfect in the laboratory.

The most efficient way of doing that was by sending only the pixels that changed from frame to frame in the scene. For every frame in a video of, say, a sun setting over a mountain, only small amounts of data need be transmitted, because there's very little change in the picture from frame to frame. If a plane flies through the scene, only those bits are sent.

In simple terms, it is a way of picking out what is important from frame to frame, storing the memory of the image, and sending only the pixels that change. And it turns out that in most pictures (except for sports), you can eliminate 90 percent of the pixels by sending only those components that undergo change.

It is quite a technical feat if you stop to think about it. In a digital format, these pictures and sounds were packed so that ten channels could glide on the bandwidth of one analog 6 Mhz channel, then be beamed up to a satellite transponder and down to a cable-system headend. From there, these digital "packets" traveled through a hybrid fiber-coax cable to the customer's home. In the home, our new set-tops decompressed the digital channel, unpacked all those digital packets, and converted them into ten analog channels that could be viewed in real time on a normal television set. Abracadabra.

Digital compression has many parents, and like most big technology advances, it required the combined efforts of scientists, engineers, and government to become a commercial standard.

Expanding channel capacity with compression was just the first thing CableLabs focused on; since then virtually every major technological advance in the industry has come from this amazing consortium, which later nurtured and advanced solutions to standards for new services such as high-speed cable modems (data), internet telephony (voice), cable Wi-Fi (wireless), and even more sophisticated cable-TV set-top boxes (video). This would lead to huge capital deployment to build and install the new capabilities, ultimately creating what is the backbone of the internet today.

In the short term, this breakthrough could change everything, particularly Wall Street's view of the cable-TV industry as a regulated monopoly with limited growth prospects and too many new competitors. And if we could clear the overhang of the 1992 Cable Act rate regulations, we could solve our capital dilemma and fund the rebuild of our wired networks.

This was especially important for TCI, which was starved for cash at the time and was trailing our rivals in upgrading systems for fiber optics and two-way switching gear. TCI was planning to spend $2 billion to upgrade its cable systems with seven thousand miles of fiber-optic lines. This made it all the more important that we deploy digital sooner rather than later, to unlock more channels and rake in more subscription revenue to help pay the bills. TCI committed another $100 million to build the National Digital Television Center in Littleton, Colorado, with massive satellite dishes capable of receiving and sending compressed digital signals to TCI and other cable operators.

What I believed strongly, and I said so at the time, was that the steps we had taken to ramp up digital compression clearly established the cable industry's technology as the preferred infrastructure for delivering video, voice, and data in the U.S.

The market was warming to a new metaphor that many in the industry and politics were using to describe the new platform cable companies were building: the Information Superhighway. The term, often conjured by Senator Al Gore, whose father, Senator Al Gore Sr., had been a strong advocate of the U.S. interstate highway system, underscored the idea that this broad, interconnected, open network would be accessible to the masses, similar to how highways connected the nation.

In 1993 cable operators began launching tests, small and large, separately and in joint ventures, offering movies on demand, video games, interactive shopping, targeted advertising, and online service. Sumner Redstone's Viacom Inc. launched an interactive TV system in Castro Valley, California. Time Warner, the second-largest U.S. cable operator after TCI, announced the Full Service Network (FSN) in Orlando, Florida, the first to "integrate emerging cable, computer, and telephone technologies over a fiber-optic and coaxial cable network"—and expensive new set-top boxes.

The FSN, which offered shopping, games, and movies on demand, was reminiscent of QUBE, the interactive project launched nearly two decades earlier, and famously allowed a consumer to order a pizza via remote control with partner Pizza Hut. The test drew global attention, and Gerald Levin, the former HBO chief who had ascended to CEO of Time Warner, led the charge, vowing it was the "keystone of Time Warner's vision and strategy."

The gargantuan task of building even a small network of interactive services from scratch required the help of other tech behemoths, including Silicon Graphics (servers and operating system), Toshiba (electronics in headend), AT&T (switches), and Scientific-Atlanta (cable set-top box). These were early days, with servers the size of refrigerators and souped-up set-top boxes that cost an estimated $7,000 each.

Wall Street and consumers were transfixed by the promise of an interactive future with videos on demand, electronic banking, home shopping, instant-response advertising, and making phone calls with the click of a button. Business plans would be scrapped and recalculated, and the largest companies in communications began to position themselves to stake claims on the most valuable pieces in this new ecosystem. The race was drawing in cable operators, computer companies, telephone giants, movie studios, TV networks, and others, all converging to create something consumers had never experienced before when they turned on the TV.

I had the creeping awareness that maybe TCI one day would need the financial heft of a Baby Bell or some other mass-scale giant if we were to build out our biggest dreams. Maybe.

CHAPTER 12

TELEPHONE TAG

If business is war, and it certainly feels like it sometimes, I was thrilled we had a new weapon in digital compression, but it was not ours alone. Soon others would exploit its power, too. And as I looked at the broader North American battle map, our flank was exposed.

The most immediate threat was the satellite companies—not the makers of the big ten-foot C-band dishes, but a new generation of smaller dishes and powerful satellites that could leverage digital compression from space—without the need for wires.

One early gambit, called Sky Cable, promised 108 channels, twice as many channels as most cable systems back then, to a dish a mere eighteen inches in diameter—about the size of a pizza pan. The venture drew deep-pocketed backers, including General Motors' Hughes Communications; General Electric's NBC; News Corp., owner of 20th Century Fox Studios; and Cablevision Systems Corporation. Lucky for us, just a year later, the high-cost Sky Cable partnership imploded.

Hughes Communications, which GM had bought from the billionaire Howard Hughes in 1985, would stay in the game and partner with Hubbard Broadcasting on a small dish service called DirecTV, which was offering two-hundred-plus channels—more than enough to steal the cable-TV industry's digital thunder.

A year after I gave the speech on five hundred channels, a rocket carrying the DirecTV satellite launched on December 17, 1993. The service would become so popular it would draw a million customers within two years, stealing most of those subscribers from cable-TV operators.

Right on the heels of DirecTV came Dish satellite TV service, the brain-child of a Tennessee-born card-counting gambler turned telecom maverick named Charlie Ergen. In 1992, Ergen secured a set of coveted orbital slots from the FCC, fueled by $335 million he'd scraped together through high-risk junk bonds. He launched the company under the name EchoStar, a bold satellite TV venture that would later be known simply as Dish.

Ergen had made a name selling C-band big satellite-television dishes in rural Colorado from the back of his truck with his wife Candy, and he, too, planned to launch a new service with smaller dishes. I liked his grit—he had built EchoStar with practically nothing, bet big on himself, and jumped into the high-stakes worlds of satellites and television, both of which had frequent blowups on the launchpad.

While the short-term threat was from satellite companies, the more dangerous menace was the telephone companies. As far as bandwidth goes, their twisted pair of copper lines was a drinking straw compared to the firehose of hybrid fiber-coax. But they were putting more fiber into their networks, overlaying their thin twisted copper. And they could do it easily, with plenty of capital and deep experience in switched, two-way communications.

Ever since the breakup of the old AT&T phone monopoly by a federal judge, the regional Bell operating companies had been itching to break into new businesses—long distance, wireless phones, and TV services. Despite the fact that telephone companies were barred from offering video in their own territories, politicians and regulators were warming to the idea.

All seven original regional Bell operating companies had applied to the FCC for technical trials to offer TV service outside their territories, and they began announcing plans for a "full fiber" network to homes—a direct challenge to TCI and other cable companies.

Three of the regional Bell telephone companies—Bell Atlantic, NYNEX, and Pacific Bell—agreed to spend up to $100 million apiece in a new service called Tele-TV, with shows, movies on demand, shopping, and other services. Hollywood talent superagent Michael Ovitz, head of CAA, had signed on, and the venture later hired former CBS Broadcasting CEO and former Sony president Howard Stringer to run it.

The Baby Bells would focus more on competing in the long-distance wars and wireless over the years, but they kept their hand in TV services, which made them dangerous as competitors, especially in the eyes of Wall Street.

In my mind, it would be far easier for cable operators, with a much bigger pipe, to offer telephone service than it would be for the phone companies, with their skinny twisted pair, to offer the bandwidth hog of video.

Still, they were increasingly aggressive in winning new business. By the end of 1993, three big phone company deals would get Wall Street to start doubting the future we had so carefully laid out. In February 1993, Southwestern Bell, a Baby Bell, made history by becoming the first telephone company to buy a cable company in the United States—$650 million for the cable systems owned by Hauser Communications. This was rather poignant: Gus Hauser was the former Warner Communications CEO under Steve Ross who had managed the first tests of two-way interactive TV with the QUBE system back in the late 1970s. Because the Hauser systems were located outside the service region of Southwestern Bell, they were therefore legal under cross-ownership laws.

In May of the same year, US West, another regional Baby Bell, caught the cable-TV bug and shelled out $2.5 billion to pay for a 25 percent stake in Time Warner's cable systems, the Warner Bros. movie studio, the HBO cable channel—and the nationwide rollout of Time Warner's Full Service Network. US West agreed to buy an Atlanta cable system serving 446,000 for $1.2 billion after that.

Later the same year, Southwestern Bell struck again, with a $4.9 billion deal to merge with Cox Communications (although that deal fell apart a year later). And Bell Telephone of Canada (now known as BCE), a telecommunications powerhouse and the largest publicly held company in Canada, agreed to pay $400 million for a 30 percent stake in cable pioneer Glenn Jones's Jones Intercable.

Keep your friends close and your enemies closer. For me it wasn't just a cliché. It was a very real way to learn how to deal with the phone company threat. And with the knowledge that TCI and other cable operators could offer telephone service, we began looking at ways we could learn about and invest more in the business. For TCI to get into the phone business, we needed to upgrade our network with two-way switching to carry phone calls to and from customers.

I made sure TCI's tentacles were touching several businesses related to telephony. In 1992, TCI had joined forces with US West in the United Kingdom, in a venture called TeleWest International, which combined our cable TV and their phone service for nearly 2 million subscribers.

That same year TCI paid $85 million for a 50 percent stake in Teleport, which provided long-distance service to businesses in large U.S. cities, bypassing incumbent local phone companies with its own fiber-optic cable and satellite network. Teleport also included Cox and Comcast, both family-run companies and longtime TCI partners in several ventures and acquisitions.

TCI and McCaw Cellular tested a service where local wireless calls were picked up by cellular base stations, routed through TCI's coaxial cable network, bypassing the phone company and connecting directly to McCaw's broader cellular system. As I was sitting on the board of Cellular One with my friend Craig McCaw, watching the dynamics of the business, I scratched my head, wondering: *How come TCI has no play in cellular?*

So when the FCC made bandwidth available for new wireless personal communication services, or PCS, we formed a consortium in 1994 with Sprint—along with Cox and Comcast—to build a nationwide network and bid on wireless spectrum, the government-licensed radio frequencies needed to transmit cellular signals. The goal: an integrated package of wireless, local telephone, long-distance service, and cable TV that would be unmatched by rivals.

As I told an industry conference around that time: "Clearly in telephony, the focus is going to be a full-service offering. It's going to be wired and wireless. It's going to be long distance and local. It's going to be narrowband and broadband all neatly packaged and customized for the customer's need, and that seems to be a concept which is gaining a worldwide acceptance."

These new technologies were causing disruption in business in other countries, including in Japan, where firms were testing PCS services and competing with the NTT (Nippon Telegraph and Telephone Corporation) monopoly there.

Thankfully, CableLabs was pushing the cable telephony agenda aggressively in the direction of achieving scale. On the morning of August 9, 1994, I was standing in the Terrace Room of the Plaza Hotel in New York City, onstage with CableLabs CEO Dick Green, Comcast CEO Brian Roberts, and representatives from Time Warner, Comcast, Cox, and Continental Cablevision. We committed $2 billion to buy telephone equipment through a CableLabs proposal, aiming to deliver phone service over coaxial cable for homes and businesses.

We were also involved with the earliest versions of Voice over Internet Protocol (VoIP), the technology that lets you make phone calls over the internet instead of traditional phone lines, in 1992. An Orthodox Jewish businessman named Howard Jonas, who worked with a talented team of Israeli engineers, was working on software to make telephone calls over the internet by embedding audio signals in IP "packets" of data.

Jonas had launched a scrappy long-distance service called Net2Phone out of a former funeral parlor in the Bronx. He wasn't really looking for money from TCI—he wanted proof his idea could work at scale. So he asked if we would test it on one of our cable systems.

We helped him try routing phone calls over a two-way data spectrum— a version of what would become VoIP. His company, IDT, eventually drew major investors, including a $1.4 billion stake from AT&T. The stock soared, Howard made a fortune, and TCI earned a solid return on our 17 percent share.

By the late '90s, VoIP was catching on, and Howard had been one of the first to see where it was going.

As CableLabs worked out standards, soon cable operators would be able to offer phone calls, too, in addition to TV and internet, something never before possible in the history of the industry.

CHAPTER 13

FAILURE TO LAUNCH

S ometimes your most carefully laid plans lead you down a dead-end road, and the prize you thought would be waiting at the end turns out to have been a mirage. This happened to me three times in one year, involving three would-be multibillion-dollar mergers that would have reshaped the television industry but for the intervention of Uncle Sam, a former drive-in theater chain owner, and a loss of nerve by the buyer.

During the entire year of 1993, I was beginning to understand the lyrics to the old Rolling Stones tune "You Can't Always Get What You Want." Even when you try, sometimes you *don't* get what you need.

That summer, at fifty-two years old, I felt the yoke of leadership bearing down on me more than ever before. On July 8, I flew from Maine to Lenox, Massachusetts, to attend a board meeting of the National Cable Television Association. From there I flew to Sun Valley, Idaho, for Allen & Company's annual media conference, where I hoped to gather intel and see some old friends. High above the clouds and headed west, I felt the same old demons preying on the quiet time in my head. I was leaving one city to go to another—and neither one was home. I would eventually return from trips like these exhausted, lost in winding tunnels of thought and, more often than not, reacting to every decision in business from a place of fear instead of fun.

Leslie and I were seeing less of each other, which meant we did not have time to discuss the everyday issues of a household, much less tell one another how much we loved each other, which is sometimes all you really need to hear. She had become the de facto CEO of our home, hardly complaining and always working to see our son and daughter were fed, picked up from practice, and tucked in every night feeling safe. She listened and bore witness to all the indignities I relayed to her of a normal day trying to make a living. I wish I had listened more.

When she wasn't so sweet, she could get a little tart, saying more than once: "I should have married a plumber. At least he would be home more."

And my daughter and son didn't get any better from me. The moments I missed when they were younger hurt twice as much because they were both now in their twenties, coming into their own, and I could feel the chasm widening. You can't make up the time playing tee-ball or with tea sets later—the moment is gone.

They are both such hardworking, good-hearted kids, and I love them deeply, and it was bittersweet to watch them grow up in the real world and eventually leave home. There is no "pause" button in life, only "play." And sometimes that feels like "fast-forward."

To help relieve some of that stress, I had been on the prowl for a partner for TCI or even a full-on buyer. The 1992 Cable Act had already constricted our rates, and this had battered the stock. And to me, running a rate-regulated monopoly as we tried to build the Information Superhighway was like driving a sports car with the emergency brake on.

I was on the hook for public promises I'd made. I had already put a ceremonial shovel into the ground for the building of the Information Superhighway with a big set-top box order, committing TCI and the industry to a five-hundred-channel digital future I knew was coming—but just not sure when precisely.

Meanwhile, the FCC was in the process of allowing the seven regional Baby Bells, AT&T, and other telcos to offer video service over their telephone wires. Cable operators could offer digital phone service, but the rollout would take years.

In order to fulfill the promises I had made, TCI would have to recast and rebuild its aging cable systems to compete against much richer competitors. I was unsure I could pull it off.

For the first time, I reached the point I suppose every person does in business: I wondered if it was all too much. So, on the plane ride to the

Allen conference, with all these issues swirling in my head, I leaned back in my chair, looked out the window, and pulled out a yellow legal pad.

I started writing out a list, "John and Leslie's goals":

- To reduce stress.
- To have more fun.
- To ensure a safe and liquid personal investment portfolio.
- To generate predictable income to support our lifestyle.
- To reduce government, media, and legal exposure by removing myself from the public eye.
- To honor commitments and moral obligations to family and business associates.

To accomplish these goals, I sketched out a second list:

- Retire from TCI.
- Reduce outside public board memberships from 11 to 4.
- Remain chairman and controlling shareholder in Liberty.
- Remain chairman of CableLabs.
- Stay on the Turner board.
- Get the government off TCI's back.
- Generate predictable income by deferring TCI compensation payments with stock dividends, which should produce sufficient cash to maintain our lifestyle.
- Say nothing publicly about the contemplated change until Bob Magness is comfortable.

The lynchpin to this litany was selling TCI, the nation's largest cable company at the time. This would mean letting go of the company I had helped Bob Magness build for the previous twenty years—and sailing off into the sunset with Liberty, which suited me—and especially Leslie—just fine.

But I could not leave Bob, who had lost his wife of thirty-six years, Betsy, a few years back. I felt the weight, too, of my debt in promises to the institutional investors with substantial stakes in TCI.

But TCI was thirsty for capital to upgrade its networks and expertise in the two-way switching required for interactive TV. The local phone company offered two-way service that generated cash and boasted a reputation for innovation and customer service. It could resolve the issues bedeviling TCI—no lobbying skills, poor customer service, and systems in need of upgrades. Cable companies, whose pipes had vastly more capacity to carry data, video, and voice, were ideal partners on paper.

So we began to get to know the heads of all the regional Bell telephone companies and launched several digital video ventures with these Baby Bells, including US West and Bell Atlantic. One of the most thoughtful leaders I met was Bell Atlantic CEO Raymond Smith. More than any of the other Baby Bells, Philadelphia-based Bell Atlantic was moving fast to transform itself from a plain old phone company into an innovative telecom prepared for a digital future.

Ray was named CEO in 1989, five years after the breakup of the old AT&T, and moved quickly to rid the place of bureaucratic thinking and "analysis paralysis." Bell Atlantic had invested $200 million in an interactive-TV navigation system dubbed Stargazer. And the phone company had won a federal lawsuit challenging the 1984 Cable Act to offer and own video in its service area covering the mid-Atlantic states.

On the surface, we were quite different. Ray had a silky-smooth speaking style, honed from years as an accomplished actor and playwright, which seemed to win over large crowds and politicians, two groups I largely shunned.

After several phone conversations dancing around the unavoidable topic of merging, we finally agreed to meet in TCI's headquarters on June 16, 1993. Within minutes of arriving in my office, Ray and I were like old friends.

With TCI cable subscribers covering nearly 25 percent of the country, and his local phone monopolies in six East Coast states and Washington, D.C., we could cover roughly 40 percent of the country, enough of a footprint for a national business, not counting the overlaps, which would be sold.

Of course, we would have to get past the cultural issues and differences. Bell Atlantic was three times the size of TCI, earning $1.4 billion on revenue of $13 billion in 1993. It also was slavishly focused on maintaining its quarterly dividend to shareholders.

TCI, by contrast, posted *cash flow* of $1.86 billion, had grown annual revenue to more than $4 billion, and never had posted after-tax net income in twenty-five years of business, much less paid dividends to shareholders. And TCI was managing nearly $15 billion in debt. We were solely focused on long-term growth in the value of our stock.

I wanted to know: What was Bell Atlantic's appetite for losses? How much would the company be willing to cut its dividend to invest in the infrastructure needed to build the so-called Information Superhighway?

And Ray had questions for me. He wanted more than just TCI and its pipes into one in four homes. He wanted my life raft—Liberty Media—included in the sale.

After thinking it over, I trusted Ray and his ability to make decisions for the combined company. More importantly, Bob Magness, who at sixty-nine was looking to ease out of TCI himself, got a good feeling from Ray.

Bob and I were both comfortable with me taking the role of vice chairman of the combined company, while Ray Smith would remain chairman and CEO, front and center, the person talking to politicians.

"Okay," I finally told Ray. "We'll put Liberty back into TCI and we'll merge the whole thing." TCI's longtime outside counsel, Jerome Kern, took the lead on negotiating the final wording. Everything was kept secret.

Ray and I and a handful of our advisors stole away for one secret meeting in a boat on Boothbay Harbor, off the coast of Maine. It was an ideal setting to talk freely, but as we were preparing to leave, we tried to lift the anchor and it got snagged on something down below. The winch strained as we pulled; we swung the boat around and pulled up again. Stuck. Then one sharp-eyed passenger looking ashore deduced we were likely stuck on a cable crossing.

Snagged on cable—is it an omen?

All I could think was if we broke the power line, knocking out power for an island, the Coast Guard would be out there, this entire area would be crawling with news crews, and our cover would be blown. We tied the anchor chain to a floating boat fender to get later and quietly motored away as Ray and I kept talking.

While the deal with Bell Atlantic was fermenting, our newly formed Liberty Media was facing headwinds, this time in the home-shopping category.

Liberty already owned a controlling stake in QVC with Comcast, and we wanted to double down by buying a stake in the other dominant network, Home Shopping Network. In contrast to his blustery testimony to the Senate about TCI's monopoly power, HSN founder and chairman Roy Speer was downright congenial when he sat down with me to discuss terms for selling HSN to Liberty. Discovering your enemy could also be the buyer of your company can do that to a person.

Liberty made a cash-and-stock purchase of a 23 percent stake in HSN in late 1992, with an option to buy twelve UHF stations from Speer called Silver King. Immediately, the Department of Justice opened an inquiry over antitrust concerns.

The ultimate aim was combining the two operations into a TV-shopping powerhouse: QVC, with 44 million subscribers, would gain from HSN's sophisticated telephone-ordering system, and HSN, with 28 million, would benefit from QVC's brand and reach. A combined QVC-HSN would have $2 billion–plus in annual revenue and could strategically grow the market.

And we had the best CEO money could buy with Barry Diller, widely hailed as a TV programming genius. He was now at the helm of QVC, persuaded into the role by the leaders at Comcast.

So, in April 1993, with Comcast, TCI, and Diller on board, QVC announced a deal to merge with HSN in a stock swap valued at around $1.3 billion. A combination of the two largest home-shopping cable networks instantly triggered antitrust inquiries from the Department of Justice, the Federal Trade Commission, and the Federal Communications Commission.

But the regulators were looking at it from the wrong perspective. True, HSN and QVC were the two biggest home-shopping channels, but they were not so much competing with each other as they were competing against other Goliath retailers such as Target, Macy's, and Best Buy. Sales for the entire TV home-shopping industry in 1993 were estimated at $2.5 billion; annual sales at Walmart that same year were $55.5 billion. With that merger on pause, we waited for a response.

Amid all of this, a storm was brewing in another part of the TV world, and I was about to get sucked into it headfirst, taking Liberty Media off course and down another road of uncertainty.

On September 12, 1993, Sumner Redstone, the well-known seventy-year-old chairman of Viacom, owner of MTV, Showtime, Comedy Central, and Nickelodeon, made an offer of $8.2 billion, or roughly $69 per share in cash and stock, for Paramount Communications, which owned one of the last big Hollywood studios.

Redstone was an old-school, self-made media mogul with real grit. Born in Boston, he left Harvard in 1944 for the military, where he deciphered secret Japanese transmissions during World War II. In 1979, as a fifty-six-year-old lawyer, he got caught in a fire at the Copley Plaza Hotel and clung for life on a third-story window ledge that became so hot it fused the fingers of his right hand together. Told he might not walk again, Redstone made liars out of the doctors, playing tennis into his seventies.

He transformed Viacom from a chain of drive-in movie theaters, National Amusements, into a global media powerhouse, controlling 70 percent of the stock. His mantra: "Content is King." Owning a movie studio meant controlling a steady stream of valuable content, fueling theaters, TV networks, and pay-per-view services.

Paramount, one of Hollywood's six major studios, followed a lucrative model: films debuted in theaters, then moved to DVD and pay-per-view, before landing on cable networks. The market for movies on demand was soaring. In 1993, TCI struck a $90 million deal just to air Carolco Pictures' films—like *Total Recall* and *Basic Instinct*—on pay-per-view before their theatrical releases.

With its studio, TV stations, Madison Square Garden, the Knicks and Rangers, and Simon & Schuster, Paramount was a prime acquisition target. I had discussed a merger between Paramount and Turner Broadcasting with Chairman Martin Davis, but nothing materialized. Meanwhile, Barry Diller, head of QVC and awaiting regulatory approval for its HSN merger, saw acquiring Paramount as his next move.

Diller had deep ties to Paramount. He had led the studio through a golden era in the 1970s and '80s with hits like *Saturday Night Fever* and *Raiders of the Lost Ark* before clashing with Davis and leaving for Fox. Now he envisioned a new media empire combining Paramount with TV interactivity and the internet.

When Viacom announced its bid for Paramount, Diller countered with a $9.5 billion offer—QVC stock plus $30 per share in cash—backed by $1 billion from TCI and Comcast. The battle escalated when QVC sweetened its bid to an all-cash offer of $80 per share for 51 percent of the company, triggering a months-long bidding war—one of the last great hostile takeovers in media history.

After marathon clandestine negotiations between TCI and Bell Atlantic, the sticking point came down to—surprise, surprise—price. At one point, Ray and I agreed to meet alone without our teams, at the Waldorf Astoria. We took price off the table, and revisited the strategy. In Ray's eyes, Bell Atlantic offered credibility. The phone company's reputation for customer service, its financial strength, and record of innovation would resolve the issues bedeviling TCI—a poor customer service reputation and systems that needed upgrades. I agreed.

We agreed that the deal would be a tax-free stock swap, with Bell Atlantic issuing new shares, the dividend still to be determined, and the final price based on valuing TCI at 11.75 times the company's cash flow.

True to our promise to Ray, TCI merged Liberty, which had spun off from TCI in 1991 over regulatory concerns, back into TCI through a $3.5 billion tax-free stock swap in early October. My hopes for shareholder value were realized in the deal: for anyone who participated in the original Liberty deal, a Liberty share bought in 1991 for $256 had soared to $3,821 by August 1994, when TCI reacquired Liberty.

We shook hands over a final document in the New York offices of the law firm Skadden, Arps. On October 13, 1993, I stood with Ray Smith on stage in the Macklowe Hotel in Times Square, as we announced to the world that TCI, the largest cable operator in the United States, would merge with regional telephone company Bell Atlantic in a deal valued at $33 billion, creating one of the largest companies in the U.S.

The combined colossus, delivering phone, cable TV, and internet, was expected to post revenue of nearly $17 billion and position us perfectly in this new world of giants.

After exactly twenty years at the helm of TCI from 1973 to 1993, I felt a small moment of relief, as if a weight had been lifted from my shoulders.

Sumner Redstone flashed his bare-knuckle legal style in the Paramount fight on September 23, 1993, when Viacom filed a federal lawsuit against TCI. Instead of focusing purely on the impact of our role in the proposed merger, Redstone took direct aim at me personally, and the initial words of his lawsuit left no room for doubt.

"In the American cable industry, one man has, over the last several years, seized monopoly power. Using bully-boy tactics and strong-arming of competitors, suppliers, and customers, that man has inflicted antitrust injury on plaintiff Viacom and virtually every American consumer of cable services and technologies. That man is John C. Malone."

The lawsuit aired out a laundry list of grievances and alleged misconduct over TCI's twenty-five-year history to show that "Malone seeks to exert monopoly power over key stages of the delivery of cable programming to the American consumer."

The primary allegation was that under my direction, TCI was illicitly trying to acquire Paramount through QVC, and the suit sought to prevent Liberty Media and TCI from participating in the QVC bid. My support for the deal was depicted as my latest effort to systematically monopolize the TV industry. Redstone and Davis led a small group of lobbyists to Capitol Hill and the Federal Trade Commission, where they handed out copies of the complaint.

In November 1993, Sumner got his wish—at least part of it. The FTC dealt a blow to QVC when it required TCI to withdraw its $500 million support to QVC, given the merger announcement with Bell Atlantic. I had to recuse myself from the Paramount discussions at QVC.

A week earlier, we had made the hard decision to shutter the QVC merger with HSN. Pulling the plug on the QVC-HSN combination avoided a two-front war; QVC's battle to buy Paramount required total focus from Barry Diller. And we didn't need more attention from antitrust regulators.

Viacom and QVC, meanwhile, brought on powerful allies. Viacom secured $1.2 billion from Baby Bell Nynex, then merged with Blockbuster Video to strengthen its cash position. QVC was backed by Comcast, Cox Enterprises, S. I. Newhouse's Advance Publications, and regional phone giant BellSouth. Both sides dug in for a long fight.

Then, in late December, it looked as if Christmas might come early for Barry Diller, when the Paramount board recommended a $92-a-share offer by QVC to shareholders, deeming it financially superior.

The recent mergers among the cable, telephone, and TV industries had drawn the scrutiny of Congress, and two weeks before Christmas, on December 16, I was called to appear before the U.S. Senate Subcommittee on Antitrust, Monopolies and Business Rights to discuss the merger with Bell Atlantic.

Days before my testimony, Sumner Redstone had appeared before the committee as a witness and riled up the chamber with the charges made in Viacom's lawsuit against TCI.

Senator Howard Metzenbaum (D-OH), the same senator who had written to the FTC and DOJ to urge investigations into the QVC-HSN deal, led the questioning, making clear he was skeptical that mergers could help competition.

Sitting at a large table facing the committee, I began by acknowledging TCI's twenty-fifth anniversary as a public company started out West by a handful of flinty entrepreneurs. I told the committee how TCI was the only source of financing for new channels like Black Entertainment Television (Robert Johnson) and the Discovery Channel (John Hendricks), adding to program diversity. I outlined the coming explosion of high-speed internet services, the potential for interactive television, and the promise of wireless.

Then I dove into the defense of the Bell Atlantic deal and phone-cable mergers. "This opportunity is just too big for TCI on our own merits. For one thing, we're entering a world of giant competitors here in the U.S. and internationally. We've got revenues of less than $4 billion a year; AT&T's revenues are sixteen times as large." And TCI lacked the political skills, financial breadth, and telecom expertise to fight these bigger foes alone.

As for the attacks on my reputation, they didn't bother me personally because character is more important than reputation. But I wanted to clear the air, nonetheless. "I can assure you that virtually all these anecdotes are either completely untrue or wildly inflated by business competitors who seek your help in gaining commercial advantage."

Finally, I turned to deconstructing each of the accusations by Sumner Redstone over what he called the "abusive monopoly power wielded by TCI." Redstone had complained that TCI's Encore movie channel had tried to lock up rights to movies with several studios, for example, by intentionally overpaying $1 billion in deals, depriving Viacom's own Showtime and The Movie Channel of a flow of films. As I pointed out: "Obviously, Mr. Redstone's complaints are nothing more than sour grapes from a losing bidder. If Liberty paid too high a price, the only party that will be injured is Liberty."

At the end of my time at the table, Senator Metzenbaum was unmoved, and he declared: "Mr. Malone, I'm not at all convinced that your description of a competitive environment accurately portrays the likely result of the Bell Atlantic–TCI merger," referring to us again as "monopolistic."

"And frankly, I'm afraid your proposed merger with Bell Atlantic is a continuation of this behavior."

On February 14, 1994, after five months of bids and counterbids, Viacom threw a knockout punch, beating out QVC for Paramount Communications with an offer of $107 a share, or about $10.7 billion based on the closing prices—a 30 percent premium over Viacom's original $8.2 billion offer.

In response, Barry Diller put out one of the shortest press releases in the history of business mergers: "They won. We lost. Next."

Viacom's lawsuit against TCI dragged on until 1995, when the chance to settle our differences finally arose. Sumner Redstone was looking to slash some of the $10 billion in debt he took on acquiring Paramount Communications, Inc., and Blockbuster Entertainment Corporation.

So Viacom spun out its cable-TV systems serving 1.2 million subscribers, and TCI bought control of the new company for $350 million, taking on $1.7 billion in debt, in a deal valued at $2.25 billion. Case settled.

With two deals in tatters—Liberty Media's QVC aborted attempt to acquire all of Home Shopping and QVC's ongoing effort to snatch away Paramount from Sumner Redstone—I was focused on the third one: the far bigger merger plan between Bell Atlantic and TCI.

We had blown past internal deadlines to complete the deal, and by February 1994, and we were still stuck over differences in valuation.

The stocks of both TCI and Bell Atlantic had dropped by more than 20 percent since the announcement, and by February TCI's stock had shrunk much further, hovering around $20—most all due to worry over the 1992 Cable Act.

Cable-TV rates were immediately frozen when the 1992 law passed, and the FCC concocted a convoluted formula to set "benchmark" rates and roll back any offending rates 10 percent by September 1993.

On February 22, 1994, the FCC struck again. Everyone I knew was glued to C-SPAN that day to see the FCC's live meeting on cable-TV rate regulation and the press conference afterward. FCC chairman Reed E. Hundt dropped the news like a brick on live TV: the FCC would impose new formulas for cutting an additional 7 percent on top of the initial 10 percent—for an overall 17 percent rate reduction.

Cable stocks dove as Chairman Hundt predicted the new rules would save consumers $3 billion a year, proudly proclaiming the legislation to be the "greatest consumer savings in the history of American business regulation."

TCI stock inched down, and to preserve capital, we suspended half of TCI's $1.1 billion capital budget, pending clarification of the FCC's rate rules. When investors saw our spending halt for hardware, they shaved the stock price of the industry's major equipment suppliers.

Over at the offices of Bell Atlantic in Arlington, Virginia, the executives watching C-SPAN felt the same gut punch. Ray Smith picked up the phone when I called, and I told him: "Ray, this is a bigger hit than we thought." He agreed. I flew to New York.

Ray always intended to buy TCI using Bell Atlantic stock, valuing TCI at about 11.75 times the cash flow from its cable systems. But after the FCC announced new rate cuts, Bell Atlantic's stock fell from around $68 in October to around $53. Ray argued the cuts hurt TCI's stock and would shrink its future cash flow—so Bell Atlantic shouldn't have to pay as much.

We continued to chisel away at price. But the FCC cuts, which had already hit the stock, would also cost TCI an estimated $300 million over the next two years.

So on a cold, sleeting day in New York one day after the FCC press conference, we had our final meeting on the matter in a forty-fourth-floor conference room of Bell Atlantic's legal advisors. As the press releases officially calling off the deal went out, I stepped toward Ray, shook his hand, and said what was in my heart:

"Nice try, my friend."

The aborted merger would put a chill on the much-ballyhooed convergence of the telephone and cable-TV industries.

The FCC cuts also TKO'ed all the big interactive TV trials and ventures. Time Warner shuttered its expensive Full Service Network project, and Viacom closed its interactive test system.

Two months after our Bell Atlantic deal collapsed, Southwestern Bell called off its deal with Cox Communications.

James Robbins, president of Cox Cable, summed it up eloquently: "The Clinton administration wants to build the Information Superhighway and the FCC keeps bombing the bridges."

CHAPTER 14

DOWN IN THE VALLEY

A t the Western Show, the same place in Anaheim where I had made the five-hundred-channel speech, I was back four years later, in 1996, and it was painfully embarrassing and obvious that TCI was late to market with the digital boxes we had promised.

One evening during the convention I was to appear onstage before the evening's performance by rock-and-roll legend Little Richard, and I was introduced by Dick Clark, whom I remembered from watching him host *American Bandstand* on TV.

When I got the signal the band needed more time, I decided to have a little fun and warmed up the crowd with a story poking TCI's tardy supplier, GI.

"A young lady goes to the psychiatrist," I said, "and says 'Doctor, you've got to help me; I've been married three times and I'm still a virgin.'

"'How can that be?' asked the doctor.

"The woman explained that her first husband was a traveling salesman and was hit by a bus.

"The doctor said, 'Yeah, but what about your second husband?'

"She said, 'He was a college professor. He used to write about it and talk about it, but he never got around to doing it, and he died of a heart attack.'

"'So what about your third husband?'

I paused for effect.

"'Oh,' she said, 'that's easy. He's a GI salesman, and he just constantly tells me how good it's going to be when I get it.'"

I savored the sting of the punchline when it brought the house down in hoots and guffaws. We all had a good laugh, but the message behind the joke was deadly serious. Competitors, analysts, and investors began to wonder aloud in the press whether the cable industry—particularly TCI—could actually deliver what it had promised.

And Wall Street was listening. Cable stocks had taken a beating when the FCC demanded a second round of rate reductions totaling 17 percent, and each passing month we failed to deliver a new product, we lost a little more credibility. Investors started to question the cable industry's strategy, and I felt like I was in the hot seat. By early 1996, *The New York Times* was asking on the front page of its business section: "Can TCI's Leader Walk His Talk, At Last?" Our reputation was taking a hit.

And we were taking it from all sides. Around the same time, competitors and others seeking an edge raised concerns about cable's two-way capabilities and the potential for congestion during peak usage since the network was shared by users. Even Intel CEO Andy Grove threw a swing when he mentioned to the press that he was not sure if cable modems were the optimal internet path, suggesting that new technology from phone companies was somehow better.

I had had enough. After mulling it over, I called in TCI Tech Ventures SVP Bruce Ravenel, the former Intel chip designer who was leading our digital set-top box effort, and asked him for more details on a crazy idea he had been pushing: to build our own cable set-top box from the ground up with all the specs we needed for voice, video, and data.

So at the same time we were negotiating with Silicon Valley companies and our traditional suppliers such as GI, we launched what I call a "Skunk Works" project, kept under wraps until we saw if it could fly.

The initial box that GI was building was capable of receiving decompressed signals based on worldwide MPEG-2 video specs. But we soon realized what we really needed for this interactive TV box would be a very powerful computer, capable of retrieving and storing data as well, since our VOD tests showed people were quite willing to pay for movies on demand with no advertising.

So we became investors in a secretive start-up called MicroUnity aiming to essentially combine memory and processing in one revolutionary new microchip that could be programmable. These cable-TV boxes could be programmed and updated remotely, so operators would not have to change out hardware (and send out trucks) for every new service or upgrade. In those days, Cray supercomputers, the fastest computers in the world, were capable of performing billions of calculations per second, requiring thousands of parallel processors in a giant room. Around TCI, we called the project "Cray on a tray."

Run by a former Harvard physicist and entrepreneur named John Moussouris, MicroUnity was funded by more than $100 million from TCI, Time Warner, Comcast, and Cox, among others, to build chips in its own factory specifically for the bandwidth, video, voice, and data specs for set-top boxes, cable modems, and computers.

After months and months of intense effort, in the end, a simple, insurmountable hurdle stopped us: the processing volume caused the chip to get too hot, and it could not be made commercially viable in the time frame we needed.

It was another big swing to try to force a play. I applied every bit of my diagnostic skill to solve for these issues of consolidation, convergence, and the conversion to digital with actual products, down to the silicon chip—that's how deeply we were thinking. I was desperate to get the answer I was looking for.

It was not the first time TCI had placed jaw-dropping bets on a technological leapfrog. Several years later, seeking to get an edge on internet delivery, TCI would invest more than $400 million in Astrolink, one of the first of several attempts to offer global internet access via satellite—long before Elon Musk. It would have been the first system for satellite internet access. The venture, backed by TCI and Lockheed Martin, planned to launch nine global satellites but folded because of lack of investment.

Right after that, Liberty Media overpaid for a stake in 360networks, a Canadian-based company that bought and built long-haul dark and lit fiber-optic lines throughout North America, many along railroad rights of way. The CEO of 360networks, Greg Maffei, the former CFO of Microsoft, had convinced Liberty Media, News Corp., and Nathan Myhrvold, Microsoft CTO, among others, to invest. Within one year of Liberty investing, the company filed for bankruptcy when the dot-com bubble burst. We lost a lot of money when the market tanked.

When you run a technology company you have to take your shots, and sometimes that means losing hundreds of millions of dollars. I call it tuition. You either adapt to new technology, disruptive or not, or die with "this is the way we've always done it."

The box delay continued to eat at me, so in the summer of 1996 I called one of the few people who could grok the box issue: Bill Gates.

"Bill, I know we can build this digital set-top box for three hundred dollars in volume—cable operators can afford that if it meets our Cable-Labs specs.

"But there are engineers at some of the vendors, namely Scientific Atlanta, saying this could be five years out now, and cost at least $600. Keep in mind, I am trying like hell to avoid a major rebuild of the entire TCI footprint with fiber—and to use digital compression to get channel expansion at an affordable price."

Vendors would point to the all-digital, interactive Full Service Network whose astronomical costs made it impractical, and they'd say the same thing: "Well, we can demonstrate it technologically, but it is far too expensive as a consumer product."

But I also knew Moore's Law meant processing power would keep doubling every two years, so it was only a matter of time before the tech caught up. I'd run the numbers and think, "Why should these components cost so much?"

"John, I am absolutely certain that that we could build such a device and deliver it at or below a three-hundred-dollar target price. Why don't you bring 'em up here and we'll have a discussion. And I'll tell them myself—Microsoft will build what you want for three hundred bucks—any volume you want—and we'll guarantee it."

And that's exactly what I did. We had arranged a trip to Silicon Valley in April 1997 to visit several companies who could vie for the software included in the next generation of set-top boxes: Intel, Oracle, and Microsoft. On the last leg of the trip, we traveled to Microsoft headquarters in Redmond, Washington.

About a dozen major cable executives, most of whom were on the board of CableLabs, attended, including myself, Dick Green, Comcast's Brian Roberts, Time Warner's Joe Collins, and Cox Communications' Jim Robbins. We were escorted to a large conference room, where we settled in.

Bill put the specs up on a slide and said, "Microsoft will guarantee—guarantee!—these specs in a box at or below three hundred bucks. How many do you want and when you want them?" Smiles broke out.

The cable operators, too, had brought a slide—showing that roughly two-thirds of the industry had been rebuilt to handle high-speed internet access. Bill perked up when he saw that Comcast was spending $600 million that year to upgrade its cable systems to launch cable modems.

TCI, Comcast, and Cox were still planning to launch the nationwide high-speed internet service @Home, and Time Warner was moving ahead with its own high-speed online service called Road Runner.

Bill liked what he heard and began talking eagerly about cable's role in the evolution of the internet. Interactive TV, which critics said was mostly hype, was still alive, just late to the party, and arriving in a different form—the internet. His enthusiasm was infectious, and it was reassuring to hear the person who had built Microsoft into the largest software company in the world telling us that cable's manifest destiny was to build the pathway for the internet.

Bill had seen, as clearly as we did, that the doldrums the cable industry found itself in were temporary. The industry's wires passed 95 percent of U.S. homes, and in key ways, the computer industry's future was hinged on the cable industry's success. Cable's pipe could deliver data hundreds of times faster than phone lines. If this so-called digital economy was to ever evolve to the next level, a system with enough bandwidth to link every one of the nation's homes and deliver fresh content was required. Hybrid fiber-coaxial cable was the answer.

Already invested in the convergence of the TV and the computer, Bill had paid $425 million for a start-up called WebTV, a service that offered TV-based internet browsing and email via wireless keyboards—but the concept failed to draw enough consumers.

Microsoft had also invested $220 million in a joint venture with MSNBC that would dissolve many years later.

And as delicately as he could, Bill just happened to mention that Microsoft would be the optimal choice to build an operating system for this next generation of cable systems.

At dinner that night, Bill hosted the group at a private club with a view of Lake Washington. Again he acknowledged the cable delegation's message—that the industry was serious about providing the main pipeline for surfing the internet. Sitting next to Bill, Brian threw a fastball.

"Hey, Bill, you know this is all great stuff, but the industry is really depressed right now, and the market is down on cable. If you really believe in us, why don't you buy ten percent of everyone in the room tonight?"

With Brian's earnest enthusiasm, we couldn't tell if he was kidding or not, and we all laughed.

"How much would that cost?" Bill asked, not missing a beat.

"I don't know, let's say five billion dollars," Brian offered, off the cuff.

"You know, I have around ten billion in cash," Bill replied. "I could do that . . . if I could get the right guarantees."

We laughed again, and the banter quickly was rendered into separate conversations and different topics.

I razzed Brian afterward. "Brian, it sure was a sad thing to see you on bended knee asking Bill Gates to bail out the cable industry." None of us knew how serious Bill was. Greg Maffei, Microsoft's CFO, reached out to Brian the next day.

Just a few months after the dinner, Microsoft made its largest investment ever in a single company—$1 billion in cash—for an 11 percent take in the equity of Comcast, the nation's fourth-largest cable operator.

Already paying off a debt load of more than $7 billion, Comcast could now ramp up plans to upgrade its wires for high-speed, two-way networks. All cable stocks jumped on the news.

From Bill's point of view, he had the exits covered: access to Comcast's 4.3 million subscribers, synergies with WebTV, MSNBC, and Road Runner, a possible seat in the larger @Home high-speed service, and perhaps an inroad into putting his software into all these new devices.

But most importantly for us, in a single movement, Bill changed the thinking on the cable industry. Such a ringing endorsement from Microsoft that our technology and strategy were aligned on the right path sent all cable stocks higher. A second wave came in because of the typical herd mentality on Wall Street: follow the smart money.

I was genuinely happy for Brian, who with his father and team were familiar partners in some of TCI's biggest deals, including the Group W cable-system purchase, the shopping network QVC, Teleport, and Sprint PCS.

Later, when we were alone, I shared my concern with Brian about Gates coming into the industry, then forcing his will, or his proprietary operating software on cable operators—and I wasn't alone in that thinking.

After the investment in Comcast, a meeting was arranged with Bill Gates and the heads of major cable companies in the U.S., at Time Warner's boardroom in Rockefeller Center.

Bill started out cordially enough, then eased into details of how Microsoft could provide the one-stop solution for cable operators. Windows software could run the servers in the cable headend, set-top boxes, and everything in between. He then suggested that beyond the standard licensing fee, Microsoft would be entitled to a fraction of the income earned on these new interactive and transactional services.

Some of my fellow cable operators sat in stunned silence at Bill's chutzpah to suggest going into *their* customers' living room controlling the operating system that drove *their* platform. Others exchanged glances. Finally, several spoke up saying in different ways the same message: "Thanks, but no thanks. We're not interested."

So now I was hanging out in the wind a bit, and trying to figure out: What do I do now? All this time, I had done everything I could through

CableLabs to bring the industry together on standards, stressing interoperability and compatibility.

A few months later, in August 1997, at TCI's annual meeting in Denver, I tried to send a message to investors and the market that the cable industry would control its own destiny. We were eager to deal with Microsoft, I told the crowd, but we would keep a tight grip on the technology inside the box.

"We have to push [the standards] in Silicon Valley, and when the smoke clears we still own it," I said. "Bill has got to accept the fact that he can't set the standard that the rest of us are going to use."

The field of potential vendors had widened for cable modems, digital compression, and new interactive TV boxes, and each vendor had a unique software or hardware that was not compatible with everything else.

A couple years later, CableLabs launched the OpenCable Application Platform, or OCAP, a Java-based "middleware" software for the new digital set-top box, in which the cable operator, not the software vendor, would have control over functions such as DVR, channel guides, and banking.

OCAP, like MPEG-2 and DOCSIS before it, would also ensure that all digital set-top boxes would be nationally portable and interoperable, regardless of vendor or software. This would also allow the devices to be sold at retail as well as supplied by cable operators.

When we returned to Denver from the CableLabs trip to the West Coast, while Bill was in talks to invest $1 billion with Brian, I called an old friend at GI, Ed Breen, who had worked on digital technology at the GI VideoCipher division.

Ed got his start at GI selling converter boxes and rose fast to be SVP of worldwide sales; less than ten years later, he would be running the company as CEO.

"Gates can make these boxes for three hundred dollars," I blurted out to Ed almost as soon as he answered the phone. Of course, he raised the specter that Gates would simply subsidize the cost until the industry was in his stranglehold.

I knew that GI needed a hit as badly as we did. Even though GI discovered the breakthrough for digital compression, business was hurting because cable operators, TCI among them, had put off costly upgrades in the rounds of rate cuts following the 1992 Cable Act, which had crimped cash flow. GI had about 60 percent market share in TV set-top boxes but wanted the new digital business.

Ed said that the best price on the box at the time was $400, more than double the cost of a typical analog box.

"Okay, let's get serious about it," I said. "How many do you have to be buying for and by when, to get your price down to a three-hundred-dollar price?" Ed knew the specs and pricing of the box better than anyone, and I trusted him.

"You know, if you ordered ten million of these things, we could get the ball rolling, because that would be a three-billion-dollar purchase order."

An order that large would be unprecedented and would require enormous amounts of arm-twisting with each one of the big cable operators, and in a hurry. It would be easier to train monkeys to play chess. "I have an idea," I said. "We can give you a bigger order than that. We just need to sweeten the pot."

"I'm listening," Ed said.

"Why don't we do a deal where General Instrument gives warrants for GI stock for every box that a cable operator buys?" I explained that if GI got a big order, for say, millions of boxes, it was safe to assume the stock price of General Instrument would go up significantly, and that way, Wall Street would essentially pay for the upgrade. We figured this would motivate people to participate. And boy did it.

Ed said he was certain he could assemble the parts and deliver the physical box for under three hundred bucks. Then came the thorny question of software to make this thing work. And that's where we got in between another set of combatants, Microsoft and Sun Microsystems, both of which made operating systems software.

Initially we contracted with both companies to work together on the product, and it was endless fighting over the best way to code it. At one point CableLabs CEO Dick Green pulled me aside and said, "No memory is going to be big enough to accommodate combined software of Sun and

Microsoft because they're both writing software to push the other guy off the platform." This elbow-pushing went on for quite a while, back and forth between the two software giants.

The delays compounded the timetable at GI. In the end, Ed Breen finally said, "This is brain damage. We'll take on the task of writing the operating software for the digital set-top box." As a result, the initial digital set-tops had GI software.

So we shook on it. TCI would put in the first order for 1 million boxes, and we devised a sweetener for cable operators of all sizes: we would offer everyone the same most-favored-nation terms for the warrants as TCI, the largest cable operator. And we would pray for a rising GI stock price.

JC Sparkman rode herd on the negotiations, and we asked everyone to keep the deal confidential—whispers could prod the stock price up too soon, thus erasing our profit.

On December 17, 1997, GI announced $4.5 billion in orders from nine cable operators including TCI, Time Warner, Comcast, Cox, and others. In addition to the 15 million set-top boxes, the cable operators would also receive warrants for a 16 percent stake in GI. This single order—three times GI's $1.8 billion in revenue—would guarantee the company's profitable future, especially since the same operators would look to GI for maintenance parts and upgrades.

As part of the deal, in 1998, GI traded 10 percent of its equity to TCI for our digital Headend in the Sky (HITS) distribution network, making Liberty Media, through TCI, GI's largest shareholder. The stock walked steadily from $12 to $50, and Liberty later raised its stake to 18 percent by buying 10 million shares from Forstmann Little & Co.

By late 1999, with GI trading above $80, Motorola bought the company for $11 billion. Thanks to our stock and warrants, TCI briefly became a controlling shareholder in Motorola, with a stake worth nearly $5 billion. GI's ownership would shift again, but for a moment, I held the reins of the company I'd once dreamed of working for. What would Monty say now?

Just as we had hoped, the profits from the warrants on the GI stock would offset the entire cost of the boxes for the cable operators. In the end,

Wall Street had more or less paid for this digital upgrade of the cable-TV industry.

Our agreements with GI gave TCI control of decisions for graphics chips, microprocessors, and software—negotiating leverage we needed against the giants in Silicon Valley.

The choice for an operating system was coming down to Microsoft and Sun. On Christmas Eve, I got a visitor to the office who helped seal the deal. Scott McNealy, chief executive of Sun Microsystems, had flown to Denver, where we agreed on a deal for Sun to supply Java software as the "middleware" in the new cable boxes.

All this time we were pushing the technology of television, believing it was going to be *the* interactive platform. I think what we've come to see is that TV is more of a sit-back, passive, mass-audience platform with limited interactivity; whereas the computer was becoming more of a lean-in, heavily interactive, individual platform.

Innovation always looks obvious in hindsight, but predicting it is really hard in real time. In Time Warner's Full Service Network, consumers could order pizzas with the remote, but it was not what consumers were truly craving; in time the press of single button on a smartphone could do the same. The most that consumers wanted to do with a big new HDTV was sit back and watch *Star Wars* again.

Looking back, what stays with me most from that time is how we changed the story around cable—how a technology once seen as a one-trick pony became a bridge to the future. We shifted perceptions by finding new possibilities in the same old wire and by showing other operators that the business case was not just viable—it was powerful. And the value we unlocked proved it.

The large end-to-end groundbreaking deal with Microsoft never materialized, though we managed to strike smaller deals with Bill later.

Bill Gates remains a friend, and I am still in awe of his intellect, energy, and relentless curiosity. Some of my favorite memories are of spending time with Bill and his team, including Craig Mundie, chief research and strategy officer, and Nathan Myhrvold, the chief technology officer—while traveling to Washington State for Cellular One board meetings.

Cable stocks started to climb higher after the Microsoft investment in Comcast, and the entire market started to heat up for internet companies and online businesses.

But while I chased the next big thing, I missed the cracks forming beneath our core business. Satellite had finally found its footing by the mid-90s, peeling away our subscribers week by week. Customer service issues dragged on, and we were bleeding money on consultants and campaigns. The old guard was stepping back, and a wave of new leadership was stepping in. Somewhere along the way, we stopped moving with purpose—and started chasing too many things at once.

CHAPTER 15

PIPE DREAMS

Allll hell was breaking loose. The massive technology shifts in the early nineties would later be called the Information Age or the Digital Revolution. This new ability to create digitized signals for voice, video, and data created a panoply of new entertainment and information options for American homes.

There was no single "Aha!" moment in this grand discovery. There was no one single inventor. We were all dreaming the same dream. Cable-based broadband, defined by its wide bandwidth capacity, would become the main portal into the home, and its growth would continue even as dot-com companies were imploding into stardust. As it remains today.

In November 1993, I made a speech about the impact of these new technologies to business graduate students at Yale. The topic was "The Broadband Revolution: How Technology and Entrepreneurship Will Override Boundaries in Telecommunications." The speech would become my internal manifesto, and, aside from the title, it was probably the most lucid explanation I ever had given about what I was thinking back then, and what I still believe today.

Standing at the lectern at the front of a small auditorium of bright, young students, I felt at home in the academic setting and lost the tightness in my stomach that comes for me with speaking in front of crowds. I explained how the worldwide communications industry was about to undergo transformative change, like nothing any of us had seen before.

And as I look back on it more than thirty years later, my words were scarily accurate. I spoke of how fiber optics, high-speed microprocessors, and new operating software were combining to enable "just about everything in the communications business" to be done in "a digital format that is much cheaper and has greater capacity than ever before."

I told them: "Everyone is going digital. It is the thing to do. It also works. Cellular is going digital. Cable is going digital. Telephony has to go digital, especially as it goes broadband, because it is a more robust transmission scheme.

"Breakthroughs in digital compression of video materials now allow movies to be treated just as another stream of digital information, just as telephone calls and the internet would be treated, at higher quality and at lower cost than before, and the cost differences are fairly dramatic.

"As a result of these technological changes, the traditional industry structures in this country and overseas are going to break down. The telephone industry can no longer be a complacent, separate entity based on a technology that was invented about a hundred and twenty years ago. And the cable industry can no longer be a complacent entity based on a technology that was invented about thirty years ago. They are converging into each other."

The computer industry, I said, was going to be dramatically affected by a surge in distribution capacity and speed, as was the television industry.

"There will be social changes, too. We will have the ability to do distance learning, messaging, very high-quality video conferencing, entertainment customized to the individual's time schedule, catalog shopping, video stores—the list goes on and on.

"A dispersed workforce could collaborate productively, rather than bringing people to their jobs. Boiler rooms will now be dispersed. Customer service representatives will be able to work out of their homes; the information will come to them rather than the other way around. This dispersal creates a very interesting change in the dynamics and productivity of those workers: it has the potential to bring new people into the workforce, to enhance their productivity, and to substantially enhance their happiness."

I also pointed out that "a positive outcome is that, once this system is deployed on a wide-scale basis, the barriers to entry come down for anybody with a new programming idea, with a new software application, with a video game, with what is now being called a 'smart agent,' or with a navigator.

These technologies will all prosper on this platform because it will be high fixed cost and low marginal cost, and therefore should be very stimulative of applications that expand on the use of capacity. We have tested the economic locomotives of this scheme sufficiently to know that there is revenue available to drive it."

As grand (or grandiose) as my vision was at the time, none of this might ever have taken shape without the lynchpin that had yet to be invented: a cable modem for every household. That little box became the gateway between cable companies and customers, translating internet signals into data, video and even phone calls. Without it, broadband was just a pipe with no faucet.

In the fall of 1990, there were just 313,000 computers on what was quaintly called the World Wide Web; by 1996, there were around 10 million computers online. New services launched to help the masses get online for the first time—America Online, CompuServe, and Prodigy—offering entertainment, message forums, games, and other software. People started "surfing" the internet, mailing letters electronically, and saving personal data on "floppy" disks.

Today it is easy to forget how dramatically high-speed cable modems changed the experience for online users, letting us tap the internet instantly, seamlessly—and silently. Before its arrival, online sessions were painfully slow because transmission speeds were limited to the phone company's twisted copper wire.

Dial-up modems made a hellacious set of noises—screeching and beeping—as it took thirty seconds or more to get connected to an online service. Since the online session was considered a call, you could be knocked off the line if someone in the house picked up the phone. But the real annoyance was the speed. Dial-up modems in the early 1990s delivered a snail-like speed of 14.4 Kbps. To download a page of text to took several seconds, and a picture or a song took several minutes, a two-hour movie more than twenty-four hours, giving rise to the slang term "World Wide Wait."

I knew the cable-TV industry could provide the one thing that everyone wanted but no one could deliver, not even the telephone companies—a fast connection. Compared to early 9.6 or 14.4 Kbps telephone modems, early cable modems delivered speeds at an eye-popping 10 Mbps, or 10 *thousand* Kbps—around seven hundred times faster.

Even when the telephone companies tweaked their dial-up speeds to a maximum of 56 Kbps, cable modems still blew their doors off. (Today, cable operators make a 1 *gigabit* service—about seventeen thousand times faster than the 56 Kbps modems—available to more than 90 percent of U.S. homes.)

On the day Netscape went public in 1995, I watched as the value of a company that existed mainly in the digital ether soared to nearly $3 billion on the first trading day. It was the start of the dot-com boom (or bubble, depending on your timeline). Netscape's new browser had suddenly made text-based websites accessible and fun to read for the first time, giving home computers a new purpose.

The novelty and promise of the new World Wide Web sparked a surge of consumer interest, and billions of dollars in venture capital followed. I knew intuitively that the cable industry could be the center of the Venn diagram of the converging TV, telephone, and internet industries. If cable companies pulled together, collectively we could be the driving force in these tectonic shifts with our hybrid fiber-coaxial cable.

To upgrade aging cable wires into fiber-rich, two-way symmetrical service, the cable-TV industry required billions of dollars to rebuild their systems for the Digital Age. Investments in—and from—computer companies could help.

AOL, with around a million subscribers in 1994, proved to be a crowd favorite, with an easy interface and a popular email service that audibly announced your latest incoming message with "You've Got Mail!" At the time, AOL was still mailing out free-trial CDs with start-up software. The rate was $9.95 a month, including five hours of connection time—and $3.50 each for additional hour. All this at the whopping speed of 9,600 bits per second; it was nothing to wait a few minutes for a page of text to download, several more if it had pictures or graphics.

I was eager to get a toehold in the nascent industry. If you believe in the laws of attraction, they were working when I got a call from an investment banker who said Paul Allen, a cofounder of Microsoft, had around 25 percent of AOL stock—and now wanted to get out of it.

Paul had left Microsoft in 1983, just eight years after founding it with his high school buddy Bill Gates, when he received a diagnosis of non-Hodgkins lymphoma. With nothing to lose and $20 billion to spend, he invested in software, internet firms, the NBA's Portland Trail Blazers, real estate, deep sea exploration, and a kaleidoscope of worthy causes.

Paul was a bona fide futurist, a believer in the societal benefits of a wired world, and by 1998 he would buy a controlling stake in one of the largest U.S. cable operators, Charter Communications, in which I own a substantial stake today. Years later, Liberty would buy Paul's stake in Ticketmaster.

I was quite fond of Paul, whose eclectic tastes were reflected in his art (works from Cezanne, van Gogh, and Warhol) and the vast problems he tackled with his generous philanthropy, across science ($100 million to wipe out the Ebola virus), medicine ($100 million to brain science), and the environment (elephant census on the Savannah). Paul left us too early, passing away from cancer in 2018 at the age of sixty-five.

A young CEO named Steve Case ran AOL, which was on the cusp of becoming a household name, but it was not there yet. I had met Steve once before, so I called him up.

I told him we might be interested in buying Paul Allen's piece of AOL and cited some synergies: "We could include AOL with every customer we've got, and let's charge them a buck a month for the service."

So Steve came in, pitched to the TCI inner circle, and made a good impression. And soon it looked as if Liberty Media would buy this block of stock. We had verbally agreed to terms, and I went to bed that night confident we had a deal.

But then Bill Gates got in the way.

A short while later, I was on the *Ragtime* boat cruising with Larry Romrell and a couple others, taking it up the East Coast to Maine, when I got an urgent message to call the office. Because of spotty service, we headed into a port in nearby Cape May, New Jersey, and I jumped on land to make a call on the nearest pay phone when we got to a marina.

When my right hand, Marty, picked up the phone, she said, "Bill Gates desperately needs to talk to you." So I called Bill. When he answered, I could tell he was perturbed.

"John, I hear you're talking to Paul about buying his block in AOL."

"Your information is correct," I told Bill. "We don't have anything on paper, but we've done a handshake over the phone."

And then Bill says: "John, you really don't want to do that."

"Why is that?"

"Let me tell you the whole story," he began. The reason Paul Allen wanted to sell his block of AOL was to avoid a conflict of interest: Microsoft was about to come out with a new operating system that would directly compete with AOL. Bill cited Microsoft's 90 percent share of the PC software market and said, "We will soon have our own web portal. It's gonna be called The Microsoft Network—MSN—and it will be a dial-up internet service provider (ISP) tucked inside the release of Windows 95."

And then Bill Gates issued the real warning he wanted to convey: "And when we release this, it's gonna be very difficult for customers that upgrade to Windows 95 to be able to find AOL . . . and we think Microsoft Network is gonna be a huge success.

"So, you know, I don't want you making the mistake of putting your money into something that we're gonna put out of business." This was rather brass knuckles of Bill, and sometimes this was his way; it is how you get to 90 percent market share of anything.

Strategically, I knew that Bill was blocking an easy play between AOL, the fastest-growing online service, and TCI, the largest cable operator in the country. But I also believed what he was saying about the market, so I asked him, "What are you suggesting? What's the alternative?"

"Well, why don't you just buy twenty percent of Microsoft Network? This is going wide fast, and it's certain to be a massive success."

"What are you going to charge me for this?" I asked.

"Well, why don't you pay me the same amount you were going to pay Paul for his block. This could be worth an enormous amount . . . who knows?"

This was a rather rich ask. Gates was seeking, for just 20 percent of his new and untested service, the same price we were about to pay for 25 percent of the leader in the online access business. It might sound a little arrogant, yet it also sounded like the truth.

TCI and Microsoft were already conducting small interactive tests in the Redmond area, and there were some discussions to develop a cable-TV network covering computing. *What is there to think over?* TCI would be a 20 percent owner of a new internet portal that would piggyback on the most successful operating software in the industry.

"Do you want cash or stock?" I asked Bill.

"I'll take your stock," he said.

So, after passing on the AOL stake, for $125 million TCI bought a 20 percent stake in Microsoft Network, which valued the service at $650 million. To pay the tab, we issued Microsoft common shares in Liberty stock.

Not long after, the U.S. Department of Justice sued Microsoft for abusing its monopoly market for personal computer operating systems. Bundling its Windows operating system with Microsoft Explorer and other services, the suit said, was a way to, among other things, get rid of competition such as Netscape Navigator and others in the web browser market.

After winning the suit, the government forced Microsoft to include AOL and other third-party players alongside its MSN service. The Microsoft Network morphed into an ISP, then a content portal, but as originally conceived, it never quite took off. (Today it is the domain for Microsoft's online news services.)

I called Bill after the antitrust suit, and we talked about the turn of events for AOL and the Microsoft Network. It was an awkward call for both of us as I recalled aloud his advice to pass on Paul Allen's 25 percent stake in AOL and to buy 20 percent of MSN instead.

"Bill, your advice didn't work out so well for Liberty, especially when I look at the stock of AOL now." (By the end of 1999, AOL's stock price would peak with a market cap north of $220 billion, making it one of the most valuable companies in the world. By my back-of-the-napkin math, if I had carried out my original plan to buy Paul's entire 24.9 percent stake, Liberty could have seen a paper profit in 1999 of nearly $55 billion.)

To his credit, Bill conceded he had been blindsided by the government's onerous restrictions and overconfident about the Microsoft Network in the early days of online. "Yeah, John, you know, I'm really sorry about that. Why don't I just return your Liberty shares?"

And that's exactly what he did, returning the shares in Liberty in 1996, even though Liberty shares over the same two-year period had increased dramatically as well. Bill saw past the profit and saw more in the gesture. He was fair, which is one of the highest compliments one CEO can give another in the blood sport of dealmaking.

This would be the first of two occasions in which AOL cost Liberty Media dearly. Three years later, when AOL bought Time Warner, TCI was forced to sell its Time Warner shares as part of the deal, we were taxed on the gains, and the government took our votes away— but that's another story.

⊶⟨∘⟩∘

As consumer demand for these faster speeds became clear, tech companies big and small jumped at the chance to be a supplier for these modems built specifically for hybrid fiber-coaxial cable lines. Soon cable operators around the country were announcing plans to deploy these modems in test markets.

A cable modem deciphering signals for the internet required a different brain than the new digital set-top boxes that could decipher compressed digital MPEG-2 video signals.

A telephone line connects two points and allows sound both ways, but it has low bandwidth. The cable industry's hybrid fiber-coaxial cable allowed numerous digital conversations at once with a neat trick: using Internet Protocol, senders could break digital data down into "packets" of information, each with a shipping address of the destination and assembly instructions. These packets then were seamlessly dropped into the slipstream of other packets traveling through the network.

As the internet began to flourish, cable operators built an entirely new business atop their existing networks: internet service provider. It was a new revenue stream that had nothing to do with TV, effectively doubling the subscription revenue from the same wire. But in order to offer these new services, we still needed capital to upgrade our lines. And cable modems to do the heavy lifting.

As fast as these new devices were, there were so many models popping up at once that it was difficult for cable operators to determine value. Few operators ordered in bulk because technology tweaks were improving the devices every day.

And there were no standards. Most consumer electronics work no matter where you buy them, but if you bought a cable modem in New York, there was no guarantee it would work in New Jersey, because each cable operator's architecture was different, and each cable modem sent different amounts of data upstream and downstream.

Just as MPEG-2 was the language for digital compression of video, this new platform begged for a similar standard that every supplier could build on.

At the CableLabs board meeting on November 30, 1995, although the agenda was packed, I had only one thing on my mind: high-speed cable modems.

Urgency was needed because cable operators, working on their own, could not possibly scale this new service quickly enough. Already the local phone companies were preparing to roll out a new ADSL (asymmetric digital subscriber line) service at 10 Mbps data transmission on the existing copper wire telephone lines to homes—but almost all of it downstream.

Everyone at the meeting knew the need for standardized, interoperable equipment to deploy high-speed internet services, so I raised the issue, and we took a vote with little debate: CableLabs would start work immediately on DOCSIS (Data Over Cable Interface Specifications), a set of vendor standards specifically for delivering high-speed data services via cable modems over a hybrid fiber-coax cable network. CableLabs solicited input and working models from more than two hundred companies worldwide.

CableLabs drove innovation through a unique collaborative model: a royalty-free licensing system that avoided patent lawsuits and complex payment schemes—the downfall of many tech agreements. This approach helped DOCSIS cable modems spread globally at remarkable speed.

CableLabs could sublicense the technology to vendors on the same royalty-free basis, opening the door for smaller players to enter the market and increasing consumer choice. It also reduced reliance on dominant suppliers like GI, which charged for licensing its digital video-compression tech. With no threat of patent litigation, engineers could build on competitors' designs, cut R&D costs, and speed up improvements.

One scary moment for me was when the folks at Broadcom, one of the biggest players in this new modem category, insisted on holding on to some proprietary technology that we needed for the DOCSIS specs. Henry Nicholas, the brash, aggressive Broadcom cofounder, liked to play hardball, but Richard Green, our firm, friendly, music-composing CableLabs CEO, stared down Broadcom and Henry, reminding him that vendors who agreed would enjoy all tech updates for free, and holdouts would be hemmed into a proprietary trap. Broadcom finally relented.

CableLabs worked like an incubator, actively helping vendors in the lab test and troubleshoot DOCSIS-certified equipment with rigorous performance reviews data flow, modulation, and, most important of all, interoperability worldwide.

To drive the effort faster, we hired an Iranian-born businessman named Rouzbeh Yassini, whose tiny LAN-city firm had beaten out bigger players for the lion's share of the cable modem market, earning him the nickname "Father of the Cable Modem."

Word spread quickly. Early users saw web pages and videos load instantly—no more waiting, no more screeching noises, and no more tying up the phone line. Always on. Cable modems weren't just faster than dial-up; they were better in every way. CableLabs' DOCSIS data transmission standard made it possible. The first version delivered 40 Mbps; today, it supports speeds up to 10 gigabits per second—250 times faster.

As the excitement over high-speed modems made headlines, I got a call in December 1994 from John Doerr, a Silicon Valley investor at venture capital firm Kleiner Perkins, renowned for his Midas touch with start-ups in the computer industry. He backed Compaq, Netscape, Sun Microsystems, and later, Amazon and Google.

I knew John by way of TCI's head of Tech Ventures, Bruce Ravenel, from their days working at Intel in the 1970s. John called with an idea he had been chewing on for weeks. He knew that cable modems were well on their way to going wide, and that this would fundamentally turn the online experience into a colossal business with implications for finance, commerce, education, medicine, media, and nearly every facet of modern society.

John saw, as we did, the cable industry's massive opportunity with broadband as a conduit linking computers via cable modems. What if we could assemble an alliance of North American cable operators that would offer a nationwide high-speed internet service at speeds unmatched by the telephone industry? With standards already set by CableLabs and the largest operators working in concert, we agreed this new alliance could dominate the field.

TCI Tech Ventures had made an early bet, buying a 2.3 percent slice of Netscape in 1994, which had grown to ten times the initial $4 million investment a year later. TCI also owned a stake in the Sega Channel, a $15 monthly gaming service over cable-TV lines, and Acclaim Entertainment, maker of the popular video game *Mortal Kombat*.

John proposed a national service marketed under one brand providing speeds of 40 Mbps, more than a thousand times faster than the fastest telephone dial-up modems at the time. He even had coined a name for it: @Home, using the @ symbol used to separate name and affiliation in email addresses, an artifact of early ARPANET users.

@Home would be a software-backed service for consumers, with email, a home site, and plenty of content exclusive to the high-speed service. We announced the venture in May 1995, and by everything I could see, it would dominate. It was an AOL-killer.

Modems were relatively cheap—Motorola was selling them for around $300—which, if we could get the price down, would help us steal a chunk of the $100 billion local telephone market.

So I reached out to my cable brethren—CEOs of the largest companies—and tried my best to persuade as many of them as I could to join @Home, by bringing them all in on the action. Under the structure we sketched out, 35 percent of the revenue would go to the central entity for developing the technology and providing the networking. And the cable operators would control 65 percent—which was an easy sell to the CEOs of big cable operators in North America, including two of Canada's largest cable operators,

Rogers Communications, led by an enthusiastic Ted Rogers, and Shaw Communications.

As I checked off the joiners, TCI as the number one operator was on board, as were the third-, fourth-, and fifth-largest cable companies (Comcast, Cox, and Continental Cablevision, respectively), among others—but the number two player, Time Warner, was holding out. A partner of Time Warner was blocking the deal: US West, which had acquired a 26 percent stake in Time Warner's entertainment businesses.

At first, it looked like a great marriage. US West, like other local phone companies at the time, was eager to break outside its service area, and Time Warner wanted to reduce some of its $16 billion in debt. But now US West was balking at the @Home agreement, one of several management quarrels between the two partners, as Time Warner CEO Jerry Levin explained the situation.

Frustrated, I made a personal pitch to Jerry on my next trip to New York, reminding him of the plan to set aside a portion of revenue for new content, which Time Warner could lead. Jerry thanked me but came back later and said the Baby Bell had veto power and was not joining the @Home alliance. No matter, we would have to launch without Time Warner.

To launch @Home, John Doerr tapped a Kleiner Perkins partner, William Randolph Hearst III, who had been the publisher of the *San Francisco Examiner*, started by his grandfather, the influential American newspaper publisher and media magnate.

To engineer the system, John recruited a NASA Ames Research Center engineer named Milo Medin, a pioneer in network connections on the budding internet. He was a no-nonsense architect who knew how to connect cable operators through a national, switched, Internet Protocol two-way fiber-optic backbone that could carry the millions of subscribers we expected.

As the chief technology officer of @Home, Milo was bullish on building the first large-scale residential broadband access service, and this gave us all confidence. Ultimately, the new backbone capacity we were building would increase our collective bandwidth one hundredfold.

Less than six months after John and I first spoke, TCI unveiled @Home

Network in May 1995 with a North American agreement for a platform to roll out high-speed connectivity in early 1996, starting out in a TCI system in Sunnyvale, California.

Within weeks, Time Warner unveiled its own new high-speed cable modem service that offered a portal of content from the company's studios, publishers, and content creators. Named after the wily cartoon character (*beep-beep!*) from Warner Bros., Road Runner was modeled much like @Home, charging $40 a month and sharing a similar cut with cable operators.

Within days of our announcing @Home, Bill Gates called, upset. He made it clear to me how he did not appreciate how TCI had kept Microsoft out of the @Home partnership, choosing instead to do a deal with his Silicon Valley competitors. Bill and I did not have what I would call a strong relationship back then, and this certainly did not help.

In his eyes this was a hostile act in the ever-shifting war of chipmakers and software designers and their alliances. As if to make a point, later Microsoft and Compaq Computer Corporation would each invest $212.5 million for 10 percent stakes in Time Warner's Road Runner, beating out Intel and Oracle. Bill would install his CFO, Greg Maffei, as his representative on the Road Runner board.

The truth is when I hung up the phone, I felt like we had walked into the middle of a pissing contest between Microsoft and the Silicon Valley clients whom Kleiner Perkins represented.

By the time we launched @Home, the goal was to upgrade our networks to a fully asymmetrical, two-way, fiber-rich, low-noise, reasonable-latency path to the home. Most every home would have a digital box, and some could still have a one-way analog box. And that was the beauty of the architecture.

At every turn, as we pressed and pushed, first with fiber, then with compression, the wire evolved and transformed before our eyes. The hybrid fiber-coax system we came up with was so infinitely adaptable and so incredibly flexible that it could be rebuilt again with constantly changing devices and technologies. And the sweet part was that it was all compatible, and the existing businesses dependent on the platform could be expanded as these new technologies made more services possible.

The future had never looked brighter.

CHAPTER 16

TURNER'S LAST STAND

By the summer of 1995, the urge to merge was in the air. The Walt Disney Company announced a stunning $19 billion acquisition of Capital Cities/ABC Inc., and its coveted ESPN channel, and the very next day, Westinghouse announced plans to buy CBS for $5.4 billion in cash.

This raised the anxieties of Ted Turner and his team at TBS. Despite the fact that TBS was growing fast, with revenue nearing $3 billion, Ted told me he still felt "vulnerable," concerned his company would one day become a takeover target.

He had exhausted even the financially elastic mind of Mike Milken to find another acquisition for TBS. With the takeover threats from Kirk Kerkorian and others still fresh in his mind, and consolidation and vertical integration going on around him, Ted felt it was time to think seriously about joining forces with somebody.

To this very day, thirty years later, I wish Ted Turner had let TCI or Liberty Media acquire Turner Broadcasting, as I had proposed to him. Ted could have stayed in place and run everything on the content side forever. He could have counted on us to support him, always, and he could have held voting control that ensured his financial independence.

It would have been the easiest thing in the world for Ted to combine assets with TCI, at which point he could have continued to run his empire forever. We would have valued a deal for TBS as a good investment *and* a good public service.

But Ted, who had joined the TCI board a year earlier in 1994, told me when I mentioned the idea of a merger, "I love you guys, but you're too far right-wing for me. I think if CNN is going to be controlled by any-body or fit with anybody, it needs to fit with somebody who's in the news business—and Time Inc. is probably the most logical choice." In truth, I'm a libertarian, believing in minimal government intervention, free markets, and personal freedom—but I could not argue the nuances to Ted. Few can.

Ted had several options he was considering, including a joint venture with Bill Gates and Microsoft for a version of CNN.com in which Gates was willing to invest $1 billion. But in each of these discussions with potential partners, Ted was held back by provisions in his agreement with powerful new cable-operator board members as a result of his bailout. He was chafing under the restrictions.

Ted was also talking to Jerry Levin, who was by this time CEO of Time Warner, the same Jerry Levin who had worked with Ted to put WTBS up on the same satellite with HBO back in 1976. Time Warner's stock price was sagging, and Levin was looking to boost it by selling off assets or buying some new ones.

These were the days when Ted and I were spending time together at his ranch, and he would ask me from time to time how to play his cards. I was disappointed when he finally told me he was close to doing a deal with Time Warner.

The combination of the Warner Bros. studio, Time's magazines (includ-ing *Time*, *People*, and *Sports Illustrated*), HBO, and Ted's networks, includ-ing CNN, TBS, and TNT, was an impressive medley of assets, but it offered little true synergy beyond financial machinations, in my opinion. Time had barely proven the validity of its merger with Warner Communications, five years earlier, in 1990. Jerry was scrambling to get the stock price up, even as he was trying to quash the internal infighting that would become a hallmark of Time Warner's corporate structure.

Compared to TCI and its cable cowboys, though, Time Warner was a step up in respectability in Ted's eyes. By aligning with them, Ted figured he could have a bigger impact on the causes he supported. The Time Inc. half of the company, with headquarters in midtown Manhattan, was at the center of the media world, steeped in the prestige and the legacy of founder Henry Luce, revered as one of the most influential publishers in American history.

Over the years, Ted had grown more passionate about liberal causes, such as the environment, global warming, and overpopulation. This was especially true during the decade he spent married to actress Jane Fonda (1991–2001), before they divorced. As his politics were swinging more to the left, I think Ted allowed CNN to drift to the left, which he regarded as key to the salvation of the planet. To Ted, the right was just a bunch of Neanderthals. That was his judgment, and he was entitled to it, just as CNN was his property to manage.

I felt like Ted would be okay, and if he was patient, he might even find a way to end up in the role of chairman of the combined company. How could he know he would be betrayed so many years later by one of his earliest partners?

In September 1995, Ted had made up his mind, and Time Warner agreed to pay $7.5 billion for Turner Broadcasting, creating the largest entertainment company in the world. Jerry Levin would keep his CEO/chairman title and Ted would be vice chairman, responsible for the cable networks of both companies, including HBO. When the deal finally closed, and the TBS shareholders exchanged each TBS share they owned for three-quarters of a Time Warner share, Ted, overnight, would become a billionaire, with his personal holdings in TBS stock worth north of $2 billion.

As part of the agreement, TCI's stake in Turner, now Time Warner shares, were placed into a voting trust controlled by Time Warner because of FCC restrictions at the time.

Ted sold to Time Warner for a lot of reasons: his price, his legacy, and his political philosophy. I also think that after thirty years of scrambling from crisis to crisis to save TBS, Ted was tired. From here on in, he could focus on the parts of the company he liked best, as he helped integrate the two entertainment giants.

In the process, someone had put a value on the sweat, sacrifice, and strategy necessary to turn a tiny billboard advertising company into an $8 billion news and entertainment empire.

I could guarantee only one thing: if Ted had joined Liberty Media, he might not have had the prestige of Time Inc., but he would have ended up being a hell of a lot richer—and in control of what he built, rather than being sidelined by lesser executives later on.

Five years after Time Warner bought Turner Broadcasting, Ted found himself in another life-or-death struggle in the media world, and this time, he wasn't at the helm to steer the boat.

"Have you heard about the AOL deal?" Ted asked me in one of our frequent calls.

"Well," I said, "I understand there are talks going on, but everybody talks. What did Jerry say?"

"He said Time Warner has been trying to figure out how the internet affects these businesses, and AOL is the biggest thing on the internet right now. Hell, John, it *is* the internet. And if we do this merger, then this new AOL/Time Warner is gonna be the biggest provider of internet and TV services, basically a new platform that'll dominate anything out there."

When he finished parroting the pitch from Jerry, I could hear in his voice just the slightest hint of skepticism. Even Ted, a born salesman, was not believing his own schtick.

Time Warner's brands, which now included Ted's CNN, TBS, and other channels, Time Inc. magazines, and Warner Bros. and Looney Tunes, were household names, but the entertainment giant's presence online was still limited.

Its Pathfinder portal—an umbrella site for Time Inc. magazine and original content on the web—launched in 1994, but failed to appeal to users as much as Yahoo and Excite, and it, too, was abandoned after four years and $100 million.

I knew that AOL was being shopped. I heard AT&T had sized up the internet service, but CEO Mike Armstrong was unmoved. At the time, AOL was the largest provider of internet service, with 25 million subscribers, and its stock price was inflated like almost any other stock with a dot-com name.

The grand plan was that the "new media" America Online would tur-bocharge the "old media" Time Warner, one of the world's biggest media companies, and turn it into a growth company. AOL CEO Steve Case and President Bob Pittman were pumping the company up, but there was very little there. It was a bubble stock, like so many others out pitching their dot-com predictions.

AOL's strength, it appeared, was its claim of reaching 45 percent of all homes in the U.S., but those figures were deceiving. A new wave of high-speed internet connections offered by cable operators, along with powerful new search engines by Netscape and others, was already silently taking root across America—a new vision of the internet *without* portals, or "walled gardens," like AOL. These connections would allow consumers to simply plug into the internet, with no need for a "portal" service like AOL.

Jerry Levin, for his part, was desperate for a transformational deal that landed Time Warner at the top of the heap, with Jerry at the helm. But he was buying a concept that was unproven, and he failed to ask the Monty Shapiro question—"What if this doesn't work?"

Like the surfer who misjudges the wave, he jumped on board too soon. The internet was coming, but not there yet, and not in the way AOL was selling it.

Time Warner's businesses had brought in $26.8 billion in revenue in 1998, five times the revenue of AOL. But in the wacky world of values during the growing internet bubble, and in part because AOL earned four times the net profit of Time Warner, the stock market valued AOL at 1.5 times as high as Time Warner. As government investigators would later learn, the company books were phony. Time Warner had also committed a rookie mistake in any merger: not enough due diligence on AOL.

The announcement to create the AOL/Time Warner entertainment and internet conglomerate came on January 10, 2000. Using its pumped-up stock, AOL paid about $165 billion for Time Warner and would also assume about $17 billion in Time Warner debt. It remains today the largest combi-nation in history, at a total market cap value of $360 billion—and the most spectacular failure in American business.

In May 2000, just months after the merger was announced, Ted invited me to visit him down at the Vermejo Park Ranch, which is next to a ranch and land I own in northern New Mexico. I thanked him for the invite and then hit on an idea I had thought about for a long time: "Ted, have you ever toured your ranch from the air?"

"No!"

"Well, I'll charter a helicopter and fly down, pick you up, take you for a tour of both of these ranches from the air. That'll take an hour or so, and then you and I can sit and talk about things."

One of the most enduring lessons I learned from Ted was about legacy and what a person leaves behind on this planet after they are gone. You can live the American dream and go from rags to riches, but what do you do with the riches? He believed that saving the land, preserving it, and protecting it from development was just *one* thing a person with wealth could do to make the world a better place. "What good is wealth sitting in the bank?" Turner said once. "It's a pretty pathetic thing to do with your money."

When Ted was negotiating with Penn Oil to buy the Vermejo Ranch in New Mexico, his first big land purchase, I also got a sense of how strategic—and rewarding—it could be. I was sitting next to him as he was negotiating on the phone when it dawned on me: this is something I should be doing.

So Ted and I went up in a helicopter, and it was one of those magical days when you wish you could hit pause on the great VCR of life. Flying in that helicopter was scary as hell at times, but the view was majestic, and you could see forever. Ted's ranch is a stunning stretch of rugged beauty, roughly 875 square miles of pristine wilderness spanning southern Colorado and northern New Mexico. The topography changed like a dreamscape as the chopper sped past the Sangre de Cristo Mountains, mixed conifer forests interspersed with aspen groves, plains dotted with sagebrush and juniper, and meadows with flowers and ponds. Bison, elk, and deer roamed across fields of pale green and gold, crisscrossed by streams filled with native trout.

In addition to many land and riparian restoration projects on the ranch, Ted's Turner Endangered Species Fund has worked with the U.S. Fish and Wildlife Service to restore several species, including the endangered black-footed ferret, a critter that looks a lot like a little furry burglar with a black mask and a tipped tail.

My fondest memories are visiting Ted and Jane at the ranch in New Mexico, where we would go fly-fishing or quail hunting or simply walk the property. Given how much we both love the water and how much we both love sailing, it is disappointing that circumstances never allowed for Ted and me to take a long sea voyage together.

One day as we were walking on his ranch, Ted suddenly got the idea to go fishing in a small, stocked pond on his land. With fishing poles in hand, he finally coaxed me to climb into this eight-foot dinghy with a tiny outboard motor that he had docked at shore.

I wish I had a picture—here I was in the same boat as the man who had won the America's Cup, and he was moving us to a spot at full speed ahead—all of two knots!

Aye-aye, Captain.

I had more fun that day with Ted at the helm than I have had on the fanciest yacht in the Atlantic.

As Ted and I would hike to his favorite vistas, I could see, literally, that this was a far bigger monument to a life than a statue or a building, and a far better gift to your fellow human. And if you do well, you can own that land to protect and preserve it for future generations.

The pinkish-coral horizon of the morning had given way to a bright cobalt sky, and as the chopper descended after the fun ride, Ted and I were ready for terra firma, eager to sit down for lunch. I noticed a moving truck by the house, a not-so-gentle reminder that Ted's marriage to Jane Fonda was over. Ted had taken it hard because he loved Jane, and I was also quite fond of her. After our ride, he spent time with an old girlfriend from his sailing days, Frederique Darragon, an attractive French former polo player whom I had met before.

Ted was reveling in another one his gregarious moods, which tickled me to no end. After Frederique told us about her latest adventure of hiking across Tibet, Ted declared, "She's being modest. This woman is in impeccable shape! Lay down on the floor, Frederique, and show John—let him walk on your stomach. She's tough!" We erupted in laughter. I politely declined Ted's invitation.

We were almost ready to eat when Ted excused himself to check his fax machine. "Aaaaaaaaahhhhhh . . . ," he began, as he always begins a sentence. "There're some press releases that they're putting together for the AOL deal."

A minute later, Ted walked in with a fax in hand, a draft press release from AOL Time Warner, including details of the management roles. "Here it is . . . ," he said and read it aloud.

It started off by saying AOL chairman and CEO Steve Case would be chairman of the new AOL Time Warner. Time Warner chairman and CEO Gerald Levin would be the new CEO of the combined company. And AOL's chief operating officer, Bob Pittman, one of the founders of MTV, would be running the Turner businesses—rather than the man who had created those businesses and still wanted to run them, Ted Turner.

Turner would be one of two vice chairmen and also hold the title of senior advisor. AOL's COO Pittman would be one of two co–chief operating officers responsible for subscription services such as AOL, Time Warner Cable, HBO, and . . . Turner Broadcasting.

Ted lost the color in his face. He would no longer run the companies he founded. "John, how . . . how could they do this? I've got a contract that says, for years, I get to run the businesses I merged in."

"Well, Ted, I don't believe that you can force specific performance on that contract, not now," I said. "They'll simply pay out the salary they owe you. Then you can sue 'em . . . but what are your damages?"

"John, what do I do?" he asked.

I told him he still was a very large shareholder of Time Warner, and now he would be vice chairman of the board. "And if I were you, I would talk to their board members and at least get in a position where you can make some changes going the other way at some point in the future."

And then I cut to the hurtful truth. "Honestly, Ted, I think you've been screwed."

He was crestfallen, genuinely hurt by the betrayal of a man he'd known for decades. "How could Jerry Levin do this? He's my friend."

"Apparently not, Ted," I observed. "Apparently not." Turner protested in calls to both Levin and Case, but to no avail. And because TCI's Time Warner shares were in a blind trust, we could not influence anybody.

So I called Jerry Levin and asked him straight up, "What are you doing to our friend Ted?"

"Well, it couldn't be avoided," he said. "First, Case and Pittman insisted on this being a provision of the deal. Secondly, Ted is embarrassing us in the corporate office with his behavior." The Time Warner executive suite was not accustomed to Ted's outbursts and blunt observations in meetings—and to the press.

Ted was bitter, and rightfully so. He was learning a lesson that several leaders, like Craig McCaw and me, would learn the hard way: When you sell your company, cash out. Go away. Do not go on the board. Do not hang around. You will be trapped. You will see mistakes being made, and you will know how to fix them, and your ideas will be ignored. And you will be miserable.

When the AOL Time Warner deal was announced at the start of the new century, Steve Case called it a "historic moment in which new media has truly come of age." It was historic all right, but not for its prescience—more for its myopia, hubris, and the value lost in the merger's implosion. In the end, more than $100 billion in shareholder value was wiped out.

Many observers have called the AOL Time Warner deal the biggest mistake in the history of business, but even that superlative doesn't begin to describe the scope of value destruction, or the scale of loss, deception, and betrayal.

Yet it is easy to forget how frothy the dot-com market had become. Anyone who didn't jump in was a sucker for missing out on easy money. After all the high fives and hugging onstage by Levin and Case, the honeymoon didn't last long—and the optimism on display at the press conference evaporated like summer dew in high country.

Then, in the summer of 2000, the dot-com bubble began its slow-motion collapse. Online advertising began to slow everywhere, making it impossible for AOL to meet the financial forecasts that had supported the deal.

In May 2000, AOL agreed to pay $3.5 million in fines and to restate earnings to settle charges with the FCC that it reported profit when it was losing money in 1994, 1995, and 1996 related to how AOL booked its marketing expenses, sparking a wave of shareholder suits. Two years later, after stories in *The Washington Post*, the SEC launched a probe into similarly unconventional deals, this time dealing with inflated ad revenue. This time AOL Time Warner was forced to pay $510 million in fines and to restate its financial results, and Time Warner was reminded again of its lack of due diligence.

Books, articles, and business school studies have tackled the conundrum of how it could have happened. Was the merger doomed because the concept was ahead of its time? Was CEO Jerry Levin too desperate for a deal? Were the two companies so incompatible that the cultures couldn't gel? Or was it simply a lack of due diligence and too many unconnected dots? Was it fraud on the part of AOL?

The answer is all of the above.

Time Warner was struggling to play in the new world of the internet, and I believe that Jerry believed he was future-proofing the company. Any firm with a .com was believed to be superior to old mainstream media business models. And the merger occurred just as the dot-com bubble was about to pop.

In December 1999, the value of a share of stock in Time Warner hit its all-time high of $254 a share; ten years later it was trading at about $25 a share. In a decade, 90 percent of the value of the company had simply vanished.

The fallout was a disaster for so many investors, employees, retirees, and investors, including TCI, whose shares in the new company also tumbled. Ted's net worth collapsed with the deal—he lost roughly $7 billion. For Ted, the ripple effects were harsh. Just a few years earlier, he had made a commitment to the United Nations to donate $1 billion. Despite the stock collapsing, he still honored it, which shows you what kind of guy he is.

Top architects of the deal headed for the door, either by choice or by request. In December 2001, Levin announced he would retire and Time

Warner president Richard Parsons, a smart leader known for a steady hand, would take over his CEO role.

By July 2002, Bob Pittman, under relentless scrutiny from the board, resigned as chief operating officer. That same year, with angry investors still cashing out, AOL Time Warner reported a quarterly loss of $54 billion, the largest ever for a U.S. company at the time. But nine months later, it topped itself and announced a $98 billion annual loss.

And in January 2003, Steve Case announced his resignation as chairman of AOL Time Warner, amid rising complaints from the largest shareholders—specifically, Gordy Crawford and me. Later that year, AOL was removed from the company name, which changed back to simply Time Warner.

Time Warner chairman Dick Parsons's stalwart efforts to get the stock price back up fell short. In 2006, with the stock still stagnating, activist investor and financier Carl Icahn threatened to take the company over and break it up into pieces.

The following year, with Time Warner still looking to improve its balance sheet, Liberty Media agreed to trade its big block of Time Warner stock—about a third of our holdings in the company—in return for $1 billion in cash and ownership of the Atlanta Braves baseball team. Ted was understandably sentimental about losing the tie to his beloved Braves, but he also knew it would be a big help to Time Warner. Plus, the team would be in good hands.

Former HBO chief and longtime Time Warner executive Jeff Bewkes was named CEO in 2008 and knew exactly what to do. A vocal critic of Case, he knew what others had observed over the years—that few people had been able to build a true team of all the various divisions. The best way to maximize value was to break the company up and exact as much value as possible for shareholders.

And so the entertainment giant began to dismantle itself, starting with the spin-off and sale of Warner Music Group in 2004 to a group led by Edgar Bronfman Jr. for $2.6 billion, and four years later spinning off Time Warner Cable into a separate public company. Eventually, it would unload its venerable magazine titles, then sell its major cable channels and programming to AT&T (which then sold them to Discovery).

By 2009, Time Warner decided to spin off AOL as its own company again, ending their ill-fated relationship. It eventually got bought by Verizon in 2015 for $4.4 billion, a sliver of its worth at the time of the merger.

I remain eternally grateful to Ted Turner for showing me a way to look at the world that made it much bigger than me and how to have a real impact. After the debacle of the AOL Time Warner deal, Ted turned his interests back to his bigger goals: saving the world.

Ted was never just about business. In 1990, he founded the Turner Foundation to support land conservation, wildlife protection, renewable energy, and efforts to curb population growth.

Perhaps his most famous conservation efforts involve the American bison, which once roamed from the Great Plains to Mexico before being hunted to near extinction by the late 1800s. Today, his ranches are home to the largest commercial bison herd in North America—more than forty-five thousand animals. He brought that mission to the public with Ted's Montana Grill, serving bison sourced from his own herds.

And even before his pledge to the United Nations, he was concerned about world peace. Earlier, during the Cold War, Turner launched and televised the Goodwill Games as a gesture of international unity through sport—undaunted by more than $20 million in losses.

Today, as chairman of Turner Enterprises, he is the third-largest individual landholder in North America, with approximately 2 million acres in eleven states and Argentina.

The number two spot is held by yours truly, and most all of the 2.2 million acres, in Colorado, Florida, New Hampshire, New Mexico, Maine, and Wyoming, is designated for what I call sustainable conservation, long after any of us are here.

In 2001, just as AOL was cratering, Ted was concerned about nuclear superpowers. In January that year, he launched the Nuclear Threat Initiative, whose goal is to curb the proliferation of nuclear, chemical, and biological weapons. Ted recruited former senator Sam Nunn, a fellow Georgian and former chair of the Armed Services Committee, to run the group. Ted pledged $250 million to the NTI over five years because nuclear weapons represent "the greatest threat humanity faces" in the short term.

There are a lot of people I respect in this industry for their energy and focus and drive. And there is a short list of people whom I feel at ease around, and an even shorter list of people I feel close to. Ted said once he would give his life for mine, and his loyalty to me and to the industry warms this old engineer's heart. The feelings are mutual—I really love the guy.

The last really good meeting I had with Ted was in 2020, up in Montana at his place. And though he needs a little assistance, we were able to do some fly-fishing. I saw him again at a bison conference in Denver, and that was the last time I saw him.

He still sends me notes occasionally. I received one on CNN after AT&T announced its acquisition of Time Warner, and the DOJ was suing to block the deal. Ted wanted to know whether we could put a group together and buy CNN out from under the whole deal.

Here is what Ted wrote to me, and the longing in it for a final crowning deal is redolent:

Dear John,

My good friend and former CNN president whom you know well, Tom Johnson, and I have been conferring with a trusted group of current and former associates about who might be most fit to lead CNN into this next chapter. I concur with a recommendation and hope you will not mind me forwarding it to you for consideration.

And so that you can get it into the hands of the leaders who will ultimately be making the decision. Please do not hesitate to follow up directly with Tom Johnson. Should you be interested in discussing it further on a personal note? Nothing would please me more than getting to see you and catching up in the near future.

Best personal regards,
Ted

After we talked at length, we concluded that CNN and the Turner networks on a standalone basis might falter financially, given the many ways the industry had changed. We dropped it, but it was a reminder that my old friend still had the passion in him for one last big deal.

CHAPTER 17

MISGUIDED

In the mid-to-late 1990s, Rupert Murdoch and I embarked on a frenzy of dealmaking in pursuit of an idea that we thought would drive our products deeper into American homes.

And like so many products and people that appeared on the horizon of the telecommunications landscape in that time, this service seems almost quaint by today's standards: on-screen guides to TV programs.

These scrolling grids of cable and broadcast program listings are extraneous today, when AI algorithms have a repopulated list of suggestions when you turn on your video screen. You can point and click at a search box, type a few letters, and watch your program instantly. You can find a movie by the name of the actor. Or simply speak into your remote control.

But for a while, electronic program guides were the Next Big Thing. Several companies, including TCI, were hot on the idea, willing to spend billions of dollars on a bet that Wall Street was more than happy to back.

The thinking was that the program guide would be the gateway to everything else on a person's TV. It would help viewers navigate a sea of new cable channels and promote new programs and services. A guide with navigational features, sold to video providers around the world, might bring in huge revenue. New guides with digital video recorder (DVR) services, such as TiVo and Replay TV, were about to launch.

From the 1950s to the 1990s, the listings business was dominated by a stubby print magazine called *TV Guide*, which Rupert bought for $3 billion in 1988. It had a colossal weekly circulation of 17 million (and millions more online) at the time, with tentacles of distribution that reached into supermarket checkout lines, newsstands, and direct mail.

TV Guide's massive print circulation had dropped along with newspapers' decline as the internet grew, to 13 million in 1997 from a high of nearly 20 million in 1970. Rupert wanted to seamlessly transition the brand to an on-screen guide.

TCI owned a firm called United Video Satellite Group, headed up by my old cable partner Gene Schneider, which ran a primitive scrolling listing service called the Prevue Channel that went out to 50 million cable-TV homes. So we merged the two services and became fifty-fifty partners in June 1998, with plans to roll out a new on-screen navigational guide nationwide.

Among TV Guide Interactive's biggest rivals was a company named Gemstar International Group, run by a litigious inventor named Henry Yuen, who touted ironclad patents and a new product called VCR Plus+. Yuen had built a reputation as a ruthless defender of his patents, unafraid to sue equipment-makers or cable operators—on grounds they were not paying for his software. We knew him well—he was suing TV Guide for patent infringement.

A year after Rupert and I teamed up, we worked to convince Yuen to stop fighting us in court and do a deal together. Finally, in 1999, TV Guide Inc. agreed to merge with Gemstar in a $9.2 billion deal, giving TCI and News Corp. each 20 percent of the new company.

After the sale of TCI in 1998, I was fifty-seven years old and was building what I always had dreamed Liberty could be: a prized portfolio of the most successful tech and media and entertainment companies in the world. We had amassed stakes in Time Warner (9 percent), Barry Diller's USA Networks (21 percent), Gemstar–TV Guide International (21 percent), and of course, 8 percent of Rupert Murdoch's News Corp. These were the bulkheads of Liberty, and if any single one of them took a hit, the ship would still stay afloat.

Rupert had a vision, too—a television empire sending an unlimited stream of news, sports, and entertainment into space, then right back down to millions of subscribers across the globe. He wanted to expand the company's footprint beyond British Sky Broadcasting, and this deal with us could strengthen his hand.

Then in September 2000, we engineered another stock swap, giving Rupert a controlling 44 percent stake in Gemstar, when Gemstar's market cap was at the heady price of around $30 billion. In return for our 20 percent stake, which had roughly doubled in value, Liberty got shares in News Corp. representing about 10 percent of the company, valued at more than $6 billion at the time.

With the roughly 8 percent of News Corp.'s stock we already owned, the deal gave Liberty an 18 percent nonvoting stake, making it the company's largest shareholder outside the Murdoch family. Liberty would also receive additional shares of a new global satellite business that Rupert was planning to take public called Sky Global, the home for BSkyB in Europe, Star TV in Asia, and other satellite assets, raising our interest to roughly 6 percent at the time of the Sky Global IPO.

On a conference call with reporters on September 27, 2000, Rupert shared his enthusiasm for the deal, citing our partnership and calling me a "trusted friend and advisor"—noble praise in few words. "John is a friend, and is and always has been welcome on our board."

"We see this as kind of a triple play," I said to reporters. "We get a substantially bigger economic stake in News Corp., which we've always regarded as having a great global strategy in a consolidating media world, we get a direct investment in Sky . . . and we continue to protect our investment in Gemstar."

Rupert and I were beginning to get to know each other as people, more than business associates. I attended several News Corp. management retreats as a guest and enjoyed them. We talked about strategy and his sons and their potential roles. In 2000, when Rupert made public his diagnosis of prostate cancer and ongoing treatment, he did suggest I consider joining the News Corp. board. If not for a long list of complicating business factors and potential conflicts, I'd have done it.

Our dream of building a digital TV program guide as a gateway to all video in a home would be short-lived—and not because of "creative destruction" or the rise of the internet. Yes, the internet bubble was moments from bursting, but it wasn't the competition, or the market, or Wall Street that put an end to our dreams.

It was a swindler named Henry Yuen.

In April 2002, a financial bomb exploded inside Gemstar, and the collateral damage was painful, particularly for Rupert. The company made a public disclosure that it was restating its finances—to Wall Street, the equivalent of a bright flare above a ship in distress at night.

To our shock, Gemstar had been illegally booking more than $225 million in revenue from 2000 to 2002.

Yuen had impressed all of us with his credentials as a patent lawyer and inventor and his aggressive defense of the patents as CEO, suing any company around the cable industry to pay him for the use of technology created by Gemstar, including Pioneer Electronics, EchoStar, and the TV set-top box maker Scientific Atlanta.

And in 1999, without our knowledge, Scientific Atlanta, refusing to settle and countersuing, stopped paying Gemstar licensing fees, and Yuen nonetheless kept booking payment from SA—and others—as if the checks were coming in regularly. What hurt the company even worse was when, in late 2002, a federal court ruled that Scientific Atlanta and other cable companies hadn't infringed Gemstar's patents. Gemstar and SA would settle all of their litigation in 2005.

As quickly as it could, News Corp. fired Yuen and CFO Elsie Leung, and they were both sued by the SEC for securities fraud. As their internal charade had grown, Yuen and Leung had raked in a windfall of around $100 million in salary, bonuses, exercised stock options, and the sale of Gemstar's inflated shares. Leung agreed to pay more than $1.3 million to settle the SEC's charges.

In 2005, Yuen pled guilty to criminal charges of destroying subpoenaed documents. The following year, the SEC won its suit and fined him $22.3 million, one of the largest fines for securities fraud for an individual at the time. Yuen never paid the fines, and in 2008, the DOJ charged Yuen with obstruction of justice after he deleted computer files related to the accounting fraud at Gemstar.

Where is Henry Yuen today? No one knows, not even the U.S. government, which, as of this writing, is still looking for him and considers him a "fugitive from justice."

Rupert and I both were utterly stunned and chagrined, embarrassed that we'd been too distracted by the prize, never considering we were getting conned. We and many others had placed trust in a man who had lied, stolen, and cheated us. How do you deal with a pathological CEO? In the old West, he'd have been hung from the nearest tree. But in real life, you accept it for what it is. And you move on.

Gemstar was a high flyer on Wall Street for a while, with a stock price around $70 and a bright future as the opening gateway to the next level of TV. In the end, as the scandal was laid bare and Yuen went on the lam, the share price dropped to a couple dollars.

News Corp. was hit hard, posting $6 billion in losses related to Gemstar— including shareholder lawsuits and SEC fines—and eventually Rupert unloaded it to Macrovision in 2007 for $2.8 billion, a fraction of the $30 billion we valued it at in 2000.

What few people know is that while we had shaken hands on a deal fair and square, the terms were never papered, and in the end there was no proof that we had agreed to something more than our word, even though Gemstar already was turning a bit foul.

When Henry Yuen betrayed us, Rupert could have reneged on our deal entirely, and I would have had zero legal recourse. He could have called me up and said, "This isn't working for us anymore." But he kept his word. And that means everything to me.

Years earlier, in 1993, Rupert had set his sights on the National Football League. His reasoning was clear: he viewed sports as a "battering ram" for his global satellite company. With just a handful of stations and no sports experience, Fox, whose biggest hit was a cartoon (*The Simpsons*), faced stiff competition from the Big Three networks, which had dominated NFL broadcasts since the league first aired games on TV in 1956. CBS, NBC, and ABC each held prized NFL packages, but CBS, constrained by cost-cutting CEO Laurence Tisch, seemed unlikely to outbid anyone.

And Murdoch understood what others missed: the NFL games were more valuable to him because they offered instant credibility, a key male demographic, and a ratings boost for Fox's lineup. Listening closely to league owners, he identified a divide: legacy owners were hesitant, but new voices like Cowboys owner Jerry Jones wanted fresh revenue and innovation.

Fox's pitch wowed the NFL with promises of better camera angles, aggressive marketing, and a fresh studio approach. Then came the shocker in December 1993: a $1.6 billion bid for a four-year deal, 50 percent higher than CBS's prior agreement. "You had to have a number that made them choke," said Fox EVP Chase Carey.

The move, initially seen as risky, was transformative. The deal gave Fox the NFL, reshaped the media landscape, and became a *Harvard Business Review* case study on bold negotiation.

Two years later, in 1995, Rupert and I danced together again. Flush with the NFL package, News Corp. bought a 50 percent ownership interest in Liberty Media's Prime Sports affiliates, a collection of regional sports networks that carried local games. In the same way we had pooled our assets with Gemstar–TV Guide, we combined a dozen regional cable sports-TV channels, as well as Fox's FX, an entertainment channel reaching 39 million homes.

Four years after that, in 1999, we sold our half to Murdoch in exchange for more News Corp. nonvoting stock worth $1.4 billion, a nontaxable transaction. It was a handsome return for Liberty Media, and it was a good deal for Rupert Murdoch, too. Fox Sports has been a moneymaker for him ever since.

By the time I made my first investment in Rupert, I had known Ted for a decade, as a major shareholder, a consigliere, and sometimes, his minder.

I had been impressed with Rupert Murdoch's media forays in the UK and now in the U.S. So, sometime around the late 1980s, I called Ted and told him: "Ted, if you're smart, Rupert's just getting rolling, you should get to know him a little better."

"I don't know him," Ted said, suspicious. "And why should I cozy up to *him*?"

I pressed him, suggesting potential joint ventures in the UK or the U.S., so Ted flew over to see Rupert personally. It went poorly. A short time later, Rupert called me from London to ask me a simple question: "Hey, John, do you think there's room for another news network in the U.S.?" Instantly I thought: Ted should have found a way to get along better with this man.

Ted Turner had started CNN in 1980, building what was first derided as the Chicken Noodle Network into a fine and proud global news operation. Today CNN is a shadow of what its founder had envisioned, frankly, financially and in its all-politics focus. Rupert would start Fox News sixteen years later, and today it dominates cable news, with more viewers than CNN and MSNBC combined.

And so it wasn't surprising to me when I got that call from Rupert, asking if there was room for a new news channel. Some radio programs were offering news from the far right, but I hadn't seen anything on cable. And I assured him that, at TCI, the largest owner of cable systems in the country, we would be happy to open up space to carry a Fox News channel.

To run the network, I suggested a hot new star on the right, Rush Limbaugh, whose archconservative views were drawing 5 million listeners a week broadcast nationally on ABC stations out of New York. But Limbaugh declined, and Rupert ultimately hired Limbaugh's former executive producer, Roger Ailes, who had served as an advisor, speechwriter, and campaign manager for Presidents Ronald Reagan and George H. W. Bush. Ailes had experience running the new CNBC business channel and later a network called America's Talking.

But while Rupert's satellite TV service, fed by soccer and cricket games, was the dominant TV provider in the UK and Australia, and elsewhere, the cable-TV industry dominated TV delivery in the U.S.

Even in the five-hundred-channel world, there was still a tight squeeze to add a new channel on a crowded dial as systems transitioned to digital technology. With many cable operators already carrying two twenty-four-hour news channels (CNN and MSNBC), many gave Rupert a cold shoulder at first.

TCI agreed to launch Fox News on all our systems in exchange for an option to own 20 percent of Fox News at any point we wanted, merely by paying 20 percent of News Corp.'s original net investment in the network. We called it the "step in when you get ready" option (which we eventually did).

When Rupert and others agreed to contribute a 20 percent stake in a new network to TCI as part of a new carriage deal, they all knew the benefit to the business, and they, too, wanted the revenue synergy between distributor and content producer. Meanwhile, in carrying Fox News on our TCI systems, we also would pay Fox News the same rate as any other cable operator—no sweetheart deals.

Concerned that other cable systems were slow to take up Fox News, Rupert made another bold bet that changed the stakes. He began offering to *pay* cable systems to carry Fox News, rather than insisting they pay him, the typical model. Going forward, he offered an unprecedented onetime cash reward of $10 or more for every subscriber in a cable system if an operator agreed to carry Fox News—by far the largest fee ever offered to carry a channel in the history of the industry.

Fox News had launched on October 7, 1996, alongside CNN and MSNBC, and Rupert began a long campaign to win over cable operators. My attitude was, "Hey, folks, this is an honorable guy trying to offer a different perspective on the news. It's another voice in the marketplace. What's wrong with that?"

Several cable operators followed TCI and gladly took the $10 bounty for each subscriber they delivered, but there was one holdout—Time Warner, which held a virtual cable-system monopoly on the largest market in the U.S. and the center of the media world: New York City.

Time Warner at the time was the second-largest cable operator in the U.S., after TCI. It also owned CNN, the leader in cable news. The tempest erupted into a storm over NYC that sucked in my friend Ted Turner, the mayor of New York City, the governor of New York, and every media outlet in the metropolitan region.

At the heart of it, Rupert felt that Time Warner chairman Gerald Levin had shaken hands on a deal to carry Fox News in New York—and now Jerry was reneging on it. "He said, 'We have a deal.' Levin gave his word," Ailes told a reporter. Time Warner denied it.

The contretemps drew in Ted, then the new vice chairman of Time Warner after the sale of Turner Broadcasting, who still lived up to his nickname of the Mouth from the South. As he told the opening keynote audience of cable executives at the industry's annual Western Show in Anaheim on November 29, 1995, "I'm looking forward to squishing Rupert like a bug." Ted, never one to hide his feelings, called Murdoch a "schlockmeister" and a "scumbag" and compared him to "the late Führer."

Then Rupert's *New York Post* ran a doctored photo of Ted, who has treated mental health issues with lithium, in a straitjacket. "IS TED TURNER NUTS? YOU DECIDE," said the headline. The paper also went after Turner's wife at the time, Jane Fonda, running an infamous photo of her in Hanoi during the Vietnam War and calling her a "scatty brained Hollywood nude-nik."

Murdoch, who by this point had launched Fox News with 17 million subscribers thanks in part to TCI, was missing NYC and LA. When he charged that Time Warner was unfairly favoring its recently acquired CNN, Time Warner shot back that it also carried CNBC.

In October 1996, News Corp. filed a fraud and breach-of-contract suit against Time Warner in U.S. district court in New York seeking $1.7 billion in damages.

When two friends are fighting, loyalties are divided. And a careful sorting of feelings and facts is required. Ted and Rupert, for all their differences, were very much alike in many ways. Both men were fearless entrepreneurs who built empires from separate but similar visions of content production.

Murdoch bought 20th Century-Fox so he could produce programs for the Fox network and its broadcast stations. Turner had nearly gone bankrupt to fund the purchase of MGM/UA Entertainment Co. for its library of films to feed the WTBS superstation on cable, as well TBS, TNT, and TCM. Both had invested heavily in sports: BSkyB airs Premier games, and Turner's Atlanta Braves are regulars on WTBS.

And both men had a preternaturally high tolerance for loss, debt, and roadblocks on the road to winning.

Rupert and his team persuaded Republican governor George E. Pataki, as well as then-mayor Rudy Giuliani, to make personal pleas on News Corp.'s behalf to Gerald Levin, in part because of fifteen hundred jobs Fox News would bring to the city, but also because a legitimate political perspective was being shut out of the news media capital.

Fearful of the city's review of its lucrative, exclusive contract to offer cable TV in the richest market in the country, in 1997, Time Warner ultimately would agree to carry Fox News.

In the end, the success for Fox News seemed destined. Despite the skeptics' predictions, FNC became the most-watched cable news channel in 2002, a position it has held for more than twenty-three consecutive years.

CHAPTER 18

EYE ON SKY

The public spat between Rupert Murdoch and Jerry Levin over Time Warner's refusal to carry Fox News in New York City had sunk to mudslinging and name-calling before both sides dropped their weapons and settled in 1997. As a recipient of plenty of both in my career, I always have found that to be regrettable, and I avoid doing it. Can't we just talk it out?

The dispute was a reminder for Rupert that he lacked an important component in the U.S. that would elevate News Corp. to the status of a truly global media empire: a big distribution platform here. In Asia, he controlled the satellite broadcaster Star TV, and in the UK, he owned the satellite broadcaster BSkyB. In the U.S., he owned content but needed distribution.

Rattled by the cable oligopoly's ability to block his channels, Rupert sought to build or buy an American satellite-TV company that could replicate his success abroad. That vision put him on an epic pursuit that ignited a burst of big deals, public fights, name-calling, lawsuits, big losses, and, ultimately, two separate interventions by the Department of Justice.

For me, it would strain the loyalties I held for cable operators I had known for decades and test a key friendship. I get dizzy thinking about it even now.

Perhaps more than anything else, though, the satellite saga I am about to tell showed me the true essence of Rupert Murdoch and why this man succeeds. He refuses to surrender. He is determined, fearless, and endlessly inventive, willing to change course instantly and repeatedly to absorb the next setback.

First, a little background information. Up until the 1980s, the most prevalent satellite dishes in the U.S. were big ten-foot-wide C-band dishes that cost each household thousands of dollars. The oversized dishes could pull down TV signals entirely free of charge. Typically they were used in rural areas, out of reach of cable or broadcast TV signals.

By the 1990s, new high-powered direct broadcast satellite (DBS) rivals were streaming TV signals to dishes that had shrunk to the size of a pizza pan, offering hundreds of channels. For the first time in a decade, cable operators, accustomed to comfortable local monopolies, faced the threat of new competition.

To stave off these satellite rivals, TCI and other U.S. cable operators were racing to announce the rollout of our own version of digital TV (read: more channels). We had been achieving advances on digital compression—the ability to carry more channels in the same old bandwidth—with Cable-Labs, our industry consortium. And instantly the media turned my casual answer into a new industry meme: Five Hundred Channels.

The problem was that the new wave of satellite rivals had the bandwidth to offer hundreds of channels right away. Cable needed a stopgap, and a year earlier the big operators had formed their own satellite service, PrimeStar. The owners included my outfit, TCI, and Time Warner Cable, Comcast, Cox, US West/MediaOne, and General Electric.

PrimeStar started off in 1990 as "mid-power" service to dishes that were smaller, around three feet wide, and by April 1997 we had announced 65 new networks leveraging digital compression, bringing the total to 160. By June 1997 PrimeStar had signed up 1.8 million subscribers in rural areas.

Duly impressed, Rupert Murdoch asked in early 1997 about having News Corp. become a partner and investor in PrimeStar.

Personally, I liked this idea a lot. By this time I had learned it was better to ally with him than to do battle against him. In fact, I was happy to step back and let Rupert take a controlling stake in PrimeStar and run it himself. This asset was a lot more important to *his* strategy than it was to TCI and its cable operator partners.

When I pitched a version of that to Rupert, he tentatively agreed, and we even drew up some papers to pursue it. Then Jerry Levin and Time

Warner got in our way—again. Still stung by their clash over carriage of Fox News in New York, Levin and Ted Turner balked at letting Murdoch take a controlling position in PrimeStar. They didn't want him at the cable table, and PrimeStar's ownership structure gave Time Warner veto power, which they exercised.

This was a bad mistake, and I knew repercussions inevitably would follow. By this time I had put in three decades in business, and still it surprised me how the personal ambitions and grudges of powerful people can shape the multibillion-dollar decisions they make for their shareholders.

Business is about relationships, and those relationships can get extremely personal. Trust is the foundation of all business, and it is difficult to earn and easy to lose. The people running Time Warner and News Corp. no longer trusted each other, if ever they had, and now that lapse had derailed a great would-be alliance.

I was so disappointed in the shortsighted decision that I would have bolted right then and had TCI break off from the PrimeStar partnership to pursue a satellite partner, but our agreement prevented it. The pact kept the cable interests aligned, despite that I disagreed with my partners and silently stewed.

As infinite as outer space is, the slots available for premiere real estate are limited in the earth's orbit. At the highest orbit of about 22,300 miles, only a few "parking spaces" had the ability to let a single, powerful satellite beam TV signals to every home in the continental U.S.

In January 1996, the FCC held a multitiered auction for the few remaining slots. In the running were TCI, the number two long-distance carrier MCI, and Charlie Ergen's EchoStar. They were hoping to win the auction and take on DirecTV, which had signed up a million subscribers in eighteen months.

MCI won the bid with a rich offer of $683 million. Its partner in the purchase? Rupert Murdoch's News Corp. I knew we would be seeing him again. Together, MCI and News Corp. planned to provide 150 channels of TV programs, music, games, data services, and software delivery.

But while MCI and Rupert had won the coveted parking spaces in the sky, they lacked the satellites to occupy their newly acquired property, and building these "birds" can take a couple of years. Meanwhile, my TCI owned actual satellites we wanted to launch—but we lacked the orbital slots that MCI and Rupert had just bought.

At the time, at TCI we were still hell-bent on becoming a high-powered player in satellite TV, our cable origins notwithstanding. So we tried to strike a deal to sell our idle satellites to Telesat Canada, Inc., the biggest Canadian satellite broadcaster, which owned orbital slots that could let a satellite cover all of North America.

We planned to then lease back that satellite capacity for our PrimeStar service, and our having a partner in Canada was an added plus: the FCC at the time was trying to expand U.S. satellite service to foreign firms to encourage reciprocal action.

The plan would have put PrimeStar in instant, direct competition with the venture planned by MCI and News Corp., so Rupert Murdoch placed a gentlemanly call to me and told me straight-out: "John, I guess you know we'll be filing to block your proposed deal with Telesat. It's in our business interest to get these high-power satellites up first."

I had assumed as much, and I thanked him for the call.

MCI then filed a petition with U.S. regulators, urging them to reject our plan because we would be using a Canadian provider while Canada blocked American satellite broadcasts into its own borders. The arrangement was blocked by regulators. Fair enough.

Rupert christened the new MCI–News Corp. venture American Sky Broadcasting, the final link in his global dish-TV strategy after BSkyB in the UK, Star in Asia, and a service in Latin America. Still, he lacked a bird aloft and ready to beam.

Making matters worse for cable stocks, phone giant AT&T had just announced a $137.5 million deal for a 2.5 percent stake in market leader DirecTV, and agreed to market the new TV service to its 90 million phone customers. Now the biggest gun had more ammunition.

This had me feeling uneasy. Rupert had just joined MCI to set up a potent competitor to cable, yet News Corp. and TCI were intertwined in serious ways. We jointly owned regional sports channels, the FX cable channel, and a direct-broadcast system in Latin America. And we carried Murdoch's Fox broadcasting network and the fledgling Fox News Channel, not to mention the Family Channel, which Liberty was discussing selling to News Corp.

I had seen the formidable threat of Rupert's strategies on the battlefield, and how often competitors underestimated how he could create an assault from nowhere, seemingly with nothing.

Which is precisely what Rupert did next. Still searching for satellite carriage, he and his MCI partners reached out to a professional gambler. Literally.

They turned to EchoStar, founded by a charming Southern gentleman who looked ten years younger than his age. Charlie cultivated the role of a simple Tennessee country boy who had made good. He was a serious poker player, just as my old partner Bob Magness had been. Industry lore had it that Charlie was banned from certain Las Vegas casinos for counting cards. In 1996, his EchoStar had rolled out a new small-dish service called Dish Network.

Unlike DirecTV and now ASkyB, Charlie didn't own a full complement of frequencies at the 119-degree CONUS orbital slot. Still, he had enough channel capacity to do real harm, like a small blade in a knife fight. Dish offered a package of forty of the most popular cable channels, including MTV, USA, CNN, and the Disney Channel, for $20 a month on a tiny dish, heavily undercutting DirecTV. Charlie also was hammering the cable industry in press releases and ads for his new service.

On February 24, 1997, on a soundstage on the 20th Century Fox lot in Los Angeles, surrounded by investors and analysts, Rupert announced that News Corp. and MCI were launching a new satellite service fifty-fifty with EchoStar, to be known as ASkyB. He had found his bird in the sky.

News Corp. and MCI would contribute orbital slots and satellite assets valued at more than $1 billion. EchoStar, number two only to DirecTV in the booming new mini-dish market, would contribute its two existing satellites and nearly half a million subscribers. Unlike rivals, Sky would offer local TV channels in its digital lineup, creating a genuine threat to cable.

ASkyB president Preston Padden, who would run the venture, stepped up to the mic and started bad-mouthing the cable industry. When ASkyB was offered, he said, cable operators would be "calling Dr. Kervorkian," a reference to the infamous doctor who assisted suicides.

Satellite companies, in the short term, could win the race to offer digital TV nationwide by simply flipping a switch to offer digital TV service to anyone, anywhere, immediately. Cable companies, by contrast, were spending millions of dollars on the ground to lay fiber and coax to every home.

The new ASkyB service could beat the cable cowboys to market with five hundred channels. In just six years, Padden declared, ASkyB expected to generate cash flow approaching $1 billion a year. Details of the plan startled investors and enraged cable operators—including me. Investors tossed cable stocks like bad milk the following day, erasing more than $1 billion in market value for the cable-TV industry.

Despite my earlier proclamations about patience, I was pissed.

In a later call with Rupert, I told him bluntly, "We have a real problem." We were in the middle of signing a new agreement with FX. I strongly suggested that if he took this too far, we should reconsider our joint ownership in the sports outlets, FX, and more.

Rupert promised to tone down the hyperbole, though his effort on this front was somewhat restrained. A few months later, Rupert and Charlie Ergen ran a full-page ad in *The Washington Post* laying out their succinct lobbying message for regulators in a dozen words in large, bold black letters: "SKY. Finally—the Cable Competition the Telecom Bill Was Designed to Create."

Their timing was ideal. Congress had just passed the Telecommunications Act of 1996, which dramatically reshaped the nation's telecom boundaries in pursuit of a competitive free-for-all. The new law allowed, for the first time, true competition in both local and long-distance phone service, and it freed the Baby Bells to get into video and encouraged cable companies to invade the local-phone monopoly.

That spring, Murdoch made a persuasive plea before the Senate Commerce Committee for changes in copyright rules that were hampering his new Sky venture. With a far lower price and fees and local broadcast station carriage, he said Sky was the answer to Congress's concerns over competition in the U.S. cable industry, which reached 65 million homes.

Murdoch told the senators, "Sky is willing to risk a $3 billion capital investment to bring consumers a better choice now. . . . If you give us the legal authority to compete, the rest is up to us."

At the cable industry's annual NCTA convention just days after the Sky announcement, the cable faithful joked about Murdoch's supposed "Death Star," but in truth it had potential to be just that, and, privately, some operators I spoke with were spooked.

At the confab, Ted Turner gave a speech and tried to rally everyone, vowing, "we're going to make it as tough [for Murdoch] as we possibly can. . . . Kind of like the Russian Army did with the German Army . . . either Murdoch is going to go hungry or we are."

Amid all the drama, Ted could still make me laugh, whether it was his off-color jokes or in serious moments like this, his now familiar word-for-word recitation of "Horatius at the Bridge," about the Roman army officer, alone against an army of invaders. Around this time, he was always ready to belt out in a crescendo the final lines of the stanza . . .

In yon strait path a thousand
May well be stopped by three:
Now who will stand on either hand,
And keep the bridge with me?

Back in Britain, Murdoch had been able to mount a serious challenge to a complacent broadcast industry by introducing satellite TV, locking up exclusive rights to movies and live sporting events, and quickly signing up millions of subscribers.

The U.S. cable operators were a far more antagonistic foe, especially when a new tech threat united them against it. They redoubled efforts to upgrade to digitally compressed TV signals, and many operators refused even to meet with News Corp. to discuss carriage for Fox News and other Rupert-owned networks.

If Rupert wanted war, the cable industry would bring it to his doorstep.

The cable opposition added to the woes of the new Sky satellite venture of News Corp. and EchoStar. U.S. cable systems began selling telephone and internet access in packages that the satellite services were unable to match. Plus, Sky would be late getting to market, and by some estimates it would have to sign up 5 million subscribers rapidly just to hit break-even.

In addition, the new marriage between News Corp. and EchoStar was having a rocky honeymoon. As Sky president Preston Padden and EchoStar's Charlie Ergen planned the launch of Sky for March 1997, clashes between Ergen and News Corp. management erupted fast, and worse, the press was writing about it.

Chemistry and culture are key ingredients in any merger, and this becomes apparent very early on—as Rupert and Charlie were discovering. The moguls couldn't get along or agree on control, and this reached a crescendo over a seemingly minor issue.

Rupert Murdoch had sent a letter to Charlie Ergen insisting their new Sky venture had to use News Corp.'s security system. Charlie disagreed.

Way too often in business, especially when expansive egos and enormous companies are involved, we go to war in court as a first resort when both sides would fare better if they were to sit down together and seek a truce.

In May 1997, EchoStar filed a $5 billion breach-of-contract suit in federal court against News Corp., which, of course, countersued. The press had a field day with the feuding media barons.

So did we at PrimeStar. With Rupert's alliance with EchoStar now shorn in court, he still needed satellite access—and we had it to offer. We rekindled our meetings with Rupert, hoping we could find a way to bring News Corp. on board—and the Sky venture's satellite parking slots up in the sky.

The specter of Rupert's thrashing cable with new tiny satellite dishes had scared the hell out of the cable guys, and the upside was that their fear helped me get them in alignment with the idea of letting him join us at PrimeStar. *Except* Time Warner still refused to bend. The lawsuit that Rupert had filed against Time Warner in NYC, and the name-calling that followed, had so angered Ted Turner that he had vowed never to forgive Murdoch.

We argued forcefully, again, that allowing Rupert into the tent would solve more problems than it created. With the full satellite slots, $1.1 billion in cash, and TCI's satellites, PrimeStar could become a real player.

Rupert, determined to heal his relations with the cable industry, offered to drop the lawsuit against Time Warner and commit the satellite slots that News Corp. and MCI owned, if PrimeStar would guarantee carriage of News Corp.'s cable networks.

The combative Australian's message was clear to cable operators: I am no longer your enemy. I am your friend.

Time Warner's Levin relented, reluctantly, to let Rupert's service join PrimeStar, while dictating that Murdoch's stake had to be nonvoting, and Time Warner wanted to share operational control of PrimeStar. So in June 1997, PrimeStar admitted Murdoch into the partnership. We rolled it up into a publicly traded company, with News Corp. holding a 30 percent nonvoting stake and 70 percent in the hands of the original cable partners.

In that window of detente, Liberty Media sold a prized asset to News Corp.—its controlling stake in International Family Entertainment, which owned the Family Channel, a popular cable network owned by Pat Robertson, who hosted *The 700 Club*—for $1.7 billion.

And then, in May 1998, Rupert's quest for nationwide satellite carriage received another setback—this time from the government. Almost a year after PrimeStar agreed to let News Corp. join it as a partner, the Justice Department filed a civil antitrust suit against it.

The prosecutor in the case was the fearsome Joel Klein, the DOJ's assistant attorney general for the antitrust division, the same man who simultaneously had just filed the government case that tried to break up Microsoft. Klein publicly declared, rather melodramatically, "Unless this acquisition is blocked, consumers will be denied competition—lower prices, more innovation, and better services and quality."

Klein's statement would turn out to be utterly wrong—if anything, the interference by the Department of Justice would result in less competition in the new satellite industry, rather than more. This happens often in government's regulation of business: noble, self-important sound bites followed by questionable assumptions and feckless, poorly executed policies.

In October 1998, PrimeStar abandoned the deal with News Corp. and MCI, and Klein called it the "right result and a big win for consumers." It wasn't.

The blowup of the deal had left both Rupert and PrimeStar hurting. When the DOJ stopped that deal and no viable partners were left, Rupert faced a delay of several years and the layout of billions of dollars to build his own satellites.

So, Rupert zigzagged yet again. News Corp., with its options waning, sold the coveted orbital slots it had bought for $683 million with partner MCI back in January 1996, and related assets, to the guy whom Rupert first had sought as a satellite partner: Charlie Ergen at EchoStar and Dish Network, for $1.25 billion.

This helped Charlie strengthen his network to better challenge the leader, DirecTV, but the deal also meant that a new entry in this space race was unlikely—future competition had just been reduced. Thanks for your input, Department of Justice.

As for PrimeStar, without Rupert's Sky as a partner, there was no way it could compete with smaller dishes, more channels, and lower prices while lacking the right slot up in orbit for a new, high-power satellite that it had still parked on the ground.

A few months after News Corp. sold its orbital slots to EchoStar, Prime-Star sold its satellites to the other dominant competitor, DirecTV, for $1.8 billion in cash and stock, just two years after buying the birds from News Corp.

With the PrimeStar deal, and after previously buying its longtime partner, United States Satellite Broadcasting, DirecTV rose to become the nation's third-largest pay television company overall, trailing cable providers Time Warner and TCI.

The weird thing was, even at this point, Rupert Murdoch was still doggedly searching for a way to get the nationwide distribution that a bird in the sky would offer Fox News and a growing portfolio of other channels. This man never gives up. Never.

Next, Rupert, having just sold Sky's space-borne parking slots to number two mini-dish service EchoStar, turned his attention to the only other player in space: number one service DirecTV. Again, his timing seemed perfect. DirecTV was owned by General Motors, and GM was looking to shed distractions, focus on its core car business, and find new ways to finance a pension fund shortfall.

But before Rupert could bid for DirecTV, EchoStar's Charlie Ergen stepped in and told GM he was interested in buying it. In October 2001 EchoStar made a $26 billion offer to buy DirecTV's parent division inside GM, Hughes Electronics. Some $5.5 billion of the offer was in cash, and Charlie himself personally guaranteed one-half of that sum.

Now, that is moxie. In the hundreds of deals I have done, I am unsure I ever would have taken such a big financial risk that was so direct, unhedged, and entirely personal. I never have.

By the end of October 2001, News Corp. dropped out of the bidding for DirecTV—and months later, the government intervened again, I began to truly believe, just to see how much it could mess things up. This time, the Department of Justice and the FCC moved to block EchoStar from buying its bigger rival, DirecTV.

This forced EchoStar and Charlie Ergen to pay a $600 million cash breakup fee to Hughes Electronics, under the terms of their agreement. And only because government lawyers and regulators decided they knew better.

This gave Rupert another opening, yet again. With 11 million subscribers, DirecTV could still offer him the entry into the U.S. pay television market that he had sought so relentlessly.

In December 2003, News Corp. bought a 35 percent stake in Hughes Electronics and its DirecTV satellite operation from General Motors for $6.6 billion—stunningly, some $20 billion *less* than EchoStar had bid for the same business just two years earlier.

News Corp. brought back Chase Carey, who had resigned as co–chief operating officer in January 2002, to be president and CEO of Hughes. Murdoch became chairman.

When Charlie Ergen went after the business in 2001, Murdoch had been ready to bid $20 billion. The alarming decline in DirecTV's market value in just a few years owed more to market factors than government interference.

In those few years, the newfangled World Wide Web was gaining viewers exponentially. Cable's terrestrial systems were catching up in laying the latest, fully digital, fiber-optic-backed network lines, able to provide interactive, high-speed internet access. The birds up in space couldn't match that ability; they were designed for transmitting TV signals one way down to receivers on earth.

Still, Rupert's News Corp. was in the television business rather than the internet-access business, and DirecTV offered him much-needed distribution for his networks—and a shortcut around the cable operators who had so adamantly opposed doing one whit of business with him.

There was one problem: my company, Liberty Media, was interested in buying DirecTV, too. By this point, Liberty no longer was affiliated with TCI, and it owned stakes in cable channels but no cable systems.

Why buy this once-beautiful but now fading star in the sky? Even a declining business offers good intrinsic value if you can acquire it on the cheap on tax-advantaged terms. Plus, people always overestimate how soon the Next Big Thing will arrive and take hold. And we also underestimate how long the old incumbent technology will hold on.

You can earn a nice return by investing in assets that fall somewhere in that gap, and DirecTV was one of them. So, once again, I would sit, looking for an opportunity, on the opposite side of the table from the wily Aussie who had founded Fox News.

When I put in that call to Rupert Murdoch, I avoided bluntness and took a subtle approach: "Geez, Rupert, we thought DirecTV would fit Liberty." Subtext: Is there any way we can own this together? I wanted to buy directly an ownership stake in DirecTV, or perhaps indirectly, by buying more shares of News Corp.

In the end, I stepped aside and took a lesser role in the deal, clearing the path for Rupert to buy DirecTV from GM and add that to his Sky satellite holdings across Asia, the UK, and Europe. Liberty participated in Rupert's acquisition, in exchange for warrants to own $500 million in News Corp. stock.

Rupert had tried to partner with every player on the board to see his vision through. He had sold everything, then bought it all back. First he had tried to partner with the cable industry in PrimeStar and was black-balled. Then he allied with MCI and turned to EchoStar, saw that blow up, and went back to PrimeStar. Justice blocked that, so Rupert tried to buy DirecTV but got bested by EchoStar, only to snag DirecTV two years later at a fraction of the old price.

The one constant through it all was Rupert Murdoch himself. The man is relentless.

CHAPTER 19

WEAK RECEPTION

I had navigated TCI through some rough waters, but nothing would prepare me for the tempest that followed the aborted Bell Atlantic deal in February 1994. After all the planning and effort, after telling the market we needed a partner to build the interactive future, now TCI and Liberty were left to complete this mission on our own.

By that July, as we were settling in for another stay in Maine, *Wired* magazine ran a cover illustration depicting me as an Infobahn Warrior, clad in black leather biker gear and brandishing a knife and gun. But in truth, I was more concerned I would look like roadkill on the Information Superhighway.

TCI had moved quickly to reassure the markets after we called off the deal, then laid out a meticulous plan to get TCI back on track. For the ensuing two years, we would start putting the right pieces in place, and I started to feel like we were going to be okay. Shedding my fears of failure, I turned my focus elsewhere. Then, in the summer of 1996, reality came crashing down on TCI as suddenly and severely as any storm on the Atlantic.

The cascade of events began with a stomachache. In the summer of 1996, on a trip to visit TCI International's cable operations in Argentina, I caught some sort of stomach bug, and on the flight home I started to feel woozy and lightheaded. By the time the plane landed in Denver, I had flu-like symptoms that damn near knocked me out.

But I could not really rest at home in Denver, as Leslie and I were due in Maine for a date we had both been keenly anticipating for weeks. We were about to launch the *Liberty*, a new boat we had painstakingly designed together, and this had to coincide with the high tides on the East Coast.

I love the Rockies, but Maine has a spell on me. The smell of the sea and evergreens is fragrant, and in the stillness there my thoughts untangle themselves, and I see things I couldn't see before.

Leslie and I fell in love with the rocky coast of Maine not from the road but from a boat, after anchoring in Boothbay Harbor one night on our anniversary. In the 1980s when TCI was busting at the seams, we spent almost the entire summer there, and it was like being a teenage kid back in Milford, driving the back roads in my sports car, puttering around the bay in a boat, and back at the house in time for dinner. It was freedom. We bought a house on a hill with a view of the water.

So Leslie and her brother laid me down in the back of our RV, a big land cruiser that we had taken many times across the country because of Leslie's aversion to flying, and I tried to close my eyes. I have always loved the open road, listening to classic books on tape, or simply talking with Leslie about nothing in particular, cruising through tiny towns, and counting the crop rows in passing fields. But on this trip, I saw a lot of the RV ceiling.

For me, the boat we were launching was a symbol of the freedom of my youth, spending summer days on Long Island Sound, racing with my teenage buddies, and walking with Leslie on the beach. It also was a gift of time to Leslie. As a practical matter, it was a replacement for the *Ragtime*, the sixty-five-foot-long antique 1928 commuter vessel, which we had under restoration yet again.

For this new motorboat, the *Liberty*, I set the performance criteria, such as speed and power, and Leslie worked on the design and aesthetics. *Liberty* was an eighty-foot-long, black-and-crimson power boat, built by Hodgdon Yachts, a longtime wooden boatbuilder in Maine. Modeled after the commuter yachts of the 1920s, the hull was made of cedar, fir, and mahogany, and the teak deck had a shine so deep you could see your reflection. Though she barely made a wake idling through the harbor, when you punched the two big MAN diesel engines, *Liberty* could jump to 30 mph—blazing for a boat this big—with a range of nine hundred miles. From time to time, even a reformed Calvinist can enjoy an indulgence. This was a reward for decades of helming TCI.

Just when I thought I could hit pause for a moment, everything moved into fast-forward. Wall Street started to question TCI's credibility on delivering new digital boxes, worried that we were failing to grow new revenue fast enough. Yet regulators in D.C. were questioning our latest acquisitions, concerned we were growing too much.

After the Bell Atlantic deal, everyone seemed to be asking, "What now?" I tried to simplify the story by splitting the company into four separate businesses: (1) the core cable-TV business, (2) programming investments under Liberty Media, (3) technology ventures including new internet investments, and (4) international cable and programming.

As part of the plan for Liberty—the company, not the boat—TCI had created a new class of tracking stock, a public stock distributed to TCI shareholders that tracked the performance of Liberty's earnings inside TCI.

Scale was still our goal, but government stood in the way. At the time, TCI was hounded with questions from the Justice Department and the Federal Trade Commission on several big deals, over concerns TCI exerted too much influence on the TV industry.

In one, I had negotiated a deal for TCI to buy TeleCable Corp. for $1.4 billion, a fair price and healthy payoff for another cable pioneer, Frank Batten, who had built the eighteenth-largest cable operator at the time, with 750,000 subscribers in fifteen (mostly southern) states.

We were also in a trade of cable systems with Sumner Redstone's Viacom and with another cable operator called Multimedia. These swaps were a part of our clustering strategy of keeping systems contiguous to save money. But the DOJ and the FTC were bothered by TCI's reach, around 26 percent of the 60 million cable-TV households in the U.S. in 1994.

And the DOJ and the FTC also were interested in the still-alive proposed $1.4 billion joint venture with Comcast Corp. to buy QVC, despite the fact that Comcast would be the controlling partner with 57 percent. TCI's 70 percent voting stake in QVC rival Home Shopping Network had triggered the inquiry, but we were competing against the entire retail industry!

All of this had the undesired effect of preoccupying TCI's top executives

(Courtesy Hopkins School)

At Hopkins School, a prestigious prep school in New Haven, Connecticut, that I attended by work scholarship, I played team sports, but I preferred the solitary pursuits of chess and fencing as a student. (Hopkins School Varsity Fencing Team, 1959. I'm seated in the first row, third from right.) (Courtesy Hopkins School)

(Courtesy of John Malone)   (Courtesy of John Malone)

My marriage with Leslie, my bride of sixty-two years, is my longest lasting—and most rewarding—partnership. She is a horse-lover, an advice-giver, and the anchor in our family, as attractive to me as the day I met her on our local beach as teenagers. (Courtesy of John Malone)

etsy and Bob Magness launched their
rst "community antenna" TV service
1956 in Memphis, Texas. In the early
ays, Bob climbed poles and strung wire,
hile Betsy tallied new customers and
alanced the books at the kitchen table.
Courtesy of Barco Library, The Cable
enter)

I joined Tele-Communications Inc. (TCI) in Denver on April Fools' Day in 1973, spurning a
top cable job on the East Coast in New York City. Bob Magness, a part-time cattle rancher up to
his Stetson in debt, believed in me, and we built TCI into the largest cable operator in the U.S.

TCI Chairman Bob Magness (left), picked a circle of advisors that would stay together for nearly three decades: Donne Fisher (second from left) as treasurer helped us stave off bankruptcy. JC Sparkman (third from left) as COO delivered quarterly numbers you could literally bank on. I was the new kid, a first-time CEO, and younger than the cable cowboys around me—yet still treated like one of them. (Courtesy of Barco Library, The Cable Center)

TCI strung wire reaching into one of every four cable-TV homes, offering new channels such as HBO, MTV, and CNN for the first time. Installers and repair crews were called "pole-climbers"; out West, we were called "cable cowboys." (Courtesy of Barco Library, The Cable Center)

Liberty Media President Peter Barton, who was instrumental in winning early cable-TV franchises for TCI, and I present Harold Washington, the mayor of Chicago, with a check for nearly two million dollars in franchise fees for the right to wire the city in 1985. (Courtesy of Barco Library, The Cable Center)

Bob Magness and I led a growing team at TCI in the 1980s, including SVP of Finance Barney Schotters (seated) and John Sie (standing), founding CEO of Starz and head of TCI's strategic planning, technology, and government relations. (Courtesy Cable Center, Barco Library)

Our investment in Black Entertainment Television was a bet on founder Robert Johnson (right) and his vision of a network for an overlooked audience. His success, buoyed by growing subscribers, and cheered on by friends like HBO SVP Don Anderson (left) led to the eventual sale of BET to Sumner Redstone's Viacom in 2000 for $3 billion. (Courtesy of Barco Library, The Cable Center)

Ted Turner is a visionary entrepreneur, dedicated humanitarian, accomplished sailor, and one of my dearest friends. Few people have changed my thinking about the world more than Ted, who gave $1 billion to the United Nations, started the Goodwill Games, and bought land—lots of it—for conservation efforts, which convinced me of the value of open spaces. (Courtesy of Barco Library, The Cable Center)

or the first time after Betsy died, the light ame back into Bob Magness's eyes when e met Sharon Costello. She shared his ove of Arabian horses, which is how they net, and they married in 1989. (Courtesy f Barco Library, The Cable Center)

Paul Gould (right), a managing partner at Allen & Company, has been more of a friend than a trusted advisor and dealmaker over the years, and the same was true for Peter Barton (left), former CEO of Liberty. Together they were trusty shipmates on voyages up and down the East Coast as we plotted Liberty Media's future. (Courtesy of John Malone)

Walter Cronkite (center, with wife Betsy) helped advise Discovery's founder, John Hendricks (far right, with wife Maureen) in the early days, and became a friend in the process. In September 1998, Walter and I talked about the "The State of Television News" in a discussion moderated by journalist Ken Auletta (far left), ruminating on the impact of twenty-four-hour TV news cycles and media owners like Rupert Murdoch and Ted Turner. (Courtesy of Barco Library, The Cable Center)

Depending on the deal, News Corp. and Fox News founder Rupert Murdoch has been either a competitor or a partner. Over the years, we've traded satellite companies, sports teams, cable networks, stocks, and cash. Today I call him a friend. (Courtesy of Barco Library, The Cable Center)

I loved traveling with CableLabs CEO Dick Green (pictured beside me) to conventions like this one and on technology trips abroad. Funny and smart, he was the ideal CEO of the industry consortium responsible for the greatest advances in cable technology: digital compression, DOCSIS, cable modems, VoIP, 5G, and more. (Courtesy of Barco Library, The Cable Center)

The chairmen of the nation's biggest cable and computer companies interfaced last week during a multimedia conference in San Jose that logged in 10,000 attendees: John Sculley, Apple Computer; John Malone, TCI; Barry Diller, QVC, and Bill Gates, Microsoft.

Malone calls cable engine of multimedia

Says TCI has plans for converter with built-in computer; Microsoft's Gates says his company wants to provide software for next-generation box

In the 1990s, when we set our sights on high-speed cable modems, Silicon Valley was scrambling to get a piece of the action. At the front of the line was Microsoft's Bill Gates and Apple's John Sculley, as well as content creators such as Barry Diller. (*Broadcasting & Cable*, April 5, 1993. Special Collections, University of Maryland)

I have been called to testify before Congress twice, and both times I felt like a piñata at a kid's birthday party, with everyone taking a swing. In 1989, I was grilled over the industry's cable-TV rate increases by a young Senator Al Gore. In 1993, as TCI prepared to merge with Bell Atlantic, I was questioned about media consolidation. (Courtesy of C-SPAN)

Bell Atlantic CEO Ray Smith was different than most "Bellheads" and wanted to transform his regional phone company. As cable and phone companies were hooking up to deliver voice, video, and internet, TCI/Liberty and Bell Atlantic agreed to merge. Shaking hands on October 13, 1993, we promised to build the Information Superhighway. Less than year later, after rate cuts ordered by the 1992 Cable Act, we called the deal off. (MRB/AFP via Getty Images)

Paramount Chairman Martin Davis (left) and Viacom Chairman Sumner Redstone (right) announce the merger of their companies in September 1993, sparking a fierce bidding war with Barry Diller's QVC. After filing a federal lawsuit against TCI to block our support of QVC, Sumner prevailed with a higher bid, expanding Viacom's empire to include Paramount Pictures, Simon & Schuster, and Madison Square Garden assets. (HAI DO/AFP via Getty Images)

After TCI started to run off track in 1996, I called Leo Hindery in to help fix it. A professional race car driver on weekends, Leo kept his foot to the accelerator as president of TCI. Within a year of his arrival, cash flow was up, Wall Street was happy, and he had found a buyer willing to pay a premium. (Photo by Adam Berry/Bloomberg via Getty Images)

When TCI Chairman Bob Magness died, I lost a friend and mentor. More than 1,000 mourners packed the church in Denver at his funeral on November 21, 1996. Among the pallbearers were Bob's sons, his grandson, Ted Turner, Larry Romrell, and me. (*Denver Post* via Getty Images)

When we sold TCI to AT&T for $48 billion on June 24, 1998, I truly believed Michael Armstrong (left), chairman and CEO of AT&T, could lead us to the Promised Land: delivering national high-speed broadband service. The merger was not meant to be—luckily, I had a lifeboat called Liberty Media. (Photo by Porter Gifford/Liaison via Getty Images)

Our initial $530 million loan to the newly merged SiriusXM in 2009 was a lifeline for CEO Mel Karmazin, who was close to bankruptcy. The loan, convertible to shares, would give Liberty its largest return on investment ever. Despite my desire for him to stay, Mel left soon after Liberty Media took over the company. (Photo by Evan Agostini/ImageDirect via Getty Images)

After I sold TCI to AT&T, we started all over again overseas with Liberty Global. CEO Mike Fries (seated, left across from me) transformed Liberty Global into one of the world's largest international broadband and television companies across Europe and Latin America. Here the entire Liberty Global board considers an issue after a meeting in Berlin. (Courtesy of Liberty Global)

In March 2013, after a conversation with LionTree investment banker Aryeh Bourkoff, (standing, left), I jumped back into the U.S. cable industry, buying a 27 percent stake in Charter Communications for $2.6 billion, based largely on the skills of CEO Tom Rutledge (standing, right), one of the best operators in the business. With Barry Diller, (sitting) they were among attendees at an event honoring me. (Photograph © Patrick McMullan)

I have known David Zaslav, the CEO of Warner Bros. Discovery, since his days at NBC, where he helped launch CNBC and MSNBC more than thirty years ago. When he took over Discovery in 2006, he transformed a domestic cable channel into a media powerhouse, expanding globally and launching new channels, such as the Oprah Winfrey Network, culminating in the 2022 merger with WarnerMedia. (Courtesy of Allen & Co.)

Former Formula One CEO Chase Carey (right), Liberty Media CEO Greg Maffei (middle) and I at an F1 race in Austin, Texas. When Greg first raised buying F1, I knew we needed a trusted CEO with intuition, vision, and drive, and we got that in Chase, who took Formula One into overdrive. (Photo by Mark Sutton/Sutton Images via Getty Images)

Open spaces are sacred—and vanishing. The Malone Family Land Preservation Foundation looks for places that need saving. When rampant development threatened to close off the last open space between Denver and Colorado Springs, Leslie and I personally worked with partners and put up $78 million to help preserve 21,000 acres —and a pristine view of the Rockies. (Photo by Helen H. Richardson/*The Denver Post* via Getty Images)

Neither of my children wanted to take over my role at TCI, so I never longed to have a family dynasty. After the intense work hours in the early days of TCI, I just wanted a connected family. Today, my son, Evan, runs his own business and sits on the Liberty Media board. (Photograph © Patrick McMullan)

Liberty Media acquired the Atlanta Braves in 2007 and improved the team's financial health through investments in the ballpark and surrounding area. Under the management of Braves Chairman Terry McGuirk, the team has thrived. Though it was spun off into its own company in 2023, Terry and I still get together for a game and to tell our favorite Ted stories. (Courtesy of John Malone)

with filling document requests from government lawyers instead of focusing on the business. A federal investigator estimated that the FTC had collected around nine hundred boxes of TCI records, with each box holding over two thousand pages, in response to three inquiries. Our statement to the FTC and the public was unequivocal: "The FTC staff's position on legal and factual issues at stake here is simply wrong."

I reminded myself that TCI lawyers could handle this, and by the time our big road rig finally passed the Maine state line, I felt like my fever had broken; my blood pressure eased and my pulse rate dropped down to normal.

The headwinds we faced blew unabated. True, digital cable-TV boxes would start shipping in the fall of 1996 from GI, and our high-speed internet service @Home Network was scheduled to roll out in homes in San Francisco by year's end. But we were nearly three years late, and Wall Street punishes companies severely when they miss stated goals. From April 1994 to April 1996, as the Dow Jones Industrial Average jumped 52 percent, shares of TCI had gone up only 24 percent.

In February 1996, President Clinton had fired the starting gun for aggressive new competition when he signed into law the Telecommunications Act of 1996, which removed virtually all competitive barriers between the telephone and cable-TV industries.

US West, which already owned a 25 percent stake in Time Warner, couldn't wait for the ink to dry. On February 26, 1996, the cable-hungry Baby Bell paid $10.8 billion in cash, stock, and debt for the third-largest cable operator at the time, Continental Cablevision, run by founder and chairman Amos Hostetter, a cable-TV pioneer who founded Continental in 1963 with an initial investment of $4,000. The new company would be renamed MediaOne.

The new satellite-TV services, EchoStar's Dish and DirecTV, had by now signed up 4 million homes to cable's 65 million in 1996—enough to take the wind from cable's sails, as subscriber growth slowed to under 5 percent a year in the 1990s.

Meanwhile, I had delegated more operating authority to the management team, hoping to see some key executives rise to the challenge. We needed fresh blood in our leadership ranks. Many of the original employees whom Bob Magness had hired twenty-plus years earlier were retiring.

I missed most the clockwork reliability of JC Sparkman, who had retired as COO in 1995 because of health issues, replaced in the role by Brendan Clouston, a former banker who had joined TCI a decade earlier from United Artist Cable. We had promoted him when he meshed UA's businesses into TCI seamlessly.

Brendan was an optimist, and not long after taking the reins as COO, he charted an ambitious course for TCI to deliver hundreds of new digital cable channels, high-speed internet access, and, eventually, telephone service.

But it was too much too fast. TCI already had committed to spending $2 billion to upgrade its aging cable systems, many in suburban and rural areas long overdue for expensive overhauls to bring them up to par. Now new costs were being added.

TCI rarely hired consultants, but in 1996, for example, consultants billed TCI close to $60 million, and the advice was typical academic hogwash. To combat a bad reputation for poor customer service and centralize for "efficiency," TCI was advised to create six elaborate (read: expensive) regional customer service centers that promised to deploy technicians twenty-four hours a day, something no one in the cable-TV industry had ever done.

To help roll out the new services, Clouston brought in a new, younger team of executives with specialized skills, including a former aerospace executive, to design something called SUMMITrak, a new software system that coordinated a customer's relationship with TCI, tracking orders, repairs, and other services.

But to centralize the functions of hundreds of different systems of varying size, age, and location through a new proprietary billing platform and database was a massive challenge. Everything looks good in a PowerPoint presentation—the real world is always harder.

All of these costs were piled on top of an astronomical $14.5 billion in long-term debt, which hung, like the sword of Damocles, just over our heads.

JC, retired but still on the board, began to openly question Brendan's decisions. At first, I passed this off as an old guard/new guard contretemps. A more serious warning came from one of TCI's (and Liberty's) earliest and largest investors, Gordon Crawford, the easygoing head of Capital Research, a Los Angeles–based money management firm that owned positions in the largest media company stocks at the time.

Wall Street was ready to see the cable-TV industry, and especially TCI, return to healthy cash-flow growth from new digital services. In a friendly but concerned tone, Gordy predicted that, based on everything he knew, TCI's upcoming financial report for the third quarter was going to miss its mark, despite management's ironclad guarantees.

"It looks ugly," said Gordy, who shared that Dennis Leibowitz, a smart equity analyst at Donaldson Lufkin & Jenrette, was equally unsettled about TCI's performance. Immediately, I flew back to Denver.

The flight, on TCI's Canadair Challenger, took all of five hours to get from Boothbay, Maine, to Denver—more than enough time for me to reflect on what had just happened. One of my largest investors had just warned me about troubles inside my own company—problems I had failed to see really. Humbling at best, a little humiliating at worst.

I had been focused on Liberty Media and its stable of media company stakes, delegating TCI to Brendan Clouston and the team of managers that he had assembled. And now I had to hear from an outsider just how bad a job they were doing.

The third-quarter numbers were worse than I'd thought. TCI *lost* 70,000 basic subscribers and 308,000 pay-TV subscribers, mostly to new mini-dish competitors, driven partly by our price increase. This was the first time since TCI's first public offering of shares in 1969 that our total subscriber rolls declined rather than grew. Cash-flow growth was a lousy 3 percent, when most analysts had expected 10 percent.

When the preliminary numbers were released later in October, investors ran out like the house was on fire. TCI shares, one of the most actively traded stocks on the Nasdaq Stock Market, closed at a new fifty-two-week low of $11.625. TCI stock had fallen 40 percent from its high in 1995.

JC was right. Not only was the plan bad, but we were rushing it. Expenses had ballooned. We had trained Wall Street to magnify our cash flow when analyzing our financials, yet we ignored it as we focused on a payoff a year or so out. If given the time and money, the overhaul of TCI might have made sense, but we had neither—cash flow had turned massively negative due to capital spending.

I didn't formally fire Brendan, at least not at first. The message was more: step aside—I am comin' in hot.

It felt like 1973 all over again. I had to cauterize the bleeding. I set new rules: any capital expense over $1,000 had to be approved by me, and those not contributing directly to cash flow would be nixed.

We cut executive salaries, including my own (I agreed to take a 20 percent pay cut in my $800,000 salary), and froze others, in conjunction with layoffs. TCI laid off twenty-five hundred people, mostly in marketing, and we sold the TCI jet. "We are going to squeeze this entire company until we turn the cash flow in the right direction," I said to anyone listening.

I told teams to simply stop paying programming increases, which had soared in the past couple years—or drop the network. I interviewed the financial teams, the marketing leaders, even the line construction managers. We scoured each office's expenses. We fired consultants and sold and outsourced the new SUMMITrak billing system.

We could still deploy digital set-top boxes even as we were deferring network upgrades, I explained, because compression technology did not require fiber optics. So we were still ordering digital boxes and planning to be in forty markets the following year. This more aggressive deployment would give all customers more, and sharper, channels—and bring in more revenue for TCI.

Next I took a bullhorn and told the world how TCI screwed up and how we were going to fix it. And although privately I felt that Brendan had let me down, publicly I emphasized my own role in letting this setback happen at TCI.

I invited a *Wall Street Journal* reporter up to my office, with Brendan by my side, and I answered every question he fired down the plate for the page-one story that ran January 2, 1997.

"My ambition was to be more of an investor and director and to be less of an operating guy," I explained. "We were just chasing too many rabbits at the same time, and the company had gotten a little overly ambitious in terms of how many things it could do simultaneously," I said.

I pay little mind to headlines and the noise of the media, but a *Fortune* magazine headline seemed to peg my current state in January 1997: "HIGH NOON FOR JOHN MALONE. THE GLORY DAYS OF THE BELL ATLANTIC DEAL LONG GONE, THE CEO OF TCI FACES THE FIGHT OF HIS LIFE—REVITALIZING HIS CABLE COMPANY AND SALVAGING HIS REPUTATION."

The old familiar feelings of insecurity and anxiety began to pull at me harder now, just as they had done two decades earlier when TCI was fighting for survival. I was contrite around Bob Magness, my mentor and TCI's largest shareholder. As TCI stock sank, Bob told me in his slow, measured drawl, "You'll figure it out, John. You always do." A good mentor is a cheerleader. I hoped to God that Bob was right.

My greatest shortcoming is avoidance of conflict, and for far too long, I wrestled with asking Brendan, who had so passionately wanted to be the savior of TCI, to step down.

In my almost two decades at TCI by this time, I had fired only one person, and that case involved gross insubordination, and he was half-drunk at the time it happened, and I still felt sorry about it the next day. So I gave him the chance to take back his job, and he declined.

In the next couple quarters, the stock started to recover as we increased cash flow. Still, I needed help, and began shaking the trees for a solid, proven cable-TV industry veteran. In February 1997, I brought in an old-school cable operator, Leo Hindery Jr., to take on the role of CEO of TCI. Leo was a forty-nine-year-old serial dealmaker who had done several partnerships with TCI and others in the industry.

With a head of graying hair, Leo drove in professional races in his downtime, speeding at nearly two hundred miles an hour, and he seemed to have a similar metabolism, often starting the workday at around 5 a.m. every morning.

After leaving Chronicle Publishing Company, which owned TV stations, cable systems, and newspapers, Hindery had built Intermedia Partners into the ninth-largest cable operator in the country by attracting investors such as

the Bank of New York, General Motors, and New York Life. Better yet, Leo
was a born politician, blessed with a schmoozer's tongue, and he knew how
to build a consensus—a few years earlier, he had orchestrated a consortium
of several cable companies, including TCI, that bought Jack Kent Cooke's
cable properties for $1.5 billion.

Just days after arriving at TCI, Leo Hindery completed the management
restructuring. Clouston opted to leave soon after. Leo scrapped the expensive
billing system and returned customer service to local offices.

To help, he brought back Marvin Jones, former CEO of United Artists
Cable Systems, which had merged into TCI in 1991, to be COO of the cable
group. With his flat-top crew cut, Jones looked like a drill sergeant from the
Marines—just what we needed.

Leo was more than I had hoped for, and he started to deliver the numbers
we wanted, in part because he was such a great promoter. He was the perfect
antidote to the scorn I had shown for lawmakers in Washington, D.C. Leo
made more trips to D.C. in his first six months than I had made in my entire
career at TCI. And while TCI executives had forgone even hiring a public
relations person for years, Leo talked to the press with uninhibited élan.

Soon, TCI was back on track and ahead of schedule in its plan to offer
digital video services. But as 1996 began to draw to a close, how could I
have known that an existential crisis would threaten TCI and devastate
me personally?

CHAPTER 20

LAST RIDE

While TCI struggled to adapt in the two years after we walked away from the Bell Atlantic deal, my old friend and mentor Bob Magness was enjoying the two great loves of his life—horses and his wife Sharon, who had married him in 1989, four years after the death of Betsy, his wife of thirty-six years.

One day in October 1996, he poked his head into my doorway to tell a joke, then said he was headed to California to bid on a ranch with Sharon. But on the trip, Sharon noticed something amiss when Bob appeared to have difficulty with motor skills. Concerned he'd had a stroke, she flew with him to Eisenhower Medical Center in Palm Springs, the same hospital where he'd had a defibrillator put in months earlier.

But the diagnosis was much worse than a stroke. Inoperable cancerous tumors were pressing against Bob's brain. By the time I flew to the hospital, Bob had lost the ability to speak. He could comprehend everything, but could only nod to answer.

As I sat alone with him in the hospital room, I filled the silence with small talk. He was frustrated, and I was glum, not even aware this would be our last visit. It was all too sudden. Also sitting in the room was a half-inch-thick final draft of Bob's will we had been working on, but he had not yet signed this latest version. Nor would he.

After consultations, Sharon had Bob flown to University of Virginia Hospital in Charlottesville, which used a new gamma knife radiation and chemotherapy to shrink the tumors. Neither worked.

In a private room on the University of Virginia Hospital's cancer ward,

Bob was fortunate enough to be able to say goodbye to close friends and his two sons, Gary and Kim, and his three grandchildren. Less than a month later, on Friday, November 15, 1996, Bob breathed his last ragged breath; the cancer had taken him. Sharon was by his side right up to the end.

But any family unity would disappear months later, as Bob's widow and his sons went to court in separate actions, contesting Bob's wishes and demanding a bigger share of what he'd left behind. This very public, nasty fight over money would pose an existential threat to the company that Bob and I had built.

For more than twenty-five years, Bob had been a constant in my life. His advice was never grandiose, never flashy. It was practical, uncomplicated, and it resonated in ways few other words ever could.

He taught me how to sift through the noise and find the signal. "Forget the critics," he would say, "and focus on what really matters." Those words, so easy to forget, became a mantra that shaped the trajectory of my life. To honor the memory of the man, the main thing I could do was carry his lessons forward, and I have done that.

Five days later, on November 20, nearly a thousand friends and family drifted into the Denver First Church of the Nazarene to pay their respects to Robert John Magness, a faithful husband, a decorated World War II hero, a former cottonseed broker, a genuine cowboy, a self-made cable-TV billionaire and philanthropist—the embodiment of the American dream.

His coffin, surrounded by white roses, was draped in an American flag in reflection of his service. Bob's cowboy hat and his black, silver-studded show saddle were displayed near a photo of Bob with one of his Arabian horses. Outside the church, Thunder, the mascot of the Denver Broncos, paced as the body of its owner lay dormant inside, where a choir led mourners in singing "The Battle Hymn of the Republic."

Family, friends, and what seemed like the entire cable industry filled the pews, including Ted Turner and his wife, Jane Fonda; Tim Robertson, son of televangelist Pat Robertson and head of the Family Channel; Glenn Jones, founder of nearby Jones Intercable; and throngs of other business partners and competitors.

"I came to love Bob," I said to the gathered mourners during the ceremony. "He was a man of enormous virtue. Quiet. Deep. Solid. Loyal. Brilliant in many ways. Self-effacing. We went through a lot of experiences together. We were partners. He was my mentor. In many ways, he was my father."

Ted Turner, who served with me as a pallbearer, praised Bob and me for stepping up to save Turner Broadcasting back in 1987, and lauded Bob's entrepreneurial mind, his cowboy ways, and his love of the land out West. "He was just about the finest man I ever met," Turner said. "I used to say, 'You build the wires and we'll make 'em sing.'"

Despite the somber mood of the church, I kept turning one thought incessantly over in my head: What is going to happen to Bob's 32 million super-voting shares?

Around the time Bob died, as if that wasn't enough of a blow, TCI's stock hit a new fifty-two-week low, hammered by Wall Street over digital product delays and satellite competition.

As often as we had talked about estate taxes and how to avoid them, I was flabbergasted to see Bob's estate plans. The twenty-three-page final will of one of the richest men in the history of Colorado was filled with scratch-out marks and lines in the margins, pointing to insertions and initials for changes made to the text. It included an attached list, handwritten in block letters, parsing out close to $1 billion in assets, including the single largest voting bloc in TCI—more than thirty-two thousand shares of TCI stock.

Roughly 90 percent of Bob's estate—cash, stock, ranches, and land—would go to his two sons, Kim, forty-four, and Gary, forty-two, from his first marriage to Betsy Magness. Bob's widow, Sharon, was bequeathed around $55 million in property and cash. And he had set aside money for his favorite causes: the University of Denver ($10 million), the Boy Scouts of America ($2.5 million), and the Denver Art Museum ($900,000).

For all his charms and winning decisions, Bob's failure to finalize his will was a grave error, one that is all too common. Some aging patriarchs think they will live forever, some put off the unpleasant task indefinitely, and others think it will magically take care of itself.

We were all astounded to learn that Bob did not take advantage of gifting, charitable trusts, or other legal, tax-sheltered ways to transfer wealth to heirs. Nor did he simply get his wife and two sons together and tell them his wishes. The result: the largest estate battle in the history of Colorado.

Because of Bob's procrastination, his $1 billion fortune would end up being drained by half a billion dollars in federal estate taxes, some of which could have been avoided if only he had taken the proper, legally allowable steps. Half of his entire wealth, accumulated over a lifetime, was handed to the government simply for the act of dying and likely went to interest payments on the national debt.

Worse, the only way for Bob Magness's heirs to raise half a billion dollars to pay this exorbitant tax bill was to sell TCI shares, which were down.

Bob had chosen as executors of his estate two of his closest friends, men of impeccable integrity. Dan Ritchie was a quiet Denver philanthropist who had once run Westinghouse Cable and now served as chancellor of the University of Denver, without pay, having donated $16 million to the university. Donne F. Fisher, who had retired as Bob's first treasurer and CFO, was a consultant to TCI and a member of the board.

After condolences, the first message the executors had for Kim and Gary was that the IRS was expecting a big, fat tax payment, and soon. Dan and Donne were genuinely concerned that the stock price could fall farther the longer they waited, making TCI even more vulnerable to a takeover.

Together, Bob and I had effectively controlled TCI and Liberty through super-voting class B shares, each of which counted for ten votes, while class A shares held only one vote apiece. Magness's shares accounted for 26 percent control of the company; I held about 18 percent of TCI's vote; most of my holdings were in Liberty Media.

I held a right of first refusal on Bob's TCI block of stock, which was valued at more than a half billion dollars, but I lacked the liquid cash to cover such a large bill. I prayed TCI could afford to buy it all back, because an open block of stock on the market was like blood in the water for takeover sharks.

In June 1997, the executors agreed to sell Bob's super-voting shares back to TCI for a 10 percent premium. They told the sons that this was what Bob would have wanted, and it was the simplest, fastest way to retain control of TCI and pay a whopping IRS tax bill.

But Bob's sons, who would each receive around $200 million in TCI, were adamant that the executors instead borrow money against the shares to pay the estate taxes due just a few months hence. They also dropped a stunner on us: they told the executors that they had heard from a new bidder who was willing to pay a higher price for the sons' shares. But they oddly would not reveal the suitor's identity.

Satisfied they were filling Bob's final wishes to safeguard the long-term value of TCI, the two estate executors sold 32.5 million shares back to TCI on June 16, 1997, for $529 million, or $16.52 a share, to settle the taxes.

Because TCI could not afford the shares, I used math to solve the problem: First, the estate would swap the 32.5 million super-voting B shares for TCI class A shares, which traded at roughly the same price as the B shares. Then TCI would borrow $529 million from two New York investment banks, Merrill Lynch and Lehman Brothers, in return for the 32.5 million A shares. TCI could then buy back the class A shares from the two banks over the next two years.

Everything went quiet for a couple weeks.

Our plan started to unravel days later, on June 24, 1997, when Sharon Magness sued to invalidate Bob's will, arguing in probate court that she was due much more than what it had set aside for her—$55 million total in assets, including the house and the horse farms. Now she demanded at least 50 percent of the estate under Colorado state law, requesting a jury trial on the issue, setting up an old-fashioned western showdown with her grown stepsons.

The brothers came back the next month with guns blazing in a countersuit that cited a 1989 prenuptial agreement, which had limited Sharon to even less than she was granted in Magness's will.

It was troubling for everyone involved, and the press had a field day with the stereotypes of a rich septuagenarian with a messy will and a presumed gold-digger younger blonde wife versus two spoiled sons in Colorado's biggest estate battle. People were hurting, and greedy, and wolfish lawyers had gotten the best of them.

Meanwhile, TCI and I, personally, reached out to investors to shore up more control, exchanging in swaps as many A shares as we could with class B super-voting shares owned by founding TCI investor Kearns-Tribune Corp., the publisher of *The Salt Lake Tribune*, and TCI shareholder Knight Ridder, which boosted my TCI voting power to 25 percent from about 18 percent. Still not enough to block a takeover.

Then on September 11, 1997, Bob's sons stopped everything by petitioning the court to remove Dan Ritchie and Donne Fisher as executors. The following month, they sued the estate to overturn the stock sale to TCI.

Both sides were angry. The sons' petition said that the "unalterable hostility between the personal representatives and the two principal beneficiaries dictates their immediate removal." The brothers claimed Donne was conflicted as an executor because he was a TCI board member and had negotiated the sale at the $16.52-per-share price, despite another offer for more.

The truth was that Bob knew damn well Donne was a TCI board member and consultant when he appointed him, and he, too, feared unfriendly raiders who might buy control of TCI and sell it piece by piece.

The anonymous offer had come from a boutique banking firm, Lazard Frères & Co., which had faxed a similar two-page offer letter to the estate. Lazard represented an anonymous buyer "willing to pay in excess of $20 a share" for the estate's 32 million series B shares—but the executors did not want to play games with buyers who refused to identify themselves.

It was not until later that the mystery bidder revealed itself: Comcast Corporation, a longtime partner! I should have known. That same month, in June 1997, Bill Gates had shocked Wall Street by having Microsoft invest $1 billion in cash in Comcast at the behest of Brian Roberts. The unprecedented investment was a blue-chip endorsement of cable's internet strategy, and stocks had spiked up on the news.

When I broached the bid for TCI control shares with Brian Roberts, he basically blamed Bill Gates, who said he was going to make the offer for TCI through Lazard. "You guys can join me, but if you refuse now, you won't ever be a part of it," Brian quoted Bill as having warned him.

I had to admit, it was a pretty bold step. Bill Gates, founder of the largest software company in the world, trying to position himself in the cable industry, had plunked down $1 billion for number three Comcast. And just days later, he tried to take a shot at a control position in number one TCI.

It stung a little. After all, I had a history of partnerships with Microsoft, and with Comcast for more than twenty years, and at various points had even raised the prospect of a merger with Comcast. Brian and his father, Ralph, both said they thought their involvement would make it "friendly."

"Well, if you wanted it to be friendly, you know what the phone number is," I said, "come through the front door and talk about it." I stopped short of getting mad about it. Business is like chess. You can feel remorse over your own bad move, but it is wasted energy to get angry at your opponent for making a good one.

While the swipe at TCI's stock was a momentary, existential threat, Gates's rapacious behavior reflected his vision of broadband delivery for computer services, and this actually helped TCI's predicament.

Microsoft bet even more on cable operators, investing $400 million into Rogers Cable of Canada, fanning the interest in broadband. Bill Gates's cofounder of Microsoft, Paul Allen, would go on a bigger buying spree for cable operators, paying $3.2 billion for cable systems serving more than 1 million subscribers.

TCI's stock price rose accordingly; stuck around $15 after the death of Bob Magness, it was at $28 by early 1998 and was flirting with $40 by early summer.

A rising tide lifts all boats, and after several weeks of separate calls and meetings with Gary and Kim, and Donne and Dan, Sharon, and me—and, of course, more than a dozen lawyers—we reached an out-of-court settlement that seemed to satisfy everyone. We hammered out the details in late December and announced the settlement on January 5, 1998.

As part of it, all the lawsuits were dropped. The estate agreed to void half of the original sale of Bob's 32.5 million B shares and retake possession of 16.2 million TCI shares—which had grown in value by almost $200 million. The stock increase created a windfall that would help the estate pay the taxes owed to the government.

Never let a crisis go to waste. To avoid future control issues, TCI agreed to pay $124 million to the Magness brothers for first-refusal rights to buy the estate's remaining 34 million shares at market price, plus a 10 percent premium in the event of a death or sale. (I was also paid for the same first-refusal rights.) We were buying stability. The Magness brothers also agreed to grant me the right to vote their shares, and Kim Magness was given a seat on the board.

I now controlled 76 million shares, or about 40 percent of the vote at TCI and its related companies, TCI Ventures and Liberty Media. And as the price of the stock took off, it became harder for anyone to complain.

The estate settlement had provided a lull in the storms around me. But TCI would still have to deliver on the promises for new lines of business that the market now was expecting from us. Meanwhile, back at home, Leslie was pressing me to be more present, especially when I was in the same house.

An emptiness I could not shake began to settle in, and I found myself craving the sight of Bob's weathered face in the doorway, sporting a bolo tie and a tan leather jacket, and hearing his drawl one last time.

I started seeing a therapist, an older gentleman, to help me map my thoughts and ward off depression. In our first session, I told him: "I'm really torn here. I do not know whether to retire or to continue to build and grow something."

But after a few meetings, this therapist told me, "John, what you're up against here is a typical Calvinist parent—you are trying to please your now-dead father. And essentially, that impulse never leaves you." And what he was really saying was that I would always be driven, so I might as well do something I enjoy.

Losing Bob made me consider these things more. I realized part of what had made my job gratifying was that Bob would feel good about it. I could live up to Bob's expectations, just like I was driven to live up to my father's. Now that Bob Magness was gone, I had lost my most important audience: my mentor, partner, friend, and father figure. With him gone, everything felt different, somehow.

So, in December 1997, I sat down with Leo Hindery and had a heart-to-heart conversation, telling him, point-blank: let us find a big investor—or buyer—to help us fund this next level of TCI's evolution.

Throughout 1997, Leo had focused slavishly on boosting cash flow, in part by driving a "partnering and clustering strategy" that created twelve new partnerships and ten system exchanges, helping TCI streamline and strengthen bonds among industry players. Leo called it the "Summer of Love."

Fueled by Leo's boundless energy, cash flow grew by a robust 20 percent in 1997. And he had delivered on a promise to offer digital video service to 5 million homes by the end of 1997; by February 1998, we were marketing digital cable to 80 percent of our 14 million customers.

My urge to sell grew even stronger when TCI's stock rose, naturally. The Liberty tracking stock was doing well, too, spiraling up to 90 percent in 1997, helped by Liberty's investments in Time Warner, Discovery Communications, Encore Media Group, USA Networks, and the Fox/Liberty sports partnership.

As we looked around for the right partner, Leo and I circled back to a company that had brushed TCI off a few years earlier under a different CEO, a company where I had started my career: AT&T.

AT&T, whose annual revenue was more than six times TCI's 1997 revenue of $7.6 billion a year, would give TCI the capital to actually build a national high-speed network. Unlike local phone companies, AT&T lacked a wire that went "the last mile" into customers' homes, and the direct customer relationship that came with it. Cable operators were the only other companies with a direct pipeline into millions of American homes.

The real prize for AT&T, however, would be @Home, the cable industry's high-speed internet service. It had signed up one hundred thousand customers to rave reviews and promised to be the winner in the race to deliver high-speed internet access. With cable's fat pipe and AT&T's brand name and bankroll, the business around internet-based services looked to be limitless.

@Home's reach went far beyond just TCI's 14 million customers; it had exclusive rights to provide internet service to a total of 55 million households

in cable systems owned by @Home's many partners—TCI, Cox Communications, Comcast Corporation, Cablevision Systems Corporation, and
Rogers Cable—where TCI was the majority shareholder with a 42 percent
stake.

We thought the current AT&T chairman and CEO, Mike Armstrong,
might bite. Before taking on that role in 1997, Armstrong, a former IBM
executive, had been CEO of General Motors Corporation's Hughes Electronics group, where he had launched DirecTV.

Mike's mission, and I believed in it, was to remake AT&T into a diversified telecom and internet company. AT&T faced an existential crisis. Still
king of the $80 billion long-distance market with a 60 percent share, it was
a sandcastle: long-distance per-minute rates had fallen two-thirds in two
years, from 15 cents to 5 cents, as Voice over Internet Protocol technology
flourished and competition increased. And those rates would nosedive to
zero—today, Americans no longer pay per-minute long-distance fees for
calls inside the U.S.

Mike had flown out to Denver to talk not long after he got the job—we
had met years before at an industry conference. Within minutes of quizzing
each other on the new alliances and competition the new law had ignited,
we turned to ways that TCI and AT&T might partner.

Armstrong bit first in January 1998, when AT&T paid $11.3 billion
for Teleport Communications Group, the partnership with Comcast and
Cox that sold phone services to businesses. The deal, structured as a tax-free
stock swap, made TCI's 30 percent stake in Teleport worth $2.9 billion, a
more than 4,000 percent increase.

Mike Armstrong observed the massive venture capital investments pouring into tech companies and internet start-ups, and he felt time was closing in
on him. So did we. One day, after we had played with the idea long enough,
Hindery called me to say Armstrong was ready to do a deal, "and he wants
to do it really fast." At the time, I had 48 percent voting control of TCI and
41 percent voting control of Liberty. And TCI owned 72 percent voting
control of @Home.

In the spring of 1998, in our boardroom on the eleventh floor of TCI
headquarters, Mike agreed in principle to terms of a merger that would be

one of the largest in business at the time. It all went down in eight days. I had met every AT&T chairman since 1964, and this was the first one, I thought, that got it.

AT&T agreed to pay $48.3 billion in cash, stock, and assumption of debt—$50.71 a share, a 30 percent premium to the share price, but roughly a 60 percent premium compared with the $30 level at which the stock had been trading months earlier.

AT&T was one of the most widely held stocks in the U.S., and it paid dividends. In those meetings, I showed Armstrong and his CFO, Dan Somers, that the best way to insulate the AT&T stock was to offload the cable assets (and their losses) to a tracking stock, a separate public stock that tracked the performance of a business unit inside the parent.

I would still control TCI's programming arm, Liberty Media, as a tracking stock inside AT&T for two years. They agreed.

We unveiled this epic merger on June 24, 1998, and as I shook hands with Mike Armstrong onstage at the AT&T building in Manhattan, I felt as if a weight had been lifted off my shoulders, or maybe my chest. It felt like freedom.

The deal would be treated as a tax-free stock merger because AT&T had used its own stock and a new AT&T-issued tracking stock representing the Liberty assets in exchange for the shares of TCI and Liberty.

The value of cable systems soared to new highs on the news. At one point that day Cablevision Systems Corporation jumped 39 percent to $76 per share. Time Warner rose 11 percent to close at $88.63; Comcast jumped 8 percent to $40.44. The price also sent the values of cable systems up to around $5,000 per subscriber. Shares in @Home, cable's high-speed internet service, rose in market value by nearly one-third to more than $6 billion with the AT&T deal. The prediction was the company would generate $7.5 billion per year in cash flow from $33 billion in annual revenue.

Mike would remain chairman and CEO of AT&T. I would be named a member of the AT&T board of directors, and I would remain chairman and CEO of Liberty Media, which would remain independent, and I would have virtual autonomy running it. I held 4 percent of its outstanding stock, 33 percent of the vote, and six of nine seats on the board.

Leo Hindery would become president and COO of the planned AT&T Consumer Services Co., serving under AT&T president and COO John Zeglis.

AT&T had paid $31.8 billion in stock, plus assumed $11 billion in TCI debt. The phone giant also paid $2.5 billion for TCI's stake in @Home and another $2.8 billion for stock given to TCI in the Teleport deal.

I had traded my personal stake of $1.7 billion in TCI and Liberty for $2.4 billion in AT&T and Liberty stock. And because Liberty was technically a tracking stock of AT&T, the IRS allowed exchange of assets with no tax penalty.

I didn't feel sheepish at all when I heard a few cracks about me not paying taxes.

"Have you ever paid any taxes?" I was asked one day, as if it was criminal to reduce your tax bill. I said, "Sure, I've paid taxes—as little as possible, and as late as possible." And I was deadly serious. Then I gave my standard speech: "I regard that as my shareholders' money. It is not the government's. It is my job to save as much of that as I can for my shareholders."

About a week before TCI shareholders were to vote on the AT&T deal, on Tuesday, February 16, 1999, many of the senior TCI executives met for a celebratory dinner at the stylish Swan restaurant in Denver, including JC Sparkman, thirty-two years with TCI; Donne Fisher, thirty years; and Larry Romrell, thirty-eight years.

On the menu was pepper-seared beef carpaccio, crab cakes, chateaubriand, and tuna steak on ginger rice with Asian pear salsa. We could have never afforded this place back in the 1970s. It was an intimate affair, and one of the rare times Leslie joined a company event. Above the laughs and one-liners, I tapped a fork to my champagne glass and spoke to a room that felt more like family.

"We're going out absolutely on top," I told the group. I praised Leo Hindery, in particular, saying, "He really has made this merger possible—a lot of us were skeptical a deal could get done. He did it with sheer energy. He drove it and drove it and drove it, and brought the deal home. Thanks, Leo, I appreciate it."

From 1973 to 1999, TCI delivered an extraordinary 30.3 percent annual compound return, compared with 20 percent for other publicly traded cable companies and 14.3 percent for the S&P 500 over the same period.

Over that twenty-five-year span, a single dollar invested in TCI in 1973—accounting for its spin-offs and stock splits—grew into an astonishing $900 by mid-1998, according to William N. Thorndike Jr. in *The Outsiders*. That same dollar would have reached $180 in peer cable companies, and a modest $22 in the S&P 500. In sheer performance, TCI outpaced the broader market more than fortyfold, a record I am damned proud to claim.

"Bob Magness would have loved this. The run-up of TCI stock and Liberty stock is close to one hundred billion dollars—which I think would even get Bob's attention. What a great run," I told my fellow cable cowboys and their wives. AT&T shareholder approval came quickly, and the FCC gave the deal a green light.

Some weeks later, inside TCI's National Digital Television Center, home to the massive satellite uplink dishes that had ushered in digital compression, I convened the twenty-sixth and final annual TCI shareholders meeting. Shareholders enthusiastically approved TCI's $48 billion acquisition by AT&T.

Onstage with TCI president Leo Hindery and Liberty Media president Dob Bennett, I told the audience of investors, "We've had a helluva run, and now we're going off to a new adventure." Little did I realize that I had used the wrong word: *misadventure* would turn out to be the more appropriate description.

CHAPTER 21

DISCONNECTED

The sale of TCI had capped a dramatic string of events for me, personally, all within a span of eighteeen months, starting with the monumental loss of Bob Magness and the emotional, public battle over his estate and ending with the agonizing decision to sell the company that Bob and I had built over three decades.

But everything was fine now, I reassured myself. AT&T had just paid us $48 billion for TCI stock, a 40 percent premium to its recent price, creating a communications behemoth that was destined to be the biggest and the most valuable provider of communications in the country.

We had just been paid in shares of AT&T stock that traded under the symbol T, in a bedrock American company founded in 1877 by Alexander Graham Bell. The stock, a favorite of pension funds and other institutional investors, had never missed a dividend payment. AT&T was home to Bell Labs, which invented the transistor, the laser, and the Unix software system, and employed the world's smartest engineers; it was an operation I knew well. We were in safe hands.

Execution was another matter. The rapid-fire, just-get-'er-done philosophy of the cable cowboys at the top of TCI would somehow have to mesh with the deliberative processes of the "Bellheads," the managers and engineers who heeded the Ma Bell way. I just hoped Mike Armstrong possessed the right skills to keep everyone rowing in synch.

My fortunes would be tied up in the value of AT&T stock for at least two years, for better or worse. When we merged TCI into AT&T, to avoid paying more in taxes than we otherwise would have to, we created a tracking stock inside AT&T for Liberty Media, with the understanding that we would wait two years and entirely spin off Liberty in 2001 without owing any tax bill. We essentially would combine assets, then separate them without a lot of tax leakage.

The TCI sale made me the largest individual shareholder in AT&T. Liberty Media, which I controlled, was still, technically, a part of AT&T, through this tracking stock. I felt a lot like Jonah in the whale.

As soon as the deal closed, I started pushing one priority: follow through on our plans to create a second tracking stock, this one linked to AT&T's newly acquired cable systems. A tracking stock, which trades separately, would also insulate AT&T's traditional shareholders, who disliked the volatility of the cable business, which often generated losses. And it could be a currency for acquiring more cable systems in the U.S.

Initially, AT&T stock had recovered quite nicely from the initial hit we expected from the TCI acquisition. It had dipped to the upper $40s from $63 when they announced the deal, but shortly after the close, by February 1999, the stock hit $94 when it was announced that AT&T had struck a preliminary partnership agreement with Time Warner cable systems to offer phone service. The 50 percent rise reflected the market's appreciation for Mike Armstrong's grand strategy.

In Mike's mind, the parent stock's rise removed the rationale for issuing a new tracking stock, and in early 1999, he tabled the idea indefinitely. Intuitively, I knew that if the market fell and AT&T shares declined with it, the ambitious overhaul would suddenly be in trouble. AT&T would have mustered a huge army but would lack ammunition. No one was asking the question that Moses Shapiro had taught me to ask, decades earlier: "What if not?"

It didn't take long for the calm to turn to chaos. One Friday afternoon in the spring of 1999, I called Mike Armstrong with news that, come Monday, Comcast, the fourth-largest cable operator in the nation, would announce a $58 billion bid for MediaOne, the third largest, with 5 million subscribers nationwide.

This threatened to torpedo Armstrong's grand plans for making AT&T the world's largest cable company. MediaOne was the last big prize waiting to be acquired, and without it, AT&T would have to spend years buying a jumble of dozens of small, separately owned systems to patch together a nationwide network.

I knew AT&T had been looking to make a bid for MediaOne for months. Now that Comcast was knocking on MediaOne's door, if Armstrong had issued a cable tracking stock for new deals, we would have had a way to bid against Comcast. Though this was gallingly obvious, I pretty much left it out of my conversations with AT&T's CEO. By now, I was beginning to doubt that he would listen.

Comcast unveiled its offer for MediaOne the following Monday, March 22, 1999, and it was a stunner. It wasn't just a bid, it was a finalized, bona fide merger *agreement*. MediaOne had accepted Comcast's now–$60 billion takeover bid. It appeared that Comcast CEO Brian Roberts had just bagged the cable industry's most impressive trophy.

And he had pulled it off before AT&T had even had the chance to pull its six-shooters from their holsters. The deal would transform the company. Comcast would nearly double in size, reaching 11 million subscribers, and adding a turnkey circuit-switched telephony business.

To me, at this point, Comcast-MediaOne was a done deal. And we had plenty of reasons to stand down.

Lacking a cable tracker meant that AT&T would have to issue still more of its own common stock to bid for MediaOne. When you issue more shares of stock, each share outstanding on the market goes down in value (it is called dilution), and earnings per share go down, as well. So you are hurting your stock price as you do it.

To tamp down how many new shares AT&T would have to issue for a bid, Armstrong would have had to augment the offer with barrels of cash—an extremely inefficient form of payment that would require MediaOne shareholders to pay federal taxes on the cash gains. Never pay taxes you legally can avoid paying. It is as simple as that.

Further, to raise the cash, AT&T would have to borrow it, and this would put more strain on its once-pristine, triple-AAA-rated balance sheet.

These various pressures might even threaten AT&T's hallowed dividend, further driving down the price of the company's stock. That would require the payment of more shares to offset the stock's decline in price.

So AT&T had many reasons to step aside and let Comcast go ahead with its costly bid for MediaOne; and I discussed these reasons in polite and brief conversations with management. Nobody listened.

A few weeks after the news of the Comcast deal, I was attending an AT&T board meeting in person in New York City. I nearly did a comic spit take with my coffee when I heard that Mike Armstrong was working on a rich counterbid to buy MediaOne. He had listened to my advice—and chosen to ignore it utterly. Exactly one month after Comcast hailed its merger, AT&T Corp. launched a surprise $62 billion bid for MediaOne—with *$20 billion of it in cash*.

To the outside world, it was impressive. Armstrong had taken a company with no presence in cable, then acquired the number one player (TCI), and now was gunning to get the number three player (MediaOne) to forge the largest cable operator in the U.S., with 16 million subscriber homes in markets covering nearly a third of the country's 100 million homes.

But in so many ways, the AT&T bid was the zenith of ignorance—and arrogance. For starters, the price was simply too rich, by billions of dollars. Cable systems were selling by one measure for $3,000 per subscriber, and now Mike Armstrong was bidding more than $5,000 per sub. Moreover, AT&T was willing to pay $62 billion for a company that the former Baby Bell known as US West had assembled for less than $15 billion, which included the $10.8 billion purchase of Continental Cablevision a few years earlier.

The worst sin, though, was how AT&T and Mike Armstrong had decided to fund the cash portion of the bid. The company was borrowing $30 billion in short-term commercial paper, which typically becomes due in weeks or months.

It was as if Mike Armstrong had walked into a real estate office and bought a new house on his Visa card. AT&T was financing its biggest deal ever on some of the worst terms possible.

Weeks later, on May 6, 1999, MediaOne accepted AT&T's sweetened offer: $62 billion, a 26 percent premium to the recent price. Because AT&T's stock price had fallen to $52, a "collar" had been triggered, forcing AT&T to pay an additional $3.6 billion in cash, on top of the $1.5 billion it had paid to Comcast as a breakup fee owed to MediaOne.

Without a cable tracking stock as I had advised, AT&T had to issue 603 million new AT&T shares in addition to the cash, and AT&T was forced to take on an extra $4.5 billion in long-term debt, pushing the company's total debt load to almost $60 billion. Considering the $48 billion for TCI, the $62 billion that Armstrong and AT&T were spending for MediaOne looked exorbitant.

Mike had reneged on our agreement for a tracking stock. If I had threatened litigation over the matter, he would have gone bananas, and any news about it might tank the stock and further hurt my own investment. Looking back on it, I should have forced the issue of the tracking stock for the cable business. I was a gentleman when I probably should have been a jerk about it.

In the end, Comcast and AT&T ended up trading systems to "cluster" their systems in adjacent cities after all; Comcast ended up with systems serving 750,000 more subscribers than it gave up, and it paid AT&T an estimated $3.5 billion.

The deal reflected another polar difference of opinion between the new management and me: Why did AT&T have to come in hot with a rival bid? Why didn't Mike Armstrong just call Brian Roberts at Comcast and ask him to let AT&T join the deal—and the two partners could split up the assets? Just as I had done in so many previous partnerships.

There might be reasons for mistrust, but never is there any need for hostility. It is why, across my career, I have alternated competing with and partnering with so-called rivals, such as Rupert Murdoch, Ralph and Brian Roberts, Charles and James Dolan, and the leaders of Time Warner.

I had underestimated how difficult it would be to overcome cultural differences in melding AT&T with its new cable operations. Cable systems arose in a business dominated by cowboys, eccentrics, and small-business mavericks, where growth trumped financial stability. Conversely, even under the outsider Mike Armstrong, AT&T still clung to its origins as a telephone monopoly, and everything it did pivoted around that identity. Its reverence for regulation, for example, and a habit of studying everything to death before making a belated decision. He had succumbed to the old Latin warning *"Illigitimi non carborundum"* ("Don't let the bastards grind you down").

At the time, I also underestimated just how directly my fortunes were linked to so many outside forces beyond my control, including the internet tidal wave that was about to upend entire industries and render obsolete dozens of technologies.

Now the company was betting more than a hundred billion dollars on cable systems, but Armstrong and his lieutenants seemed more interested in cable as a conduit for getting back into the business of local phone service. Back then, cellular phone service was just beginning to take off, and AT&T had completed its $12.6 billion purchase of McCaw Cellular Communications right before Mike Armstrong arrived.

But audacious cable operators were upgrading their hybrid fiber-coax networks to sell their own brand of phone service, all of which was causing problems for the new CEO of AT&T's cable and internet unit, Leo Hindery, who had been instrumental in turning TCI around a few years earlier. Now he was having a nettlesome time trying to persuade cable operators to agree to the AT&T local-phone partnership.

AT&T was getting close to an accord with Time Warner Cable for access to the 19 million households the cable giant passed in thirty-three states, a plan it hoped to replicate around the country.

In the fall of 1999, Leo was asked by reporters if AT&T was in talks with AOL about access to its upgraded broadband wires. Leo defiantly denied it. To cable operators, this was a big deal. All their bets were on the white-hot dot-com start-up for internet access known as @Home or At Home, and AOL was a competitor agitating with federal regulators about open and equal access to the high-speed cable lines to compete with the cable companies' @Home service.

Weeks later it came to light that, yes, indeed, AT&T had been in secret talks with AOL. Leo Hindery was livid for having been deceived by his own bosses at AT&T—and the cable operators he had been trying to round up were even angrier. They saw it as a breach of trust, and they blamed Mike Armstrong personally.

It was the last straw for Leo Hindery, and he quit as AT&T's cable CEO in October 1999, leaving AT&T with no real legacy link to the cable-TV industry. Meanwhile, the company's stock continued to slide down from the $60 range into the mid-$40s on pressures in its mainline long-distance business.

Leo Hindery's successor atop AT&T's newly acquired cable business was the company's chief financial officer, Dan Somers, a man who always reminded me of Candide, an eternal optimist who thought the world was in the best possible state. He had no problem guaranteeing the value of the AT&T stock, or borrowing short-term money, or spending outrageous sums of money to buy agreement with partners.

@Home was backed by over a dozen cable companies as their chosen gateway for the new internet access they wanted to sell to their cable customers. AT&T was the largest holder of @Home, with a 26 percent stake, which it had inherited when it bought TCI. Cox and Comcast were the other leading owners.

The original idea for @Home was a winner: pooling our resources for a universal North American business offering a high-speed network and services such as mail and a home page of news, entertainment, and sports for $40 a month. So the scale, the economics, would've been extraordinary, and we had a fair revenue split.

@Home's stock price had zoomed past $125 in February 1999, giving the year-old company a value of $12 billion. In 1999, against the wishes and advice of AT&T's Leo Hindery, @Home's new CEO Tom Jermoluk had taken the inflated currency and spent a crazy $6.7 billion to buy Excite, a second-tier internet portal with a few million customers in the frothy days of the dot-com bubble.

The newly-merged Excite@Home went on to pay $780 million in stock and cash to acquire an online greeting card company, Blue Mountain, with scant revenue and millions of loyal fans who liked the free service. With each deal, cable operators' stakes were diluted.

It was fool's gold. After the internet bubble burst in 2000, Blue Mountain was more like a crater, sold two years later for $35 million to American Greetings alongside the plummeting asset values of troves of dot-com companies.

Amid the tumult of mismanagement and mixed motivations, Excite@Home CEO Jermoluk left the company in April 2000. Part of the tension between management and cable operator owners was that the Silicon Valley contingent was buying traffic, while we were looking at cash flow.

In early 2000, impatient with cable partners over the direction of the Excite@Home partnership, AT&T moved to buy Cox's and Comcast's respective 8 percent stakes, raising their bid to a stiff $48 a share for a total of almost $4 billion in new AT&T stock. For this hefty price tag, AT&T's voting control in what was now Excite@Home rose from 56 percent to 74 percent.

It was a terribly rich deal—and terribly reckless, really. It is what happens when a company is too big and has pockets that are too deep. AT&T paid up because it could afford to pay up. This problem persists in business still. After AT&T agreed to pay $48 per share, for @Home and its newly acquired Excite portal, the share price fell to $10—yet AT&T still owed some $3 billion to Comcast and Cox for shares that now were worth only $550 million.

Excite@Home was having operational issues, as well. While the cable partners wanted a nationwide, high-speed access business with a good return on their investment, Excite@Home began pursuing a loftier notion, a model much like that of AOL, with a "walled garden" of exclusive content. This failed utterly. The net consumes all.

By March 2002, Excite@Home had shut down entirely, having filed for Chapter 11 bankruptcy after AT&T withdrew a last-gasp offer of $307 million for its cable assets. Excite@Home's shares had bottomed out at 13 cents a share. In April 1999, the stock sold for nearly $100 a share. All the while, the slo-mo implosion of the $165 billion AOL Time Warner deal had been starting almost as soon as it was announced in January 2000.

It showed how crazed and crazy the dealmaking had gotten in the dot-com bubble; there was little value there. The cable operators ended up selling internet access as merely another add-on service under their own brand names, and users had no need for a particular branded on-ramp. What had started as an entirely new industry—websites as portals to the internet—became an afterthought.

Because I had sold my stake in TCI to AT&T in exchange for stock in the company rather than cash, I was able to avoid paying any federal taxes on the gain: that is the way the law works. The downside was that this tied much of the personal fortune I had built in three decades to the price of AT&T stock. By this time, my net worth already had gone down by $1 billion; though, if you don't sell, you haven't had a loss.

What bothered me even more, however, was something I had noticed while studying the company financials at the most recent board meeting. AT&T, one of the most formidable corporate giants on the planet, was in danger of running out of cash.

In the summer of 2000, while sitting next to Citigroup CEO Sandy Weill at the AT&T board meeting, I gave him a nudge and asked: "Are you aware that these guys could run into a liquidity crisis, maybe even a bankruptcy, here?"

"What do you mean?" he asked. I told him AT&T had a ton of commercial paper out in the market—around $28 billion. Commercial paper is a short-term, unsecured, and low-cost substitute for bank loans, for big creditworthy issuers, that typically matures in thirty days. Now, looking at the company's declining cash flow as long-distance prices kept falling, I knew Armstrong and his people would have trouble rolling over the debt so as to avoid having to pay off $28 billion all at once. I told Sandy, "And there's no backup. You know, they could be in serious financial trouble, and pretty fast."

A nightmare scenario was forming in my head. If AT&T went bankrupt, its stock would be worthless, and so would my stake in the company. Worse, I was at risk of losing the lifeboat, Liberty Media, which technically still was a part of AT&T.

So, ultimately, if AT&T faltered and couldn't pay off its commercial paper, the holders of those notes would start looking at selling off Liberty assets to recover their loans. In a worst-case scenario—the "What if not?" question—Liberty could be seized by creditors and sold off in pieces, with nothing going to the holders of Liberty tracking stock. It would be a financial disaster for the employees, shareholders, and customers of four companies: AT&T, TCI, MediaOne, and Liberty itself. When this prospect first occurred to me, I literally started to sweat.

To put out the debt fire, AT&T raised cash from a wireless IPO for $10 billion and sold a 16 percent stake to Japanese mobile phone giant DoCoMo for $9.8 billion, and as a safety net, paid banks high interest for backup lines of credit. And finally, they brought in a seasoned CFO, Chuck Noski. The measures that the AT&T executives had to take to save themselves were very painful in terms of loss of future value.

For me, the frustration was that I had to sit there and watch, powerless and unable to simply pick up the phone and demand answers, as I always had done. Without the authority of being the CEO or chairman, it was harder to bend wills my way, or, at the very least, demand accountability. Instead, I gave my advice gently and politely, and it felt like no one was listening.

Then, one afternoon in July 2000, I got a call from a *Wall Street Journal* reporter asking about my views of what was going on at the company. She had caught me at just the right moment—maybe it was the wrong moment. Either way, I gave her an earful.

Since the TCI deal had closed, AT&T shares were down 38 percent, while Liberty's class A shares, adjusted for splits, had soared 78 percent. In speaking for the article, I made sure to be polite and upbeat, insisting that "AT&T has fabulous assets, great people and a solid business plan. I still believe in the end AT&T will get there." I added: "I'm a little frustrated, like everybody else, that the market is not seeing value in the company."

The story pointed out that AT&T shares had lost more than 40 percent of their value since March and reached an all-time low of just below $32 earlier that week in trading on the New York Stock Exchange. Speaking to the reporter as if she had the ear of the board, I rattled off a list of things AT&T could do to help itself, and of course, I raised the issue of a tracking stock for its broadband unit, which held the cable assets.

I received a letter one day from Mike Armstrong, whom I like personally, basically acknowledging that a tracking stock would have indeed solved many of these issues. So we talked about it, and he ultimately floated the idea publicly. But it was too late.

By October 2000, Armstrong had had enough, and he announced what amounted to a breakup of the company. Suddenly, he was a big fan of tracking stocks, and he set new plans to create *four* of them.

AT&T announced a restructuring that would give shareholders the ability to invest in any or all of three newly autonomous units with four separate trackers: AT&T Wireless, AT&T Broadband, and the long-distance business, the last of which would have two trackers, an AT&T Consumer stock linked to the consumer business and an AT&T Business tracker for corporate accounts.

Thus ended a thoughtful strategy with poor execution to remake an icon of American business. AT&T had spent $110 billion to build a national telecommunications conglomerate able to deliver everything from local phone calls to cable television to the internet. The effort had died amid harsh criticism from analysts and investors alike, as AT&T stock continued to flounder.

Armstrong was carving up AT&T not because of a government-mandated breakup, like the one that had created the Baby Bells in 1984, but because of poor management. Now, by splitting itself into pieces, it would do what I had said all along: allow investors to focus on the high-growth sectors without having to also buy into the faltering long-distance business.

Of course, by taking these steps, Armstrong was unintentionally setting up a legendary American icon as an easier target to be broken up and sold off in pieces.

In November, AT&T finally agreed to spin off my baby, Liberty Media, which, since the TCI deal, had been operating free of the parent company's control under a tracking stock that had been outperforming AT&T shares rather handily.

At TCI, we had formed Liberty Media in 1991 as a holding company for the stakes we acquired in cable channels (as opposed to the cable *systems* that TCI operated). And by 2000, Liberty Media owned stakes in twenty-two of the top fifty cable channels, including the Encore pay-TV service, Discovery Communications, USA Network, and QVC. Liberty was the largest shareholder in AOL Time Warner, with a 9 percent stake, and it also held 8 percent of News Corp., which I would increase over time.

Some months later, in early July 2001, I traveled to Sun Valley, Idaho, for the annual Allen & Company conference again. Early on, I came across Comcast's chairman and founder, Ralph Roberts, and his son and successor, Brian. I skipped exchanging pleasantries and cut to the point, basically asking them, "Why don't you take AT&T out of their misery?"

I suggested they could buy just the cable systems out from under the stumbling, debt-burdened giant, and either keep them or spin them off. My argument was: "Do something. Because at this point, I am the largest individual AT&T shareholder, with twenty-six million shares, and I can see that these people don't know what they are doing."

The Robertses already had an offer in the works. On Monday, July 9, 2001, Comcast Corporation announced an unsolicited bid of $44.5 billion for AT&T Broadband, the collective cable systems that AT&T had spent $110 billion to acquire. Comcast would assume $13.5 billion in cable debt as part of the offer. By this time, AT&T had 13.5 million cable subscribers, the largest base in the U.S. If Comcast succeeded in buying the business, it would serve an unprecedented 22 million customers in eight of the ten largest U.S. markets.

Instantly, the Comcast bid marked a reversal in my genteel relations with Mike Armstrong and the AT&T board. Things got adversarial, fast.

As a member, I would have been happy to advise the board of my view of the Comcast offer—it was way too cheap. Alas, the board disinvited me to the meeting for discussing the bid, largely because I would soon be an outsider, with Liberty officially spinning out of AT&T in August 2001.

Around that time, I handed in my resignation letter, then made public my intent to sell 5 million shares of AT&T stock, or about 20 percent of my stake in the company.

By the time Liberty Media broke free, AT&T shareholders had watched the stock tumble down. I empathized. With AT&T's stumbles, coupled with the dot-com bust fallout, I estimate I had lost as much as $4 billion on paper in my personal holdings, Liberty Media, and the value of my AT&T stock, salvaged by my ownership stake in Liberty Media. All things considered, I was enormously relieved. The lifeboat had saved us.

Then, in December 2001, AT&T sold AT&T Broadband, encompassing the cable holdings for which it had paid $110 billion, to Comcast for $47.5 billion in stock, plus the assumption of $25 billion in cable-system debt.

The move left AT&T essentially where it had started. Liberty Media was gone. AT&T's wireless business was spun off (and in 2004 it would merge with Cingular Wireless, co-owned by BellSouth and Southwestern Bell). Now cable would be gone, too, and AT&T would be left with only long-distance and data services for consumer and business accounts. Its stock was trading around $18 at the close of 2001.

Two years later, in January 2004, AT&T agreed to sell itself for all of $16 billion to the former Southwestern Bell, later SBC Communications, which AT&T had spun off in 1984. The company that bears the AT&T brand now was really one of Ma Bell's seven progeny.

I have made many mistakes in business and life, and selling TCI to AT&T might have been the biggest whopper of them all. Losing more than half my wealth at the time was jarring, but also it was galling: I blamed myself. More painful than that, however, was watching TCI, the company that my friend Bob Magness and I had built with a lot of blood, sweat, and tears, simply fade away and get sold for 50 cents on the dollar to our occasional archrivals at Comcast.

My harshest personal critique is that I failed to look hard enough at what we were getting in return for selling TCI to AT&T. We were raptly focused on the handsome premium that AT&T was willing to pay. We were too optimistic. Other TCI shareholders could sell their stock and take the premium, but we were stuck. Aside from my own losses, it was even more painful to acknowledge the stock funds and 401(k) plans laden with the wobbly shares of AT&T.

Once the TCI sale to AT&T was complete, I should have cashed out and gone away. Craig McCaw learned that lesson when he sold McCaw Cellular to AT&T in 1994. Ted Turner learned the same lesson after selling Turner Broadcasting to Time Warner.

Don't go on the board. Don't even hang around. It will make you miserable, because the company you built belongs to someone else now. It is theirs to screw up in whatever way they choose.

Some days were better than others, but more often than not in the months following the spin-off, I suffered through silent self-interrogations over how things ended. These questions were fueled by self-doubt and bottomless remorse, two things I knew were meaningless in the real world.

There are two kinds of regret in life. The first kind eats at you, and you can feel energy drain away with each negative question you torture yourself with.

The second kind drives you and fires you with energy you never knew you had. Watching AT&T, this giant in American telecommunications, simply disintegrate into bits and pieces had been hard to watch. But the whole sordid ordeal was in my rearview mirror, and I couldn't look back anymore.

CHAPTER 22

GOING GLOBAL

While I was stewing over the reckless decisions that led to the inevitable and ignoble end of the last remnants of the old AT&T, one person kept sneaking into my thoughts—a cigar-smoking, brandy-drinking, knee-slapping old Texan named Gene Schneider.

Together with his brother, Richard, Gene was known widely in the U.S. cable TV industry as a pioneer from the earliest days. In 1952, he and his brother had erected a giant microwave on a mountaintop between Laramie and Cheyenne, and they delivered the signals of a Denver TV station to their cable system in Casper, Wyoming. Partnering with Bill Daniels, they were responsible for the first television picture seen in the state of Wyoming.

Gene ultimately would be responsible for my cannonball leap back into the cable-TV business, just months after I had gotten out by selling to AT&T. But my comeback, if you can call it that, would unfold outside the U.S. Gene had opened my eyes to something much bigger that could replicate the model we had assembled in the U.S.: a broadband pipe carrying voice, video, internet data—and wireless—to homes around the world.

A UT-Texas Longhorn, Gene had an unbridled Texas twang, a boisterously loud laugh, and big glasses that covered much of his face. All of that concealed one of the sharpest business minds I have ever known. Our relationship dated back to my days at Jerrold, when I sold cable system components to Gene, while playing countless games of eight-ball pool and talking with him about the future of the industry. Our visions were fueled by big snifters of brandy, a nightly presence in his house in Oklahoma.

Gene and his brother were bitten by the cable bug early. Virtually inseparable since birth, they had both volunteered for the U.S. Navy, where Gene served in aviation and radar electronics, and they eventually went into business together. By 1980, they had built the eighth-largest cable operator in the U.S.

I had maintained a close friendship with Gene ever since my days at Jerrold, periodically checking in on business; his brother Richard had passed away, and his son, Mark, was just getting into the business. Gene had also been a partner of ours in cable systems in the U.S. in the TCI days.

As the U.S. cable industry began to mature, Gene was one of the first to recognize the hunger abroad for American entertainment, and by the late 1980s, he had assumed some small cable television interests in Europe and elsewhere. Viewers around the world, especially Europeans, were hungry for video, which gave Gene a great entrée into markets that were looking to expand their offerings.

Gene had wisely replicated the business lessons he learned from his pole-climbing days in Wyoming: if you build out high-capacity networks where there had been none, it opens up a bounty of new entertainment and information choices, and it can pay dividends for decades.

In 1991, after a series of deals, we had merged Gene's U.S. company, United Cable Television Corporation, into TCI. Gene and his team kept some of the international cable television holdings they had developed, which would ultimately be known as UnitedGlobalCom (UnitedGlobal).

Gene saw virgin territory where others saw complications, currency issues, and unfamiliar rules. He understood that while the start-up tasks were challenging, the potential for scale in certain areas was enormous. Viewers in Europe began to warm to the U.S. style of programming. MTV, for example, had localized versions of its flagship channel, including MTV Europe, which, on a fall day in 1989, actually covered the fall of the Berlin Wall in its own unique style, to the beat of rock music.

Mark Schneider, Gene's son, was even more optimistic about the international markets than his father. VOIP—Voice Over Internet Protocol, which has virtually replaced the old public switched network for homes and businesses today—was just being perfected for mass rollout and fine-tuned for cable modems by CableLabs. Strategically, cable could now go after the telephone companies' turf. To the Schneiders, any investments made now would surely pay off huge, just as they had in the U.S.

UnitedGlobal began spending more and more to rip out and replace aging cable wires with new hybrid-fiber coaxial and broadband systems, and borrowing even more on acquisitions.

In early 2000, at the height of the Internet bubble, UnitedGlobal— public since 1993—had a market capitalization of $10 billion and more than a million cable subscribers across Asia, Australia, and Latin America. And its crown jewel was a controlling stake in United Pan-European Communications (UPC), then Europe's largest cable television operator, serving 10 million subscribers in sixteen countries. UnitedGlobal had taken UPC public in 1999 on the Euronext Amsterdam exchange. And in July 2000, Forbes had dubbed CEO Mark Schneider "Europe's New King of Fiber."

But Gene Schneider's overseas operation had just one problem: it was burning up cash a lot faster than it could take it in. The debt load was too great, and the ROI would take years to be realized.

During the late 1990s and into 2000, UPC was able to buy new systems in Europe with relatively cheap debt, but these acquisitions required continued access to capital to offer the digital "triple-play" of voice, video, and data. More than sixteen acquisitions in five years saddled UPC with $10.5 billion in debt, which would, in short order, pull it down like a weighted anchor. UPC's stock dropped from a high of around 80 Euros in March 2000 to under one Euro, threatening the company's listing on Euronext.

When the internet bubble burst and tech stocks collapsed, UPC's digital momentum vanished. The growth story seemed over—Gene and Mark were no longer building the future; they were trying to keep the company alive.

It was a classic start-up problem. The existential crisis the Schneiders found themselves in had nothing to do with the quality of their product— the new services were hands-down better than anything offered in the sleepy markets of Europe. And it wasn't a demand problem—it was almost a given that penetration rates in upgraded markets shot up. It was a money problem, and in this case, the culprit was debt.

In the summer of 2001, with shareholders restless and the company's options waning, Mark Schneider, the CEO of UPC, then Europe's largest cable operator, resigned after the firm reported one of its worst quarters.

My decision to get involved took all of five seconds. Gene was in trouble. Here was one of the pioneers of the industry, flat on his back, and the vultures were circling. If nothing was done, the company's European subsidiary and biggest operation would have to file for bankruptcy. A dream would die, and one of my oldest friends would go under financially. All the while, the possibilities became more visible to me:

- We already owned 35 percent of UnitedGlobal, a stake we acquired from Apollo in late 1999.
- We were sitting on a pile of cash that wasn't doing anything.
- We couldn't get back into the cable business in the U.S. because I personally had a noncompete clause in the contract with AT&T, while all of Gene's cable TV assets were in foreign countries.
- And we served a few markets ourselves in Europe, Asia, and Latin America through our Liberty Media International unit.

This could work. By moving a few chess pieces on the board, Liberty could become the dominant terrestrial broadband player outside North America.

During the whole process, Gene and I talked things through like the old friends we had always been. His son, Mark, had uncovered some remarkable opportunities in Europe, Gene said, but had simply gotten ahead of himself. I was warming to the idea of becoming the largest shareholder of the largest cable operator outside the United States. Why not replicate the success of TCI on a broader canvas?

Gene said the window was open: Goldman Sachs had provided UPC with a $1.0 billion bridge loan when things looked better but was now having second thoughts and would consider getting out.

We'd be stepping into Goldman Sachs's shoes as a financier and investor, becoming the senior-most creditor of UPC in the process.

We spent the next two years executing some of the most complex deals I've been involved with, all with the goal of fixing UnitedGlobal's European subsidiary and righting the ship that had been blown off course with too much leverage.

Once Liberty Media became the most important creditor to UPC through the Goldman bridge and public debt we had purchased in the market at distressed prices, we turned around to Gene and offered to trade him these positions plus about $1 billion of cash in exchange for 75 percent and control of UnitedGlobal.

This made a lot of sense for both of us. Gene would have the tools he needed to force his European debt holders to restructure UPC—which they agreed to nine months later by swapping $7 billion of the $10.5 billion of debt for 35 percent of the European operation. He would ultimately buy out the bondholders with UnitedGlobal stock, leaving him once again with 100 percent of a much healthier business in Europe.

By this time we had invested about $2 billion into Gene's company, but we were not done. My ultimate goal was always to consolidate everything we had into one large international cable company.

So in 2004 we spun out Liberty Media International, which owned the 75 percent of UnitedGlobal and some of its own cable interests, and later merged in the remaining 25 percent of UnitedGlobal.

In 2005, the newly combined public company started life as Liberty Global, which quickly became one of the largest broadband providers outside the U.S., with stakes in businesses serving more than 15 million customers across nineteen countries and reaching 30 million homes. Gene graciously handed over the chairman title to me.

What we needed more than anything was a global leader who was good at many things—someone who understood the financial markets, capital allocation, the dynamics of M&A, the changing technology, and consumer demand. Someone, also, who could tell the story to investors and local media in different countries, often with different cultures and languages.

But we wouldn't need a search firm to find our next CEO. We already had one who was essentially doing the job: UnitedGlobal president and COO Mike Fries.

Mike had joined the Schneiders in early 1990, shortly after Gene founded his international cable business; he was the fifth employee at the firm at twenty-seven years old and by all accounts a cofounder. Mike was one of the few Americans who could adapt quickly to complex operations, local politics, new regulations, and foreign tax systems.

By contrast, several U.S. cable operators and telephone companies had rushed into international markets in the 1980s and 1990s, only to retreat back to U.S. shores as they gave up on the complexities of doing business outside them.

Mike also had good reason to hustle. Like his colleagues, the challenges of the European business in 2001 had wiped out most of his equity in the firm he had helped build. He was also right by Gene's side as we all worked through those transactions in 2001 to 2003 that gave UnitedGlobal a second shot.

From the beginning, Mike was a driving force behind UnitedGlobal's expansion around the world. Just as Eastern Europe was opening up in 1990, Mike and Nimrod Kovacs jumped on an airplane to Hungary. The way Mike tells it, they basically rented a car and drove to every large city. And in thirteen of them, they convinced formerly communist mayors in newly capitalist economies to privatize their cable networks, which were of mediocre quality, for about $10 million dollars. That first operation in Eastern Europe was ultimately sold to Vodafone for €700 million.

After launching Liberty Global, Mike drove rapid growth with laser focus—pushing products people truly wanted, like local sports and a sleek, Netflix-style interface. In 2012, Horizon TV transformed tablets and smartphones into remote controls or extra TV screens, even letting users beam personal content to their TVs wirelessly.

Then, in a bold, judolike move, Liberty Global embraced Netflix rather than fighting it. In 2013, just as Netflix spread across Europe, it became an app on Liberty's platform. Instead of losing customers, the company found they watched more, paid more, and stayed longer. Seamless access to both CNN and Netflix on the same box? Customers loved it. And other portfolio companies like Discovery started feeding Liberty Global's systems—a dose of ever-elusive synergy, something many giant media companies chased in the 1990s to little effect.

Over time, we upgraded networks, acquired local partners, and refined content. As demand surged, so did profits. Despite navigating complex regulations and political landscapes, Liberty Global outpaced its U.S. peers in the broadband race—delivering the coveted triple-play of voice, video, and data with 100 Mbps speeds as early as 2008. We consistently outperformed incumbent telcos, capturing broadband market share across Europe. Even today, many customers enjoy speeds from one to two Gbps—two to three times faster than rival ISPs—cementing Liberty's long lead in the two-decade race for broadband dominance.

Over the next two decades under Mike's leadership, we began buying, building, selling, and trading cable assets across the globe, completing over $200 billion in deals in more than fifty countries.

While many of my peers in the media and entertainment business were empire builders, I always advocated for smart capital allocation and good timing—like exiting Japan and Australia at high multiples and reinvesting $5 billion into Europe, where the cable market was fragmented and ripe for consolidation.

One of those markets was Germany. In 2010 and 2011, we bought two companies for $9 billion just as private equity was retreating. After scaling the businesses and boosting broadband, Mike orchestrated a sale to Vodafone for $21 billion—turning a $2 billion equity stake into $13 billion in proceeds and dividends. Big mobile operators were focused on adding fixed broadband to their portfolios and we were willing to oblige. Similar deals followed, with Deutsche Telekom buying our Austrian cable assets and Iliad acquiring our Polish operations.

In markets where we had broadband scale, we saw the same convergence opportunity with mobile. In the Netherlands, we merged Ziggo with Vodafone's mobile business in a fifty-fifty joint venture, becoming the country's largest consumer telecom provider. In the UK, after acquiring Virgin Media for $23 billion, we struck a similar deal with Telefonica, merging it with O2, becoming the leading national challenger to British Telecom.

Bundling broadband and mobile proved smart—customers were more loyal and spent more. Despite the complexity of fifty-fifty deals, Mike and the team have made them work. The only question now is how they'll eventually unwind.

While Europe was consolidating, our presence in Latin America took a major leap forward in 2015 with the $8 billion purchase of Cable & Wireless Communications, which added two dozen new markets to our existing operations in Chile and Puerto Rico.

By the end of 2017, in classic Liberty style, we spun off our Latin American operations into a new public company—Liberty Latin America—led by CEO Balan Nair, a longtime Liberty Global executive and tech-savvy strategist always focused on what's next. More recently, we did the same with Sunrise in Switzerland. As part of Liberty Global, Sunrise was valued at just 5.5 times EBITDA. Now, on the Swiss exchange, it trades at 8 times. That's the kind of upside we target—unlocking value through smart, tax-efficient spin-offs, capitalizing on strong market multiples, all while focused on share buybacks. Since 2017, Liberty Global has spent nearly $15 billion to buy back over 60 percent of its shares, boosting long-term investor value.

Liberty Global continues today as one of Europe's leading broadband and mobile providers, with consolidated operations in the United Kingdom, Ireland, the Netherlands, Belgium, and Slovakia. Today, Liberty Global has 30,000 employees serving 30 million gigabit homes, 80 million fixed and mobile connections, and generating $22 billion in aggregate revenue. And over his twenty years as CEO, Mike has collected more passport stamps than most diplomats.

He's also a literal rock star—lead singer of a band made up of Colorado CEOs who trade spreadsheets for Stratocasters. When he's not onstage or in the boardroom, he's hurling himself down mountains, heli-skiing, or mountain-biking places I can only observe from a distance. Legal tried sneaking a "no life-threatening hobbies" clause into his contract. Mike politely declined. At one board retreat, he was last seen waterskiing behind my float-plane, smiling like a man who's never heard the words "risk management."

What impresses me most about Mike is his treatment of everyone on his team. Over the years he has assembled an extraordinary group of loyal executives who represent some of the best operating, legal, financial, technical, and M&A talent in the business. And I've never seen him take credit, only share the limelight. He mentors newcomers over dinner in his home and stays grounded by giving back to his hometown.

And he has built an entrepreneurial culture that closely resembles the DNA that Bob Magness and I shared. A division called Liberty Growth with $3 billion of media, tech, and infrastructure investments looks an awful lot like Liberty Media when we started.

These days, Liberty Global's priority, getting wired and wireless together, is number one. Over the last twenty years, revenue has grown from $5 billion of mostly video services to more than $20 billion with half of that attributable to mobile services and most of the balance to broadband. Consumers want seamless connection—at home or on the go—and delivering that is more valuable than ever.

The combination of terrestrial and mobile assets is increasingly potent in Europe, driving scale and synergies, as it will be at some point in the U.S.

So in the Liberty Global camp, connectivity is king, not content, which is why it continues to strike deals melding cable and wireless into a single, seamless service. Now the future will blend these two fronts into a single virtual pipe offering all manner of functions, services, and content via land or air, via cable or cellular. How it all got there to the palm of your hand will be utterly invisible, and which route it took will no longer matter.

CHAPTER 23

CLEARING THE LEDGER

By the time of the presidential election in 2004, Rupert Murdoch and I had come to know each other well. We had formed a pretty good friendship, competing and cooperating on a number of fronts and building the mutual trust that is integral to doing business.

That trust can be damaged by a single phone call. Or by the lack of one, and that is what happened to Rupert and me in this next go-round.

On Tuesday evening, November 2, 2004, my wife and I were watching coverage of the election returns for Republican George W. Bush and Democrat John Kerry when the phone rang. The caller surprised the hell out of me.

Our Merrill Lynch contact in Sydney was calling me back to confirm an earlier call in which he told me that, inexplicably, a big block of News Corp. *voting* stock, the kind of shares that Rupert and his family owned, was coming up for sale on the Australian stock market. As he had asked earlier, were we interested in buying it?

News Corp.'s business properties were becoming more valuable than Rupert's holdings in Australia, and he had decided to delist the company's stock from the equivalent of the S&P 500 on the Australian exchange and have it join Nasdaq in the U.S.

Moving News Corp. to Nasdaq forced Australian index funds to sell their shares, including a large block from the Australian Index Fund, which had to auction off its stake by the end of the day under its rules. As the Merrill caller told me: "The entire holding of News Corp. will be liquidated from this fund. Those are the rules. So, if you're interested in buying some of this, have somebody there with the authority and the wherewithal to bid for it."

Liberty already had built up a 9 percent stake in News Corp. with non-voting shares and was the largest single shareholder in the company after the Murdoch family, which held 27 percent. This was a rare opportunity for us to own an even bigger stake by acquiring voting stock—on the open Australian market.

Even from the first time Liberty Media invested in News Corp. stock, I had always known in the back of my mind that at some point down the road, Rupert and I would sit down, and he would swap us out and trade some attractive assets he owned for our stake in his company.

At the time, I had no idea why so much precious voting stock in Rupert's company was coming up for grabs, and neither did Liberty's CEO, Dob Bennett, but I knew a cheap stock when I saw it. I advised Dob to buy the shares in the Sydney auction, telling him, "If News Corp. or the Murdoch family show up to bid for it, stand down. If no one from the Murdoch family shows up, then go ahead and bid for it."

"How much do you want to buy?" Dob asked me. "It's gonna be quite a bit."

"All of it."

Liberty Media entered an open auction for News Corp. stock, trading 21 million nonvoting shares plus cash in exchange for a 9 percent voting stake. In 2004, Liberty increased that stake to 17 percent, making it the second-largest voting shareholder after the Murdoch family, which held 30 percent.

To me, this was a continuation of our strategy to accumulate News Corp. stock on the open market because I genuinely regarded News Corp. as undervalued and I trusted the leadership. If we were ever going to swap out with Rupert, it would be better to have the voting shares.

As I saw it from Rupert's point of view, he was low on cash, and stock was the one asset he had in his company for doing deals. And Liberty was a friendly company with a lot of firepower.

I knew that in any transaction with any company, voting equity will have a greater dollar value, and greater psychological value, than nonvoting stock. This especially was true for a family-controlled company like News Corp., where it was especially important to Rupert Murdoch to retain control and hand his company to his two sons, James and Lachlan.

The statement from Liberty was succinct, or so we thought: "News Corp. is one of the few truly global media companies, and we are very pleased we were able to leverage our substantial equity interest in News Corp. into a larger equity and voting stake."

News Corp., officially, at least, said it welcomed the investment. "In our view this is another sign of confidence in our company's health and future strategy by Dr. Malone," a News Corp. spokesman told AFP.

Still, the media swirled with wild speculation about Liberty's intentions, eagerly suspecting we were plotting a takeover with the second-largest voting stake.

Looking back, I made a critical mistake, especially when dealing with a friend: I failed to be absolutely clear about my intentions. Having failed to call Rupert when we first heard about the stock coming up for sale, I should have called him after the news broke to tell him what had happened. But I didn't. And so the speculation that we were going to make a move on his company only intensified.

An article in *The Independent* described me as Darth Vader in the opening sentence and said I had "parked [my] tanks on the lawn of Rupert Murdoch, their cannons aimed squarely at Murdoch's own media empire." The story went on to say that "it is not unreasonable to wonder if he is in the first phase of an all-out campaign to acquire News Corp., owner of *The Times*, BSkyB, Fox Television and countless other assets for himself." This had to have unnerved Rupert. Publicly, he was unflappable. Was he concerned? a reporter asked him.

"No, not at all. I think it's an endorsement of the company. I say that quite sincerely. I'm not losing any sleep over it."

For a few days, he didn't return my phone calls, and I couldn't blame him. We were both trying to figure out what had happened.

Someone must have made a mistake for a family dynasty to allow that much stock to go on the open market. I knew from his people talking to our people that Rupert was pissed, but I also knew that he was a hell of a lot more pissed at his own people.

But at that point, a deep, primal defense instinct, honed over decades, had awakened in my old friend, and there was little I could do to put him at ease. Rupert then took some very public defensive measures, rallying allies, including a Saudi prince who moved to acquire 5 percent of the stock on the open market.

And yet Rupert never called me screaming, demanding answers. He never attacked me or Liberty publicly. He was, always, a gentleman, and that is important to me in business dealings.

Of all the companies in media where we owned sizable stakes, including Discovery, QVC, and Starz, the News Corp. stake was Liberty's most valuable asset. I had no intention of taking over, or even threatening to take over. I knew once we had that block of stock, we would be able to work something out with Rupert that was mutually beneficial. As chairman/CEO, it was my obligation to increase the value of Liberty's shares.

When I finally did talk to Rupert a few days later, it wasn't hostile, but it wasn't friendly. He didn't cast blame or chide me or say I should have told him. It was simply, okay, these are the facts, what are we gonna do about it?

I expressed to him that we would have stayed out of it if he wanted to buy the big stake, but we saw no one from News Corp. at the auction, and we loved his company, so we bought it.

"Rupert, we've always had great relations. There's no need to go into panic mode."

Then I did what I could in the press to dispel any rumors of hostile intentions and show support for Rupert. We put out a statement saying News Corp. was "the best run, most strategically positioned vertically integrated media company in the world." Liberty CEO Robert Bennett would later reaffirm the statements: "We are a large happy friendly shareholder."

The press fed the intrigue, and five days after the news of our stock purchase broke, Rupert unveiled his board's plans for a poison pill, specifically aimed at preventing me from increasing my stake further. The "poison" is different in each pill; with this one, if Liberty were to purchase any more shares, it would trigger a plan letting existing shareholders increase their shares at half price, making a takeover by Liberty all but impossible.

He was assuming that we were playing with his legacy, and he didn't like it. The company said the poison pill was a precaution, and Rupert was doing exactly what I would have done had I felt threatened—protecting all shareholders from a takeover without getting paid a premium.

So we scheduled a series of meetings. Rupert and his sons, James and Lachlan, flew out to see me in Denver, and we met in a conference room at Liberty Media. I reassured them that we were happy, passive investors. Maybe we could do something creative here. There might be some assets they would like to swap for some of our News Corp. shares. Or if this was too much, maybe we could discuss a way to take us out over time.

They wanted to talk about a trade. And that is when Rupert Murdoch offered to swap us DirecTV.

James Murdoch, who was running Sky at the time, was concerned about the future of the satellite business and the fact that it lacked the two-way, interactive capacity of cable broadband networks. Cable operators were offering the Triple Play—voice, video, and data over one line—while satellite looked to be limited to a future as a robust one-way system with minimal internet delivery.

In the fall of 2006, we finally shook hands on a deal. I agreed to swap Liberty's 19 percent voting stake in News Corp., valued at $11 billion, in return for Murdoch's 38 percent stake in DirecTV, valued at roughly $7.4 billion, plus three regional sports networks owned by News Corp. and $550 million in cash.

In the end, it worked out extremely well for us both.

Because it was largely a swap of assets, both sides avoided taxes. Secondly, it monetized a healthy 26 percent gain on the $6 billion Rupert had paid for DirecTV after so many labyrinthine moves a few years earlier.

And our latest transaction gave Rupert the one thing that he cared most about—family control of the company. In redeeming the shares, he popped from 28 percent of the vote to a virtually unassailable 42 percent.

Considering the volume and value of News Corp. stock involved, it amounted to one of the largest buybacks in corporate history.

For Liberty, and for me, personally, this was the apex of three decades of dealmaking with Rupert Murdoch, one that would even up the ledger between me and an old friend and respected competitor. We got out of a noncontrolling stake in News Corp. and into effective control of DirecTV, at a good price, and I was back on good footing with Rupert.

Now, here is one thing that gets me: all of this came about by serendipity and the randomness of business and market events, and by our reacting and adapting and finding a way to work things out. Yet the media and gossips in the business started to say that it was all planned, an elaborate, premeditated plot to increase Rupert's control of News Corp.

That gives Rupert Murdoch and me far more credit for brilliant foresight and Machiavellian maneuvering than either one of us might deserve. I can promise you here and now, we arrived at that day more by accident than anything else. And an awful lot of deals happen that way.

Life is like that. Sometimes you have to experience a setback or a surprise to change your way of thinking. I look back and wish I had done some things differently, but I know the mistakes I made are an important part of what I learned, and they helped shape my thinking and make me a better person.

I had turned sixty-five the year that Liberty prepared to take over DirecTV. At a time when most people retire, I was about to become a new chairman.

When news spread that a onetime cable cowboy was now the owner of DirecTV, the largest satellite service, it was as if I had walked across the field at halftime and switched team jerseys. Many found it dubious that I had chosen to get into the satellite-TV business just as General Motors and News Corp. were getting out of it to focus on buying internet properties.

I could see what Rupert and his sons could see—the day when cable operators and broadband would eclipse satellite-TV services like DirecTV with broadband capacity. We just thought this doom was farther off in the future than everyone else thought, and we could make it a pretty good asset for a couple of years. And we did.

Under Michael White, a former PepsiCo executive, DirecTV had grown net subscribers each year, and by 2010, it had signed up 19 million subscribers. DirecTV was close to taking Comcast's title as the largest pay-TV provider in the U.S. All it took was a bit of patience. Liberty had turned deferred gratification into an investment philosophy. We were willing to make investments that could take years to mature in an uncertain environment.

In June 2010, just a couple of years after Liberty had officially taken control of DirecTV, I stepped down as chairman and resigned along with two other Liberty members of the DirecTV board. We announced a stock swap meant to reduce my voting control in the satellite giant from 24 percent to just 3 percent.

This was not by choice, but by government demand—the FCC was concerned about potential overlap between Liberty Global's Puerto Rico cable operations and the DirecTV subsidiary there. It was a rather picayune point, and too often this is precisely the FCC's raison d'être, but there you have it. And let me also say, bless those same unelected bureaucrats. Their order ended up being a lucky setback that may have saved Liberty Media billions in losses at DirecTV.

Five years after the FCC bounced us out of DirecTV, AT&T acquired the service in 2015 in a diversification move beyond wireless for $67 billion (including $18 million in DirecTV debt), combining its subscribers with AT&T video customers to claim the title of largest pay-TV provider in the nation, serving 26 million customers.

So-called cord-cutting was a new troubling new phrase among cable operators as viewers began to abandoning cable for streaming video. Just as this disruption hit, AT&T paid $67 million in stock and debt for DirecTV in 2015 and made a bad situation worse: it raised prices, killed promotions, and watched nearly 8 million subscribers walk away between 2016 and 2020. Pay-TV overall shrank by 20 million in those years, but DirecTV's fall was steepest—plunging from number 1 to number 3, and ending with a $15.5 billion write-down in early 2021. Bad timing, worse execution.

These days Rupert and I still talk, and now and again we still compete for the same prize. Always, though, we operate with the same decorum and respect that are part of our implicit agreement that we are going to play to win but not at the cost of our principles or reputation.

Liberty Global jumped into the ring against BSkyB in the UK in 2013 when we bought UK pay-TV company Virgin Media for $23.3 billion. Three years after that, we saw an opportunity for Formula One, owned by a consortium of companies led by CVC Capital Partners and run by longtime CEO Bernie Ecclestone.

We saw Formula One as an interesting turnaround proposition. Eyeing the field, we compiled a short list of our possible rivals in a bidding war, and the top three were Apple, a Qatari businessman, and my old friend Rupert Murdoch.

In late 2016 I got another call from Rupert, who this time told me, "John, I guess you know the boys [Lachlan and James] are going to be bidding against you on this. I don't know why they want it, but I thought you ought to know." It was a gentlemanly thing to do.

In the end, Liberty was willing to pay more, outbidding News Corp. and agreeing to $4.4 billion for a 35.5 percent stake in Formula One in January 2017, which valued the entire enterprise at around $8 billion including debt. We brought in one of Rupert's most trusted executives as Formula One's new chairman, Chase Carey, former executive vice chairman of 21st Century Fox.

Some time later, Rupert made another call to me, and this one would prove to be especially memorable. Rupert, as he always did, moved past any pleasantries to get to his point.

"John," he said, starting out carefully, "I guess you heard the news. I've got offers from three bidders to buy 21st Century Fox and Sky. What do you think?"

CHAPTER 24

OWNER'S MANUAL

The most critical issue for any large investor is control—or the lack of it. How big of a stake do you need to control the company and block hostile or aggressive shareholders from staging a coup? I don't know what the exact answer to that is. Some people say it is around 15 percent. I think it is probably closer to 50 percent.

Throughout my business career, I have done everything I can to be in control of the companies in which I invest. I am haunted by memories of living by your wits; the stock drops 20 percent and you have to start thinking about finding another job. Control is a necessity rather than a luxury—it is the primary reason we have succeeded. At Liberty Media, our controlling stakes in our various properties let us avoid having to spend all of our time looking over our shoulders, making short-term decisions for antsy Wall Street analysts looking for quarterly gains.

For the most part, Liberty has opted to own stakes of companies, rather than take full control, and then to spin those stakes out at the right time to create more public companies with their own separate stocks, creating still more value for shareholders. Among the companies Liberty has spun out are Discovery Communications, Starz, DirecTV, QVC, Liberty Broadband, Expedia, and SiriusXM.

Of all the business leaders in my orbit, few people appreciate ownership control more than Barry Diller. Barry and I feel much the same way about the topic. The push for control would come to shape Barry's destiny. And at one point, the battle for control would come damn close to tearing apart our twenty-year friendship.

In his twenties, Barry was a Hollywood wunderkind. He had started his career in the mailroom at talent agency William Morris. Later, as head of programming at ABC, Diller brought in a protégé, Michael Eisner. They all but invented the TV movie of the week and the big-event miniseries. In his thirties, Barry ran Paramount Studios, serving for a decade as chief executive and green-lighting megahits such as *Saturday Night Fever* and *Raiders of the Lost Ark*.

Diller left that job in 1984 and joined up with Rupert Murdoch to pursue the implausible dream of starting Fox, a fourth broadcast television network to compete with the oligopoly of ABC, CBS, and NBC. Eisner, who had followed Diller to Paramount, quit and ended up becoming CEO of a then-ailing Walt Disney Company.

The network Diller built, Fox Broadcasting Company, grew into a spectacular success, altering the TV landscape and ushering in a new, subversive style of programming. Fox gave the world *The Simpsons*, which started as a cartoon short, became its own series in 1989, and as of this writing is the longest-running scripted prime-time TV show in U.S. history.

Barry had programming skills born of real passion, the type of creativity that is impossible to learn. I am in awe of this, because I will never be a gifted programmer, able to divine what audiences are craving to consume when they don't even know it themselves.

All my career, I have tried to nurture a curiosity to learn. But for all the knowledge I have accumulated, there are things I will never know how to do. I have learned that no matter how brilliant you are, there will be other people who are better than you are at executing your ideas. And if you are smart, you will politely step out of the way and leave them to it.

This was the instinct that I usually followed, and over the years, this would help free up Barry Diller to create billions of dollars in wealth for his shareholders, including Liberty and our shareholders to boot.

Despite the amazing feat Diller achieved in creating the fourth broadcasting network, he sensed that no matter how well he performed, he would never really be in control of Fox Broadcasting. It was part of News Corp., and Rupert had made it clear that his sons, Lachlan and James, would inherit the throne. Someday. (Albeit that someday has been looming now for thirty years, and Rupert is still around.)

So Diller resigned at Fox in 1992. His next pursuit was to take on the CEO post at shopping channel QVC, which he hoped to use as a platform for bigger ambitions. Really big: in 1994, he had QVC bid to take over CBS and came close to pulling it off.

But less than twenty-four hours before CBS and QVC boards were to vote their approval of the merger Barry had orchestrated, Comcast owners Ralph and Brian Roberts stepped in with a $2.2 billion offer to buy QVC and thwarted Barry's bid. He left soon after and got fascinated with the interactive-shopping possibilities of the newly emerging internet and World Wide Web.

Barry and I stayed in touch after he left QVC, as he was spending increasingly more time on his new boat searching the horizon for the Next Big Thing.

The whole time he was looking around, we had fun talking about our shared passion of sailing vessels. I had just finished restoring my boat *Ragtime*, and now I was looking at building a new boat, with no sails. Later, we would christen it *Liberty*, in part because it was one of the few places where I felt like I was free from the chains of duty and responsibility.

In the spinning flywheel of my mind, I started grinding out an idea. At Home Shopping Network, founder Roy Speer was leaving, and we needed someone with retail and TV experience to drive that business, with more than $1 billion in revenue every year.

We already had concluded that neither Liberty CEO Robert (Dob) Bennett nor I was a retail merchant. Barry would be perfect—given his programming savvy and his recent stint running competitor QVC, in which Liberty also owned a stake.

More to the point, Home Shopping Network owned a bunch of UHF local broadcast stations it originally had purchased to increase HSN viewership, but Liberty Media, as part owner of HSN, was forbidden by federal cross-ownership rules from owning the station group. So HSN had spun off the stations and named the new business Silver King Communications.

It occurred to me: Who better to run this new outfit than programming genius Barry Diller? So, in mid-1994, I briefed him on this national network of broadcast stations made up of a dozen UHF stations that covered roughly 20 percent of the country in big metro markets like New York, Chicago, and Los Angeles.

We discussed him creating a network with Silver King. I told him it was even possible we could recombine Home Shopping Network with its much smaller spin-off to create a more formidable balance sheet for acquisitions and growth.

When I asked Barry if he would be interested in taking on a bigger role as head of both HSN and Silver King, he paused. His answer went right to the heart of a truth Barry had come to realize after so many decades of being an employee, with negligible ownership and little real, formal control.

"I've built businesses for other people," Barry said earnestly, referring to Paramount, ABC, and Fox, "and I've ended up out in the cold. I never *owned* anything, and I don't want to go into another role where I can't make the decisions because I'm not the owner."

His words struck a chord with me, as someone who had spent half his career at TCI working for someone else. So I made him the offer of a lifetime. "Okay, Barry, here's the deal: If you agree to take on the role of chairman of the combined HSN/SK for me, you've got a lifetime proxy. As long as you want to do it, you have our votes, and we won't interfere."

Though Barry owned just shy of 4 percent of the vote, I would offer him, in writing, lifetime control over Liberty's super-voting and ordinary shares, as if Barry himself owned those shares. Now Barry would control around 70 percent of the vote of the combined company until he quit or died.

It was an extraordinary arrangement, one that I never had contemplated doing before, and one I have never done since. This revealed how vital and valuable Barry's skills and instincts were going to be in building the consolidated company.

So Barry agreed to become chairman and CEO of Silver King Communications as well as Home Shopping Network, which we merged in 1996. Barry remained chairman of both, and Liberty ended up with a stake of about 20 percent in the new HSN Inc.

Barry and I had some things in common—boats and business—but it is our differences that have enriched my life. Barry cultivates diverse interests and lives in a different world than I do. On any given day, he may be chatting up a Hollywood celebrity, dining out with his delightful fashion-designer wife Diane von Furstenberg, or cutting deals with internet tycoons at headquarters, a signature, chic, white glass–paneled tower designed by the renowned architect Frank Gehry, along the Hudson River in New York City.

My interests in business differ. I could very well be negotiating to buy land for timber, looking at hotels in Ireland, or heading out to the ranch office for a wolf sighting near the fence line. So Barry helps me tap into a talent and a worldview that I would not otherwise have.

Often CEOs hire agreeable, focused, hardworking operating clones, but they are less likely to innovate the business they are in or find a new business to enter. At Liberty, we were good at investing in cable channels, our core roots, but the internet boom was igniting, and we lacked the knack to bet big on this new wave—Barry Diller could be our guide.

E-commerce platforms drew the earliest and largest bidders, and Barry already had handicapped many of them. He set out on a mission to identify the best online banking, dating, shopping, travel, and entertainment companies. And he bought scores of them.

At first, Liberty CEO Dob Bennett was skeptical about investments in the internet, abiding by the old notion that pioneers get arrows in their backs. But Barry was a seasoned, aggressive CEO looking for opportunities to grow. Barry was willing to make big bets, and I trusted him. Plus, I liked his nickname: "Killer Diller."

And happily for Liberty shareholders and those who bet on Barry Diller, this man truly did "kill" it. In the ensuing years, the newly formed HSN Inc. would morph into USA Networks, then Universal, then Universal Interactive, then IAC/InteractiveCorp, and finally IAC. Along the way, the company cobbled together dozens of online businesses that started out being worth millions of dollars and ended up growing into companies worth billions of dollars.

In one of his first and most prescient investments, Barry in 1997 bought a controlling stake in the ticket sales giant Ticketmaster from Paul Allen, cofounder of Microsoft, in a stock swap that granted Allen an 11 percent stake in HSN. With Paul's 48 percent stake in Ticketmaster and shares he bought on the open market, Barry had 50.1 percent control of the number one events ticket-seller.

Barry's HSN then paid $4.1 billion in stock and cash to Edgar Bronfman's Seagram Company in 1997 to buy Universal Studios' TV assets, which included USA Network, Sci-Fi Channel, and the TV production and distribution businesses. The price would turn out to be a bargain for Barry; the same assets would prompt an even richer bidder to make an offer to Barry two years later.

Meanwhile, Diller's newly renamed USA Networks was scouring the internet for e-commerce sites, acquiring the leaders in various categories. In 1998, Barry merged Ticketmaster with Citysearch, a digital travel-guide service, and the public stock took off. A year later it bought Hotel Reservations Network, which became Hotels.com.

At Liberty, which still held around 60 percent equity stake in the whole combination, we were impressed and pleased with Barry's picks. And even if we had disagreed, he had sole authority to proceed anyway, having lifetime control over our shareholder vote. This is the great thing about control: it freed up Barry Diller to place big bets without having to worry about getting fired.

In 1999, Barry made another prophetic bet with online dating, paying just $50 million to Cendant Corp. for a dating site called Match.com. IAC would spin out Match Group as a separate public company twenty years later. Today, Match Group Inc. owns the largest portfolio of online dating services in the world, including Tinder, Match.com, Meetic, OkCupid, Hinge, Plenty of Fish, OurTime, and other global brands. Match Group's market cap now approaches $7 billion. Based on Barry's original $50 million price tag, this amounts to an annual return of 28 percent over those two decades. Extraordinary.

In 2001, USA Networks bought Expedia, intending to combine it with Hotel Reservation Networks. It closed the deal in the wake of the travel market collapse after the 9/11 attacks. By this time, Barry's digital businesses had become so significant that he renamed the company IAC/InterActiveCorp, and focused almost solely on rolling up digital brands to combine them, build them, and spin them out into separate stocks later on.

Barry's dream of launching another broadcast television network withered next to the velocity of deals in the digital world that was forming before our eyes. Despite his bold efforts to transform Silver King into a hyperlocal broadcasting programmer in metro areas, the U.S. broadcasting strategy failed to get traction. Sometimes even the dreams you hold on to the longest just weren't meant to be.

But the stations' value had skyrocketed thanks to the 1992 Cable Act, which included a retransmission consent/must-carry clause that *required* broadcasters to carry all broadcast stations in any given market. In 2001, Barry sold the stations to Univision, the nation's leading Spanish-language broadcaster, for $1.1 billion in cash—almost double what Liberty had paid for voting control of the entire HSN company in 1993.

The following year, in 2002, IAC sold the Universal cable-TV network assets that Barry had bought from Seagram five years earlier for $4 billion. He sold them to a French company called Vivendi for $10.3 billion in stock and cash—with a nice profit for IAC, and thus for Liberty. An annual return of 15 percent in those five years.

That is, if the currency paid to IAC—the stock of Vivendi—was worth what it was stated to be worth. And therein lies the problem. What seemed like a good deal would turn out to be a catastrophe for everyone involved.

You can choke on a deal if you rush through the numbers or get too emotional about a prize. You must learn the other company's business as fast as humanly possible before you commit money, even after assurances from the seller. A lesson I've come to embrace: there is no such thing as too much due diligence before a merger.

All of the due diligence in the world, however, will fail to rescue you if you are dealing with a deceitful person. And in this case, that deceitful person was an ambitious, egotistical French businessman named Jean-Marie

Messier. Vivendi's chairman and CEO, Messier was hell-bent on remaking his company, a French water utility, into a global media empire. Which sounds far-fetched on its face, even so many years later.

In 2000, Messier had embarked on a $60 billion acquisition spree to remake Vivendi into a media giant in league with AOL TimeWarner, Viacom, and the Walt Disney Company. Vivendi agreed to put up $12 billion in stock to take full control of Europe's biggest pay-TV company, Canal Plus, and $34.4 billion in stock to buy global liquor giant Seagram and its entertainment assets—which included the Universal studio, music business, and theme park—while also taking on nearly $9 billion in debt from both companies.

Now Vivendi's Messier would reunite those Seagram businesses with the TV assets Seagram had sold to Diller's USA-turned-IAC. It was an era of media mergers, and Messier saw a kindred soul in Edgar Bronfman, the young scion of Seagram's. Bronfman was fueled by the longing to change his family's liquor fortune into a media empire.

In exchange for a 3.6 percent stake in Vivendi, Liberty had thrown in the controlling stake in USA/IAC, along with shares of a French cable-TV company. This made Liberty the largest institutional shareholder of the new colossus. Barry, still IAC/USA's chief executive, agreed to take on the role of CEO of the newly formed Vivendi Universal Entertainment on an interim basis, leaving in less than a year.

Over the next two years, the bottom fell out of the stock, which would lose 80 percent of its value as the dot-com boom turned into a crash. Vivendi Universal reported a loss of more than $25.6 billion for 2002, the largest in the history of France.

We would sue Vivendi later for "outright fraud, misrepresentation and concealment" of a liquidity crisis that made their stock worthless. This was one of the few times I was more than happy to testify in front of a judge. The whole ordeal was especially costly for the Bronfmans, who would lead the effort that eventually ousted Messier from the company; Edgar would end up watching much of his family's liquor fortune get washed away.

Justice for Liberty finally came ten long years later. In 2013, a federal jury awarded Liberty Media close to $1 billion in damages for fraud and breach of contract, affirming Liberty's claims that Messier and Vivendi had concealed the deteriorating state of the company's finances. Vivendi later agreed to pay Liberty Media $775 million in cash to settle all claims.

We had been cheated, yet we settled for a sum that was 23 percent less than the billion-dollar award we had demanded. Why do this? Because, while a lot of macho CEOs might liken business to war, going to war is a regrettable last resort. So you end hostilities as soon as possible, even when you are in the right.

In 2004, General Electric, which had owned NBC since 1986, agreed to spend $3.8 billion in cash and assume $1.7 billion in Vivendi debt to acquire its entertainment properties and merge them into a new joint venture called NBC Universal. (Which, years later, it would sell to Comcast.)

Barry, meanwhile, still was serving as CEO of the newly named USA Interactive, which still held a controlling stakes in Home Shopping Network and Ticketmaster. USA Interactive continued to gobble up internet companies at a furious pace, buying a stake in discount travel-booking site Expedia, which Microsoft had spun out earlier, and in 2003 buying the whole thing for $1.5 billion. By May 2004, and now known as IAC/InteractiveCorp, the combined company was worth around $25 billion, more than Amazon ($18 billion) at the time.

The same year, Diller spent $212 million on Tripadvisor, a travel media company, then bundled the travel-related sites together and spun them off as a new public company, Expedia Inc. In the wreckage and aftershocks of the dot-com crash, IAC was surging. Tripadvisor thrived under the Expedia umbrella, growing revenue by more than 30 percent YOY and in 2011 was spun off tax-free into a separate public company, to the delight of Expedia shareholders.

Not every investment was a winner. IAC spent $2 billion on search, buying the also-ran Ask Jeeves, which turned into Ask.com. Five years later, it would abandon search as a business in the shadow of Google, which would come to own the business.

At Liberty, amid the dot-com bubble burst, we were sitting on more than $5 billion in cash when a lot of companies were starving for it. So there was enormous opportunity. And without his daredevil copilot Peter Barton, Liberty CEO Dob Bennett remained cautious, reluctant to target big acquisitions.

When I pressed him on the matter one day in my office, he said, "John, Liberty needs a CEO who is willing to make big bets in a shifting world, but that's not me." Know thyself. I respected his honesty. Dob, a trusted advisor on countless mergers, splits, and spins, remains one on the Liberty Media board today.

In 2006, as we looked to expand anew, I offered the role of Liberty Media CEO to Greg Maffei, the smart, ambitious dealmaker I had met at the Allen & Company conference who had served as CFO at Microsoft and briefly at the software giant Oracle.

Greg could stack five meetings through the afternoon and tear through every one of them. He was a quick study and fast on his feet in negotiations. In this environment, he would need to be.

As decisive as Greg Maffei was as the new CEO of Liberty Media, he had not done as many partnerships as I had. When you grow up at a formidable, dominant company like Microsoft, as Greg did, you get used to dictating what your counterparts must do, rather than accommodating them.

And this is how Greg, focused solely on protecting Liberty at all costs, went to war and nearly wrecked a twenty-year partnership and friendship with Barry Diller.

In 2007, IAC announced a plan to split the company into five public entities to make it easier for investors to identify the unique mission of each and realize more value for the sum of the parts. Under the plan, Barry would run the core entity, IAC, which included its internet businesses Ask.com, Citysearch, and Match.com. The four spin-offs would comprise separate stocks for home-shopping network HSN; the online lender LendingTree.com; Ticketmaster, the ticketing giant; and Interval, an online service that sells time-shares in vacation homes.

I liked the idea in principle of simplifying the company with separate stocks, and Wall Street warmed to the concept.

At the time IAC stock was getting dragged down on Wall Street because it had paid high for LendingTree and was hit hard by the mortgage crisis. With IAC's stock price faltering, Greg Maffei and Barry Diller began making noise about unwinding the IAC-Liberty relationship, but the talks went nowhere.

Liberty held a 30 percent financial stake in IAC, but thanks to our 1995 proxy agreement, we still had full voting control—control that Barry Diller had the right to exercise on our behalf.

That control became the sticking point in Barry's plan to split IAC into five separate companies. But his proposal included a key provision: the new companies would have just one class of stock, each share carrying one vote. On the surface, this was about giving new shareholders more value and a stronger voice. But the real impact was this—it would eliminate the special class B shares Liberty held, which carried ten votes per share. Our super-voting power, roughly 60 percent of the control, would be slashed to 30 percent. In other words, Liberty would lose control of the new companies.

Barry intended to use the proxy I had granted him years ago to vote Liberty's powerful class B stock against Liberty's interests—effectively dismantling the control structure we had built and agreed on.

He argued that the one-share, one-vote model was cleaner and better aligned with the idea of companies free from dominant shareholders. But from our perspective, it stripped away a significant piece of Liberty's value without offering anything in return. That wasn't just a tough pill to swallow—it was unacceptable.

Looking back on it now, I realize my mistake was that I was happy to leave it to Greg Maffei, as Liberty's CEO, to handle this unpleasant negotiation with Barry Diller and push back. I was focused on DirecTV and Liberty's other holdings.

The core question evolved, once again, around control. If Barry was willing to stay, I was perfectly happy with him voting our control shares in the five new spin-offs, just as we had agreed in our original deal. Instead, Barry wanted to scrap those terms to stay in control. What we really needed was for a judge to look at the facts and make a ruling as to whether Barry was right or we were right. Period.

I learned more details about the spin-off plan in a fiery phone call with Barry in December 2007, a plan that would blow up into a destructive legal fight.

Business leaders could learn a lot from big predators in the wild. Bare your fangs, but never expend energy fighting unless it is absolutely necessary. Litigation can sometimes go careening out of control, and the injuries you incur to assert dominance can be fatal.

Unfortunately, Greg, frustrated with IAC/InteractiveCorp's intentions, hired a law firm in Delaware to go after Barry in court in January 2008, suing to block the spin-offs and nullify the proxy agreement we had with Barry. I counseled against it but reluctantly agreed with my CEO.

IAC countersued to proceed with the deal, then Liberty sued to remove Barry from his post. Meanwhile, I was focused on acquiring control of DirecTV in a swap to give Rupert Murdoch secure control over his News Corp. empire. So I was less involved than I should have been. And the lawyers we picked were too pugnacious, in my opinion, too ready to go to war with the meter running, and too eager to attack the character and intent of my longtime friend Killer Diller.

At the trial, the lawyers attacked Barry for his compensation package ($295 million in 2007), the lagging stock performance of IAC, which had a $6.4 billion write-down on LendingTree, and IAC's few bad bets. The lawyers made it personal, attacking Barry's integrity, insinuating he was wasting corporate assets and wanted "to provide himself liquidity."

This was no way to treat a partner, especially one who had created so much value for Liberty shareholders. I was mortified to be on the stand, and when an IAC lawyer asked me about Barry, I said honestly, "I think he's terrific. Barry is a genius—a great guy." I noted he was well compensated, but more to the point, he was breaking our original agreement.

Diller conceded he, too, was frustrated with IAC's anemic stock and insisted that his effort to unlock each company's true value was driving the breakup plan he proposed.

But Barry was trying to make a statement, too. He referred to Liberty executives as "insane" and called Greg an "irresponsible executive," testifying that his disparaging public comments about IAC were hurting turnaround efforts.

The bad blood went back years, as I would later learn, over expired stock options Greg was awarded when he became chairman of Expedia, and he blamed Barry for the loss. When emotion gets into a business decision, reason and rationality can fly out the window.

When pressed on the witness stand, Greg said that he felt like he was used as a go-between to pressure Diller on my behalf, or as he put it, "Because of the friendship, [Malone] was reluctant to tackle some of the issues." Maybe that was partly true—if I had tried harder, earlier, to talk with Barry, maybe things would have been different.

Deep down I felt the yearning Barry felt to be an owner, not just an operator, and I had thought I was helping him back at the start, when I handed him lifetime voting control over our stake in the original HSN/Silver King. What do you do when you know you have hurt a friend, whether in life or in business?

Finally, I wrote a note to him: "I apologize, Barry. This was never supposed to spiral into a courtroom battle. This was supposed to be a simple determination on these spin-offs—what was right and what was wrong. It got out of control."

And the key thing was, none of these businesses would be as valuable without Barry at the helm. Who would run these things for us if he left? And how smart and aggressive would they be?

In March 2008, a Delaware Chancery Court judge ruled that Barry could go forward with the split-up plan, thwarting Liberty's challenge. It wasn't fair, but then, life is unfair.

We agreed to drop our appeal and lay down our weapons. We struck a deal with IAC to cap Liberty's ownership at 35 percent of the vote in any of the five businesses without the approval of the boards. So we were prevented from having hard control.

This courtroom loss was easily forgettable once I considered the billions of dollars in shareholder value that Barry had created during my relationship with him. Ultimately, I was happy for Barry because he had secured the dream of ownership control that had eluded him for so many decades, in much the same way I had with Liberty Media.

In the choppy seas of the internet, Barry never shied away from market chaos and uncertainty, which made him a good captain. His purchase of Ticketmaster was no different, and pulled it Liberty into the music business, which had been even more disrupted by the internet's rise than the TV industry.

The digital revolution had hit the music industry first and hardest. Music fans went from browsing vinyl records, then CDs, in big brick-and-mortar music stores like Tower Records (in malls!) to scrolling through songs on their mobile phones.

Spotify and Apple Music became the new DJs, and listeners were so content with the convenience they barely noticed the shift from owning records and CDs to monthly paid access to streaming services. As record stores shuttered across America, artists were forced to adapt, and they turned to concerts for revenue.

In February 2009, IAC's Ticketmaster announced an all-stock merger with Live Nation, which dominated concert promotion, artist management, and venue operations after having rolled up dozens of regional promoters to increase its national scale. The newly formed giant Live Nation Entertainment would have $6 billion in revenue, own more than 140 concert venues globally, sell around 140 million tickets a year, and promote 22,000 concerts annually.

Politicians, competitors, and consumer advocates complained that the combined company would act as gatekeeper in the concert business, with the ability to dictate ticket prices. But merging the largest ticket company with the largest concert promoter was an unavoidable natural evolution of business. It would streamline operations, creating a one-stop shop for artists and venues, and make the whole process easier for fans. On the business side, it would drive down costs and turn up the volume on profit.

The Justice Department antitrust division approved the merger with several conditions, such as requiring Ticketmaster to license its software to competitors. After the Ticketmaster–Live Nation Entertainment merger closed in 2010, Liberty created a tracking stock representing its 30 percent ownership so investors could narrow their focus on the music assets.

As is typical with trackers such as the SiriusXM tracking stock, the LNE tracker traded at a discount of as much as 30 percent of its asset value, but investors in Liberty hopefully did not mind. If you had been invested with Liberty since we announced our tracking stock structure in late 2005, by January 2010 you would have earned a compounded annual rate of return of about 18 percent compared to 4.1 percent for the S&P Media Index and 1.6 percent for the S&P 500 Index.

Fast-forward to 2022, when I got a call from Michael Rapino, CEO of Live Nation Entertainment, the largest live-entertainment business in the world, who had been CEO since he launched Live Nation in 2005.

Not only had he successfully integrated the companies, but the stock was at an all-time high, and Rapino had performed like a death-defying acrobat from Cirque du Soleil during the COVID pandemic, which should have killed a live-events company.

As revenue plummeted with canceled shows, Rapino declined to take a salary, improved refund policies, and started relief funds for unemployed music crew employees. He took advantage of the downtime, improving the deals with venues, and signed more creative win-win deals with artists in the face of cancellations. He showed real leadership.

He called me up as the stock was hovering around $110. "John, can you believe this? Remember when you wanted to buy the company for eight bucks a share and you finally tendered the stock at twelve bucks?"

Live Nation's revenue surged 36 percent in 2023 to $22.7 billion, edged up in 2024, and despite a slower start in 2025, the company returned to Q1 profitability on strong concert and ticketing demand. Nice work.

Barry and I finally untied the knot in 2010. Liberty Media gave up its control stake in IAC in a $360 million deal—$220 million in cash plus two IAC businesses, Evite and Gifts.com. Barry swapped his IAC shares for Liberty's class B voting stock, giving him control of the company going forward.

When we announced the deal, I pointed out that when Barry and I shook hands back in 1993 for him to become CEO of Silver King Communications, the company had revenue of $46 million. "Since then, the entities involved have grown to revenues of over ten billion dollars and a combined market capitalization of 13.8 billion dollars," I said. "IAC itself has grown over 20 percent this year and has outperformed the S&P by 31 percent this year."

Barry was nostalgic. "These last seventeen years of my association with John Malone and Liberty Media have been a great, and occasionally wild, ride. We began this grand tour of interactivity a few years before the internet became widely used, and we were able to create, acquire, and build up substantial businesses over that time."

More than twenty-five years after I made a promise, I regard it as honoring a lifelong commitment that Barry would end up with the company that he built. And I'm a shareholder, and all my shareholders are now also Expedia shareholders.

Has it been a good investment? When Barry Diller took over as chairman and CEO of Silver King Communications in 1995, the television station holding company was worth some $250 million. Twenty-five years later the resulting IAC/InterActiveCorp has created equity value estimated to be $100 billion, counting the value of the numerous media and internet subsidiaries and spin-offs of IAC.

Barry's "calving" strategy of acquiring companies and nurturing them before spinning them off as separate public companies to shareholders, similar to Liberty, was a successful tactic for growing shareholder value that he executed with remarkable efficiency with Expedia, LendingTree, Match Group, and Vimeo, all of which trade separately now.

Barry later stepped down as CEO of IAC, but he remains chairman and the largest single shareholder. IAC is now a very long-term asset for Barry and his family, and my guess is he will be a great steward of the company in the years to come.

Today, IAC still controls a portfolio of promising e-commerce services that could be potential spin-offs, including Angi home services, a stake in MGM Resorts, car-sharing service Turo, and Meredith Corporation's publishing assets, including *Better Homes & Gardens* and *People* magazine.

As business partners go, Barry Diller was one of the best in my long career in doing deals and building businesses. Millions of viewers were entertained by his programming and the channels he grew. Millions of individual shareholders in his companies and hundreds of retirement funds and other institutional investors reaped billions of dollars in wealth and income from his efforts. And thousands of couples met and married on the online dating apps his company created.

That is a lot of impact on a lot of lives, from one driven man, and I am fortunate to know him.

CHAPTER 25

THE GREAT KARMAZIN

In the fall of 2008, as Liberty Media was on the prowl for investing opportunities, I heard that SiriusXM CEO Mel Karmazin was in a heap of
trouble. The satellite music service he had assembled only months earlier,
by combining two failing competitors, Sirius and XM, needed money. Fast.

The company owed $3.25 billion in debt, $600 million of it in bank
loans and the rest in high-yield bonds, with a bond payment of $175 million
coming due in a few months. The company was out of cash and unable to
pay it; a default would push it into bankruptcy.

Worse, SiriusXM's bank lenders were unwilling to loan any more money
to the wobbly enterprise. The Great Meltdown of 2008 was underway, and
the credit and lending markets were frozen. And worse still: that $175 mil-
lion due in a few months was for bonds held by Charlie Ergen, the crafty
satellite-TV pioneer and founder of EchoStar and Dish Network. He figured that SiriusXM's satellite music service could mesh nicely with Dish
satellite-TV service.

Charlie had descended at just the right moment. Sirius shares, which
had traded in the $3 range in 2007–8, had dropped to 14 cents following
the merger. The combined companies' entire market cap was roughly $500
million, and much of its debt was trading at a steep discount to its face value.
Which is why Charlie bought it. Vulture capitalism.

He had offered to bail out Karmazin and SiriusXM by putting up a few
hundred million in cash in exchange for control of the company. Karmazin,
while eyeing Charlie's overture, had put out the message that filing for

Chapter 11 bankruptcy was an imminent possibility: he had hired bankruptcy lawyers to start preparing papers.

A shot across the bow. A bankruptcy filing would wipe out the value held by shareholders—including the holdings of Mel Karmazin himself—and put debtholders first in line for recouping whatever they could. Creditors were so upset to hear Karmazin's threat that they publicly let it be known that if SiriusXM went Chapter 11, they would fire him.

It was a bad case of "Would you rather," the kids' game in which the players must choose between two horrid choices. And both options that Mel was contemplating would lead to his ouster from the company he had spent the last five years nurturing back from the brink. Chapter 11 reorganization or Charlie Ergen in control—either way, Mel was a goner.

So in February 2009 he turned, instead, to me and Liberty Media for a rescue. This led to one of the biggest returns on investment in the history of business. *Any business.* For Liberty shareholders, SiriusXM shareholders, and Mel personally.

For me, it was a massive financial windfall driven less by strategic, long-range planning and more by happenstance, unexpected opportunity, and the other side's dire straits.

Liberty had briefly invested in the XM service years earlier, but we had bailed out, in part because of the early losses due to high operating costs, competition from free radio stations, and a costly, two-company marketing war ahead. Never profitable alone, Sirius and XM were like two cats with their tails tied together, scratching and biting each other in a race toward bankruptcy.

In my mind, Mel was a bold, hardworking CEO who already had pulled off the impossible. When the FCC granted satellite licenses to the two rival new services in 1997, the terms banned any future merger between them. Yet Mel knew the industry could not support two businesses and had first looked into the idea of a merger in 2005, soon after joining Sirius. In 2008, he embarked on the deal without seeking FCC permission, betting he could push it through. And he did, with alacrity.

Over the previous year and a half, he had painstakingly convinced the Federal Communications Commission, the Justice Department, and

Congress that it was fair to merge the two largest satellite companies into one, thereby preventing the collapse of either of them.

Mel Karmazin always had been a world-class salesman, able to sell almost anything, especially broadcast ad time. He grew up in Long Island City, Queens, and still carried the brash attitude and "deeze guys" accent of a streetwise, in-your-face New Yorker.

He had started out selling advertising for CBS Radio after college at Pace University, then worked for Metromedia, a TV and radio stations owner. In 1981 he joined Infinity Broadcasting, which owned a handful of radio stations, until he built the stable up to twenty-two stations, and then seventy-five after the deregulation in 1996 lifted ownership limits.

In 1996 he sold Infinity, the number two radio company, for $3.9 billion and $1 billion in debt to the number one competitor, Westinghouse, which also owned CBS. Now Karmazin would run the combined radio group, right back where he had started his career in radio ad sales. Karmazin later added CBS Television to his portfolio, and he offered, in vain, to buy Viacom out from under Sumner Redstone.

Spurned, Mel then sold CBS to Sumner in 1999 in a $35.6 billion all-stock deal and became president and chief operating officer of Viacom. Almost instantly, he clashed with Viacom founder and chairman Redstone, who was seventy-six at the time. They butted heads over acquisition strategy, advertising decisions, and Mel's sale of company stock. He finally quit on June 1, 2004, and joined Sirius five months later.

Satellite radio was a novelty when it appeared in 2002. For the first time, listeners were offered crystal-clear reception of commercial-free music, news, sports, and talk regardless of where they lived—or drove. This technical advance, another aided by digital compression, represented yet another ripple in the fabric of media, a shift in the way people consumed content.

Mel saw the future and understood the business, and he made Sirius a player in satellite radio, striking key partnerships with auto companies and cultivating big-name talent such as Martha Stewart and the shock jock Howard Stern.

Sirius had signed Stern just before Karmazin started running the company. Mel had helped make Stern rich back in his Infinity days, but nothing like this: a stunning $500 million five-year deal, $80 million a year in cash and $20 million in stock to Stern and his production company. Upon renewal, Mel cut it to $400 million for the next five years (2010–2015).

But Sirius had piled on too much short-term, high-yield junk debt in its effort to merge with XM. This almost killed the company when the economic meltdown of late 2008 shut down the credit markets. Any company with short-term debt was left standing in a high-stakes game of musical chairs.

So Charlie Ergen "had 'em by the short hairs," as my old partner Bob Magness liked to say. Charlie's naked opportunism to scoop up Sirius debt amid this struggle infuriated Mel Karmazin, for they had clashed before. Years earlier, they had locked horns when the Dish satellite-TV service negotiated to carry MTV, VH1, and Nickelodeon—all cable channels carried by Viacom, where Mel was president at the time.

On the theory that the enemy of my enemy is my friend, Mel then reached out to DirecTV, the main rival to Charlie Ergen's Dish satellite-TV service. At Liberty Media, we had a controlling stake in DirecTV, and Chase Carey was running it for us. Chase suggested to Mel that he should give me a call.

There were a lot of bargain hunters, but not many companies eager to jump in and back SiriusXM when it was on the brink of bankruptcy. In the Great Recession of 2008–09, car sales were down, hurting satellite radio's biggest market. Credit was frozen, and the economy was limping along.

SiriusXM, which charged subscribers a monthly fee, looked doomed. Budget-conscious consumers could get their music free of charge via AM and FM radio, new online competitors, and mobile phone apps.

When Greg and I visited Mel in his office in midtown Manhattan, I praised him for bringing the company this far and said I hoped our proposed investment, in the form of a loan, could help him pull off the turnaround he was plotting.

He leaned over and took out the actual proposal document to refinance the company following the merger approval, which had been assembled by . . . Lehman Brothers, whose later bankruptcy had set off the financial crisis we were now enduring.

After Greg Maffei and I visited Mel, we proposed terms for a deal, the ratio of warrants, etc., and made an offer that would keep Mel in control and the barbarians at the gate. In February 2009, Liberty announced that it would make a two-phase loan totaling $530 million at a stiff 15 percent interest rate. In return, we would pay just $12,500 to receive preferred shares that were convertible into a 40 percent stake in SiriusXM—if the company could survive.

Mel would remain as CEO. Greg Maffei, Liberty Media CEO, and I as chairman would join the SiriusXM board.

In my career, I had been cast as a ruthless villain in so many media stories and called a colorful list of names: Darth Vader. Genghis Khan. Robber baron. The ensuing coverage of the SiriusXM deal was one of the first times I can recall the press calling me a "White Knight."

By June 2009, SiriusXM's stock price had gone from just 6 cents to around 35 cents. Liberty's preferred shares, which had cost us $12,500, were now worth more than $900 million. By 2010, the cost savings and synergies from the merger kicked in, and the combined company started gaining subscribers, just as Mel had promised.

As time went by, the auto market picked up, and Mel posted solid results, increasing the operating margins and cash flow, and we acquired more shares. The company had a loss of more than half a billion dollars in 2009, but by year's end 2011 it had turned a net profit of more than $400 million. Nearly a billion-dollar turnaround.

By 2012, SiriusXM was up to nearly 23 million subscribers, an all-time high compared to fewer than one million when Mel arrived. Under Mel's direction and with our loans, and carry-over losses that reduced taxes owed, SiriusXM had made a full recovery.

Not only had Mel saved several billion dollars of value from getting wiped out, he had also made SirusXM one of the fastest-growing stocks from 2009 to 2012. SiriusXM shares had bottomed at 6 cents apiece in early 2009, and by mid-2012 they were up past $2.30—a thirty-seven-fold increase, up 3,700 percent. Our initial investment of $12,500 was now worth upward of $5 billion, an annualized return of more than 7,268 percent!

All of this upside because we took on the high risk of loaning $530 million to SiriusXM at its lowest point. SiriusXM was able to pay us back in full later, four years after the company damn near went belly-up.

Now we were sitting there feeling pretty good with 40 percent of the company, and the questions started rolling in my head. *Do I spend money to increase Liberty's stake in SiriusXM? Should we buy the rest of the company outright?* This would cost $9 billion or so, assuming we could pick up the shares at market prices. Maybe we just wanted to own another 10 percent to have full voting control.

Or do we give Liberty's 40 percent stake in SiriusXM back to our share-holders in a tax-efficient way, so SiriusXM management can make its own decisions about further investing? There were no right answers, which is why the questions kept fermenting quietly in the back of my brain.

We had agreed to a three-year standstill to win regulatory approval of our bailout of the company in 2009. Now that this had lapsed, we took our first step toward gaining control, attempting to take over SiriusXM without having to purchase any extra shares.

We petitioned the FCC in March 2012 to recognize that we now had de facto control, given our 40 percent stake, and to transfer SiriusXM broadcast licenses to Liberty Media. But SiriusXM opposed our proposal. Mel Karmazin publicly said Liberty Media shouldn't be able to take control without paying a premium. He was looking out for all other SiriusXM shareholders (including himself). More tellingly, though, Mel had made it clear that he was unwilling to have a boss at SiriusXM. As he had told an audience at a media conference the year before: "I'm not really good at working for somebody. I just could not be a number two."

I would have been happy to have Mel stay on board and stay in charge— he would do a better job at running SiriusXM than just about anyone. Still, whether he might choose to leave SiriusXM under Liberty's watch was going to be up to him; we were going to do what we set out to do.

After the FCC nixed our first request, we filed a second application to take de jure control over SiriusXM, requiring us to raise our stake to 50 percent. We had been buying SiriusXM shares for several months by this time, lifting our stake to 48 percent, with plans to buy enough to go over the 50 percent threshold.

Two months after filing our second FCC petition, in October 2012, Mel Karmazin informed the SiriusXM board that he would be leaving the company on February 1, 2013. I was genuinely sorry to see him go. And on January 3, 2013, the FCC issued a formal order granting control of SiriusXM to Liberty Media. It noted that this transfer of control "will serve the public interest, convenience, and necessity."

Mission accomplished.

We named Jim Meyer, the president of sales and operations, as the interim CEO. He stayed in the role for eight years, until 2020, when he retired and we hired the company's first female CEO, Jennifer C. Witz, promoting from within.

SiriusXM has grown into a national audio entertainment company reaching more than 150 million people, and it continues to be a well-run, rational business. The entire company today is valued at $21.5 billion.

Mel did a great job—and he was handsomely compensated for it, leaving the company he rescued with $255 million. He has passed on his love of the radio business to his son, Craig, who is founder and CEO of Good Karma Brands, which owns a dozen radio stations in four states.

Liberty's initial investment of $12,500 for the preferred stock, plus $1.7 billion for the 10 percent chunk of stock to get us to the 50 percent mark, is worth more than $10 billion today. The return on investment capital is unfathomable. I knew we were gonna hit a home run when we first bailed out Mel and SiriusXM—but never did I think it was going to be one of the grandest grand slams in business history.

But as satisfying as the ROI in that deal was, I know intuitively that a stock profit is as fleeting as a breath. A deal or piece of news ignites the market, and the stock surges. Hold on too long, believing the ascent will continue, and the market's mercurial tides can surprise you. The stock's price may retreat as quickly as it ascended, or slowly, over years. Analysts rethink, investors cool off, technology invades, and the excitement, over time, can dissolve into anxiety. The moment fades, and so does the profit. SiriusXM would have challenges later, but for now we were, as Sinatra (and so many others) sang, on the sunny side of the street.

Liberty Media CEO Greg Maffei had executed the deal perfectly. Liberty Media eventually gobbled up a majority stake in the company, and Liberty SiriusXM became a tracking stock that owned a 71.5 percent stake in SiriusXM.

One of the largest owners of Liberty SiriusXM (now just SiriusXM) has been Berkshire Hathaway, which owns about 35 percent of the company. Warren Buffett, a SiriusXM listener, happens to be a fan of the Siriusly Sinatra station that plays the hits of Frank Sinatra (the real Chairman of the Board!). The man has good taste in music—and great taste in stocks.

Liberty was shaking up the music business with our ownership stakes in SiriusXM and Live Nation Entertainment, which included Ticketmaster, but new threats loomed, and we needed to build a moat around the castle.

Just ten years earlier, AOL Music was the hottest online music service, but it quickly faded after the iPhone took off, and music buffs suddenly had an array of new apps offering digital music services in their hand. All of this would test consumers' willingness to pay $15 a month for SiriusXM, which was available mainly on car radios.

We were concerned about new streaming services that were gaining popularity, including Amazon, Apple Music, Pandora, Spotify, and Tidal. SiriusXM's success was still largely tied to car sales, and already new models were arriving in showrooms with the electronic brains to mate with mobile phones and play any streaming app.

Greg Maffei began eyeing Pandora, an internet radio service that could give SiriusXM a big footprint in the streaming business with 80 million (mostly mobile) listeners. Jim Meyer and Greg agreed that a youth market, internet-vs.-satellite delivery, and the novelty of Pandora's mission could have long-term synergies with our other music businesses.

A young musician from Minnesota named Tim Westergren launched the service in 2000 with two friends after creating a music discovery tool in 2000 called the Music Genome Project, by which details of every song were analyzed to build a profile based on some 450 attributes related to harmony, instruments, rhythm, vocals, and more. Do you like "Hotel California"? Pandora, powered by this interactive map of music, will deliver a digital radio station of similar songs by artists old and new, in the vein of the Eagles.

So, in 2017, SiriusXM invested $480 million in Pandora for a 16 percent stake in the music-streaming platform, which was ad-supported (with an on-demand version) and worked much like radio. Pandora could give Liberty an internet-delivered music service that could hold the new streaming services at bay—and give us a dual revenue stream of subscription service and ads.

The following year, SiriusXM took ownership control of Pandora Media Inc. in a $3.5 billion deal. The combination of SiriusXM, by this time up past 36 million subscribers in North America, and Pandora, which offered free and paid streaming music to more than 70 million monthly listeners, would create the world's largest audio entertainment company.

In 2023 we shuffled the deck again. SiriusXM had two kinds of stock—one for the company itself, which you could buy on the Nasdaq, and the other for a Liberty Media tracking stock representing our ownership of the company. Now we would call in the Liberty tracker and swap it with real shares in SiriusXM. The aim was to make SiriusXM a more liquid public company, trading under one stock, and still operating as SiriusXM, in order to move forward with acquisitions and such. Plus, now the company's shareholders could participate more directly in the performance and governance of SiriusXM.

The former Liberty Media SiriusXM shareholders would collectively own about 84 percent of new SiriusXM, and the rest would be owned by minority shareholders. The entire transaction was tax-free for both SiriusXM and Liberty, and their respective shareholders. That same year, at a big shindig in New York City, SiriusXM unveiled a new streamlined, streaming-anywhere app—setting it free from the car—with a boatload of big-name talent, including Kelly Clarkson, Kevin Hart, and of course, Howard Stern, who had signed a five-year extension to 2025.

While the music industry continues to get buffeted by technological change—here comes the AI wave, next—we believe our two largest investments can innovate and sustain their competitive advantages.

SiriusXM, Live Nation, Ticketmaster, and Pandora are investing in new technology as the way music is owned and monetized undergoes continuous evolution. All this change in the industry makes for fertile hunting ground for Liberty Media. Stay tuned.

CHAPTER 26

CHARTERING A COMEBACK

By 2013, Liberty Global had assembled the world's largest collection of cable systems, with 24 million subscribers across fourteen countries, eclipsing even the old TCI, and all of them outside the U.S. market, which I thought I had left forever.

But like Michael Corleone in *Godfather III*, "Just when I thought I was out . . . they pull me right back in."

It began on a plane ride. On a jet flying from Denver to New York, I sat next to my longtime friend Aryeh Bourkoff, head of the boutique banking firm LionTree. At the time, he had been advising Liberty Global on the $23 billion purchase of UK mobile provider Virgin Media, which was set to close in June 2013. When the discussion changed to the trajectory of Liberty Media, he calmly dropped a line that got my attention:

"By the way, John, does Liberty have any interest in getting back in the domestic cable-TV business?"

A struggling cable operator in the U.S., Charter Communications, was about to emerge from Chapter 11 bankruptcy reorganization, and some of the bigger investors were interested in selling their stake.

"It's a control stake—around thirty-five percent of the company," he said.

"Tell me more."

After selling TCI in 1998, and especially after becoming chairman of cable's number one nemesis, satellite-TV giant DirecTV, the idea of getting back into the U.S. cable market seemed remote to me. But as Aryeh described the possibilities under Charter CEO Tom Rutledge and the potential price point, I started thinking to myself:

Okay, maybe I can go back home again. We just sold most of our stake in DirecTV, and here is a major U.S. cable operator with impeccable management and a clean balance sheet? I'm in!

Charter Communications was a growing private cable operator when Microsoft cofounder Paul Allen bought the company in 1998 for $4.5 billion and took it public a year later. Paul's dream of a "wired world" required high-speed connections to advanced digital interactive services, and he jumped in big.

Paul bought out the industry's biggest pioneers, paying $3.6 billion for Falcon Cable, $3.1 billion for Bresnan Communications, and $2.7 billion for Marcus Cable, all founded by industry pioneers and partners of mine.

When Paul had finished, he had spent $13 billion and assembled the fourth-largest cable operator in the U.S., with more than five and a half million subscribers.

When the financial crisis hit in 2008 though, Charter, creaking with more than $20 billion in debt, was forced to file for bankruptcy protection in 2009.

When Apollo Global Management and other equity firms jumped in to resurrect it, they wisely hired Tom Rutledge as CEO in 2011. Tom, well known throughout the cable industry as an experienced leader, had served as the COO of Cablevision Systems, one of the largest cable operators in the U.S., controlled by cable pioneer Charles Dolan, who had founded HBO, and his son, James.

Under the watchful eye of the Dolans, Tom made Cablevision perform like a circus lion on command, posting gains in cash flow as he was upgrading to a fiber-optic network. At Charter, Tom did much the same, leading the company through significant restructuring, all the while improving customer service and expanding the company's broadband offerings. Tom knew, as we did, that there was a lot of potential in Charter.

So, in May 2013, Liberty Media bought a 27 percent stake in Charter Communications for $2.6 billion in stock, taking out some of the investors who had stepped in after the bankruptcy, including Apollo Global Management, Oaktree Capital Management, and Crestview Partners. As I told the press, I saw Charter as "a horizontal acquisition machine" that would seek more scale buying other cable assets.

To help investors see the value of our plan, Liberty Media spun out the Charter stake and other cable assets into a new, separate company—Liberty Broadband Group. This would create a pure-play investment vehicle, making it easier to raise money for cable-TV acquisitions in the U.S. In just eighteen months after the spin-off, our investment in Charter had increased in value by 55 percent.

One of our first targets was a giant: Time Warner Cable, the second-largest cable operator in the U.S.—and three times Charter's size. In December 2013, Charter made a $37.3 billion bid, plus $24 billion in debt assumption, offering a 20 percent premium. TWC's board, led by CEO Rob Marcus, dismissed it as a "low-ball offer."

With Comcast circling, I floated a plan: Let's carve up TWC between Charter and Comcast to avoid a bidding war. Despite multiple meetings, we couldn't agree on price or division. Brian Roberts, Comcast's CEO, finally called me, frustrated. "John, I'm heading to Sochi for the Winter Games [which NBC Universal bought the rights to air]. If we don't have a deal by the time I'm back, I'll go it alone." And he did. In February 2015, Comcast announced a $45.2 billion stock-only offer for TWC—outbidding us at $158.82 per share.

But the regulators balked. Combining the top two cable operators to control 55 percent of U.S. broadband sparked immediate backlash.

Meanwhile, Tom Rutledge and his Charter team pivoted, acquiring Bright House Networks, the sixth largest cable operator, for $10.4 billion in March 2015. Steve Miron, the CEO of the Advance/Newhouse Partnership; his father, Bob, before him; and the Newhouse family had been engaged, loyal partners of Liberty Media for more than three decades, going back to the early days of Discovery.

In April, as the regulatory heat intensified, Comcast dropped its bid. A month later, Charter moved decisively: In May 2015, TWC accepted our revised $78.7 billion offer—$195 per share, nearly 75 percent higher than our initial bid.

That kind of premium is, admittedly, a lot richer than I typically would want to pay for an asset. Then again, after Comcast pulled out, number two

Time Warner Cable was sitting there naked and open to offers, and some-times you have to pay more than you want so you can get hold of a prize before your competitors can grab it for themselves.

With Brighthouse and Time Warner, the newly combined Charter would serve nearly 24 million subscribers in forty-one markets, compared with number one Comcast's roughly 27 million customers at the time.

After months of rigorous antitrust scrutiny given the size of the two cable operators, the FCC imposed several conditions on Charter Communications as part of its approval process in 2016. Under these conditions, imposed by the DOJ and the FCC, Charter agreed to expand broadband access to underserved areas and offer more low-income programs. You do what you have to do to get done what you want (or need) to get done.

The key condition that stuck in my craw, though, was related to data caps. Concerned that Charter could prevent "current and future online video rivals from expanding, becoming more competitive or starting up in the first place," the FCC forbade Charter Communications from imposing data caps—usage-based pricing—on its broadband internet services for a period of seven years.

This was the FCC's imposing, de facto, a form of the regulatory regime that would come to be known as net neutrality, without having to take a formal vote or win approval in Congress to do it. This was an onerous condition. The new streaming services coming online would grow into data hogs. Cable operators should have every right to charge the biggest users of their bandwidth in ways that reflected the true costs. In 2021, before the FCC ban was to expire, Charter tried to get the FCC to end the order, arguing that "by every metric imaginable, [streaming services] are seeing record-breaking growth and gains across all performance indicators, including in the number of subscribers, the number of [streaming] platforms, streaming hours, revenue, and the amount and success of original content on those platforms." The FCC kept the restrictions in place.

When Liberty Media made its initial $2.6 million investment in Charter in 2013, it was a bet on cable. Our stake had doubled to over $5 billion in

2015, and we added another $5 billion tied to Charter's acquisitions of Time Warner Cable and BrightHouse. As of this writing, that combined investment is worth about $15.5 billion.

In November 2024, we made another move that had been a long time coming. Rather than keep things layered and complicated, we struck a deal for Charter to acquire Liberty Broadband outright, folding that stake back into the business. It was a logical step, simplifying ownership and governance, giving Charter a cleaner structure as it entered this next phase.

Our early bet on Charter came full circle on May 16, 2025, when we made Charter the largest cable operator in America. A $35 billion combination with Cox Communications gives us unmatched scale, expands our business services reach, and ensures Charter can compete—and win—against wireless disruptors and streaming giants alike. This all-stock (and tax-free!) combination was a defining moment for Charter, for my longtime partners in the Cox family, and for me personally.

Cox brings business services strength and a customer-first reputation that complements Charter's scale. Together, with 36 million subscribers, we're better positioned to deliver the broadband and video experiences consumers demand.

Competition has intensified. Wireless carriers like Verizon and T-Mobile are offering home broadband over 5G, rapidly gaining customers with lower prices and competitive speeds. Still, selling a wired broadband connection remains the most reliable—and profitable—way to serve the internet economy, from streaming to gaming. No one does it better than we do.

The Charter corporate name will eventually shift to Cox Communications, but for customers, Spectrum remains the brand they know. Titles and names may change, but make no mistake: the foundation, the strategy, the execution—that's all Charter, built on the legacy started by Tom Rutledge. Tom guided and grew the company through the Time Warner Cable and Bright House integrations with excellence. In 2022, he passed the baton to Chris Winfrey, who continues that legacy with focus and precision.

For me, this is finishing strong—cementing cable's leadership with Charter at the top. Right where it belongs.

Once I got pulled back into the U.S. cable industry I had exited twenty-five years earlier, I wanted to believe things were just like old times, but the business was changing vastly in fundamental ways. The arc of the old cable television business was cresting by 2013, and it would go into an undeniable, irrevocable decline.

Viewers began to shift to cheaper, more convenient new streaming services from broadcast networks and cable-TV apps. This accelerated the rise of so-called cord cutting and threatened the entire industry.

It would set off a disruptive bust-up of the cable dial into separate programming fiefdoms. Internecine warfare would break out between cable operators and some of their biggest and most valuable partners—the channels provided by Disney, Paramount, NBCUniversal, Time Warner, Discovery, and more. Suddenly, these programmers had found a way to bypass local cable systems and deliver their content directly to viewers. And viewers no longer had to subscribe to tiers of hundreds of channels to get the couple dozen they watched a lot.

However, the popular term "cord cutting," which typically refers to the cancellation of cable-TV services, is technically inaccurate and oversimplifies the evolution that took place. When cord-cutting consumers cancel the channel packages of their cable suppliers, they still are very much attached to the "cord," the broadband wire required for internet delivery. Cable operators dominate the internet-access business.

This would insulate the cable business for another decade and offset some of the losses as more homes canceled their TV service. More recently, though, wireless giants such as T-Mobile have started offering competing internet service, posing a threat to cable.

The explanation for how this big bang happened is as old as business: in the cable industry I so admire, we took our eye off the prize. For decades, the television industry operated under some pretty reliable ways of doing business. Broadcast networks—ABC, NBC, and CBS—relied solely on advertising. When new cable networks came along, they took advertising revenue—and they also charged local cable operators an "affiliate fee" per subscriber for their networks. And the pay-TV distributors—cable-TV systems, satellite TV, phone companies—would pass along those fees and increases to subscribers.

Cable's dual revenue stream from both advertising and fees paid by cable systems was a golden goose for the industry, producing operating margins as high as 40 percent—for programmers and distributors. (Operating margin is a simple measure of how much cash a business keeps from sales after paying for basic running costs, like salaries and supplies; the higher the percentage, the better.) The more channels we added, the more subscribers who signed up, and the more revenue we could take in, financing more channels, and drawing still more paying subs. Everyone in the circle was happy.

Subscribers ultimately paid for these increases in content costs, but they were the beneficiaries, too: this business model was enormously successful in delivering a Golden Age of Television to viewers after years of predictable half-hour sitcoms and hour-long cop shows paid for by detergent ads on broadcast networks. Cable-TV networks offered deeper dives into niche areas and showcased a new type of storytelling, giving rise to such seminal shows as HBO's *The Sopranos* and AMC's *Breaking Bad*.

As big content companies like Viacom and Disney built up a stable of networks, they started to squeeze more money out of the carriers . . . because they could. The new negotiating ploy: bundling their entire roster of networks together and refusing to rent them to cable systems individually. This problem got worse immediately after the 1992 Cable Act, and it continues as of this writing.

Under the 1992 Cable Act, cable operators were required to pay or negotiate to carry broadcasters' signals. I flatly refused to pay cash—especially as cable operators' revenue was getting strangled by the rate regulations imposed by the very same law.

Cable operators and broadcasters clashed over cash payments for carriage, and we finally compromised, agreeing to carry (and pay for) new cable networks started by the broadcasters, as the de facto fee for carrying ABC, NBC, and Fox Broadcasting. TCI led the way because it was a reasonable alternative. But content companies would quickly turn the tables on me—and the entire industry.

ABC launched ESPN2 in 1993 (and other versions later); Fox launched FX in 1994; and NBC launched MSNBC in 1996. CBS failed to offer new channels and largely stuck with compensation for the signal. And at each renewal, the companies piggybacked an upstart or low-rated network on their top-rated networks to gain distribution.

As cable operators like TCI were consolidating into fewer, larger players, the big content companies launched a consolidation craze to take advantage of scale in the new digital world, just as the cable operators were doing. Disney bought Capital Cities/ABC and its 80 percent–owned ESPN in 1995, bringing together the dominant player in sports; the kids juggernaut Disney Channel; and a national broadcast network, ABC. Viacom, with music channels MTV and VH1, followed with its CBS merger in 1999, and NBC bought USA and other networks in parent GE's Universal deal with Vivendi.

By this time, in most cities, cable-TV operators were competing with satellite and telephone players. As the programmers got more powerful, their all-or-none packaging left distributors with little choice. Who was going to risk losing monthly subscribers because they lacked MTV, or the NFL on ESPN? And the leagues took full advantage: consider that ESPN's *Monday Night Football*, which cost $550 million a year in 2005, had ballooned to $1.9 billion annually by 2013.

Pay-TV providers carried it, and all of them calculated the same odds as if in a real-life exercise of game theory: we all were paying roughly the same price for ESPN, so nobody has an advantage. We were making ESPN rich (and inflating league revenue, which was inflating athlete salaries) and overpricing our product to cover the high costs, but everybody was doing it, so . . .

This mentality lasted for more than two decades, until they could raise the price no further.

I always have wondered why the antitrust division of the Department of Justice never investigated bundling in the TV business. At the very least, it seems to me, it looked like a restraint of trade. It is like a farmer telling the store: you can sell my milk but only if you sell my eggs, fruits, and vegetables, too.

Bundling networks this way was akin to the outlawed practice of "block-booking" once used by Hollywood studios in the 1930s and 1940s to force theaters to take a package of films vs. only the hits that theaters wanted. It also is akin to practices for which the government prosecuted IBM in the late 1960s and early '70s in mainframe computers, and Microsoft in the 1990s in PC programming.

Fed up with the take-it-or-leave-it ploy, my old friend Chuck Dolan at Cablevision Systems filed a federal lawsuit against Viacom in 2013, alleging it broke antitrust laws by forcing "Cablevision's customers to pay for and receive little-watched channels in order to get the channels they actually want."

Cablevision showed how, in order to get popular channels such as MTV or Nickelodeon, it had to buy fourteen channels, including Palladia, MTV Hits, and VH1 Classic, or pay steep penalties. Cablevision ultimately settled out of court.

Around the time of Cablevision's lawsuit, Senator John McCain, the powerful Republican from Arizona, jumped into the fray by introducing the Television Consumer Freedom Act of 2013. He lambasted cable-network bundling as unfairly and artificially raising prices, as he had as a senator in 2004 and 2006. And he offered a new way for pay-TV companies to unbundle channels—wholesale and retail—and go "à la carte," as you can order in restaurants.

"My mother is a hundred and one years old," he liked to say. "She watches television all the time, but she doesn't like football anymore. So why should she pay five dollars or six dollars extra for her cable service a month for something she doesn't watch?"

ESPN at the time had raised the monthly carriage fee it charged cable systems to a lofty $5.54 per month for each home they reached, vastly higher than the average 16 cents other channels cost at the time. And although every one of the 100 million homes where it was available was forced to pay for ESPN in 2013, only 2.2 million homes were actually watching it regularly.

Research consistently showed the average home watched only ten to fifteen channels, which helped fuel the à la carte debate. Still, there was wide disagreement in the cable industry on whether to support the McCain bill. I liked the bill because it was voluntary, giving cable operators (and satellite TV) the option of buying and selling cable networks individually.

Content companies—and some cable operators—warned prices might actually go up for popular channels (one estimate was $30 for ESPN) in an à la carte model while resulting in lower revenue overall. New niche networks might die if not bundled with popular channels, opponents said.

Yet I told John McCain I supported it, even though most times I oppose too much government meddling in the market. Despite my efforts, I was unable to persuade most of my fellow cable operators to support it. When the McCain bill failed in 2013, Senator McCain told me, rather pointedly, "I'm not going to be the industry's Don Quixote again."

Ultimately, free-market competition and the advance of streaming, rather than federal legislation, would end up breaking up the cable channel packages and yielding the benefits of greater consumer choice. This is the way it should be.

John and I had many memorable discussions on bundling and business regulation, and though we disagreed on some points, I admired his perspective on national security, bipartisan cooperation, patriotism, and resilience, which was shaped by his time as a navy pilot POW in Vietnam. He was a hero in my eyes.

Meanwhile, cable-TV bills kept climbing. The average monthly bill had grown at three times the rate of inflation, and it had tripled in twenty years to more than $64 by 2012—but so had the number of channels, to 160. Over forty years, the pay-TV business soared from around 2 million cable-TV subscribers in 1970 to about 98 million cable, telco, and satellite-TV households in 2010, as customers paid more for bigger bundles.

But after 2010, the climb stalled.

Streaming arrived—cheaper and more convenient—and frustrated viewers began to drift away. Networks, instead of reinforcing the old system, followed the money to streaming, turning their backs on the financial model that had built them.

Initially limited to computers, streaming content soon expanded to TVs via plug-in devices like Apple TV (2006), Roku (2008), Chromecast (2013), and Fire TV (2014). Smart TVs with built-in internet connectivity further accelerated this trend, while a surge of services—such as Hulu Live, Sling TV, and YouTube TV—emerged to meet growing demand.

Many cable companies were like frogs in a pot of water, not noticing the water getting warmer and warmer—until, ever so slowly, they would be cooked. Many TV executives did not fully appreciate how profitable the cable-TV business model was and how quickly consumer behavior was shifting, and they refused to prepare for the change that was descending on the industry.

At first, when the cable-TV industry realized there might be a threat from new streaming companies such as Netflix, the national trade group and the largest content companies got behind a campaign called "TV Everywhere" in 2009. Cable subscribers could watch their usual TV shows online, on iPads, or phones, so long as they "authenticated" their sign-ons as paying subscribers to their local cable system.

This step, however, was a way for the program suppliers to buy peace from their cable distributors, as the programmers started to open up an entirely new and rival distribution system: streaming.

One of the first "TV Everywhere" evangelists was Jeffery Bewkes at Time Warner, whose HBO was launching a new online service, HBO GO, available to "authenticated" HBO subscribers. Many cable executives were cocky and confident that Netflix had no chance of taking over the cable-TV industry or its content providers.

In an interview with *The New York Times* headlined "Time Warner Views Netflix as a Fading Star," in 2010, Jeff made a quip he has not lived down to this day: "Is the Albanian army going to take over the world?" he said dismissively of Netflix. "I don't think so." (Netflix CEO Reed Hastings would later hand out berets emblazoned with the Albanian Army insignia, stoking his troops.)

The cable-TV industry had the right idea with TV Everywhere, but as the months wore on, cable companies never really coalesced around the campaign, and the industry also broke a cardinal rule of rolling out a new product: make it easy to use.

Cable customers became annoyed dealing with a cumbersome authentication process just to sign in. Then cable programmers began to demand more money from cable-TV operators since their content was now being "streamed" to different devices other than the TV. Somehow, the channels lost sight of the fact that the same customer was watching the same content, one way or the other.

The long-standing architecture of the deals that had worked so well was crumbling. Unlike broadcast TV, which relies only on advertising, cable networks seemed to forget their second revenue stream: fees paid by cable operators. Charter, for example, pays Disney roughly $2 billion a year to carry all its channels, including ESPN. Now some networks were going outside the cable ecosystem and beginning to explore direct-to-consumer models with digital streaming platforms to reach audiences.

It reminded me of the old Aesop fable of the dog and his reflection. A dog with a piece of meat in his mouth is crossing a bridge over a stream. Thinking his reflection in the water is another dog, he greedily goes for the other dog's meat. As he goes to attack, the meat drops into the stream and is swept away.

In 2013, when HBO and Netflix had roughly the same-size audience in the U.S., around 30 million, Netflix co-CEO Ted Sarandos said Netflix's goal was "to become HBO faster than HBO can become us." The quote would come to be prophetic. Five years later, Netflix would double its subscriber count to 60 million; HBO was still pushing in the upper 30 million range. Netflix was beginning to reach escape velocity and leave HBO and every other streaming service behind.

Around this time, overall pay-TV subscribers began trickling away across all providers: cable, satellite, and telephone companies, slowly at first, then in a torrent of millions every year. Traditional pay-TV homes peaked at 99 million in 2011, and by 2023, the total was down to 52 million. Devastating disruption, really.

If you were to go back fifteen or twenty years ago and ask a cable operator for a count of customers, they would cite total TV households and mention a smaller number of internet customers, maybe 70/30. Now those numbers have flipped as more customers go online for video entertainment. Charter today has more than 12 million pay-TV subscribers—and 30 million internet customers.

These days, some smaller cable operators have dropped video programming as it shrinks in importance and profits, while others simply pass rising programming costs on to customers with little effort to retain them.

Analysts predicted that the cable operators were on their way to becoming "dumb pipes"—simple conduits for transmitting digital bits—as consumers favored new video services on the net. When the falloff in video subscribers began accelerating, though, cable operators could rely on those broadband subscriptions to backfill the video losses. Pretty ingenious trick for a dumb pipe.

Then began the ripple effects of this shift. TV ad budgets followed consumers as they started to watch more digital and mobile media—and shifted away from live TV.

Traditional TV ads are a lot like billboards. They will serve up the same commercial for all, without any real personalization. An advertiser of air conditioners, rather than buying a billboard ad on NBC, might fare better by inserting an ad into the search results of a homeowner whose air-conditioning just went on the fritz.

Somewhere in the middle, you could get a broader audience, and a little higher valuation, and that is where Facebook landed, and why it got so big so fast.

Today more than 3 billion global users are active on Facebook, and they pay nothing for the privilege. Yet revenue at the largest global social media platform is at $135 billion a year—virtually all of it in ad revenue.

The growth in ad spending on social media networks and streaming services accelerated because of this powerful way to gather information on, and target individually and with higher precision, the growing numbers of viewers. This went way beyond the capabilities of the traditional currency of TV advertising—Nielsen TV ratings.

Throughout the 2000s, businesses increasingly allocated their advertising budgets to digital platforms like Facebook because of the technological ability to target specific demographics and measure campaigns based on their direct line into customer relationships. Meanwhile, traditional media outlets, particularly newspapers and broadcast television, saw declines.

The departure would be swift, too. Online ad revenue in the U.S. would surge from $37 billion in 2012 to more than $209 billion in 2022 for search, display, and video ads.

The TV networks were badly outflanked on advertising. Rupert Murdoch called me some years ago and said, "John, the television ad market isn't disappearing. It's just moving over to social media and the streamers." That is one more reason why Rupert, in 2017, would get out of entertainment programming, selling Fox to Disney, and hang on to sports and news.

As more customers canceled their cable-TV service, cable operators' payments to broadcasters were squeezed. From 2006 to 2015, the compounded annual growth of these fees grew 40 percent a year. Since then, the growth rate has slowed to around 14 percent.

Cable operators were betting the rate of attrition in the video subscriber base would be offset by broadband customers—and that this trade-off would be in balance. And in some quarters it was true, but in some quarters it was the wrong assumption.

I can still step back from time to time and admire the extraordinary forces the cable pioneers unleashed from a simple coaxial cable wire meant for better reception. By adding amplifiers to it, infusing it with optical fiber, we made it more reliable over longer distances. By compressing the signals sent over it, we were able to increase the capacity for more TV channels. With modems and new standards, we constructed the actual architecture of today's internet, spawning millions of new businesses.

Cable operators surfed the net wave that might have destroyed them, innovating and adding fiber a lot faster and at cheaper cost than the telephone companies. The telephone companies would focus instead on wireless and all but abandon their wired, land-based networks. AT&T did a little of both to buy TCI, then DirecTV.

What drives me nuts, though, is that while the cable industry was able to evolve technologically to anticipate and take advantage of the opportunity presented by the internet, collectively we were unable to harness the dynamics of the rapidly changing content side.

When I was at TCI, the industry's biggest players had often come together to make big things happen—saving Turner, creating CableLabs, financing @Home—but perhaps the interests of the biggest players were too balkanized in the end.

I always had believed it was possible for cable operators to become the retailer of streaming services instead of fighting them. Imagine offering customers a regular cable-TV package and any combination of streaming services—Amazon Prime Video or Netflix or HBO Max or Starz or Showtime. Cable operators could organize the streamers and provide a search platform to make sense of picking a movie—which can be quite a technical chore some nights given the splintering of services.

After the jarring breakup of the cable dial, cable operators could still survive by assuming this role of curator and packager of various streamers—and start reassembling the whole system all over again.

For me personally, it was frustrating to watch an industry miss such an achievable goal. We had a clear pathway and a unique solution to offering three services over one wire—voice, video, and data. We had a head start on all the streaming services that exist today. On both the programming and distribution side, we could not imagine defeat at the hands of an upstart. Little did we know what was coming in the next few years.

Why did it happen? Was it because cable operators were trapped in adverse bundled contracts with big programmers like Disney? Was it because the programmers couldn't get along with operators? Or because the operators couldn't pull together enough to create a streaming product with scale? Was it the high cost of cable bills due to sports? In some ways, the answer, collectively, is . . . yup.

One thing is for sure: the cable operators failed to pivot quickly enough. Rather than accepting the inevitable long-term transition, they decided to try to stonewall it. Eventually, the large operators would hold on to some customers by offering some combination of streaming and search alongside traditional cable TV, but in the end, the fifty-year-old cable model was fading.

What we could not fathom, though, was just a short while from happening: a tiny company that once sent out cute little red mailers for its DVDs was about to crush every business in its path.

CHAPTER 27

STREAMING DREAMS

You can divide the potential partners I've met in my career into three groups: those I was lucky to have as allies, others I was lucky to avoid, and an elusive group of those I sure wished I had been able to join.

Reed Hastings of Netflix falls into that last category. In twenty-five years of original thinking and fearless gambles, he has built a great American success story, a streaming colossus with more than 300 million paying subscribers in 190 countries. It earns $8.7 billion a year in net income on $39 billion in subscriber revenue.

Today, Netflix is the tail that wags the dog in entertainment media. In the first ten years of its meteoric rise, Netflix surged ahead, leaving giant rivals such as Disney, Amazon, and Apple in the dust. In the "streaming wars," Netflix is the undisputed victor.

In recent years, Netflix has spent as much as $17 billion annually on programming. The massive sum dwarfs the budgets of the biggest TV programming buyers. Netflix produces over a thousand pieces of programming in a year; huge studios churn out maybe a dozen films and a couple dozen TV series annually.

Reed Hastings and Netflix paved the way for the streaming revolution that now is all but shattering the traditional TV business I've been a part of all my adult life. Netflix sparked an era of mergers, collaborations, and bidding wars that continues today. Brilliantly, Reed beat the cable giants at their own game, using the content they sold him and the platform they had built.

The cable industry funded its own demise, and cable networks added to their troubles by selling their movies and TV series to Netflix, helping it lure away more viewers. Netflix gained traction with network series reruns like *The Office* and *Friends*; only later did to come up with its own original hits.

As early as 2011, Netflix was streaming so many off-network shows to U.S. homes that it was the single largest consumer of internet bandwidth in North America, hogging 33 percent of all traffic in peak nighttime hours. Just a year earlier the portion was at 20 percent, far surpassing Amazon Prime Video, Hulu, and HBO GO.

Here's the really hard part to swallow—Netflix's business was using the wires that cable operators strung and spent hundreds of billions of dollars to upgrade, then slurping up the lion's share of usable bandwidth—and paying almost nothing for it.

In the streaming era now upon us, thanks to Netflix, the cable dial is going à la carte, fragmenting into dozens of separate programming packages that you can get without having to pay for the entire cable bundle—and without buying them from your local cable system at all. By June 2025, Netflix, Disney, and other streamers collectively reached a historic milestone, surpassing the viewership of cable and broadcast TV *combined* for the first time, with a record 44.8 percent total of U.S. TV usage, according to Nielsen.

For the industry, letting itself get so disrupted by Netflix was an astonishing misstep, and this owes in part to the fact that the cable giants consistently underestimated Reed Hastings and his company at every turn. In business, as in life, you can be blinded by the confidence that comes from "That's the way it's always worked."

I knew better, because I had seen this movie before: In the 1990s, the hottest, newest cable networks, such as TBS, AMC, Discovery, and FX, started out by licensing reruns of series that had run on broadcast television, shows like *Law & Order* and *Friends*. Once established, the cable nets began creating original programming that could outperform the old broadcast reruns—and lure away still more viewers from the Big Three. Now Netflix was doing the same thing to cable. By the early 2000s, I had started warning my friends in the business, and my own company, about Netflix and the disruptive force of direct-to-viewer service via the internet. We needed to partner with Reed Hastings, buy his company, or band together to compete with him, and we succeeded in doing none of these.

In defense of my cable brethren, it was easy to underestimate the Netflix threat. The company started in 1997 as a mail-order shipper of DVD copies of movies and TV reruns to people's homes, which by 1999 you could order on a website and receive via the U.S. Postal Service.

Movies by mail? What did that have to do with broadband cable? The early Netflix, with no late fees and cheap rentals, looked like a disruptor of Blockbuster and the video rental store. Three years before Netflix began, Blockbuster was acquired for $8.4 billion by Sumner Redstone's Viacom, and it had 3,600 stores nationwide (peaking at over nine thousand) satisfying the desires of every American movie buff.

In fact, in early 2000, when then privately held Netflix had just three hundred thousand subscribers and $57 million in losses, Reed Hastings offered to sell 49 percent of his company to Blockbuster for just $50 million, combining forces under a new Blockbuster.com.

Had Blockbuster accepted, that $50 million would have grown one-thousand-fold to $50 billion by mid-2022, with Netflix recently trading in the $225-a-share range, with a total market value of more than $100 billion.

Instead, the video store chain dismissed the offer out of hand, and a decade later Blockbuster went bankrupt; today all that remains of it is a single, lonely store in Bend, Oregon, sustained by nostalgia buffs.

Hastings, by contrast, went out on his own and took Netflix public in 2002. Then, in 2007, he launched Netflix's first internet streaming service, complementing—and threatening—its own mainstay DVD business. I could see the damage this posed to incumbent cable companies, and a year later, in one of the few brushes I had with Reed, I offered to buy Netflix, then priced at $8 a share. He declined instantly, and who could blame him?

By 2009, Hastings had begun betting the entire company on that new internet-based business, sidelining the DVD business. He ended up managing one of the most amazing transformations ever achieved by any corporation, in the trapeze swing from the business it built to the new business that otherwise might have destroyed it.

He was on the way to building a vertically integrated business that bypassed traditional TV providers (broadcast, cable, satellite), avoiding old ratings expectations and ad models and able to reach a global audience that dwarfed anything achievable by other media companies in the U.S.

A traditional cable network, to take hold, had to sell itself to a cable operator that held a choke point over the network's ability to reach viewers. Netflix, by contrast, circumvented the cable operator as the retailer of video content and sold directly to the consumer—and then delivered the product over the cable systems' highway without paying them for the transit.

Reed saw the world differently, telegraphing his intentions from the start by naming his company Netflix, as in internet. Somehow, he had reinvented the wheel, and it rolled downhill a hell of a lot more smoothly.

It all seemed so predictable, and I watched it unfold as if in slow motion, unable to stop it or even slow it down. Cable operators, assuming life would go on undisturbed, simply passed along the fee increases of programmers, who were pushing the financial model past the breaking point. Prices rose 122 percent from 1995 to 2008, more than triple the rise in the consumer price index in the same period. They continued to spiral upward at the same rate, in part to fund the soaring costs of sports contracts.

This price surge encouraged some consumers to start bailing out of cable-TV service in favor of cable internet access and Netflix, which was charging them $8 a month starting out.

Another mistake: arming the enemy. One of the first important offenders on this front was a cable network in the stable of Liberty Media: the Starz movie network. I was as guilty of this gaffe as anyone, I suppose.

In October 2008, Starz agreed to sell Netflix the rights to stream twenty-five hundred popular movies and TV shows, including hits like *Pirates of the Caribbean: At World's End*, *Ratatouille*, and *Spider-Man 3*. The four-year deal gave Netflix a massive boost in the eyes of customers, the media, and, more importantly, Wall Street. The headline the next morning in *The New York Times* was distressingly accurate: "Starz Gives Netflix Fans a Reason to Stream."

It was a terribly short-term decision, in hindsight. Starz got somewhere between $20 million and $30 million a year on the deal but gave up so much more. Showing Starz movies from Disney and Sony and Columbia suddenly gave Netflix the whiff of credibility, and subscribers saw another reason to defect. In three years, Netflix's subscriber base almost tripled, from 9 million to 24 million homes.

Some of the smartest CEOs in the industry replicated the Starz error. Netflix was writing ever-bigger checks for content, and the traditional TV players couldn't resist the easy money.

One of Hastings's few missteps briefly tanked the stock. In 2011, he tried to split Netflix's DVD rental business into a separate company called Qwikster, effectively raising prices and confusing customers. The idea was scrapped when eight hundred thousand subscribers left in a single quarter, and the stock dropped 75 percent. Around this time, I suggested to Greg Maffei that Liberty should invest.

Greg demurred: if we invested in Netflix, our cable partners would likely get offended and retaliate by refusing to carry Liberty's Starz network.

So I decided to invest personally and called the guy who handles our family finances. He tried to wave me off Netflix, telling me, "This company is going bankrupt."

My response: "I'll bet you anything, all the money you have, it won't." (When we spoke in 2012, Netflix stock was at $17 a share; six years later, in 2018, it was up twentyfold to around $350.)

That rise was helped by Netflix's signing ever-bigger content-licensing deals, which drove more consumer sign-ups, which then provided it with the cash flow to finance still more content, especially new originals made by and owned by Netflix.

Already, broadcast networks were happily milking their hit reruns in off-network syndication to streaming services. Even as late as 2018, the three most streamed shows on Netflix were still reruns: (1) *The Office* (NBC), (2) *Friends* (NBC), and (3) *Grey's Anatomy* (Disney's ABC). Before Starz, CBS and Disney already had struck deals with Netflix for CBS's *CSI*, Disney's *Hannah Montana*, and a few other popular series.

In 2012, Walt Disney CEO Bob Iger sold some of the most popular franchise films of all time from Disney, Marvel, and Pixar, including the *Star*

Wars films, in a three-year streaming deal for an estimated $300 million per year. For Disney, it was a good way to boost their quarterly numbers; for Netflix, it was the foundational stock to draw legions of new subscribers looking for quality movies.

Knowing legacy content owners would shut him out if he became a threat, Reed raced to get big fast, and started investing money in his own original programming. By 2013, with 34 million paying subscribers, Netflix became the first streamer to win an Emmy when its original series *House of Cards* won three awards and was nominated for nine (including Outstanding Drama Series). By 2021, Netflix would pull in forty-four Emmy Awards, more than any other network or streaming platform.

Reed had used the cable industry's wires, and their shows, to build a new rival right under their noses. And now with his own programming, he was getting stronger by the viewing minute.

Federal regulators played a key role in letting Netflix run rampant over the cable industry, which they seemed to regard with suspicion and disdain. And cable incumbents were outgunned badly, in terms of their lobbying power vs. Big Tech.

In 2002, a Columbia University law professor named Tim Wu coined a concept that Google and Big Tech would use like a cudgel for years to come: "net neutrality," the idea of imposing regulations on cable operators to ban them from discriminating in terms of content or pricing against content owners they carried over their internet service.

This notion grew out of antiquated regulations for common carriers, dating back to the railroads and the early Bell telephone system and forcing them to carry all traffic, regardless of who was accessing the service, at the same basic cost.

On its face, net neutrality is anticompetitive and ridiculously intrusive: a cable operator sees Netflix sucking down one-third of its total bandwidth every night, yet it should be barred by unelected government bureaucrats from charging Netflix differently than a home user?

If internet service providers like cable operators are banned from managing their own traffic, the data hogs eventually will drive up the price for everyone. It is akin to the government's forcing a restaurant owner to charge the same price for every single customer, no matter what they order.

Google, part of the tech oligopoly beloved by Wall Street and dubbed FAANG—Facebook, Apple, Amazon, Netflix, and Google—turned net neutrality into a rallying cry. It started warning regulators and congresspeople of the embellished dangers of a cable-system operator's refusal to carry their content someday.

A phone or cable giant might intentionally slow the internet speeds of rival content providers, the tech titans argued, or charge them higher fees to access the viewers of the cable systems they controlled. Or the cable demons might favor their own allies by granting them exclusive access to higher speeds and special services.

None of this ever has happened in the market in the twenty years since net neutrality first emerged. The first, and really only, case, involved the FCC forbidding Comcast from "interfering" with the traffic of BitTorrent, a file-sharing platform that consumed vast amounts of bandwidth, often for copyrighted (read: stolen) material, music, and movies. The FCC ruled against Comcast, but a 2010 federal court case overturned the decision, highlighting the need for clearer net neutrality rules.

But in reality, competition and the free market prevented it: users, third-party speed-trackers, and the media would excoriate any cable provider that intentionally throttled or held off a competitor, and there are plenty of antitrust laws on the books to deal with violators.

But no matter. In the media business, even if you have a great product and a smart strategy, you can falter if you fail to bow to regulators and politicians in the right way.

Eric Schmidt, then Google's CEO, proudly played a key role in advising Obama's campaign data operations, and Google executives were among his largest donors, even leaving to join the Obama administration—hence virtually no government intervention.

Big Cable, by contrast, was beaten down by decades of scrutiny from regulators and antitrust officials, and it was reluctant to move against Netflix and start demanding compensation for the internet bandwidth it was consuming.

In 2015, after heavy lobbying from FAANG, the Federal Communications Commission adopted new net neutrality rules to reclassify broadband providers as "common carriers" under Title II of the Telecommunications Act, passed in 1934, forcing twenty-first-century internet firms into the same category as utilities and railroads. Eventually, Netflix would negotiate "peering" agreements with cable operators, which let it connect directly to ISP networks and meant it fell outside the purview of the new protections.

The U.S. cable industry grew up as a local business, licensed by small towns and big cities. By contrast, Netflix sold video directly to the consumer, anywhere in the world—without the cable-TV middleman. In time, it was just as easy to connect a customer in Denver as in Denmark.

Suddenly, big media companies started to see Netflix's point. Let's say half a billion households worldwide can pay $10 a month apiece. That's $5 billion a month, or $60 billion a year. CEOs in the TV industry eventually had a moment of clarity: if they were going to be a top-tier player, they had to get on this global direct-to-consumer platform fast. They faced a new class of competitor: Big Tech.

Google, which bought YouTube in 2006 for $1.65 billion when it was just a user-content website, saw potential in the future of TV over the net. Today YouTube has an ambitious streaming service that commands more "watch time" on TVs than mobile phones—and more daily viewing hours that Netflix.

In 2008, the unlikely partnership of NBCUniversal, Fox, Facebook, MSN, Myspace, Yahoo, and AOL launched a site called Hulu. Amazon launched Prime Video the same year. In later years, Disney+, Paramount+, Peacock from NBCU, and others would join the fray.

By the time the biggest cable companies seriously responded to Netflix, it was too little, too late. Like Time Warner and other cable operators, Comcast struggled to get customers to adopt its cumbersome TV Everywhere online service, so over time it launched its own rival solution: Xfinity, a brand for new TV products such as talking remotes, a sleek user interface, and digital music, movies, and entertainment. But Xfinity, too, failed to stem the incursions of Netflix.

When I consulted later with Comcast's Brian Roberts on what went wrong with TV Everywhere, he cited a lack of trust among the programmers and operators and a reticence to allow a giant such as Comcast or Time Warner to take the lead in such a venture. They pivoted too slowly, and simply expanded the limited video-on-demand options on the cable box, allowing Netflix to keep growing.

Early on, cable operators should have remade themselves as bundlers of all these various streaming services, even if it meant undercutting their own mainstream business on the TV subscription side of the house. Only recently have some cable operators started to look at this approach.

The reluctance to disrupt and even cannibalize your incumbent business is too strong to overcome for most companies. Harvard's Clayton Christensen famously labeled this "the Innovator's Dilemma." He argued that successful companies by nature focus on big-market, high-profit pursuits and how to sustain them, leaving them vulnerable to disruptive technologies that usually emerge from the outside.

Such "low end" disruption occurs when a company enters a market with simpler, more affordable products that are "good enough" for many customers—drawing in price-sensitive buyers and gradually eroding the incumbents' market share.

At Netflix, Reed created the streaming business at the expense of his DVD-mailing business, all but forcing his customers, and his own employees, to switch over to streaming earlier than many of them were ready to.

The entire world of what we knew as television shifted in a matter of a few years. Over time, most of the incumbent players that had sold shows to Netflix—Starz, Disney, NBC, and others—would unwind their deals, largely because they were launching their own streaming services.

In 2016, Time Warner bought a 10 percent stake in Hulu for $583 million, joining 21st Century Fox, Disney, and Comcast in an online TV/streaming platform. The following year, Time Warner's HBO pulled shows from Amazon for its own platform, HBO Now. And later, Warner Media would buy back the rights to *Friends* from Netflix for $425 million to carry the series on the HBO Max streaming service. NBCU paid $500 million to buy back rights to *The Office* in 2021, taking it away from Netflix for its new streamer, Peacock.

And Disney got the *Star Wars* franchises and other shows back from Netflix. Bob Iger himself would give perhaps the most eloquent mea culpa for all of us in the traditional TV industry in an interview: "And I woke up one day and thought, 'We're basically selling nuclear weapons technology to a third-world country, and now they're using it against us,'" he said. "So, we decided at the time that we would stop licensing to Netflix, and do it ourselves. And it resulted in a substantial decrease in our revenue, because we weaned ourselves off all that licensing money, but it thrust us into a business that is the most compelling growth engine in media today."

Suddenly the money flowing into fresh content for the streaming business became a tsunami, as big Hollywood players were joined by even bigger tech giants like Amazon, Apple, and Google. All the new players wanted to make a splash with the biggest stars and the best producers, and they were willing to pay top dollar.

Content budgets started rocketing upward. Competition for quality original programming was already stiff, so the new, deeper-pocketed players made it even more expensive—and riskier.

While HBO and other premium cable networks increased their spend on programming by a few percentage points a year, Netflix poured profits back into content. Netflix was spending $4.5 billion on programming by 2015; three years later that sum had tripled to $12 billion. In 2021, Netflix spent $17 billion on content.

Heads turned, even in Hollywood, when Amazon announced a deal in 2017 to make *Lord of the Rings* into a TV series at the unprecedented cost of $1 billion, the most expensive TV show of all time. For now. Apple joined the game in 2019, poaching a string of top talent with big money, and becoming the first streamer to win an Academy Award for Best Picture, for *Coda*.

The reason these Big Tech players could afford to pay more is because their business models differed sharply from those of traditional TV players. For these newcomers, streaming is merely an add-on, or even a loss leader, for their lifeblood business.

Amazon is the largest online retailer in the world, with sales approaching half a trillion dollars a year. Its server business, Amazon Web Services, boasts torrid growth and 40 percent profit margins on more than $107.6 billion in annual sales to business. Prime Video is a lesser sideline business for Amazon, yet it has 200 million subscribers, almost as many as Netflix, and subscribers are its soul source of sustenance.

Similarly, Apple's main business is the iPhone, fat and rich enough to fund years of losses in the AppleTV streaming service. And Google is the largest advertising-supported online business in the world, rivaled only by Facebook, as this duopoly dominates digital advertising and leverages massive reach to fund expansion into other markets.

All of the Big Tech players had one thing in common: they were making money with a model that had suddenly changed from wholesale/retail to direct consumer, affording them control over pricing, the flow of information, and deep data on customer preferences and activities.

Surfing on the rise of Netflix, a raft of smaller streaming services emerged with names like Crackle, Tubi, and Fandor. Shudder was a horror service created by the AMC cable network. Acorn offered Agatha Christie from the BBC. And new hybrid services—YouTube, Sling, and Hulu + Live—began delivering a package of live TV, cable networks, and on-demand video content over the internet—known as "virtual multichannel video programming distributors" or vMVPDs.

Consumers were gradually forced to subscribe to several different services to see their favorite shows. Up until this point, U.S. TV providers had been skeptical of linking their subscribers to Netflix directly, fearing it would lure them away from their longtime cable network packages. But customers were getting access to Netflix anyway, and they wanted a dominant aggregator, one place to find a particular title.

Who better to offer this service than the cable internet provider? We had pioneered this approach in 2016 at Liberty Global, which got a percentage of the revenue for signing up subs to Netflix. Comcast and others followed.

By 2018 Netflix had grown to 125 million subscribers globally, and Wall Street was valuing the company at a total market cap north of $150 billion, on par with Disney, despite the fact that Netflix had a fraction of Disney's revenue and was reinvesting every dollar it brought in, and then some.

I'm sure this caused some consternation in the C-suite at Disney, with its theme parks; Disney, Pixar, and Marvel studios; eight broadcast TV stations; cable networks including the Disney Channel and ESPN; and line of consumer products, music, and more.

Disney had the content, the reach, and the expertise to give Reed Hastings a run for his money, and so Disney CEO Bob Iger started to turn the ship into the stream. He shifted all priority to the streaming-engine compartment and put all his firepower into achieving a global presence for its direct-to-consumer video services Disney+, Hulu, and ESPN+.

Iger commanded results: In 2021 Disney+ hit the 100 million global subscriber mark in sixteen months—a feat that took Netflix ten years. Yet by May 2025, Netflix's market cap was in orbit at $494.2 million—up 89 percent over the previous year—and larger than the market cap of Disney, Comcast, Fox Corp., Paramount Global, and Warner Bros. Discovery is $330.7 billion—combined.

Unlike WBD, Disney, Paramount, or Fox—companies still rooted in domestic markets—Netflix is truly global. Around 60 percent of its revenue now comes from outside the U.S. They bet early that American content would resonate worldwide, and they were right. That global scale validated their model and gave them the reach to invest in local programming, reinforcing their presence in every market.

No other company can match its subscriber base, infrastructure, or content investment now. A year ago, Netflix and Warner Bros. Discovery had nearly identical revenue and EBITDA. Yet Netflix's market cap was worth more than twenty times WBD's. Why? Wall Street likes Netflix's growth trajectory.

At Netflix, Reed Hastings was watching the life cycle of his own business evolve. New rivals made it harder to raise prices for customers, and they bid up the cost of new shows by competing against Netflix for every deal. As growth slows, valuations moderate.

As Netflix achieved global scale, it was becoming increasingly clear that in this new era, companies like entertainment giant Time Warner, or even AT&T, the third-largest mobile carrier in the U.S., were starting to look subscale, something that would have been unthinkable twenty years ago.

Reed Hastings's tiny mail-order company had snowballed into an existential threat that launched a flurry of multibillion-dollar bidding wars, collaborations, and mergers. The ensuing stretch of dealmaking coming next would remake some of the biggest names in the global media and entertainment industry.

CHAPTER 28

FORMULA ONE

A passion for fast cars runs deep in my DNA. My mom, an elementary school teacher, cruised around town in a charcoal-silver 1954 Corvette that turned heads wherever she went. My dad preferred the feel behind the wheel of a white 1957 Porsche Speedster, which could hit 100 mph with little effort. His need for speed got the better of him, however, and in his late fifties, after earning two speeding tickets with the Porsche, he reluctantly returned to driving his 1947 Fleetwood Cadillac.

As for me, my heart has always belonged to my 1954 Jaguar XK, sleek and aerodynamic, despite its bad brakes and constant need for a tune-up. The best thing about the car was that it cost me $400, and at fifteen, I turned that broken-down, race-wreck jalopy into my dream car.

Few things compare to the feeling I got flying down the road with my foot crushing the gas pedal on a screaming six-cylinder with a dual-overhead cam—hanging on to the wheel and racing down a back road, seeing nothing but contrails of dust and swirling leaves in the rearview mirror.

So, in 2016, when Liberty Media CEO Greg Maffei and an executive named Yavor Efremov started unwinding the story about an opportunity to buy Formula One, the most popular racing circuit in the world, I was instantly intrigued. Formula One, or F1, is a racing circuit featuring some of the fastest high-tech, open-wheel cars in the world. Formula One vehicles race at speeds up to 200 mph in the tight curves of city streets in exotic international locales. A European private-equity firm, CVC, held a controlling stake in Formula One, and after more than doubling its money and dealing with a sometimes exasperating longtime part owner and CEO, Bernie Ecclestone, it was looking to sell.

CVC itself had acquired its 47.5 percent stake in F1 in 2005 from a German bank, which had come into the F1 stake as the collateral on a defaulted loan it had made to Kirsch Group, a Germany media business. The CVC deal allowed Bernie to stay in place as CEO, with 18 percent ownership.

Bernie, nicknamed "F1 Supremo" by the British tabloids, was a flamboyant, bespectacled CEO with shaggy silver hair. A race-car driver in 1958, he became a team manager and owner for twenty years before taking over Formula One in the 1970s and building it into a global sport. He did this by pushing Formula One into the television age.

But in more recent years, Formula One had failed to live up to its potential, and it looked more like a fixer-upper. I like fixer-uppers, in both cars and companies: they are a lot cheaper than buying something shiny and new.

Formula One had slavishly focused on securing the highest TV and promotion rights and failed to cultivate its following, especially new, younger fans, by tapping digital and social media. Its marketing was behind—F1 didn't start posting video clips to its website until 2008, years behind other sports. And Formula One's television audience had been stagnating even in its traditional strongholds of Latin America, Germany, and Italy. Unless F1 fans attended actual races, which are truly pulse-racing to watch live, they didn't get a real opportunity to engage with the sport. By 2016, F1's combined audience had fallen by one-third, from 600 million viewers down to 400 million.

Its revenue suffered accordingly, with many teams reporting losses. And while Formula One could draw massive audiences in far-flung locales such as Monte Carlo, Sao Paulo, and Singapore, the sport had failed to crack the biggest market in the world: the U.S., where NASCAR's souped-up stock cars were drawing the most motor-heads.

F1 also was afflicted with what were politely called "governance issues," including rumors of bribes and tax problems. Bernie ruled the circuit like a fiefdom, favoring popular teams and lavishing them with money while short-changing smaller teams that struggled as a result.

The prize fund for the top ten racing teams in 2014 totaled $863 million—and almost half of it went to the top five teams, led by Ferrari. The rest each earned only around $40 to $60 million a year. Sounds like a lot—until you consider that the cost of just one car is $15 to $20 million to build and tens of millions of dollars to maintain.

The unequal revenue distribution wrecked parity in the circuit, and this resulted in the same dominant teams winning the races, over and over again. Bernie Ecclestone lavished special bonuses on Ferrari, based on the number of races it had won in prior seasons and for being F1's longest-standing team. In 2015 (the company paid in arrears), Ferrari was paid $164 million from this bonus pool. As other teams struggled, Ferrari made more money than most teams that year before the driver even turned the key.

Bernie was a colorful character, though I never spent much time with him. He spoke his mind a bit too freely, and the media jumped on him for this over the years. In 2009, he said in an interview with *The Sunday Times* that Hitler was "able to get things done." Never praise Hitler. Zero upside.

He also sparked criticism for deploying comely female fashion models on the grid before each race, as they held placards emblazoned with driver names. In early 2016, he expressed doubts on Canadian television that a woman would be racing in F1 anytime soon: "If there was somebody that was capable, they wouldn't be taken seriously anyway, so they would never have a car that is capable of competing."

Bernie faced bribery allegations in court in Germany in 2014; an associate got eight and a half years in prison, while Bernie avoided a verdict by paying 60 million pounds in penalties.

Once we started kicking the tires on the company, we heard rumors of corruption, and we were told it was why the outfit had never gone public. It also was one reason other potential bidders had balked at pursuing a deal: too much uncertainty about what might be going on under the hood.

We looked hard beyond the known allegations and turned up no verifiable evidence of corruption. Still, in short, Formula One was misfiring, not living up to expectations. We also knew that Wall Street would do a double take at such a purchase, given the condition of F1 and Liberty's complete lack of experience running a racing league.

But it was live sports. And while it wasn't the NFL or the NBA, it was a live competition, the elixir of a profitable ad strategy in a sea of on-demand entertainment. Plus, you could buy the whole shebang for maybe $4 billion or so, less than the cost of just one NFL team.

Just one piece of this puzzle was missing, and it was, perhaps, the most important piece: we needed a professional CEO who could unlock the value we intuitively knew was there. By this time, I was in control of three companies—Liberty Media, Liberty Global, and Discovery—and the CEOs of all three stepped up to buy Formula One. They concocted partnerships and combinations, and every time Greg Maffei or Mike Fries or Discovery CEO David Zaslav asked my opinion on buying it, I'd ask how it would get paid for, and each of the plans typically ended with their company writing a big check.

Paying cash is a horrible option, taxwise. It saddles you with new debt, and the seller ends up having to share a big chunk of the windfall with the government. This means we have to pay a higher price than we would if the deal could be done tax-free.

My response to all three men: "No way. Can't we get creative and come up with a simple, tax-efficient way to buy it? Moreover, who would you get to run the thing? It's as big and complicated as any sports league in America, and it's got governance issues."

Greg walked into my office at our base in Denver one day, and he had untangled the Gordian knot.

"It can be a tracking stock," he said, which, of course, played right to my soft spot. I like tracking stocks and their advantages almost as much as I like muscle cars.

Greg was a persuasive CEO, and sometimes he could be overly confident in his strategy, but he made a great case for why we should go for it. The idea: We could use as currency our 69.6 million shares of common stock in Live Nation, worth $2.6 billion. Take those (along with $1.3 billion in debt) and swap them for controlling equity in Formula One, taking the combination public in the form of different tracking stocks. This would give us a public currency that reflected the value of the entire enterprise—while letting us avoid taxes on the transaction.

A year earlier, we had recapitalized Liberty Media's stock into three tracking stocks: (1) Liberty SiriusXM Group, (2) Braves Group, and (3) Liberty Media Group. Upon completing the F1 deal, the third stock was renamed Formula One Group. The idea, as ever, was to recognize the market value of this discrete asset and have it valued as one Liberty Media tracking stock, under the Formula One name.

In many ways it was like a SPAC, a company created solely to raise capital through an IPO and then merge with an existing company as a faster way to do an IPO. And what we were risking was essentially the value of our equity in Live Nation. If the market disliked our deal and sent the price of the new tracker plunging, Liberty Media shareholders would take the hit.

The only question in my mind lingered still: Who in the hell would we get to run an international racing circuit?

Greg Maffei finally had worked out that piece of the puzzle: Chase Carey. By this time, Chase was the vice chairman of 21st Century Fox. A decade earlier, I had watched him turn around DirecTV, which was running a poor third to Charlie Ergen's Dish when Rupert bought it in 2003.

After Chase took over as DirecTV CEO, he instinctively drove strategies that supercharged the company's subscribers, revenue, and market share. He pushed high-definition, DVRs, more channels, and international expansion. And within a year or two, DirecTV was the superior player in the satellite space.

Three years after I took over the News Corp. stake in DirecTV in 2006 and became its chairman, Rupert was begging to take Chase Carey back as he worked out governance issues with his two sons. "John, I know you have Chase on a long-term contract, but can you please turn him loose?" And so Chase left to become president and COO of News Corp. in 2009.

Lachlan Murdoch rejoined the family business in 2014 as cochairman of both News Corp. and 21st Century Fox. Following Disney's 2019 acquisition of 21st Century Fox's entertainment assets, he became chairman and CEO of the newly formed Fox Corporation, which retained Fox News, Fox Sports, and the Fox broadcast network.

Perfect timing for us: Chase, no longer with an operating role at News Corp., was looking for something in sports.

So, in January 2017, Liberty Media bought a controlling interest in F1 from CVC Capital in two stages, paying $4.4 billion in cash and a newly issued tracking stock. Our F1 bid valued the company at $8 billion when debt was included. Delta Topco and CVC Capital Partners, which had owned the sport since 2006, made a healthy return on their initial investment of $2 billion.

After we won approval from the sport's governing body, the Fédération Internationale de l'Automobile (FIA), Chase threw himself into the driver's seat, becoming F1 chairman and CEO, replacing Nestlé chairman Peter Brabeck-Letmathe.

Bernie briefly held the title of chairman emeritus, but his contract was not renewed. Some years later, he pleaded guilty to UK tax-evasion charges involving assets hidden in a Singapore trust and agreed to pay $800 million. In 2023, a judge sentenced him to seventeen months in prison and suspended the sentence because of Bernie's ailing health and his age: ninety-two. He is still hanging on.

Chase, with his trademark handlebar mustache and git-'er-done attitude, instantly saw potential in Formula One and vowed to make it financially successful by reconnecting to the global fan base. To understand the sport's core issues and challenges, he embarked on a listening tour, meeting with team owners, marketers, even the drivers, identifying pain points that hampered growth.

Afterward, he observed quite bluntly to the press: Formula One "doesn't tell any stories. The goal in this is to make the fans connect to the live experience as much as possible, and the tools you have to do that, we're not using at all." Chase changed not only the tools, but the entire culture, toward long-term growth instead of short-term gains.

Immediately, he invested in the digital platform, drawing new (and younger) fans. In 2018, Chase launched the F1 streaming service, letting fans in the U.S. and Europe pay to stream races directly from Formula One itself, complete with new TV graphics and type design, a new Formula One theme song, even a new F1 logo. This gave fans unprecedented access to behind-the-scenes content, interviews with drivers, and in-depth analysis. For gamers, a new Formula 1 E-sports Series was launched.

F1 opened up access to the track, with new levels of ticketing and hospitality, including the F1 Garage, where fans could actually watch the race in the paddock next to the teams along the pit lane. New fan festivals and live events created a spectacle around Grand Prix weekends.

Greg and Chase put together a crack team who worked like a pit crew to get each facet of the business running better. To maintain the F1 legacy, he tapped racing legend Ross Brawn, part of the group who guided Michael Schumacher to five Formula One titles at Ferrari. Ross became managing director of motor sports for Liberty Media's Formula One Group.

To ramp up sponsorship and marketing, he brought in Sean Bratches, former ESPN head of marketing, a salesman so smooth he could sell a gas can to a Tesla owner. Sponsorships provide 60 percent or so of a race team's annual revenue, and Chase saw nothing but open highway ahead.

Social media engagement skyrocketed with this more open and fan-friendly approach, revving up attention on Facebook, Instagram, X (formerly Twitter), and YouTube. F1's YouTube channel drew fewer than three hundred thousand viewers when we took over the business in early 2017; today it has 12.5 million subscribers. F1 now attracts almost 6.5 million fans to its twenty-two races, generating more than 8 billion video views. In 2022, F1 attendance grew 36 percent to 5.7 million from 2019, the last year before the pandemic, and it is driving growth still.

Because of his experience in TV, Chase quickly secured new deals with major networks and streamers in Australia, Europe, Latin America, and the U.S., widening the sport's global footprint to Vietnam, with an eye on China next, attracting new sponsors and partners along the way.

And he renegotiated TV rights packages with justifiably sharp increases. In 2022, Formula One's contract with ESPN soared to $90 million per year in a three-year deal—a 1,700 percent increase over the previous $5-million-per-year deal. Overall, total revenue from media rights hit $936 million in 2022, up 40 percent. ESPN set viewership records, posting an average of 1.21 million viewers per F1 race across ESPN, ESPN2, and ABC, a 28 percent increase over the previous U.S. TV record set in 2021.

Formula One's popularity exploded when the series *Drive to Survive* debuted on Netflix in 2019. Fans could experience the stories behind their favorite drivers, and by 2022 *Drive to Survive*'s global audience had made it the most popular show on Netflix in thirty-three countries during its first three weeks.

The Abu Dhabi Grand Prix, the final race in 2024, drew 109 million simultaneous viewers, more than the U.S. audience for Super Bowl LVI (101 million). The Miami Grand Prix roared onto the scene in 2022 becoming the most watched live F1 telecast with 2.1 million U.S. viewers—then blew past that record in 2024, hitting 3.1 million U.S. viewers.

Formula One has quickly planted roots in three key U.S. cities: Las Vegas, Miami, and Austin, Texas. This recent expansion has reignited enthusiasm among longtime fans, opened the door to a growing U.S. market, and even captured Hollywood's attention—most notably with Brad Pitt starring in a high-profile F1 film being shot amid actual race weekends. It's a smart fusion of sport, entertainment, and global brand building.

Big crowds are not my thing, so when I was in Austin for the race, I sought refuge down in the pits on the field, checking out the technology under the hood. I wish I'd had these guys with me back in my dad's old barn.

To revive competitive drama in the sport, Chase worked closely with teams to bring about some parity, imposing spending caps and lavishing funding and support on weaker teams close to dropping out. This, in turn, fostered closer competition, which ensured more unpredictable outcomes for longtime fans as well as first-time watchers.

This, in turn, benefitted the race teams. The average team value in Formula One was up 276 percent since 2019 to $1.88 billion in 2023, *Forbes* estimates. Average yearly revenue, at $220 million per team in 2018, has surged up to $600 million per team. Meanwhile, total F1 revenue grew to $3.6 billion in 2024, up 14 percent in a year. And it's not the same teams winning.

There are precious few CEOs today who understand the opportunity and have the people skills and the energy to pull off a job they never have done before. Chase got so wrapped up in the running of Formula One in the first few years that his wife called me up one day and complained: "He feels like he has to go to every Formula One race!" She told me she was headed my way—to rough me up because she never saw her husband anymore. Fortunately, she was joking.

Today Formula One is one of the fastest-growing sports the world, and it reaches a cumulative TV audience of 1.6 billion people, or an average 70 million per race, four times the size of the 17.1 million average for an NFL football game.

From the time Chase took the wheel in 2017 to 2024, revenue has doubled, to $3.6 billion. Satisfied it was running right, he stepped down in 2020 to make way for a new CEO, Stefan Domenicali, a fifty-five-year-old, widely respected former Ferrari team boss. Since then, my hope is that Chase has been spending a lot more time with his wife.

Just a few years later, Liberty Media jumped into the motorcycle racing world. Amid suitors such as UFC, TKO Group, and Qatar Sport Investments, Liberty recently agreed to acquire a majority stake in Madrid-based Dorna Sports, the owner of motorcycle racing circuit MotoGP, in a deal that valued the firm at $4.5 billon.

The Formula One deal wouldn't have worked without the flexibility that a tracking stock offered us. In fact, 2016 marked the twenty-fifth anniversary of the very first tracker we ever created. On March 28, 1991, Liberty for the first time traded on the NASDAQ under the tickers LBTYA and LBTYB, with content assets previously owned by the old TCI. Those who participated in that rights offering in 1991 and held LBTYA shares through its various incarnations would now be sitting on over twenty different tickers and significant capital gains.

I am often asked why we use tracking stocks and spin-offs, which, to the casual observer, might seem to complicate our value and create a shadow stock that trades below the price of the stock that inspired it. But we believe the tracking stocks actually provide more transparency and diversity for the investor, while giving Liberty enormous flexibility, tax advantages, and greater access to capital.

A tracking stock tracks the performance of a specific business inside a company, as a way to highlight how that business is faring and trade up or down accordingly. Yet the specific assets of a business remain on the balance sheet of the parent company. Shareholders can choose which part of the company to invest in. It is typically a transitional structure while you are trying to grow an asset to a point where it can be spun out and stand on its own. The SiriusXM tracking stock, the Live Nation tracking stock, and the Braves tracking stock were created to give us more options.

Tracking stocks trade at somewhat of a discount because of skepticism over the complexity and the uncertainty of when they might be spun off or treated as a separate asset. In the short term, a tracker structure may not actually yield the highest value.

Tracking stocks let us buy back shares cheaply when undervalued and raise capital when overpriced, benefiting long-term Liberty shareholders. With control, we can choose when to grow and spin off a tracker tax-free, avoiding heavy taxes from selling the business outright. Plus, we can off-set profits from one tracker with losses from another on consolidated tax returns, reducing overall taxes.

In addition to Formula One, a tracking stock was instrumental in the purchase of Charter. That acquisition was created largely with Liberty Interactive tracking stock created by the consolidated tax savings from QVC.

When COVID shut down Formula One and Live Nation in 2020, their stocks tanked—but Formula One had margin debt it couldn't quickly repay. Thanks to Liberty's tracking stock structure, we avoided forced asset sales by moving Live Nation's stake (plus cash and debt) to the stronger SiriusXM Group. This reattribution shored up Formula One, kept Live Nation safe, and let us support F1 tax-free. In the end, both rebounded remarkably, and the tracker structure made it all possible. Trackers let us reallocate assets and liabilities across stronger balance sheets, protecting value and avoiding forced sales in a downturn.

A tracking stock was the keystone in the biggest deal of my life—selling TCI to AT&T. Imagine if TCI had been forced to sell Liberty assets in order to do the merger with AT&T—the tax leakage would have been substantial, and you can't time the market, so billions of dollars in value could have simply floated out the window. For Liberty, a tracking stock is also an equity that reflects the specific business for the reward of the people running that business. Chase, for example, was paid in equity in Formula One.

Trackers are an incredibly flexible currency, in large part because they make tax planning easier. And by tax planning, I mean current tax *reduction*. So long as your tactics are legal under the tax laws, you have the right to reduce your tax liability as much as possible.

I have always believed that the government is your partner in business—they just don't come to the meetings. And if your partner shows you a way to reduce taxes, you are obligated on behalf of shareholders to save that money.

So, for example, if one business is losing money, you use the losses to shelter, or defer, taxes—not eliminate them—for the company. If you've ultimately made money, you'll pay taxes. By analyzing how and when you'll pay, you will be more efficient with your capital.

Cable operators, including TCI, were able to build and upgrade a national network mainly because we could take a tax break on the depreciation we claimed on the physical cable-system plant, deduct the interest payments on our debt, and amortize the franchise fees over time, spreading out the tax burden and reducing annual taxes. Tracking stocks were one more tool in the box.

Liberty Media was maturing. When it began inside TCI, I was head of TCI and head of Liberty, which in many ways was a holding company, owning interests in a diversified set of media, cable, and technology assets. We brought Liberty Media back into TCI for the (aborted) Bell Atlantic deal, then spun it back out. And when AT&T bought TCI, Liberty became a tracker of AT&T, then a stand-alone company, in which I held a controlling interest, 33 percent voting control.

And in each of these incarnations, Liberty became more and more of a holding company, an investment company, almost like a mutual fund. I hope its structure is sustained and protected when I am gone, because, to create value, what management needs more than anything else is flexibility.

And it works, with returns that have on occasion bested my friend Warren Buffet. A holder of the original Liberty Media from 2004 to 2016 would have realized annualized returns of 13 percent, compared with 7.5 percent for Berkshire Hathaway and 7.7 percent for the Standard & Poor's 500 index, according to an analysis by Gamco Investors.

Liberty Media has been a portfolio of companies with infinite possibilities. And to me the opportunity to add and arrange pieces, or spin them out at just the right time, is maximum flexibility, what I call structural Nirvana.

At Liberty, we have one board of directors, multiple public equities, and you can rearrange these pieces to optimize performance. And it is all on one consolidated tax return. And if you start to calculate what combinations are possible, the optionality becomes limitless.

Often, I get asked about the "endgame" for the Liberty Media structure. I don't know what that is, but I will let you know when we get there. Liberty is in a constant state of evolution as a business. Nothing is forever at Liberty, but there is one element that remains constant: a focus on growing long-term shareholder value.

CHAPTER 29

TAMING BIG TECH

In the 1990s, as the head of TCI, the largest cable operator in the U.S., I unwillingly became the poster child for critics who said the cable industry had too much power and wielded a monopoly choke hold over the television business. No one said running a company was a popularity contest.

I had to spend way too much time thinking about onerous government regulations and how to oppose them or devise creative and legal ways around them. The entire creation of Liberty Media, spun off from TCI and home to most of whatever I have built up in half a century in business, arose in part out of too much regulation.

My desire for freedom was in the new company's name, Liberty. If TCI had dared to start buying media companies on the whole, our opponents in Congress and at the FCC, the FTC, and the Justice Department would have descended on us with torches and pitchforks.

So, instead, Liberty Media made minority investments in an array of media and entertainment companies, exercising neither ownership control nor management power but holding enough of a stake to be able to influence events and decisions at those firms.

Just hold on loosely, but don't let go, as the old rock song advises.

That worked out exceedingly well, but we never should have held back in making acquisitions. The concerns about TCI's market domination were overblown and politicized, and they were off target: we held our holdings to under 30 percent of U.S. households, and we had an abundance of multibillion-dollar rivals eager to eat into our business.

The regulations the government spun out over the years were interfering, intrusive, and often wrongheaded. I always have had a healthy suspicion of regulations and the unelected bureaucrats who draft and enforce them. These people know too little about business, and they know even less about the advanced technologies they are so eager to rein in and take down a peg. They lack an abiding respect for capitalism and competition. Which is why it surprises me to make this next point:

We need a new regime of government regulations designed to rein in and monitor the gigantic companies of Big Tech—the biggest, most powerful corporations ever to rule media, entertainment, and personal communications around the planet.

For the good of the country and our people, it is critical that we defang FAANG. Facebook, Apple, Amazon, Netflix, and Google are so massive in scale, reach, influence, customer data, and profitability, and so far out ahead of any other company with any shot at challenging them, that only smart and specific government regulation has any chance of keeping them honest.

Google, whose old founding motto, ironically perhaps, was "Don't Be Evil," and its behemoth brethren have committed a multitude of abuses against millions of unsuspecting users. Though Google, Facebook, X (Twitter), and the rest of the social media peddlers rely on a two-hundred-year-old business model—advertising revenue—they stoke it with twenty-first-century AI, sparking conflict and hate as engagement to keep their coffers humming.

Consider that each day, Google and Facebook harvest our personal data, often without our clear consent, and slice it up, sell it, and exchange it in digital ad auctions they run and rig to favor themselves over rival bidders, according to lawsuits. Facebook and X use AI to bar individuals and groups from their platforms, a new form of digital discrimination.

A *Wall Street Journal* exposé, complete with a congressional whistleblower, exposed startling misdeeds at Facebook in the fall of 2021, showing that the company often risked the safety and health of its users, especially girls and young women on Instagram, in a relentless and amoral push for profit. The same was true of TikTok. In October 2024, a lawsuit by more than a dozen state attorneys general revealed TikTok knew the platform was harmful to kids, yet maintained the algorithm that kept them hooked.

The Big Tech platforms also censor or suppress high-profile individuals and controversial topics they deem to be out of bounds. At times they do so at the behest of the government, thereby complicitly aiding an administration's effort to impose an unconstitutional prior restraint on expression and information, in violation of the First Amendment.

X (Twitter), Facebook, and Google have ominous powers to influence entire elections by skewing their algorithms to play up certain newsfeeds, running get-out-the-vote messages in only certain districts, and snuffing out the voices of candidates they dislike. Overseas, Facebook has been used to evil ends, utilized by mobs to organize their attacks against their foes and by despotic governments to quell dissent.

Meta, Facebook's parent company, announced in January 2025 that it would end fact-checking on its platforms after censorship complaints. By allowing the unchecked spread of falsehoods and hate speech, social platforms can destabilize governments. We've already seen, thanks to digital operatives in Russia and China during the recent 2016, 2020, and 2024 elections here in the U.S., how incredibly easy it is to create phony news by using the algorithms that firms like Facebook use to surface news.

Yet in the U.S., nobody in government or in the media is demanding that these companies reveal the algorithms they use to amplify certain news stories, or the standards they apply for deciding whom to ban from their platforms. Instead, we are supposed to trust these gigantic, data-sucking tech companies—when they have shown us repeatedly that they are unworthy of our trust.

Now, most times, given my love of business and competition and innovation, I would look to private enterprise to set all this right rather than appealing to government. If the giants of an industry overstep and abuse their customers and business partners, a new raft of competitors should be able to rise up and topple them—see David and Goliath.

The problem is that the gargantuan heavyweights in Big Tech now are Too Big to Assail. They possess massive global scale and financial firepower like we've never seen before. These global tech purveyors, blessed with acquiescent regulators and surfing almost free of charge atop a distribution platform paid for by the cable industry, have grown like six-foot land iguanas on the Galápagos, free of any true competitors relative to recent history.

The speed at which they appeared and expanded has been astonishing. Amazon went public in 1997 at a total value of half a billion dollars; today it controls 40 percent of the e-commerce market, with sales over $638 billion and a market cap of more than $2 trillion. In 2007, after a decade as a DVD mailer, Netflix introduced its streaming service; ten years later, it had 110 million subscribers globally, more than the entire U.S. cable TV industry combined. Today more than 300 million homes pay to watch Netflix.

Regulators and politicians pilloried Tele-Communications Inc. in the 1990s as being too big and powerful, and we never reached more than 21 million cable homes in America. Facebook reaches more than 200 million people in the U.S.—and more than *three billion people* around the world. X's (Twitter's) audience is barely one-tenth as large as Facebook's, at 336 million worldwide, and that still is an unimaginable sum in my old cable business.

These tech giants dominate their respective markets with a lion's share that might have drawn the envy of the nineteenth-century oil baron John D. Rockefeller. Google has 95 percent of the market for all online searches.

The sheer financial magnitude of FAANG is unheard of in modern business—these five top internet-based services have a combined market capitalization exceeding $9 trillion in mid-2025, vastly outweighing the combined market cap of the five largest internet service providers by subscriber count (Comcast, Charter, AT&T, Verizon, and Cox), around $600 billion, less than one-tenth the mass of FAANG. Nowhere is the imbalance more outrageous than with C-SPAN. For decades, cable companies quietly funded this nonprofit nonpartisan civic lifeline, giving Americans direct access to their government. Now, as C-SPAN loses traditional cable-TV viewers, streaming giants like YouTube TV and Hulu + Live TV flat-out refuse to carry it, even amid bipartisan calls from Congress. The truth is brutal: public service has no place in their profit-driven algorithm.

Netflix likely faces the least opposition on the antitrust front. It is the smallest of the FAANG bunch by far, with a market cap of around $520 billion in June 2025. So far, its first-mover status has insulated it from a raft of latecomers, but the rapid rise of Disney+ and others shows Netflix has vulnerabilities. This, in turn, is why government prosecutors are likely to focus elsewhere. Competition will take care of Netflix.

Apple, too, may escape some antitrust scrutiny. Its iPhone commands 23 percent of the worldwide mobile phone market, with number two Samsung at 16 percent at the end of 2024. In streaming, Apple has perhaps 25 million subscribers, a tenth the size of Netflix and Amazon, and it spends up to $6 billion a year on new content, compared with $17 billion at Netflix and $25 billion at Disney.

The other three members of FAANG—Facebook, Amazon, and Google— pose a far bigger threat on antitrust grounds given their size, scale, market share, and rapacious and preternatural tactics.

Facebook parent Meta dominates social media through Instagram, WhatsApp, and Messenger. Along with Amazon and Alphabet (Google), Meta accounted for about half of all global digital ad spending in 2024. Despite ongoing FTC lawsuits over anticompetitive practices, Meta's market cap has soared past $1 trillion. Its AI-driven algorithms shape public discourse, but regulators have struggled to keep pace.

Google controls nearly all of online search and faces multiple lawsuits from the DOJ and state attorneys general. Allegations include monopolizing digital ads, paying billions to remain Apple's default search engine—perhaps a ransom to keep Apple from entering the search market themselves—and tracking users without consent. A 2024 ruling found Google violated U.S. antitrust laws, and the DOJ is now pushing for potential breakups—possibly targeting Chrome, its web browser.

Amazon controls 40 percent of U.S. e-commerce and continues expanding into cloud computing, AI, and entertainment. The company penalizes sellers who don't use its warehouses or who refuse to buy ads, and it competes directly by copying top-selling products and pushing Amazon-branded versions. Despite growing scrutiny over these practices, its consumer-friendly image has helped it avoid major regulatory blowback. Its financial power enables massive content investments, disrupting competitors in both streaming and retail.

For the most part, regulators and politicians are nowhere to be seen.

Compare the free rein that Big Tech gets from government today with the onerous laws slapped on the cable-TV industry: the Cable Communications Policy Act of 1984, the Cable Television Consumer Protection and Competition Act of 1992, the Telecommunications Act of 1996, and net neutrality rules in 2015.

This struck me when I had my one significant face-to-face with Meta CEO Mark Zuckerberg. In 2014, when Facebook's reach was approaching 900 million people, more than forty times the size of TCI's reach at our most powerful point, I sat down with him at the behest of Allen & Company managing director Paul Gould.

The idea was to chat about my experience building TCI, Liberty Media, Liberty Global, and the various stocks created from those assets. Onlookers were interested in how TCI evolved, how it ended up with its corporate structure, how the government reacted to our growth, and what common lessons could be learned—from both of us. Little did they know I was just as eager to ask questions of Mark Zuckerberg.

Mark is a brilliant wunderkind, and he looked so damned young, then just thirty years old when I was seventy-three. It was the young Turk meets the old guy, and he was gracious and inquisitive as he mapped out the future of his growing social media empire.

When he asked me how we expanded beyond the cable-laying business, I told him it was clear the government would block TCI, a distributor, from growing vertically by acquiring cable channels. But I could be an investor, and we could help a cable network succeed and own 20 percent of it, and the government would allow that.

Zuckerberg pondered that, and he said, "Well, I don't know why I would do that when I can sort of own everything." He was serious rather than joking, and he said it without an ounce of pomposity or arrogance. He was simply stating a fact and thinking like a businessman. He added: "At least for now, I'm not facing any government pushback as I try to buy things like WhatsApp or Instagram."

But the FTC in 2025 is now looking at those two purchases as the basis for its latest antitrust suit against Meta, claiming that the company vastly overpaid for Instagram and WhatsApp as part of a "buy or bury" strategy to eliminate competitors. Taking the stand on April 14, 2025, Zuckerberg defended the company's actions.

But Zuckerberg was right back in 2014. Up until now, Facebook and a handful of other tech giants have grown formidably powerful in this country with virtually no scrutiny. Their ties to the government are too cozy, and since media need these platforms for their survival, too, their dominance is rarely genuinely challenged.

There's a bigger question about how we, as a society, should deal with companies this big and powerful, which control the newsfeeds, communications, messaging, media, and entertainment consumed by hundreds of millions of people. What can be done? We need a better framework for laws to deal with the titans of Big Tech before these giants become untouchable.

First, Congress should require far more transparency about the algorithms they use (to moderate content and recommend ads), as well as how ad auctions are run and the terms of third-party alliances they strike. As Rupert Murdoch pointed out to shareholders years ago, "Algorithms are subjective, and they can be manipulated by people to kill competition and damage other people, publishers, and businesses." There are several bills aimed at these issues, but they seem stalled in the wake of the latest political crisis.

Second, we must resolve privacy law. Unlike Europe, we don't have a cloak of privacy protections ensconced in the laws of the land. With the passage of GDPR (General Data Protection Regulation), lawmakers in the UK and Europe are, somewhat embarrassingly for us, out in front of the U.S., enshrining the protection of privacy and personal data as a fundamental human right. In addition to imposing restrictions on business regarding collecting personal data, the law empowers consumers with rights to access, restrict, and object to who is tracking them, including the right to demand erasure of their data.

Here in the U.S., we have no broad, tough federal protections covering data security or online consumer protections. Frustrated by the inaction, several states have passed their own privacy laws.

The easiest thing in the world, literally, for governments to do is say,

"You have to opt in." Forbid all tracking, selling, and sharing of personal data unless consumers expressly agree to allow it, on every website and in every app. In fact, Big Tech should have to pay consumers for sharing the personal data that are letting these companies reap billions of dollars in profits. Tesla, for example, knows where you drove, what roads you used, how fast you drove, and whether you came to a complete stop at every single stop sign, and it knows this for every car sold. Imagine the companies eager to buy this data.

These are real issues, warranting inspection and government hearings if we had a Congress that was doing its job. We can lead the world in developing an evenhanded approach to regulating these global, U.S.-based firms while still letting them breathe free.

CHAPTER 30

LATEST DISCOVERY

In April 2022, Discovery CEO David Zaslav called me to share the biggest news of his life. Over the course of a volley of texts in a single weekend, he had just plotted the rough outline for a jaw-dropping deal with John Stankey, the CEO of AT&T.

The telecom giant, which had paid $85 billion to buy the content portfolio of Time Warner in 2016, betting big on a convergence of distribution and media, was willing to sell it to Discovery for little more than what it had put in—a costly detour. Known as WarnerMedia, it owned some of the greatest, most venerable brands in media and entertainment: Warner Bros. films and TV shows, HBO, CNN, TBS, TNT, and more.

As he spoke, I found it hard to keep my thoughts from racing—decades of deals, familiar names, and well-worn firms flashing through my mind, all somehow intersecting here, in this one unexpected moment, which now all were coming together in this moment in time and space.

A wave of nostalgia washed over me, and I drifted. Each company for me represented a deal, and behind each deal was a person, and behind each person a memory that ricocheted through my mind like a pinball, lighting up places in my past that I had forgotten long ago.

AT&T had paid for my education; it was the place where I first learned about transistors and computer science. Nearly forty years later, I shook hands with the CEO of AT&T on its acquisition of TCI, which was everything to me. About seventeen years after that, the phone giant would buy DirecTV, where I had been chairman.

Time Warner was founded by the charismatic Steve Ross, who started in the parking garage business and first offered me a job to run Warner's fast-growing cable business when I was just twenty-six years old. Those very cable systems, which were spun off in 2008, would come onto my balance sheet, in part, when they were bought by Charter Communications.

The new deal with Discovery also involved CNN, which I helped Ted Turner nurture. Before it became part of Time Warner in 1996, CNN was the lifelong dream of Ted, who founded Turner Broadcasting, which TCI and other cable operators had banded together to bankroll as he teetered on the edge of bankruptcy in 1987. His main goal was to save TBS and CNN. I was a proud board member and good friend.

And I smiled when I thought about the day in 1985 when TCI wired $500,000 to John Hendricks, who had a second mortgage on his house, to help him finance his dream of a network called Discovery, devoted to nature shows and documentaries. Burning through cash and turned down by Disney and Universal, he was desperate, and I had wired the money within forty-eight hours. The value of my personal stake would grow to well over a billion dollars at its peak.

And now here was David Zaslav himself, Discovery's energetic and affable CEO, whom I had first met as a young executive when NBC, then owned by GE, was launching CNBC with NBC Cable President Tom Rogers. What I liked most about David was his enthusiasm for the business. We had persuaded him to come run Discovery in 2006, and it gratified me to no end that he had taken Discovery so far, right up to this seminal moment.

If anyone was up for this job, it was David. He had practiced law before joining NBC and becoming a young protégé of legendary General Electric CEO Jack Welch.

Discovery founder John Hendricks built a business on people's interest in knowledge-based, educational nature shows. David took it further, growing Discovery into a powerhouse of programming—and profit—and expanding it to include sister channels TLC, Animal Planet, and Destination America. When he arrived at Discovery, he knew his way around a balance sheet. He cut money-losing businesses with discipline, reduced overhead in the C-suite, and brought on top-notch executives.

He assembled Discovery's family of assets, investing big in marquee shows like *Blue Planet*, and brought aboard the megawatt appeal of Oprah Winfrey for the OWN network. His biggest coup was buying Scripps Networks, home to HGTV and Food Network, for $14.6 billion in 2017. Zaslav also brought in ratings-driven reality shows that stretched the range of his networks, from *Deadliest Catch* to some shows I can do without, like *My 600-Pound Life*. His greatest impact was in driving a global strategy early at Discovery, putting it in more than two hundred countries.

It was remarkable to think now that Discovery—not traditionally known for scripted drama or classic film—was now poised, thanks to its global reach and complementary programming, to carry the full weight of Warner Bros.' legendary library: from Bugs Bunny and *Casablanca* to HBO, CNN, and TBS. These were some of the very assets that AOL had paid $160 billion to acquire in what was then the largest (failed) corporate merger in history. I would have given anything to sit and talk with the late Steve Ross, just to see the grin on his face.

On my call with David, he outlined the agreement in rough terms: AT&T CEO Stankey wanted a combination of cash and debt, and more than anything, he wanted a simple ownership structure, with just one class of shares to make it easier to buy, easier to run, and ultimately, easier to sell or merge.

With my supervoting shares in Discovery, I had around 26 percent voting control, and with longtime partner Advance-Newhouse Partnership, we effectively controlled Discovery.

I respect that a supervoting structure may not appeal to everyone, but there's no shortage of investing alternatives in the market. The same governance has worked at companies such as Cablevision, controlled by the Dolan family; Comcast, controlled by the Roberts family; and ViacomCBS, controlled by the Redstones. Now David Zaslav wanted to know: Would I relinquish control of my ten-for-one super-voting shares if this was the only route to a merger?

I agreed to AT&T's request to give up the shares to avoid conflicts going forward. I went a step further, declining to seek a premium for my super-voting shares to avoid any objections that might hold up the deal. Together with the Advance/Newhouse Partnership, I pledged to approve the deal, and we were offered seats on the board of the new company.

On May 17, 2021, Discovery agreed to pay AT&T $43 billion in cash, debt, and the assumption of previous WarnerMedia debt for the Warner-Media business, which AT&T had spun out as a stand-alone company. One of the best parts of the deal was that shareholders of both companies got a tax-free ruling from the IRS. AT&T shareholders got 71 percent of the stock in the new company, while Discovery shareholders ended up with 29 percent. The new service would reach 100 million homes—some 77 million from HBO Max and 24 million at Discovery+.

As stunning as this deal was, it also was an inevitable exit for a humbled and beleaguered AT&T. It was likely a relief for the company to unwind its $85 billion purchase of Time Warner, just three years after CEO Randall Stephenson called it a "perfect match."

With growth slowing in its core wireless business, AT&T had set out to diversify. In 2014, it paid $67 billion for DirecTV, becoming the largest U.S. pay-TV provider, with more than 25 million subscribers and $4 billion in annual cash flow. But satellite TV, with its one-way signal and lack of broadband, couldn't compete with cable's full-service "triple play" or the rising tide of internet-based streaming.

Timing couldn't have been worse. Streaming giants like Netflix were gaining ground, and by 2015, pay-TV subscriptions across the board began a steep decline.

Undeterred, AT&T doubled down. In 2016, it agreed to buy Time Warner for $85 billion, aiming to marry content with distribution and become a vertically integrated media powerhouse. But from the start, the deal was rocky. Time Warner was a maze of internal silos and clashing egos, and the cultural gap with AT&T was wide. CEO Jeff Bewkes knew he couldn't scale the business and opted to sell, securing a strong price—though not necessarily the right partner.

To finance the deal, AT&T took on a $40 billion bridge loan, ballooning its debt to $180 billion. It pledged $2 billion for content—a fraction of

Netflix's $8 billion annual spend—and now faced the challenge of funding prestige media while also rolling out a 5G network, fending off Verizon and T-Mobile, and propping up its fading landline business.

What began as a bold move was now a liability. AT&T was shopping DirecTV, which had gone from 25 million subscribers (DirecT+AT&T U-verse) to just 15 million in only five years. In 2021, after shedding 40 percent of its customer base and 75 percent of its value, AT&T spun off DirecTV to TPG for just $16.25 billion—less than a quarter of what it had originally paid.

Meanwhile, AT&T installed its own executive atop the newly acquired Warner content shop, rather than stay hands-off and let the current leaders remain in place. The new president of Warner Media was John Stankey, who was long on telecom experience and short on small talk. Stankey, who would rise to be CEO of all of AT&T in July 2020, made it clear HBO would have to scale up in programming and subscribers.

WarnerMedia's streaming service, HBO Max, launched in May 2020, combining all of its existing HBO customer brands with all of WarnerMedia's content. HBO Max was late to the streaming party, trailing Netflix, Amazon, Disney, and Peacock, among others, and it was priced too high, initially $14.99, double Disney's introductory price of $6.99.

HBO Max stirred controversy right away with a strategy to stream movies on the same day they were released in theaters. This enraged many in Hollywood, and it ended up costing AT&T an estimated $1 billion in lost box office revenue and license fees.

Legacy media companies had perfected the art of maximizing revenue from a film or TV show by strategically reselling it through a series of timed release windows: first in theaters, followed by pay-per-view, then cable, and finally syndication. Now streamers were collapsing windows to win subscribers, much to their pricing peril.

Despite WarnerMedia's movies and TV shows winning the most Oscar, Golden Globe, and Screen Actors Guild awards in 2021, the company ended 2021 with 74 million subscribers, up just 31 million subscribers from the HBO network in 2019.

It wasn't enough. Heavy with debt, bleeding cash, and closing retail stores during the pandemic, AT&T was doing the right thing by reversing course to focus on wireless and plowing its resources into a 5G network buildout.

Just two months after AT&T and Discovery had announced the Warner transaction in May 2021, CNN boss Jeffrey Zucker rolled out plans for CNN+, a streaming service that would feature CNN stars, films, and original shows, at a cost estimated at $300 million.

Though some CEOs might hesitate to retreat on a project so big so soon after taking over, David and his team pulled the plug. Understandably, shuttering CNN+ one month after launch was a blow to the morale of the place, but it had drawn fewer than one hundred thousand subscribers.

As David and his team sifted through the company finances, he toured Warner and identified projects and businesses that were too risky or too costly to go forward, and he put executives on notice that he wanted revised budgets and fresh business plans.

At Warner Bros. Studios, home to DC Entertainment, Warner Animation Group, and Harry Potter, David made good on his promise to return movies to the theatrical premieres. And he went through the place with a scalpel, focusing on those projects that were most assured of making profit and canceling those that weren't. Following the deal's close, Discovery had canceled eighteen projects or existing shows by mid-2022, including the $90 million film *Batgirl*.

David brought in his lieutenants from Discovery, including J. B. Perrette, the new CEO and president for streaming, and Bruce Campbell, the new chief revenue and strategy officer.

Early on, David made it clear to Wall Street, with my blessing, that this direct-to-consumer streamer would avoid overspending to drive subscriber growth, telling analysts in an earnings call, "We are not trying to win the direct-to-consumer spending war."

Moreover, I begged David to stay out of the trap that Disney had found itself in not so long before: being viewed by shallow Wall Street investors as only a streaming service, ignoring the other pieces of the empire. The stock price of Warner Bros. Discovery already had fallen more than 40 percent in the months after Discovery closed on the merger, along with a broader market tumble.

I told David it would be a mistake to get into a situation where this new company's total economic value was reduced to one number—how many streaming subscribers it had. This was where we set ourselves apart from Netflix, I advised him.

WBD launched a cheaper, ad-supported version of its service, in addition to the commercial-free version, just as its progenitors Discovery and HBO Max had done. While most consumers prefer a program without ads, a lot of folks don't mind minimal ads and you get higher CPM (cost per mille, or thousand, views of an ad) because you know a lot more about consumer behavior if it is being watched via the internet, instead of over cable.

David and the CEO of every legacy entertainment company are facing headwinds right now. Warner Bros. Discovery's stock dropped to its lowest point recently after reporting a $9.1 billion write-down on its legacy TV networks, including TBS, TNT, Discovery, and TLC, due to the continued migration of customers and ad revenue to streaming services.

To incentivize David and other top executives, the compensation committee has adjusted their pay based on their success in generating cash and helping the company reduce its leverage.

David is buffeted daily by headlines raising the specter of his firing, or worse, as some analysts have suggested, the company splitting up and being sold in pieces.

It's noise, I tell him.

You can't captain the ship if you listen to all the voices yelling at you. I have watched David in sticky situations many times. When Discovery was going global, the stock was down for a while as he invested in growth, and eventually we were rewarded. We ended up with a dozen channels in every country. When Discovery needed more content, David seamlessly integrated Scripps Networks. And when the Oprah Winfrey Network couldn't find its ratings groove, David rolled his sleeves up and helped her get on track. I trust him to get this right. You don't shoot the captain of the ship because the seas are stormy.

What happens next? WBD's trajectory is still being drawn. David has said publicly he believes the newly combined streaming service will reach

400 million subscribers one day. And why not? It's got the best studio, the best library, and the most energetic CEO. Less than half the audience of HBO Max (HBO, Warner Bros., DC Films, Discovery, TBS, etc.) is international, compared to about 70 percent at Netflix, leaving enormous potential to grow.

At one point early on, the discussion was, were we going to be a major platform competing with the Goliaths, or were we an arms merchant supplying content to them? All of Hollywood's biggest studios face the decision of licensing their content to the highest bidder or staking their future on their own streaming platforms. Sony, through Columbia Pictures, has fully embraced the first path, focusing on premium content and selling it to streamers rather than competing with them. Others, like MGM, have been absorbed by tech giants—Amazon in MGM's case—while Paramount and NBCUniversal continue to struggle for profits.

Confronting the realities of a fractured entertainment world, Warner Bros. Discovery said in June 2025 it will split into two public companies—one focused on streaming and studios (HBO Max, Warner Bros., DC), the other on legacy cable networks like CNN, TNT, and HGTV. The goal: to unlock value, streamline operations, and give investors clearer bets in a rapidly shifting media landscape. The move follows a steep decline in cable subscriptions and mirrors an earlier shift by Comcast's NBC Universal, which plans to spin off channels like CNBC, USA, MSNBC, and E! into a standalone unit, allowing greater focus on NBC, theme parks, sports, and Peacock.

But the large question looms: Can any of these companies produce enough standout content to sustain a global streaming empire? Some will fold into larger players, others will bundle services to stay competitive, and a few will break through as dominant forces in the streaming wars.

As a board member of Warner Bros. Discovery, I shared my concerns with David about the new realities setting in and the need to cut debt and grow cash flow—and we have. WBD's direct-to-consumer service aims to clear more than $1.3 billion in cash flow in 2025, a reflection of international expansion and ad revenue rising. After 20 percent YOY growth in global subscribers in 2024 (123 million at last count), it has a clear path to reach 150 million global subscribers by the end of 2026.

In the end, Warner Bros. Discovery—like many other media giants—is caught between the fading glow of legacy TV and the unrelenting pull of the streaming future. It must wring every last dollar from the remnants of its once-dominant cable empire while simultaneously staking its claim in an unforgiving digital landscape. The challenge isn't just survival—it's reinvention. Can WBD master the delicate alchemy of pricing, packaging, and partnerships before the tides of disruption wash away the old order entirely? The answer may well determine the fate of one of Hollywood's most storied empires.

CHAPTER 31

CNN: HARD NEWS

Just months after Discovery agreed to buy Warner Media from AT&T for $43 billion, one of its crown jewels, CNN, got sucked into a New York political scandal so tawdry it felt like a Netflix series already writing itself.

CNN has always been a bright star in the media world, especially given its history, a daydream my friend Ted Turner turned into a reality that set a worldwide standard for fair and balanced news coverage on television. For four decades it fearlessly covered live-fire wars, international crises, disasters here at home, and presidential elections.

In recent years, CNN began to veer away from straight, middle-of-the-road reporting in favor of more of an advocacy-style of journalism. New management, led by former wunderkind producer and NBCUniversal CEO Jeff Zucker, decided to veer hard to one side—liberal, urban, Democratic, and decidedly anti-Trump.

Now, maybe this was a strategic necessity in this age of social media, fragmenting audiences, and fickle young viewers. I tend to doubt it: instantly, you lose half of your potential audience from the get-go by leaning so hard in only one direction.

Somewhere in the digital age, some of the news media seemed to lose sight of the invisible wall between facts and information on one side, and commentary and opinion on the other. The media have abandoned the middle and bifurcated, going liberal or conservative: CNN, MSNBC, and the ABC, CBS, and NBC news divisions on the left, and Fox News, Newsmax, Blaze Media, and OAN on the right. *The New York Times, The Washington*

Post, and Politico.com on the left, and *The Wall Street Journal*, *Forbes*, and Breitbart.com on the right.

The nation is worse off for it. We have lost the certainty of one consensus version of the truth, and many outlets leave out the facts that undermine their narrative, while replaying the points their allies make without challenge or verification.

On August 10, 2021, Andrew Cuomo, the governor of New York, announced his resignation after several women came forward with allegations of sexual misconduct, which had dominated the headlines. Three months later, CNN got pulled into the investigation.

Transcripts from the New York Attorney General's Office revealed that Chris Cuomo, CNN's top prime-time host and the governor's brother, had advised him on handling the fallout. After an internal review, CNN president Jeff Zucker suspended Chris Cuomo, then fired him on December 4, 2021, following a new allegation of sexual assault from a former colleague.

Two months later, Zucker abruptly resigned on February 2, 2022, admitting to a long-rumored affair with CNN's chief marketing officer, a former Cuomo aide who had joined the calls strategizing with Chris Cuomo. The undisclosed relationship, a breach of WarnerMedia's code of conduct, complicated the inquiry into Chris Cuomo and deepened CNN's public crisis.

The scandal fed criticism that CNN, long seen as anti-Trump, had top figures advising a potential Trump rival—even as they were embroiled in their own misconduct allegations.

Zucker, once a ratings kingpin, had positioned CNN as a counterweight to Fox News, but its viewership had declined 25 percent among key demographics since he took over in 2013. Meanwhile, Fox had gained 23 percent, with a prime-time audience over three times larger.

Infamous for boosting Trump's fame with *The Apprentice*, Zucker was faulted for CNN's obsessive coverage of his 2016 campaign. Later, seeking redemption—or ratings—he steered CNN into advocacy journalism. By 2022, it was clear that CNN, like Fox and MSNBC, had become more about political commentary than broad-based news.

Now, CNN has some fine journalists who have devoted their lives to their craft—even risked their lives for it. They want to tell stories that matter to the people of this country, but we are hearing too few of them. Too much airtime is devoted to opinions and dissent, as if all Americans view life through a political prism. It is worse at Fox and MSNBC.

David Zaslav is still fine-tuning CNN. After a brief, bumpy tenure with CNN CEO Chris Licht, which saw a decline in ratings as well as some internal morale issues and controversial programming decisions, David bought in Mark Thompson, the former CEO of *The New York Times* and director-general of the BBC, in October 2023 to stabilize the network and harness its digital potential. We're all behind him.

David Zaslav and I both agree that a news service like CNN is a public trust, driven by fairness and accuracy and unmoved by fear or favor, and free of meddling from corporate ownership as it covers the news. The media have—if not an obligation, then a moral imperative—to help unite the country, rather than endlessly exposing and exacerbating our differences.

Since taking over CNN, Zaslav has said repeatedly he wants CNN to be a *news* network first, as well as a platform for all political parties, Republicans, Democrats, and independents. In the rare interviews I gave, I said I would like to see CNN evolve back to the kind of journalism that it started with—a more centrist, inclusive approach. (Even for that comment I was roasted in the press.)

Ted Turner, even though he was always a good deal more liberal than I was, never intended for CNN to be a one-sided network. In 1980, when he gave a speech hailing the launch of the new Cable News Network, Turner set out his aims:

"To act upon one's convictions while others wait, to create a positive force in a world where cynics abound, to provide information to people when it wasn't available before, to offer those who want it a choice."

It has been hard for me and most Americans to watch our news devolve into a bunch of shouting heads preening before the camera, commentary with no hard facts, reporters interviewing reporters. And everyone saying the same things.

Instead of illumination, rudeness and divisiveness abound. We can disagree while being polite to one another. Viewers, buffeted by a steady, negative drumbeat of the same political topics, are looking for news and information to help them understand the complexity of their lives and society.

Personally, I have always supported fair, impartial, and independent news, from my earliest days in business. On my watch, TCI and Liberty did the same. To me, freedom of speech ensures a diversity of voices and perspectives. If it is taken away, "then dumb and silent we may be led, like sheep to the slaughter," to quote our first president.

I especially liked the solid, august, even-keeled approach of Robert MacNeil and Jim Lehrer, who first collaborated at PBS covering Watergate in 1973. Together, with quiet intensity, they turned *The MacNeil/Lehrer Report* into something unique and sorely needed: serious, fair, long-form journalism that explored a variety of topics across the American experience.

Their earnest search for the truth won an Emmy and a cabinet full of journalism awards and drew the biggest newsmakers because guests were assured of a fair shake, and more importantly, civil and earnest debate.

In 1994, when public funding for the program all but dried up, we invested to buy two-thirds of what was by then *The MacNeil/Lehrer NewsHour* because it was the right thing to do. I loved meeting them, but not once did I ever pick up the phone and ask the producers to cover a story or change a single thing. Ever. Nor would I do it at CNN. We gave them unlimited say in what went on the air.

And we definitely were supporters of CNN. Hell, one of the reasons we wanted to save Turner Broadcasting back in 1987 was to save CNN, based on Ted's vision of the network as an impartial and independent voice. CNN has some of the best journalists in America.

Critics often cast aspersions on my friendship with Rupert Murdoch, whom they label as far-right, and on Fox News. Yet Fox is watched by more viewers than CNN and MSNBC combined, in part countering a perceived liberal tint of the mainstream media. I dislike some aspects about Fox coverage, but it would be dangerous to live in a world of uniform hegemony, devoid of dissenting opinions.

So I take exception to people depicting Rupert Murdoch as being on the extreme right. I don't see him that way at all. I see him as libertarian, pro-Western civilization. He definitely is Australian in heritage, and he loves America, his adopted country. On the morning of the 9/11 terrorist attacks on the World Trade Center in 2001, he told me "God damn it, John, how can they do this to America? We need the strongest, most militarily prepared forces in the world."

That doesn't make Rupert a conservative: it makes him an American.

In this "fake news" era, when on-air hosts and contributors slur those they oppose, and good journalists struggle for respect, it is hard to remember there was a time when news anchors were exemplars of journalistic integrity, held in high esteem. A time when Walter Cronkite of CBS News was named the Most Trusted Man in America.

In the late 1950s and 1960s, the *CBS Evening News with Walter Cronkite* and NBC's *Huntley-Brinkley Report* featured nightly news at 6 p.m. local time, and most American households were watching news at the same time. Only a limited number of voices were on air, compared with the thousands of news services available today, but the news had relevance. It was useful in people's lives and enriched their understanding of their government and the community. We need more of that today. Everybody back then was engaging on issues based on the same basic information. And TV news was beginning to assume a very powerful role in setting the national narrative.

Long after he left news, I got to know Cronkite, who was instrumental with introductions and advice in helping Discovery get off the ground. We had long discussions on the role and influence of the news business in the U.S.

Cronkite, whose calm, forceful editorials helped change the country's opinion on the Vietnam War, believed fervently that an educated public was key to a democracy's survival. He was famous for dispensing many maxims of journalistic wisdom, and there's one that is particularly apt today: "It is not the reporter's job to be a patriot or to presume to determine where patriotism lies. The job is to relate the facts."

Trust in the media is at unprecedented lows according to most every poll. What can be done to improve the product? I would advocate two suggestions at CNN, Fox, and every other news network out there. First, simply and clearly label the content on their programs as "News" or "Opinion." At least let viewers know what they are watching.

Separate journalism from opinion. I like to point out that *The Wall Street Journal* is a very good publication, offering a tremendous compendium of accurate facts every day. It does a good job of keeping opinion out of the news pages, even though a lot of reporters there lean left of center. Meanwhile, its editorial board is proudly politically right.

What concerns me is that the world is complicated, and after the news is minced into bite-sized pieces with no context and put through a spin cycle by partisan hacks, viewers would rather just put their heads down, live their lives, and rely on political leaders to make decisions for them. And the terrible thing is those leaders are so politicized, on both left and right, that they need our engagement.

The second thing I would ask of every news organization is to put the news in deeper context. It drives me nuts when an anchor talks about the huge growth rate of, say, COVID-19 cases, without saying the rate is down from in 2020. Show us what numbers mean, whether the story is about COVID cases or gun deaths or stock-price trends. Go deeper.

I just want the news without all the filters of politics, sexual orientation, and religion—and with a lot more context. Call it news, separate it from opinion, and tell the audience, "We're going to give you the news in the best way we can: timely, truthful, and informative. And then at 7 p.m., we have a personality who will spin their opinions on the news."

Ask a simple question: When you watch the images and coverage and debates on the news shows, do you get the feeling America is headed for the trash heap and a bunch of looney tunes are in power? Would it be better for the country if, instead, the media were focused on helping us get on top of some of this stuff?

CHAPTER 32

HORSE POWER

A cowboy and his horse have graced a passel of old westerns in film and TV series, novels, and country songs, and this is because the relationship is so true and pure. Horses are amazing creatures of the earth, and even two hundred years after the West was settled, these proud, sensitive, intuitive animals remain crucial to the operation of a good ranch.

You may see a few four-wheeler all-terrain vehicles on our ranches, but they're outnumbered by horses, which do a better job at herding cattle and crossing the terrain, and they are a lot less noisy than ATVs. And kinder.

Given the landholdings we have accumulated, most of it undeveloped farmland, forests, and ranch land in particular, we rely heavily on the services of a good horse. We own several hundred of them.

Part of our fascination with horses owes to my wife, Leslie, whose captivation with their athleticism led her to dressage, an Olympic sport in which horse and rider are basically doing a ballet. She is an expert rider and has a sharper eye than mine for judging a stallion or mare. She sees a lot of detail that I miss. I still am learning.

Leslie and I love these animals, and it is hard to put into words the power and elegance of a twelve-hundred-pound creature whose thundering hooves literally shake the ground in a herd, yet who is also gentle enough to let a person ride on its back. Hardworking, never-complaining ranch hands. Intelligence beyond any other domesticated animal. Soft, velvety necks on a foal and eyes so big they look like tumblers of whiskey. Born to run. These are the things that move me when I am up close to my horses.

Yet no matter how much Leslie and I love horses, it is all still a business to me. The hardest thing for me is to turn a blind eye to inefficiency. Because I trained at Bell Labs in analyzing systems, everything is a system to me based on mathematics, even how you go about buying, breeding, feeding, and caring for horses. This goes for whether they serve the ranch or train for the Olympics or live out their lives earning stud fees.

And while most investors adhere to the old saw that "past performance is no guarantee of future results," past performance plays a huge role in the business of raising horses. Historic bloodlines are usually a good indicator of future performance, and there are certain characteristics we look for on a cattle ranch: a strong animal, easy to work with, good with cows, and can stop on a dime. A horse small enough to be agile, but big enough to stand up to a bull.

Value is hiding everywhere, and most of the time, people have a hard time finding it. This turns out to be true for buying horses, too.

Horses are bought and sold for all sorts of reasons—to work cattle, win races, or serve as a twelve-hundred-pound pet that sleeps out back in the barn. A ranch must have a pool of workhorses, a remuda, ready and waiting for cowboys who need a fresh horse. Most of our remuda horses are born and raised at the Bell Ranch in New Mexico.

A good working ranch horse is an incredible athlete. In competition, a rider must cut one cow away from a herd of cattle inside the fence and hold it at the center of the pen, a common maneuver during medical treatments. As the cow tries to go left or right to get back to the herd, the horse pivots this way or that and keeps the animal separated and at bay.

The trick to finding a good remuda horse is finding someone who knows horses. For all things related to the ranch, that falls to Thad York, who manages our Silver Spur Ranches. Thad, as ranch manager, is as much a part of the ranch as the Silver Spur brand that identifies our cattle. With a history that stretches across generations, he can also read people, like a cutting horse reads a cow, and we are lucky to have him. Thad's grandfather, Old Jim, managed the ranch under Bob Magness. When he retired, Thad's father, Young Jim, became the ranch manager for Silver Spur, and Thad practically grew up on the ranch, working summers there as a kid.

After earning a master's in finance from University of Wyoming, Thad joined TCI International to work on Latin American cable acquisitions.

Then one afternoon, his father died out in the field, on the tractor while baling hay. Shock and grief hit all of us hard. A few days later, Thad walked into my office and said plainly: "I'd like to be the ranch manager."

Though the pay was less, he didn't mind. "I like the lifestyle. I don't like the international travel. I wanna settle down, get married, and build a life." And that is exactly what he did. He's been at the helm ever since, and along the way, he's added timber, farming, and general management to his portfolio, and I've made sure he's paid his worth.

What I admire about Thad is that he pursued dreams of happiness for him and his future family, without any focus on wealth or any yearning for a life of ease. He is a cowboy.

Having plenty of good cow horses for the remuda is critical to the operation, and the Silver Spur ranch, like TCI in the cable-TV business, was always known as a bargain hunter when it came to buying studs and stallions. One of the best stallions we ever owned was a horse no one else wanted, because he had been blinded in one eye as a foal, so he couldn't work on a ranch, and he was selling for only $1,200.

The foal's father was named "WR This Cat's Smart," a stallion who had won several big competition purses, including a National Cutting Horse event. The owners were looking for a good home for him, so we took him in, named him WR One-Eyed Jack, and put him out to stud. And waited.

Turns out, a horse with just one eye can manage to breed a mare just fine. WR One-Eyed-Jack paid off handsomely, siring generations of offspring that still carry all the cow-horse characteristics we like.

That little one-eyed foal that had been all but forgotten became a champion stud, living out his days in clover fields in flagrante delicto, siring SS Hey One Eye, a Versatility Ranch Horse world champion, and several national cow-horse-competition champions. Though he died several years back, his spirit lives on in the ranch horses that still kick up dust at the Silver Spur.

Quarter horses, a breed named for their original reputation, running quarter-mile races, make a good ranch horse, but Thoroughbreds are the racing horses.

Thoroughbred racing involves money, performance, rankings, analysis, and egos—just like business. In truth, horse racing is nothing more than a parlor game, but it is a little closer to the strategy and thinking in business. And it is always more fun winning than losing.

But how do you define winning? Well, some folks would define winning as going out and buying the most expensive racehorse you can find, and when it wins, you jump up and down and scream as it crosses the finish line first, and you jump into a sea of roses in the winner's circle, surrounded by fans and the flash of photographers.

For me, winning is the gratification of creating a successful system of long-term involvement that yields cascading benefits as we move forward. If you have created good job opportunities for people and watched them prosper or forged business deals that helped your partners retire comfortably, that is winning. If your business improves the quality of life in some way and enables you to support other efforts you value, that is winning.

One way of winning is to be able to engage in some level of philanthropy that you regard as being positive—you feel good about it. So, to some degree, the money aspect has that tail on it. I enjoyed playing the game and winning, as measured by the money involved, but I also then enjoyed what I could do with the money in terms of wanting to help others. The efficiency and the productivity of that are powerful.

Years back, our horse team was at an auction in Saratoga, New York, when a striking gray colt named Tapwrit came up for sale—the son of the legendary Tapit. He was being sold by My Meadowview Farm, owned by Barnes & Noble chairman Leonard Riggio, whom knew through Liberty's short-lived investment in the company. The sharp-eyed general manager of our Bridlewood Farm in Central Florida, George Isaacs, suggested we join a three-way deal to buy him.

So on August 10, 2015, at the first session of the yearling sale, we partnered with two others and placed the winning $1.2 million bid. Our share was about $400,000. Tapwrit was shipped to Bridlewood in Ocala to spend the winter getting familiar with the track. Of the two-hundred-plus horses trained there each year, we were keeping a special eye on him—he looked promising.

In the spring, we turned him over to Todd Pletcher, the legendary trainer known for peaking a horse's natural talent. Tapwrit won a few regional races, earned enough points, and ran in the muddy Kentucky Derby on May 6, 2017, finishing sixth after a bump at the gate. It happens.

We skipped the Preakness to rest and prep for the Belmont in June—and this time, Tapwrit ran hard and won, convincingly. We watched it on TV. It was electric.

Tapwrit ran his final race in 2018 in Saratoga, finishing eighth. Sometimes, you only have a certain number of wins in you—I can relate to Tapwrit on that count. By then, Tapwrit had earned more than $1.3 million in purse money. A stud farm soon approached, buying a 25 percent stake at a price that recouped all of our investment.

We still owned a quarter—and had already more than doubled our money. Tapwrit is now living a stud life, so it was a happy ending for all. If anybody could do all that anytime, everyone would be in the horse business.

With the same focus, we became owners in a horse called Journalism, who was favored to win the Kentucky Derby. At the finish, though, Journalism was beaten by a length by a horse named Sovereign, who also happened to be trained at Bridlewood. Less than a second separated our horse from history, but he's already left us with guaranteed stud fees and a story worth retelling.

How much does luck have to do with business? Sometimes, everything.

Beyond the relationship with people, we've cultivated relationships with the animals. I might have mentioned how much Leslie and I love our pugs, and we know many of the horses as well as we know the pugs—by name and personality.

In Ireland, Coolmore Stud, which operates successful farms around the world, came to us with an offer to partner up to buy a couple of yearlings. We stepped up together with some pricey bids for a colt and a filly, which we trained and raced.

The colt was disappointing. He had all of the physical characteristics but not the right mental makeup. I don't know. Maybe he is like me, overthinking it. It was an expensive investment, and disappointing.

Meanwhile, the filly came out of the gate winning several big races, but not consistently, so she could become very valuable as a broodmare for the next ten or fifteen years. Every time we go to the farm, we'll be looking at her charts, brushing her, petting her, feeding apples to her, talking to her, looking over her prospective mates, and watching her foals.

Out West, horses end up abandoned or mistreated, if you can believe it, and often these animals are seized by the authorities. It is a burden on the local government, and the ending is not often a good one for the horses. Sometimes, starved for food, these abandoned steeds end up eating sand, and they die a painful death.

And since the last U.S. horse-slaughter plant closed in 2007, horses had been bought at auction by Mexican dealers, crammed into double-decker trucks, and taken to Mexico to be slaughtered. It was heartbreaking, and Leslie and I could do nothing to fix it.

So we put up $20 million, matched by the Harmony Equine Center, to complete a $40 million project that included a private rehabilitation and adoption facility for abused and neglected horses, ponies, donkeys and mules, dogs, and cats that have been removed from their owners by law enforcement authorities.

The two-hundred-stall, 168-acre facility includes three sizable, well-equipped barns for intake, training, and adoptions, twenty-six pastures and turnouts, two indoor riding arenas, and an education center.

We run a matchmaker program, not unlike online dating, where we match the right horse with the right adoptee. Since Harmony opened in 2012, more than 2,300 horses have been helped. We are as proud of this as we are of our racing horses, Tapwrit, winning the Belmont, or Journalism, winning the Preakness.

CHAPTER 33

LAND OF OPPORTUNITY

Anyone who says money can't buy happiness has probably never made a final loan payment. I still remember us clipping coupons, skipping dinners out, and holding our breath at the bank, wondering if the check would clear. We pinched pennies so hard you could hear Lincoln cry.

After years of saving, stock options, and sheer persistence, Leslie and I have reached a point where we can finally turn outward—toward the causes we care about most: education, health, and the land we'll leave behind. For the first time, I find myself thinking less about the next quarter and more about the next generation. What do you leave behind that matters?

It's the same question for a blue-collar worker or a billionaire: How do you use what you've earned to give something back? You can't change the whole world—but you can change your corner of it.

What makes my heart happy is that so many of my colleagues who made their fortunes in the cable-TV industry, where I made mine, have given back in a big way.

Besides Ted Turner, Bill Daniels gave millions to education and addiction recovery. Alan Gerry transformed the old Woodstock grounds into a world-class arts center and helped revive his struggling hometown. Amos Hostetter poured his energy into the environment. Len Tow's foundation lifts up underserved neighborhoods in New York and Connecticut.

As for me, I've come to believe the real return on wealth is what outlives you. A onetime donation helps—but it fades. An endowed lab, a scholarship that runs for generations, a protected piece of land—that's legacy.

The wealth I've been fortunate to build now gives me a chance to invest in what really matters: education, medicine, land preservation—and ideas I never had time to dream up during the business day.

As Leslie and I started to build some excess capital, we set up the Malone Family Foundation, and it was especially rewarding for me to watch my daughter become instrumental in organizing and defining our mission.

My first instinct was to pay back the institutions that I had benefited from personally, and the first place that truly changed me was the Hopkins School, the prep school I attended as a teenager on a work scholarship in New Haven, Connecticut.

When I returned for my thirty-fifth reunion, I learned Hopkins was struggling financially. The trustees launched a capital campaign that allowed me to leverage my $10 million gift through matching donations, which helped raise enough to secure the 330-year-old school's endowment.

Alongside need-based scholarships, we funded construction of the three-story Malone Science Center, named for my father. It opened in 1999 with state-of-the-art chemistry, biology, physics labs, and classrooms. A commons and lunchroom were also built and named for my favorite math teacher, John Heath. Including the buildings, scholarships, and donations, over the years I've given north of $50 million to Hopkins—money well spent. It was the first time I had given so generously, and the joy of that act still lingers.

Over time, we've endowed fifty private secondary schools across the U.S. to provide full annual scholarships on a purely merit-based basis. We've also strongly supported Denver's charter school movement, especially the Denver School of Science and Technology, which has proven that minority students from noncollege backgrounds can achieve at the highest levels and break generational assumptions.

To help rural schools access advanced coursework, we've funded the Stanford Online High School, a fully accredited and rigorous program offering live classes through Stanford University.

Medical breakthroughs now allow us to detect and target individual muta-
tions using the body's own tools: the immune system, stem cells, blood
platelets, gene therapies, and advanced vaccines. We've focused our funding where these "personalized medicine" innovations show the greatest
promise—and potential for rapid progress.

In 2000, we donated $24 million to the Daniel L. Malone Engineering
Center, a five-story building on the Yale campus devoted to the research and
teaching of biomedical engineering, materials science, and nanotechnology—
all areas of great potential. It was a nod to my father, an engineer most of
his life, and a way to say thanks for the lessons he once gave in the barn.
More than just giving back to Yale, it also was a way to leverage the school's
strength in medicine, provide a direction in engineering, and keep Yale
competitive in a global environment.

In 2011, we gave $50 million to the School of Engineering & Applied
Science, shared with the Yale School of Medicine, to help fund ten chairs
across curriculums that connect engineering and business.

That same year, with the same intent, we gave $30 million to Johns Hop-
kins University's Whiting School of Engineering to help build a facility—and
faculty—devoted to engineering in medicine, including artificial intelligence,
computer learning, and deep database analysis.

Along the way, my curiosity led me to invest in a business here in
Colorado called RegenXX, which was the first in the world to apply stem
cells from bone marrow concentrate to treat many orthopedic injuries
and diseases.

When a gelding of Leslie's named Blixt showed some lameness, we tried
stem-cell injections in addition to orthoscopic surgery at the Colorado
State Orthopedic Research Center, and the horse recovered especially well.
Impressed by the advances, we put down a lead gift of $42.5 million (with
matching requirements) for the Translational Medicine Institute facility at
Colorado State University's vet school. The idea was that treatments developed for horses or dogs or other animals could translate well biologically to
human beings. It is thriving today.

You can't appreciate what a precious commodity open land is until you see it vanish over time. And then one day you look, and it's gone.

Forever.

When Leslie and I first moved to Denver some fifty years ago, we fell in love with the powder-dusted peaks of the Rockies, the cowboy culture, the clean air, and the freedom of the West.

We were mesmerized, like so many before us, by the infinite detail, texture, and color of the land that slopes up toward the Front Range. Out West you can be swept away with the very same sense of physical freedom you feel on open water. The view connects you in a way that transcends the physical beauty of the place. You feel it.

We bought a ranch, just to the southeast of the city limits, and learned how to run a tractor, plow fields, paint barns, and plant oats. We didn't own a boat so far inland, so we set about living a more Western lifestyle.

We learned a lot about cattle. We raised a white registered Charolais bull, a muscular breed originally from France raised around the world, and crossed it with a black Angus, hearty beef cattle from Scotland popular in the U.S., an effort to produce offspring that essentially grow faster and bigger and healthier, something known as "hybrid vigor."

We had help, but it was all hands-on for us—moving cows in snowstorms, injecting penicillin into the shoulders of sick calves, even castrating steers. For me it was a way to spend time with Leslie and to distract my brain from the stress at TCI—a refreshing (and sometimes exhausting) change from the social pressures in the Northeast.

Bob Magness owned a ranch from the time I first knew him, called the Hidden Valley Ranch, about 40 miles southwest of Denver and at pretty high elevation in the mountains. Up there he would go to unwind, rub the silky necks of his Arabian horses, and entertain guests. Bob liked to say that once a banker had a few drinks at the ranch, especially at such high elevation, he would agree to damn near anything by the end of the evening.

It is where he and his first wife, Betsy, are buried now. I have not been to their graves in a while, I'm sure in part because I buried a small piece of myself up there when he died.

TCI bought its first company ranch in Encampment, Wyoming—Cow

Creek Valley, a twenty-two-thousand-acre spread just north of the Colorado border, in the late 1970s, which would become the original Silver Spur
ranch. It was a working cattle ranch, but often TCI would hold meetings
there with investors, suppliers, and politicians. When Bob died and TCI
was sold to AT&T in 1998, I bought the ranch to keep it in the family.

And so my love affair with the land and the West started with Leslie
during those early ranch days, grew stronger in my time with Bob, and became
manifest later, during my days with Ted Turner.

We felt the West disappearing even back then. Over the years, Leslie and
I moved three times because we felt the city encroaching on us. Even now,
what used to be a pleasant twenty-minute drive to the office now takes me
an hour in traffic that feels more like midtown Manhattan, depending on
the hour of the day. And when I look up from my dash, all I can see are red
taillights snaking through waves of concrete.

Open spaces: this pursuit will consume most of the material wealth that
Leslie and I have built up in our lifetime, a key reason we formed the Malone
Family Land Preservation Foundation. We will designate a vast portion of
the 2.2 million acres in six states with a protected status that will ensure it
stays natural and utterly undeveloped forever, and I hope to expand this
even more.

The foundation, run by Rye Austin, seeks investments where we can have
a multiplier effect, either through matching funds or working cooperatively
with preservationist groups, or local and state governments.

Though our first ranch in Denver is surrounded by development, I can't
imagine selling it. Every Coloradan deserves to see the state—in its natural
state.

By 2000, the concrete corridor along the seventy-one-mile trek of I-25
from Denver south to Colorado Springs had grown so aggressively that
the sprawl was close to meeting somewhere in the middle, completing an
unbroken sea of commercial buildings, chain restaurants, and subdivisions
in between—all the way to the base of the Rocky Mountains.

There was only one natural buffer in between that afforded uninterrupted views of the Front Range of the Rockies to the west. It is a view you could have witnessed easily from the same spot standing there two thousand years ago: a twelve-mile-long panorama of grasslands, mesas, and meadows, with elk, trout, and bear, leading up to the base of the majestic snow-crusted Pike's Peak.

The largest piece of the twenty-one thousand-acre spread is the Greenland Ranch, east of I-25, one of the longest-running cattle ranches in the country, dating back to1900.

When the 17,700-acre ranch went up for sale in 2000, we paid $55 million to take it off the market and prevent development. Working with the State of Colorado and the Conservation Fund, we contributed another $23 million to secure conservation easements from the sellers. Douglas County purchased the remaining land west of I-25 for open space.

By leveraging the like interests of partners and nearby landowners, we were able to preserve a bigger piece of land, with more engaged caretakers than if I had gone in alone. Now the land is in a conservation easement and can never be developed.

Going forward, the Colorado Cattlemen's Agricultural Land Trust will be the steward of the easement because we are trying to preserve something just as important as the land: Colorado's culture. The developers called it a waste of badly needed space for a fast-growing city. I call it a permanent benefit, because in the end, we saved a sliver of Colorado that still looks like Colorado.

And it serves many beneficiaries. Aside from the carbon containment from undisturbed soil, the land supports a substantial wildlife population, including deer, elk, and bighorn sheep. And most parts are open to the public for hiking, biking, even hunting, based on a licensing lottery.

Every deal is put through a rigorous litmus test of scale, value, impact, and sustainability.

Sometimes we have stepped in to save a beautiful spot in the line of a developer's bulldozer. In 2007, we bought a six-hundred-acre Thoroughbred farm in Maryland that was on track to becoming a residential development, and we also protected it legally through a conservation easement.

To help us overhaul the facility, we called on two men from the Amish community in Pennsylvania who've known each other since boyhood. And if it hadn't been for the rudeness of a more renowned contractor Leslie had approached, we might never have met Ben Esh and Daniel Glick at all. Feeling as if one of the bigger builders we were interviewing was disrespectful toward women, Leslie turned to a small shop in Amish country we had heard about.

Building the equestrian facilities would be their first major project, but they were smart, inventive, and willing to listen.

As we reviewed the extensive plans for Riveredge Farm, I wondered aloud: *Are we sure we want to take a risk on a multimillion-dollar project with a couple of Amish pals who have built only outdoor sheds?* Leslie had a feeling about them, so of course, they were hired. For a period of a couple years, we would fly back east to Riveredge and check in on the progress, and each time we visited, we were more impressed.

The attention to detail, from the hand-hewn pegs and accent posts to the intricate millwork, gave their buildings a singular, rustic, elegant look, bringing life to Leslie's sketches. It was stunning.

Today I can show you a mighty impressive book of all the projects they have built in the past twenty years. We have helped finance their growth, and today B&D has several locations around the country. I loaned them money so they could invest in a bank, the Bank of the Bird in Hand in Lancaster County, Pennsylvania, so other small Amish businesses could get a helping hand.

They still owe me the money and pay a low interest rate. The collateral is the stock in the Bank of the Bird in the Hand, and a lot of trust. It's a great working relationship.

Today at Riveredge Farm, the carbon remains trapped in the undisturbed land, not to mention the wood used in the barn. Looking up at the rafters from the inside feels almost like you're inside a cathedral. The entire facility has been transformed into a world-class sport-horse training facility used by the U.S. Equestrian Federation, among others.

Sometimes, you do a good deed in part because you simply enjoy doing it. We have investments in hotels in Ireland in part because of the real estate market there, but also because I like doing business in, and making trips to, the land of my ancestors. I trace my roots to ancestors from Ireland who arrived in the 1830s in Pennsylvania, where my father's family worked a farm when he was a kid.

Our love affair with Ireland began in 2013, when Barry Diller suggested we borrow his yacht *EOS* to celebrate our fiftieth wedding anniversary with our oldest friends. After a delightful two-week cruise on the Adriatic, we decided to go to Ireland. On the trip, thumbing through magazines, Leslie felt a yearning to own a place there.

We returned to tour several estates, including the grounds of a bona fide Irish castle called Humewood Castle, a granite fortress built in the 1860s with turrets and towers. I was intimidated—it was huge, and in very bad condition. But Leslie, whose dad was a builder, was enthusiastic about taking on a historic restoration project.

The sale price ($10 million) was down roughly 60 percent from seven years earlier, in 2006, near the peak of the Irish economy. Plans to develop it as a luxury hotel with a golf course were dropped when the bubble popped in 2008, taking the estate developers down. The property was bankrupt and owned by the Irish government, home to a massive garden, equestrian quadrangle, and farm complex—and it was a bargain.

Over two years we painstakingly restored and furnished this old jewel, peaking at over 320 craftsmen on-site at a time Ireland needed jobs. In the process, we met more great people and had the time of our lives—and fell in love with Ireland!

The restoration turned into a business opportunity when two people who had volunteered to shepherd our project became partners in purchasing, building, and operating hotels in Ireland—Paul Higgins and John Lally— and today MLK Hotel Collection is up to fourteen great properties. This affection then led to the purchase of a historic stud farm, Ballylinch in County Kilkenny, and the picturesque Castlemartin estate out of a bankruptcy in County Kildare with its own stud farm and cattle—both places modernized by Leslie's magic touch. We were able to retain John O'Conner, a renowned equestrian trainer, as general manager of our Thoroughbred activity and now have one of the finest operations in Europe, both at the track and in the breeding barn.

We love Ireland and the Irish people, especially reviving interest in the history of the place. This is a site that will sustain history for a lot of people and, hopefully, last for a couple hundred more years.

I believe in protecting the environment, and I pursue *sustainable* approaches to farming, ranching, and timber on the land we own. But I stop short of embracing the environmental, social, and governance (ESG) movement.

Most "net zero" pledges are empty gestures rooted in the flawed idea of stakeholder capitalism—where companies seem to answer to everyone except their actual owners.

The environment that we say grace over needs to be managed in such a way that it is productive, sustainable, and enhanced over time. In the timberland we own in Maine, windmill farms lease the land atop mountains in exchange for a percentage of revenue from the sale of electricity.

Nor is every tree sacred. I see timber, too, as a "crop" that's beneficial to humans and that we can replant as a form of sustainable, long-term agriculture. In the very forests where we harvest timber, we replant and enrich the land—boosting plant diversity and stronger habitats for wildlife. These aren't pine farms; hardwood acreage is growing in our forests, not shrinking.

Once you buy land to protect it, the next decision is, what is the best use for it? Just to look at something pretty isn't enough. Ted Turner and I debated this often.

Ted and I both have working ranches, but I am not as pre-Columbian as Ted is in his view of land ownership. Ted brought back bison to his ranches and worked assiduously with experts on bringing back threatened, and endangered species, even removing any signs of human habitation on his Flying D Ranch near Bozeman.

I am trying to figure out how to enhance the productivity of farm- and ranchland, for multiple purposes, including sustainability.

One big goal for me across the board on all the property we own is the sequestration of carbon from the atmosphere. This may seem odd at first, for someone whose land is comprised of mostly ranches where horses and cattle are raised. Livestock contributes around 15 percent of greenhouse gases, according to the United Nations.

I would point out, though, that ranches and farms are doing a pretty good job of helping feed 8 billion hungry people on the planet. A solution can't be all-or-nothing. In the broad equation of life, the earth should sustain and support quality of life for human beings, and we are smart enough to make it sustainable and even improve on it.

At our Silver Spur Ranches out West, we make a constant effort to ensure sustainable grazing, protect healthy native grasses, and prevent erosion. We are trying to optimize productivity *and* sustainability, which isn't always easy in a part of the country known for a dusty landscape, with tumbleweeds and sagebrush.

Our ranch manager, Thad York, is responsible for making sure this happens, and his love of the land and cowboy traditions, combined with his financial background, made him an ideal pick for the job.

We are working on these environmental challenges one at a time. Grazing is part of maintenance. Overgrazing causes erosion and carbon consumption at any cattle ranch. If you don't graze the land at all and you don't deal with invasive species, you have erosion and a mess.

And the idea of moving the whole herd, combined with fencing costs, would be prohibitively expensive and disruptive.

At our fifty-five-thousand-acre Red Top ranch in southeastern Colorado, we have experimented with satellites and high-tech cow collars that work a lot like "invisible fence" systems used by pet owners. The cows in the herd are given audible warnings and a tiny, tingly charge, if necessary, when they approach a border of the virtual pen created by the rancher, whose coordinates are locked into GPS satellites twelve thousand miles overhead in space.

The idea is that you can rotate grazing areas without the need to drive the cattle or use fencing. In my work with the Nature Conservancy (I am a former board member), along with other groups, the goal is to help researchers better understand why cattle make the choices they do about where they graze. Horses, too, are selective in what they graze. They'll eat the grasses they like and avoid the plants they don't like.

So, in Ireland, twice a year we bring in dense flocks of sheep to the pastures at the horse farm we have, and they eat everything down to the ground, which aids the native grasses. Otherwise, only the undesirable or noxious or invasive weeds become dominant, with no competition from the natural grass.

We are most excited by the prospect of perennial grains. Our family land foundation supports the groundbreaking work at Land Institute, a not-for-profit gaining traction in the field of perennial agriculture. Unlike annual crops, perennials don't require reseeding every year, or plowing or herbicides, which in turn prevents soil erosion, improves the structure of the topsoil, and leaves carbon trapped beneath undisturbed soil.

Perennial grains capture carbon from the atmosphere and create organic compounds that go deeper into the soils with their roots. Imagine a world where grains, which now make up over 70 percent of global croplands, could transition to a regenerative model where no one had to plant, till, or spray with poison.

After forty years of testing, the Land Institute recently introduced its first commercial perennial grain, trademarked Kernza, a type of wheatgrass. And it is applying the same breeding and research into perennial rice, which now produces eight consecutive harvests over four years from a single planting.

Imagine what we could do worldwide if we could make agriculture sustainable, regenerative, and with de minimis impact on the environment? Beyond our investment, we've brought on like-minded investors who share our vision and commitment.

One of the most frightening experiences I've ever had looking at land was with Craig McCaw, and it was nowhere near a banker.

Craig is a telecommunications legend, a maverick who jumped into the cable industry while still a senior at Stanford, taking the reins of the small family-owned cable company in Centralia, Washington, when his father died.

Craig ate risk like Corn Flakes for breakfast every morning, taking on debt and expanding the tiny company with a few thousand subscribers into McCaw Cablevision, one of the top twenty cable operators in the country in the 1970s.

By the early 1980s, when the FCC licensed the first cellular phone companies, Craig bought as many licenses as he could. What frightened analysts and competitors alike was that Craig loaded up with stomach-churning levels of debt.

His confidence paid off. Craig scooped up enough spectrum before the Baby Bells to beat them into the new market for newfangled mobile phones. Cellular One was known as the first truly national cellular phone company, beating out the Goliaths in the telephone industry.

Craig asked me to join the Cellular One board in 1989. Craig and his brothers would ultimately sell McCaw Cellular to AT&T for $11.5 billion. The company was renamed AT&T Wireless and would go on to become the nation's largest wireless carrier at that time.

Around that time, Craig and I were on the board of the Nature Conservancy, and we had planned a trip with its president, David McCormick, a small expedition to British Columbia to take a hard look at an eighteen-million-acre tract of land known as the Great Bear Rainforest. It ran for 250 miles along Canada's Pacific coast, including the offshore islands.

The Nature Conservancy at the time was involved in a deal to help resolve a longstanding legal dispute that involved the native tribes, the BC government, logging companies, and other groups.

Crag and I were the anchor donors and helped raise $100 million for a trust fund that today provides for education and stewardship programs for indigenous tribes.

We made our way up the Pacific coast in Craig's eighty-foot-long boat, having scouted the emerald topography of the land from a float plane. Along the way, on the boat, we would stop to meet with local tribal leaders in native villages.

One day Craig and I took two kayaks to explore the coastal interior, paddling upstream through quiet creeks. As we went farther, salmon swam alongside us, and I soaked in the peaceful surroundings—until a loud, low noise shattered the calm.

It sounded like an outboard motor, and I turned to Craig, baffled. "How could anyone get a motorboat in here?"

The sound stopped. We froze. Then, as we rounded a bend, the source became clear: not a motor, but a ten-foot-tall mother grizzly, growling, her cubs tucked behind a stump just fifty yards ahead.

"Easy," I whispered, gripping my paddle. Without a word, we let the current carry us back, putting as much distance as we could between us and her.

In a few minutes we were paddling furiously and laughing with the nervous energy of two people who had escaped a *grisly* death.

Craig and I worked together with others on the board on several projects, but none bigger than the Great Bear Rainforest. In the end, after more than decade of negotiations, the Nature Conservancy, the British Columbia government, logging companies, and two dozen First Nation tribes reached agreements that settled lawsuits, created a fund for education, and protected most of the land from logging. To me, it remains one of the most beautiful places on earth—now essentially preserved forever.

Ten years later, I worked with several groups to help protect one of the last undeveloped islands in the archipelago near Vancouver, British Colombia—a pristine sanctuary of old-growth evergreens called Moresby Island, located at the southern end of the Gulf Islands.

The fifteen-hundred-acre Moresby Island is a little over a mile wide and over two miles long, covered in Douglas fir and cedar trees. Settled in 1863, the island's gardens and apple orchards were once a source of produce for grocery stores in Vancouver and Victoria. The buildings on the island were in poor shape, so we called Ben and Daniel and their team of Amish craftsmen, who helped build a new tenant farmer's house and visitors' center.

Today, the island is open to conservation groups by prior arrangement, and anyone bold enough to hike the trails will eventually come up to a hill in the middle, about 650 feet high. It offers a magnificent view of the island terrain and the bay. If you are lucky, you will see a humpback whale breach in the distance.

CHAPTER 34

ADAPT OR DIE

We seem to be in a slow-motion big bang moment in communications. Irrevocable and indelible change is sweeping over media, thanks to many of the advances that I and others helped enable: digital, broadband, Wi-Fi, streaming services, the Internet of Things, 5G, and of course, the social networks that consume so much of our attention span.

What happens under such extreme forces? Like stars, or any living thing for that matter, businesses have life cycles. Some media companies die off due to age or environmental change. The cosmic dust that spins out of this explosion will be reassembled into other companies and applications. And the bigger, more agile players will change to adapt. As they always have.

The early "cable cowboys" like Bob Magness who pioneered the industry in the mid-twentieth century never envisioned that their systems, originally designed to enhance TV reception in remote areas, would one day be the very infrastructure enabling the rise of Big Tech. Over the decades, cable evolved from a linear-channel business to a digital transmission powerhouse, offering broadband and high-speed internet that now serves as the foundation for the modern digital economy.

Despite the tsunami of stories about the decline of traditional subscription cable TV, cable's broadband has become the industry's primary growth engine. The transition was never about cable versus streaming—it was about the continuous evolution of technology and consumer demand.

By 2024, more than 90 percent of U.S. households have access to fixed broadband service with speeds of at least 100 Mbps download and 20 Mbps upload, enabling everything from remote work to high-definition streaming.

Broadband providers have invested nearly $2 trillion over the past thirty years to build and maintain these networks, essentially subsidizing the infrastructure on which today's digital giants operate for free.

Cable companies, including those I'm invested in—Charter, Liberty Global, and Liberty Latin America—once viewed purely as TV providers, have repositioned themselves as leaders in connectivity, bundling internet, Wi-Fi, streaming subscriptions, and even mobile wireless services into single packages.

Cable operators are now among the fastest-growing mobile providers in the U.S., offering phone service by leasing network access from major carriers and bundling it with broadband and TV—without building a single cell tower or spending billions on infrastructure.

The growing demand for faster internet speeds, better connectivity, and seamless access to content has only reinforced the importance of broadband. These companies are not merely surviving; they are adapting to a world where connectivity is the primary product. Their vast wired network is capable of delivering faster, more reliable internet than most wireless or DSL alternatives. As 5G and next-generation wireless technologies evolve, cable's hybrid model—combining fixed broadband with wireless services—only strengthens its market position.

Few industries have this much resilience in their DNA, which led us to leverage new technology at every turn. Starting out with a few analog TV channels, coaxial cable quickly evolved through pioneering leaps like digital transmission technology, enabling cable operators to provide hundreds of TV channels. We exploited satellite technology as it emerged in the 1980s, beaming TV signals to and from virtually anywhere, rapidly expanding our market reach. And in the 1990s, when web browsing felt like watching paint dry, cable's high-speed modems came to the rescue, turning the internet from a crawl to a sprint.

Cable started small, rose to dominance, and today faces a turning point as shifting consumer preferences upend the industry once again. The disruptors have been disrupted. This cycle isn't unique; businesses across all sectors navigate similar trajectories marked by growth, maturity, disruption, and adaptation.

"Adapt or die" isn't just a catchy phrase—it's the brutal truth. The companies that evolve prosper; the ones stuck in the past get left there. Cable's ability to pivot, from TV into broadband and telephone and wireless connectivity, demonstrates precisely how industries not only survive disruption but surf it for new opportunities. Adaptability is a pillar of the industry's enduring success.

Cable and broadcast still make up around 45 percent of TV viewing time, according to Nielsen, but both are in undeniable decline. Fifty years ago, *All in the Family* drew 50 million viewers a week on CBS. Today, *Tracker* is a hit with just 7 million. The audience hasn't vanished—they've splintered across cable, streaming, and digital platforms that barely existed back then.

Pay-TV subscriptions (traditional cable, telco, or satellite TV—*excluding virtual MVPDs*) have taken a steep dive—down to just 35 percent of U.S. households from their towering 87 percent reach in 2010. By the end of 2024, only 46 million subscribers remained, a staggering 54 percent drop from the peak of 99 million. That's 53 million homes gone, and assuming $30 a month in lost revenue, over $19 billion a year in lost revenue. Meanwhile, the infrastructure costs haven't budged.

Advertising migrated along with the viewers, with digital ads in the U.S. growing fivefold in ten years to $259 billion in 2024, from less than $50 billion in 2014. Conversely, advertising on broadcast and cable television fell 20 percent. This decline is even worse than it looks. In 2025, retail media—digital ads on Amazon, Walmart.com, etc.—is set to surpass TV ad spending as advertisers shift budgets toward data-driven platforms where consumers buy things.

One of the biggest flaws in the cable-TV package, as discussed, was the skyrocketing price of live sports—the NFL, the NBA, and MLB. Programmers such as Disney bundled ESPN, historically the most expensive network by orders of magnitude, into their wholesale package.

For years, cable passed these rising costs on to customers for its basic package, but subscribers bolted when cheaper, no-contract streaming services appeared. The once-mighty ESPN, boasting 100 million cable subscribers at its peak, counts only 66 million now, and that's falling.

At first, streaming platforms operated on the belief that aggressive content spending would lead to surging subscriber growth. Investors backed the strategy, confident that the numbers would eventually justify the up-front losses. Netflix, leading the pack with 300 million subscribers worldwide, and Amazon Prime Video, with around 200 million, drove up bidding wars for movies and series, pushing the industry into an era of extravagant spending.

Suddenly, there was more television than anyone could watch. A content bubble of TV shows was inflating, and we were entering an era of so-called peak TV. By 2021, streaming content surged—new scripted and unscripted shows and movies on Amazon Prime Video, Apple TV, and Netflix nearly doubled to 1,380, then climbed to 1,543 in 2022, flooding a market already nearing saturation, according to researcher Diesel Labs. But by 2023, the flood of programming had slowed: output fell 14 percent to 1,324. Peak TV was no longer rising.

Still, Netflix is expected to spend $18 billion in 2025, compared to just $2.4 billion on content in 2013, with a war chest of more than 7,500 titles, more than half original titles, in its library.

But even as streaming platforms flooded the market with original programming, something unexpected happened: audiences weren't sticking around. They signed up for buzzy releases like *Hamilton* on Disney+—then canceled as soon as they had binged what they wanted. Ironically, some of the most-streamed content wasn't even new. Reruns of old cable hits like *Friends* and *Suits* dominated the charts, proving that, in the end, audiences crave great storytelling more than endless novelty.

With thousands of video options at their fingertips and no easy way to navigate, viewers have become overwhelmed. Research found that they spent an average of ten minutes just *searching* for something to watch—after which 20 percent simply gave up. This paradox of choice, coupled with economic pressures, led to rampant "churn," forcing streamers to raise prices. But price hikes came at the worst possible time—just as inflation squeezed household budgets—leading to even more cancellations.

By 2022, Wall Street's patience ran out. Streaming giants, once celebrated for growth-at-any-cost, were now expected to turn a profit. Disney CEO Bob Iger later admitted that Disney+ had "invested too much way ahead of possible returns," a miscalculation that helped fuel more than $11 billion in losses since 2019.

When Netflix reported its first subscriber loss in a decade, its stock plunged 35 percent, sending shock waves through the industry. Disney, Comcast, Paramount, and Warner Bros. Discovery collectively racked up more than $20 billion in losses between 2020 and 2023. The operating costs assumed by cutting out the (cable/satellite) middleman became evident fast.

Most all of the major streaming platforms now offer ad-supported options, and budget-conscious viewers seem willing to accept a few commercials in exchange for a lower price. The shift is evident: ad-free streaming declined in 2023 and 2024, while ad-supported viewing grew.

Yet even with streaming ad revenue reaching $17 billion a year, it's nowhere near enough to make up for the collapse of traditional TV advertising. At the same time, streaming companies have hit a financial ceiling—content spending has either flattened or been scaled back to match the economic climate. The industry has woken up to a new reality: Growth alone is no longer enough. Profitability is now the only metric that matters.

How did we get here? Two major regulatory decisions—retransmission consent and net neutrality—played pivotal roles.

The 1992 Cable Act's retransmission consent rules forced cable operators to pay broadcasters billions of dollars annually to carry signals that broadcasters were already offering freely over the air. The law was designed to ensure local broadcasters remained financially viable as cable TV's reach expanded. Instead, it turned into a windfall, funneling an estimated $100 billion into broadcasters' pockets from 1992 to 2022, allowing them to afford increasingly expensive sports rights and fueling cost increases for all.

Flush with cash, networks aggressively outbid each other for exclusive sports rights, inflating deals to unprecedented levels. By 2024, the NFL, the NBA, and MLB were pulling in a combined $30 billion a year from media contracts, turning leagues into financial powerhouses and athletes into some of the highest-paid figures in history. By 2032, the NBA's top earner is projected to be making $100 million annually in salary alone.

The escalation shows no sign of stopping. In 2021, the NFL locked in an eleven-year, $110 billion media deal—nearly double the previous agreements. ESPN alone committed $2.7 billion annually through 2032, a 42 percent hike. In 2024, Disney, ESPN's parent company, expects to shell out nearly $11 billion on sports programming, with long-term commitments exceeding $57 billion.

Sensing a tipping point, ESPN announced plans for a stand-alone streaming service set to launch in 2025. This move will accelerate the decline of traditional cable TV and also signals a fundamental shift—premium live sports will increasingly bypass cable, catering directly to younger, streaming-savvy audiences. And when struggling local broadcasters, which now trade at historic lows, lose sports, there will be even less to draw in viewers.

Even as a rival, I respect Dish's Charlie Ergen for standing firm on sports costs—dropping Sinclair's RSNs in 2019, battling Disney in a 2022 ESPN blackout, and refusing to let sports become a mandatory tax on every household.

If you think sports rights are pricey now, just wait—the next bidding war will be more brutal as Big Tech muscles in. Live sports remain TV's last bastion of appointment viewing, making up ninety-six of the top one hundred broadcasts in 2023. Tech giants see them as a golden ticket.

Amazon set the tone in 2021 with an eleven-year, $1-billion-per-year deal for exclusive Thursday night football. Apple TV+ followed, securing Friday night MLB games in 2022 and a ten-year, $2.5 billion MLS contract. By 2024, Peacock was streaming exclusive NFL playoff games, and Amazon took a stake in Diamond Sports, the largest regional sports network operator, giving it a direct pipeline to local NBA, MLB, and NHL games.

Then came the game-changer: Amazon, NBC (Comcast), and ESPN (Disney) shattered records with a $76 billion, eleven-year deal for NBA rights. Amazon locked in $1.8 billion per year, while longtime NBA partner Turner Sports was priced out. The result? Viewers are left scrambling to figure out where to watch their teams.

If Big Tech takes over major sports, it could gut broadcast TV. Live games are the last thing keeping viewers—and ad dollars—tuned in. Without them, audience drop-off accelerates, ad revenue craters, and local stations fade into niche status with little left but news and reruns.

Now consider the strain of streaming a future Super Bowl: 50 million *individual, simultaneous* HD and 4K streams, placing an enormous burden on carriers, who see no added revenue from the surge in demand. As live sports and ultra-high-definition streaming continue to grow, the same tech giants that have enjoyed a free ride will be the loudest voices demanding expanded bandwidth at lower costs. But if we want an internet that is fast, widely available, and affordable, shouldn't providers have the right to charge those consuming the most bandwidth?

One potential solution: Allow internet service providers to charge streaming giants like Amazon and YouTube a tax or fee for premium bandwidth access during peak times, ensuring smooth, lag-free delivery of live events. A tiered system for high-priority traffic could reduce network slowdown from congestion, improve reliability—all while making the system fairer for all players.

The meteoric rise of Big Tech wasn't just a matter of innovation—it was also the result of a regulatory gift. When net neutrality was passed in 2015, it was hailed as a landmark policy to keep the internet open and free from interference. But in reality, it was a solution in search of a problem: aside from a brief episode involving BitTorrent—a platform often used for pirated content—cable companies had never actually restricted content.

Lawmakers were warned that cable providers might throttle or block content, favoring their own services over competitors. Big Tech—companies like Google, Facebook, and Netflix—lobbied aggressively for the rules, framing them as a necessary safeguard against corporate greed. But there was one problem: cable companies had never actually restricted content. Instead, the new regulation shackled broadband providers while giving tech giants a free ride.

The FCC's net neutrality order classified broadband as a telecommunications service under Title II of the Communications Act of 1934, giving the agency the oversight of internet service. But while supporters saw it as a victory for consumers, the order mainly served to benefit Silicon Valley. When Republican FCC chairman Ajit Pai repealed the rule in 2017, critics predicted disaster—slower speeds, content blackouts, and a fractured internet dictated by corporate interests. Pai dismissed the outcry as "hysterical prophecies of doom."

And he was dead right. Average U.S. fixed broadband speeds have doubled in five years to over 200 Mbps, while investment in network infrastructure surged once government micromanagement was out of the picture. The real issue had never been content blocking; it was a lack of competition and limited broadband access, particularly in rural and tribal areas.

But the policy barred volume-based pricing, forcing internet providers like Charter and Comcast to shoulder the cost of delivering Big Tech's enormous traffic loads—without compensation. By 2024, streaming video and audio made up more than 70 percent of all downstream traffic, with Netflix alone consuming 15 percent. The very companies that once relied on broadband networks for free distribution were now billion-dollar content empires themselves, competing directly with traditional TV.

Consider that as of early 2025, YouTube TV has reached more than 9 million subscribers, making it the fourth-largest pay-TV provider and on track to overtake traditional giants like Comcast. Unlike regular YouTube, it doesn't feature creator content—it's a live TV service that streams 100+ channels of traditional cable channels over the internet.

Over the years, cable operators have been subjected to layer upon layer of regulations—the Cable Act of 1984, the Cable Consumer Protection Act of 1992, the Telecommunications Act of 1996, and net neutrality in 2015. Meanwhile, Big Tech maneuvered through Washington largely unscathed, avoiding meaningful restrictions and cementing its dominance.

A full decade later, long enough for Big Tech to dominate, in January 2025, a federal appeals court delivered a victory for internet service providers, striking down net neutrality rules, ruling that the FCC had overstepped its authority in trying to reinstate outdated Obama-era policies in 2023. Talk about closing the barn door after the horse is out.

This leaves the government with a pressing dilemma: Should it allow legacy media companies to consolidate in order to compete with Big Tech,

or is it already too late? For traditional media, this is an existential moment—
and the outcome will shape the future of entertainment and information.

For now, big traditional programming companies are forming alliances and
bundling services to counteract subscriber losses—ironically mirroring the
same bundling strategy cable operators pioneered years ago.

All are experimenting for the right mix, but so far one of the most
successful collaborations has been Disney and Warner Bros. Discovery
partnering to package Disney+, Hulu, and WBD's HBO Max into a joint
offering in 2024. The discounted package is available in two pricing tiers:
an ad-supported plan at $16.99 per month and an ad-free option at $29.99
per month. Since launching, there's been strong subscriber retention, as
high as 80 percent over recent periods.

Cable operators, too, are regaining lost customers who realize that piecing together individual streaming subscriptions is both inconvenient and
costly. Charter is now a video retailer offering innovative packages that
combine traditional cable TV with streaming services through its Spectrum
brand; Spectrum TV Select Signature includes 150 channels plus Disney+
Basic and HBO Max with ads at no extra charge.

Comcast offers a bundle of NBCUniversal's Peacock Premium (with
ads), Netflix Basic (with ads), and Apple TV+, and it recently threw a smor-
gasbord of offerings in a $70 monthly Sports & News TV package: a mix of
Peacock Premium, fifty networks, a cloud DVR, and more than 100 free,
ad-supported streaming channels.

Charter and other cable operators are also innovating their connectivity
service with new features and technological advancements. For example, if
you're a Charter customer with high-speed internet, your mobile device
seamlessly switches to Wi-Fi the moment you walk into your home. This
automatic transition significantly boosts both the speed and quality of your
connection, and allows Charter to avoid usage fees for Verizon's cellular
platform.

As of 2024, an estimated two-hundred-plus streaming services are available in the U.S., catering to a wide range of preferences. Traditional TV

programmers offer their linear content on new streaming apps. New streaming services such as YouTube TV, Hulu + Live TV, and Sling deliver live TV channels over the internet, mimicking traditional cable packages. As well, a new breed of free, ad-supported streaming television (FAST) channels have popped up, with names like Plex, Tubi, and Haystack, and perform like old cable networks but without a subscription.

For now, Netflix dominates, with Apple and Disney following, and Warner Bros. Discovery's HBO Max, Apple, and Paramount+ in contention to be another contender. Comcast, which owns NBC, cable TV, and theme parks, has positioned its Peacock service strategically and can insulate it from losses.

In the future, successful content companies must have global scale, but there will be no more "mass media." The world of content is splintering beyond recognition now.

Quality, story, and characters still matter more than anything else, but there is unlimited capacity, and the choices for consumers are overwhelming.

Technology will continue to shape the viewer experience. Cable operators were disrupted by streaming, but content creators will face similar disruption from AI. What once united millions now plays out on personal screens, each one feeding from vast AI-driven databases designed to serve up exactly what an individual wants to see.

Yet I remain energized by the relentless reinvention of this industry. The companies that stay sharp, anticipate change, and adapt will survive—because media, at its core, is a living organism. It evolves or it dies. And that instinct to adapt, to thrive in chaos—that's what drew me to this business in the first place.

EPILOGUE

You can hold on too tightly to something, to anything, for too long. An investment, an entire company, a partner, or even a title. Anyone who lives to their eightieth birthday knows there comes a time for letting go.

I am reminded of my old friend (and alleged nemesis) Sumner Redstone, a visionary businessman who ruled a programming empire (Viacom) that dominated the entertainment world. Though his life was filled with triumphs in business, it reached a sordid ending in 2020 at the age of ninety-seven, marred by betrayal, legal battles, and public family squabbles.

This was caused, in part, by Sumner's trying to hold on for too long. At one point in the mid-2000s, he feuded with his daughter, Shari, a capable executive in her own right who was running his original company, the theater owner National Amusements. Sumner bestowed future control to a hired CEO, Philippe Dauman, who earned multiple millions on the arrangement for the ensuing years. Later, Sumner, with his own health deteriorating, reconciled with his daughter and tried to give her control, prompting litigation filed by Dauman and others. Despite her efforts to stabilize the company, Shari made the painful decision to sell Paramount Global in 2024.

I stayed in touch with Sumner on a friendly basis long after TCI bought the Viacom cable systems. One of our last conversations was when he called to warn me about prostate cancer after he had a scare, and he was pushing me on a diet regimen which was actually the Mike Milken plan that Rupert had been on. Somewhere therein lies a scene for another Chuck Lorre sitcom: a pair of aging media moguls talking about their prostate issues.

When Sumner merged Viacom with CBS in 1999, it had a market value of $80 billion. By the time of Sumner's death in August 2020, it was down to around $16 billion. Four years later, Shari Redstone brokered a deal to sell the rechristened Paramount Global for $8 billion, down 50 percent in four years and one-tenth of its high long ago.

Sumner's story serves as a stark reminder why it is important to put your affairs in order and find the right successors to continue on after you exit, whether into retirement or the great beyond.

In business as in life, the old saw that familiarity breeds contempt is often true. But after so many years of crossing swords with the same people, I have found that familiarity can also breed something far more unexpected: friendship.

Over the years, the lines have blurred, the rivalries have softened, and some—not all—of those fierce adversaries became trusted allies. We still haggle and spar, but we have been through too many market crashes, company implosions, and product launches to see each other as only business rivals. Instead, we are bound by an intimately shared history and mutual respect. Who would have thought that the media business, with all its cutthroat competitiveness, could foster such enduring camaraderie?

In February 2024, I sat down to lunch with two old friends, Barry Diller and Brian Roberts, and we commiserated over the apocalyptic state of legacy media these days. Barry had sailed down to Florida in the *Arriva*, a sleek 156-foot long superyacht with advance technology and understated luxury.

Soon the conversation rolled around to me and my plans for Liberty long term. Barry had mentioned that his son is really coming into his own in business, and he likely would play a central role in IAC and Expedia Group going forward. And I knew without asking Brian Roberts that Comcast would stay in family control long after he passes from this earth. His father, Comcast founder Ralph Roberts, entrusted Brian with the family legacy—the Comcast Corporation—when Brian stepped up to president in February 1990.

Brian owns a tiny fraction of Comcast—less than half of 1 percent—but he holds 33 percent of the total shareholder vote. That is the family jewel. So, even if you know that Comcast stock is going to fall by half in a few years, Brian likely would say: "This isn't for sale." He holds the power to do it.

Similarly, Rupert Murdoch now serves as Chairman Emeritus of News Corp and Fox, having handed control to his son Lachlan—now Chairman of News Corp and CEO of Fox—in 2023, a move that triggered legal disputes over the family trust and highlighted the complexity of dynastic succession. You no longer are optimizing your economics for the present, you are riding out cycles for the long term. Around a third of the businesses on the Fortune 500 list are family-controlled or family-owned according to estimates.

But I never sought to turn TCI and Liberty into any kind of family dynasty. I never got married with the idea our kids would one day take over the family business.

My kids never had an interest in the business, and I never really tried to force it on them, although I did test that hope on several occasions, and they politely passed. Some parents, fathers who run businesses in particular, would be disappointed by that, but I believe my kids should be afforded the same independence that I was. Nobody told me I had to work on the family farm or take a job at GE where my father had worked. It is repugnant to think that you could force your kids into succeeding you in your business; they will never forgive you for taking away their freedom.

I can give my kids options and opportunities, but taking me up on the offer is up to them.

My son, Evan, a businessman of his own making, has been on the Liberty Media board now for quite a few years, as well as QVC Group and SiriusXM, but that's the closest he's come to working with me. He watched the amount of time and stress that building TCI cost me, the complexity of the operations, and the hold that it still has on me today.

What Leslie and I have learned over a lifetime of parenting and making sacrifices to give our kids a better life amounts to this: our kids are separate human beings with their own lives, views, interests, and experiences, and that is just how it is. We love them every bit as much.

I struggled for years to get control of companies I ran, fending off hostile attackers in the down cycle. But wielding control loses value when your heirs are uninterested in succeeding you. And simply selling my stake to the highest bidder, as inviting as it sounds, is wrong because it would be unfair to other shareholders.

What gives you satisfaction looking back is that you were a good steward of Other People's Money, and that you dealt with people honorably and honestly.

My mother and particularly my father, coming off a dairy farm in Pennsylvania, would have said the Malone legacy was education. He and his four siblings all earned college degrees, with some going on to get PhDs. My parents never had big money, but what they left with me was more valuable: a love of learning and proof that education could change a life. For them, success wasn't measured in dollars—it was measured in curiosity, effort, and growth. That's the inheritance I carry forward in my philanthropy, trying to give others the same chances.

Today, my kids have their own kids, and I respect their need for independence, while offering guidance and support when they ask for it. We have tried to pass on the same good values, and we've been lucky enough to give them more than money—we gave them choice. That is true liberty.

I currently hold the title of chairman of three Liberty-related companies: Liberty Global (since June 2005), the largest international cable company; Liberty Broadband (since November 2014), which owns a 26 percent stake in Charter Communications, the largest cable operator in the U.S.; and Liberty Media (since March 1991, not counting mergers with TCI and AT&T), whose main asset is Formula One. In November 2024, Charter agreed to buy Liberty Broadband, a deal they expected to close in 2026. But overall, I have given up more titles and responsibilities than those I have taken on in the past five years.

I ask myself from time to time: Is my history as CEO and big investor casting a larger shadow of influence and causing decisions to be made today that are followed without question? Am I swinging a bigger ax than I should on decision-making? Am I putting in enough time?

Every board member every day should ask, "What is my willingness to learn, find out what I need to know on a real-time basis to be a good decision-maker, even when I am not motivated?"

The truth is that my role at the company—and at home—has been changing all along, and I have found myself adapting even more in my eighties than ever before. What I miss more than anything is being the CEO and the feeling that you have the authority and resources to make good things happen (and even great things). Yet technically and on paper, I left my last CEO role some twenty years ago, when I handed the top job at Liberty Global to Mike Fries in June 2005.

There was so much stress related to the responsibility of being CEO running TCI in the 1970s that I literally flinched when I peeked into my mailbox, afraid it was a letter from the IRS or the FCC or the DOJ.

And yet, even now, I miss the responsibility and the instant gratification of making critical decisions, good or bad, that set things in motion.

These days, there is only so much influence you can have in the role of chairman. It is akin to pushing on a string. Sometimes, no matter how good your idea is, all you can do is suggest it.

A big part of any chairman's role is making sure you have hired a CEO who is focused on long-term wealth creation for shareholders—and themselves. Self-interest is a driving force in capitalism. You must avoid micromanaging—and trust them.

Because even with the title chairman, I have found myself at times sitting in a room alone and thinking, *How do I, as chairman, get the management team to recognize that the path they are on is going to destroy wealth for my shareholders and me if we don't change course?*

Retirement is going to be an imperceptibly slow transition, a gradual contin-uation of backing away from things that require time and travel. I am trying, in a dignified and rational way, to back away from the commitments I have made to investors. And in doing so, I have largely held on to the ownership stakes in these firms, while shedding the board titles.

After Bob Magness died in November 1996, I took on my first title of chairman, adding that to my role as chief executive officer at TCI. After selling TCI to AT&T in June 1998, I stayed on as chairman of the board and was a controlling shareholder. Then as controlling shareholder in Liberty, I (again) took on the role of chairman when it got spun out of AT&T in August 2001 and began charting its own destiny.

My grip started to loosen in July 2018, when I retired as a director from the board of Charter Communications, which is 26 percent owned by Liberty Broadband. I was able to do so because Charter is a well-run company, with great management and a strong board. I was not able to make the board meeting in person unless the board met in Denver, and the shareholders deserved better.

A year later, in 2019, I agreed to give up my super-voting shares and ownership control of Expedia to deliver control to Barry with no premium to me.

In July 2023, Liberty Media spun off the Atlanta Braves into a stand-alone public company. I opted not to join the board, assigning my 49 percent control to Terry McGuirk—Ted Turner's longtime confidante and a trusted friend. Under Terry's leadership, our $1.1 billion investment in Truist Park and The Battery Atlanta turned passion into performance, blending sport, real estate, and commerce. The result: a 2021 World Series title, a loyal fan base, and strong recurring returns. With the spin-off, shareholders now share directly in a winning model built for the long haul.

In December 2023, Liberty Media simplified the ownership of SiriusXM by combining its Liberty SiriusXM tracking stock group (LSXM) with SiriusXM to create a new public company trading as SIRI. We essentially gave up two layers of control to create a single class of stock with a single-vote structure. We spun SiriusXM into its own company in 2024; I hold no title there today.

In April 2024, five years after I retired as director and more than eleven years on the board, I stepped down from my director emeritus role at Charter to comply with DOJ rules that ban corporate directors from serving on the boards of competitors. This because of my stake in Warner Bros. Discovery at the time. As chairman of Liberty Broadband, which we have agreed to merge into Charter by 2026, I am confident in Charter's leadership team.

Most recently, in April 2025, I stepped down from the board of Warner Bros. Discovery, transitioning to chairman emeritus. It's a half step back, with less travel, and I remain active in my advisory role.

In each of these cases, I've given careful thought to how I exit—relinquishing control in a way that ensures all shareholders are treated equally and fairly. I am trying to loosen my grip slowly, pull away without damaging the underlying enterprises where some shareholders may still think that having me involved is a good thing.

What began as a small regional cable operator in 1973 became one of the most remarkable investment stories in modern financial history, a testament to collective grit, well-timed risks, and the invisible hand of fortune. By the time AT&T acquired TCI for $48 billion in 1999, a $1 investment had grown to more than $900, outpacing its peers and the broader market, according to calculations by Ashe Capital Management. Then Liberty Media expanded into media, sports, and entertainment, and by 2024, that same $1 investment had grown to $3,950, compared to $234 for the S&P 500, with an annualized return of 17.4 percent. *Not bad, eh Bob?*

At Liberty Global, I have granted Mike Fries a right of first offer over all of my B shares for many reasons, but foremost is trust and continuity.

And earlier this year, after Liberty CEO Greg Maffei stepped down, Liberty brought in a new CEO, Derek Chang, who will drive Liberty Media into its next incarnation. I've known Derek since he worked at TCI in the 1990s, and he brings experience from the NBA, DirecTV, Scripps, and Charter.

As I back away from my corporate roles and ponder the obligations, I still can't fully answer the real question staring at me: What happens when I am gone?

One recent week in winter, Leslie and I decided to visit our son and his wife and their three children near Atlantic City. They had adopted foster kids from Eastern Europe, and we were eager to see our new grandkids. The two girls, eleven and seven, and their eight-year-old brother arrived just before Christmas, and they spoke only a few words of English.

Leslie and I arrived at their house early on a Saturday morning. The weather was freezing, but our hearts warmed with anticipation. We took the kids to a bike shop to get new bikes, helmets, and all the gear, then headed to the barren boardwalk on a frigid day.

Their giddy delight was contagious. After hours of riding, they couldn't wait to go again Sunday, cold weather be damned. Bundled up, we walked and talked while they biked, their laughter echoing on the old wooden planks. Watching their unbridled joy choked me up, transporting me back to my own childhood. For a moment, I felt young again.

It was our first meeting with the grandkids, and we fell in love with them as we had with all of our other grandkids. I was so deeply touched by our son and his wife, and the way they were navigating all the unprecedented challenges of parenting—even learning to cook Bulgarian dishes—as they opened a path for these children's lives. It was heartening to see my son become the father I wanted to be. We're equally blessed to have a daughter with these same gifts.

Wealth is never what drove me, though I have been incredibly successful, beyond anything I ever could have expected. What really drove me was a desire to bring order to chaos. I want to take the bulk of the wealth I have been lucky enough to accumulate and do good things with it.

In the commotion and confusion of life, I find myself constantly searching for order. Like most people, I sift through memories now, carefully selecting which moments to hold on to, letting go of the ones that caused me pain, and trying to make sense of them all. It is, perhaps, an illusory effort to reshape my own history.

You cannot gain immortality with a statue, or a building named after you. You live on in the memory of family and friends and the impact you had on the lives of people who were helped by your actions on earth. I have made peace with my past, and this process of shuffling through those recollections, and reflecting on the people who made this journey possible, allows me the one emotion that unlocks all others: gratitude.

Beyond Cable-TV: The Remarkable Rise of TCI and Liberty Media

What began as a small regional cable operator in 1973 evolved into one of the most remarkable investment stories in modern financial history. Under John Malone's leadership, Tele-Communications Inc. (TCI) grew through strategic acquisitions and financial discipline, becoming the nation's largest cable provider. By the time AT&T acquired TCI fo˜ $48 billion in 1999, a $1 investment had grown to more than $900, significantly outpacing both its industry peers and the broader market. But the story didn't end there. Through a series of spin-offs and strategic restructurings, Liberty Media built on TCI's foundation, expanding into media, sports, and entertainment. By 2024, that same $1 investment had grown to $3,950, compared to $234 for the S&P 500, with an annualized return of 17.4% versus the S&P's 11.1%. TCI's transformation into Liberty Media reflects not only the evolution of the cable industry but also the long-term value created for shareholders who stayed the course.

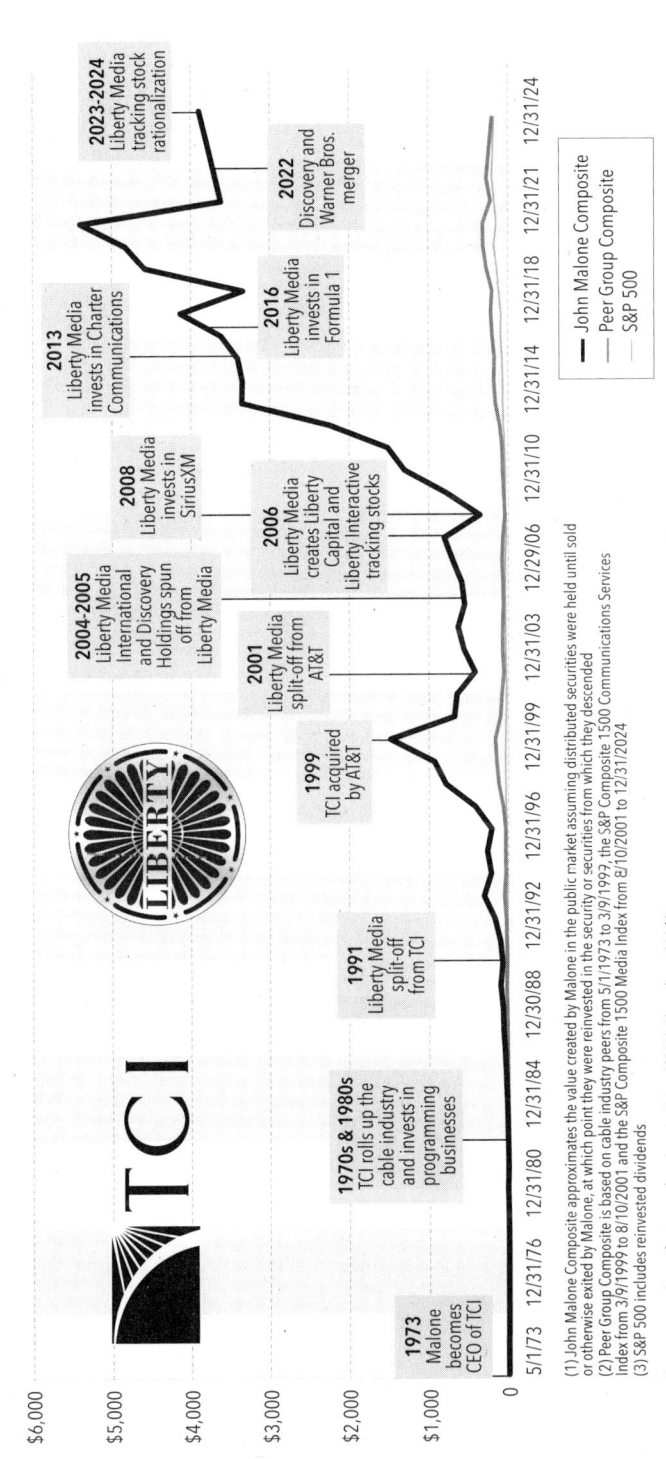

(1) John Malone Composite approximates the value created by Malone in the public market assuming distributed securities were held until sold or otherwise exited by Malone, at which point they were reinvested in the security or securities from which they descended
(2) Peer Group Composite is based on cable industry peers from 5/1/1973 to 3/9/1993, the S&P Composite 1500 Communications Services Index from 3/9/1999 to 8/10/2001 and the S&P Composite 1500 Media Index from 8/10/2001 to 12/31/2024
(3) S&P 500 includes reinvested dividends

Data sources: Center for Research in Security Prices (CRSP), Bloomberg, SEC filings
Research: Ashe Capital Management

ACKNOWLEDGMENTS

No book is just one person putting their story to the page. Even the most personal stories require the insight, support, and effort of others, and this one is no exception.

I am deeply grateful to the people who helped bring this book to life because while my name is on the cover, their fingerprints are on every page.

First I owe a lifetime of thanks for the support of my wife and family—through late nights, missed moments, and long stretches away. Time with them now is a luxury—and a priority, and their presence in my life means more than I can ever put into words.

Old friends are a gift, and Larry Romrell has been at my side for more than forty years, through every hard-earned victory and near disaster, and through it all he's given the same dependable guidance. Marty Flessner, my executive assistant, has been the steady force behind the chaos, keeping everything—and me—on track. For this project, she fielded calls, helped with research, and tamed my impossible schedule.

I appreciate the many colleagues who stood by me, steadfast investors like the Naifys, Mirons, and Newhouses, and reliable board members like Dave Wargo, Dave Rapley, and Dan Sanchez. Liberty's longtime tax advisor, Peter Zolintakis, not only kept us compliant, but kept us alive—and helped us win.

And I am indebted to every unnamed employee—past and current—for their contributions at TCI, and at Liberty Media, Liberty Global, Formula One, and the entire Liberty-related family of spin-offs and large investments.

Special thanks to Brian Kenny (and the whole team) at the Cable Center for help with photo research and for keeping the industry's stories alive and relevant. And a tip of the hat to those who helped with the charts and research, especially Steve Blass and Brent Humphreys at Ashe Capital, William N. Thorndike Jr. at Housatonic Partners, Chris Marangi at Gamco Investors, and Craig and Jessica Moffett at MoffettNathanson.

At Simon & Schuster, editor in chief Priscilla Painton saw the sweeping tale I did, and editor Stephanie Frerich nurtured a better story out of the manuscript. Attorney and agent Bob Barnett was as easy to work with as an old friend.

Finally, I'm deeply grateful to Mark Robichaux, a trusted friend and writer I've known for more than twenty-five years. Through long conversations and his steady hand, I began to hear my own voice more clearly. This story wouldn't have found its shape without him, and I'm thankful beyond words.

BIBLIOGRAPHY

This book is based on extensive research of primary sources, including news reports, company records, oral histories, lawsuits, government studies, and firsthand accounts. Every effort has been made to verify facts and present them accurately, relying on reputable sources and cross-referencing information whenever possible.

This story is also based on memory, inherently selective, swayed over the years by perspective and personal experience. But the events presented here all happened, and where differing accounts exist, I cross-checked sources and weighed context to get as close to the truth as possible.

The Federal Communications Commission's trove of records was invaluable, and lawsuits filed by the Department of Justice and others annoyed me just as much rereading them.

Of all my research, the oral histories best captured the grit, hustle, and raw invention of cable's earliest days.

Below is a list that serves both as a record of my research and a guide for those who wish to explore these topics further.

BOOKS

Auletta, Ken. *The Highwaymen: Warriors of the Information Superhighway*. Random House, 1997.

Cauley, Leslie. *End of the Line: the Rise and Fall of AT&T*. New York: Free Press, 2008.

Ciciora, Walter, James Farmer, David Large, and Michael Adams. *Modern Cable Television Technology: Voice, Video and Data Communications*, 2nd Edition. New York: Elsevier Inc., 2004.

Eisenmann, Thomas R. *Structure and Strategy: Explaining Consolidation Patterns in the U.S. Cable Industry.* Ph.D. Thesis, Harvard University, 1997.

Hendricks, John. *A Curious Discovery.* New York: HarperCollins, 2013.

Lockman, Brian, and Don Sarvey. *Pioneers of Cable Television.* Jefferson, NC: McFarland & Co. Publishers, 2005.

Mullen, Megan. *Television in the Multichannel Age: A Brief History of Cable Television.* Malden, MA: Blackwell Publishing, 2008.

Munk, Nina. *Fools Rush In: Steve Case, Jerry Levin, and the Unmaking of AOL Time Warner.* New York: Harper Business, 2004

Noll, A. Michael. *Highway of Dreams: A Critical View Along the Information Superhighway.* Rahway, NJ: Lawrence Erlbaum Associates, 1997.

Novak, William. *An Incredible Dream: Ralph Roberts and the Story of Comcast.* Comcast Corporation, 2012.

Parsons, Patrick R., and Robert M. Friedman, *The Cable and Satellite Television Industries.* Allyn & Bacon/Viacom, 1998.

Pulley, Brett. *The Billion-Dollar Bet: Robert Johnson and the Inside Story of Black Entertainment Television.* Hoboken, NJ: John Wiley & Sons, 2004.

Redstone, Sumner, with Peter Knobler. *A Passion to Win.* New York: Simon & Schuster, 2001.

Robichaux, Mark. *Cable Cowboy: John Malone and the Rise of the Modern Cable-TV Industry.* Inshore Publishing, 2002.

Thorndike, William N. Jr. *The Outsiders: Eight Unconventional CEOs and Their Radically Rational Blueprint for Success.* Boston: Harvard Business Review Press, 2012.

Turner, Ted, with Bill Burke. *Call Me Ted.* Business Plus, 2009.

Satkowiak, Larry. *The Cable Industry: A Short History Through Three Generations.* Denver: The Cable Center, 2015.

Vogel, Harold L. *Entertainment Industry Economics*, 3rd edition. Cambridge University Press, 1994.

Williams, Christian. *Lead, Follow or Get Out of the Way: The Story of Ted Turner.* New York: Quadrangle–New York Times Book Co., 1981.

PERIODICALS/WEBSITES

Advertising Age
Barron's
Broadcasting & Cable
Denver Post
Rocky Mountain News

Deadline
Financial Times
Forbes
Fortune
Hollywood Reporter
The Mediator/Doug Shapiro/substack.com
Media War & Peace/Evan Shapiro/substack.com
Multichannel News
NCTA—The Internet and Television Association
New York Times
New Yorker
Nielsen
Reuters
Variety
Wall Street Journal

SECURITIES & EXCHANGE/COMPANY ANNUAL REPORTS

Tele-Communications Inc.
Liberty Media
Liberty Global
Warner Bros. Discovery
Gemstar
SiriusXM
DirecTV
News Corp.
AT&T
Formula One
Atlanta Braves
Charter Communications

U.S. CONGRESS

Testimony of John Malone before the subcommittee on Communications, U.S. Senate Committee on Commerce, Science, and Transportation, November 16, 1989.
Testimony of John Malone before the subcommittee on Communications, U.S. Senate Committee on Commerce, Science, and Transportation, December 1993.

Cable Communications Policy Act of 1984. October 1984.
Cable Television Consumer Protection and Competition Act. October 1992.
Telecommunications Act of 1996. January 1996.

WHITE PAPERS/ STUDIES

Hazlett, Thomas W. *Regulating Cable Television Rates: An Economic Analysis* No. 3 (July 1994). Working Paper Series, Program on Telecommunications Policy, University of California Davis.
1991 Survey of Cable Television Rates and Services. U.S. General Accounting Office. July 1991.
Noll, A. Michael. *Memories: A Personal History of Bell Telephone Laboratories*, 2015.

SYNDEO INSTITUTE/CABLE CENTER—ORAL HISTORIES

Bob Magness
Ed Breen
Peter Barton
Julian Brodsky
Mike Fries
Richard Green
Leo Hindery
John Malone
Bob Magness
Ralph Roberts
Brian Roberts
Larry Romrell

John Sie
Bob Stanzione
JC Sparkman
Robert Tarlton
Rouzbeh Yassini
Alan Gerry
Amos Hostetter
Glenn Jones
Gerry Lenfest
Jeff Marcus
Ed Parsons
John Walson

INDEX